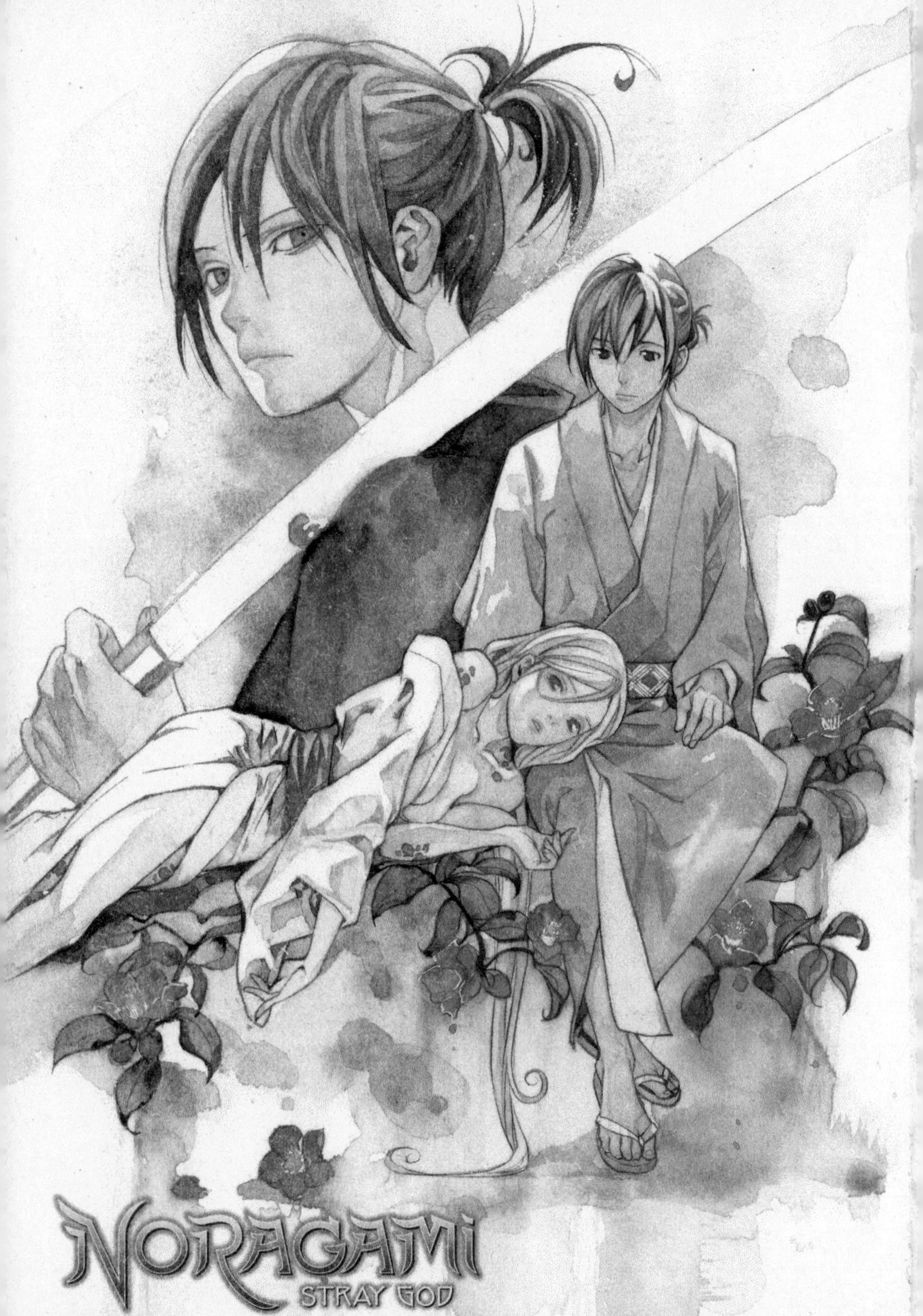

NORAGAMI
STRAY GOD

ADACHITOKA

characters

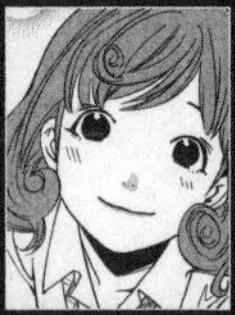

KOFUKU

A goddess of poverty who calls herself Ebisu after the god of fortune.

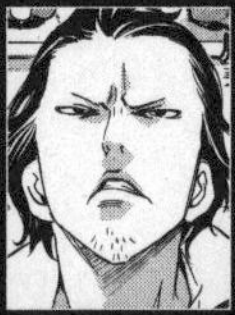

DAIKOKU

Kofuku's shinki who summons storms.

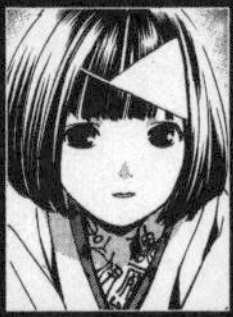

STRAY

A shinki who serves an unspecified number of deities

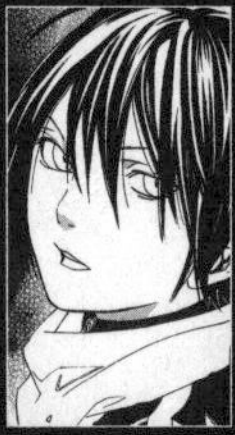

YATO

A minor deity who always wears a sweatsuit.

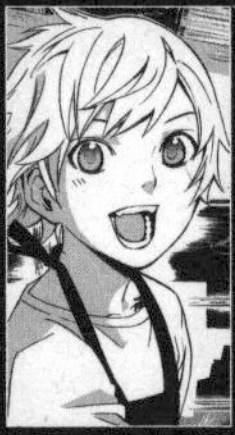

YUKINÉ

Yato's shinki who turns into a sword.

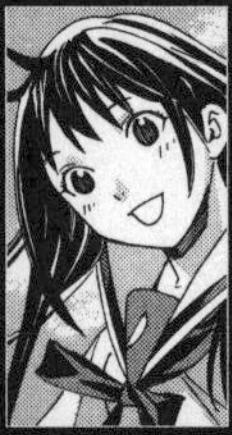

HIYORI IKI

A middle school student who has become half ayakashi.

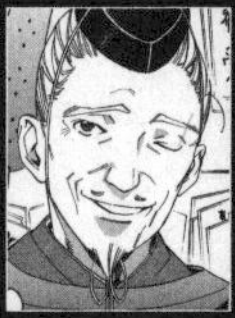

TENJIN

The God of Learning, Sugawara no Michizane.

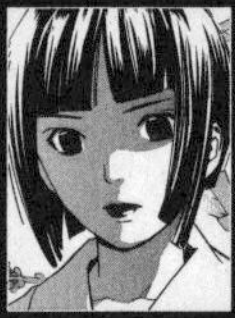

MAYU

Formerly Yato's shinki, now Tenjin's shinki.

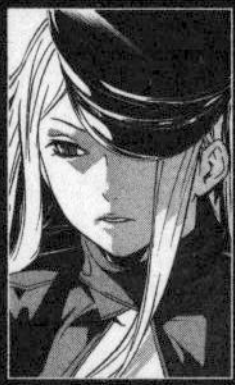

BISHAMONTEN

A powerful warrior god who seeks vengeance on Yato.

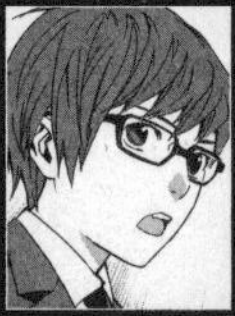

KAZUMA

A navigational shinki who serves as guide to Bishamon.

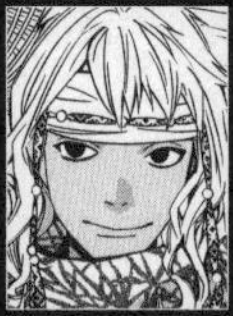

KUGAHA

A medicine man who is plotting to have Bishamon replaced.

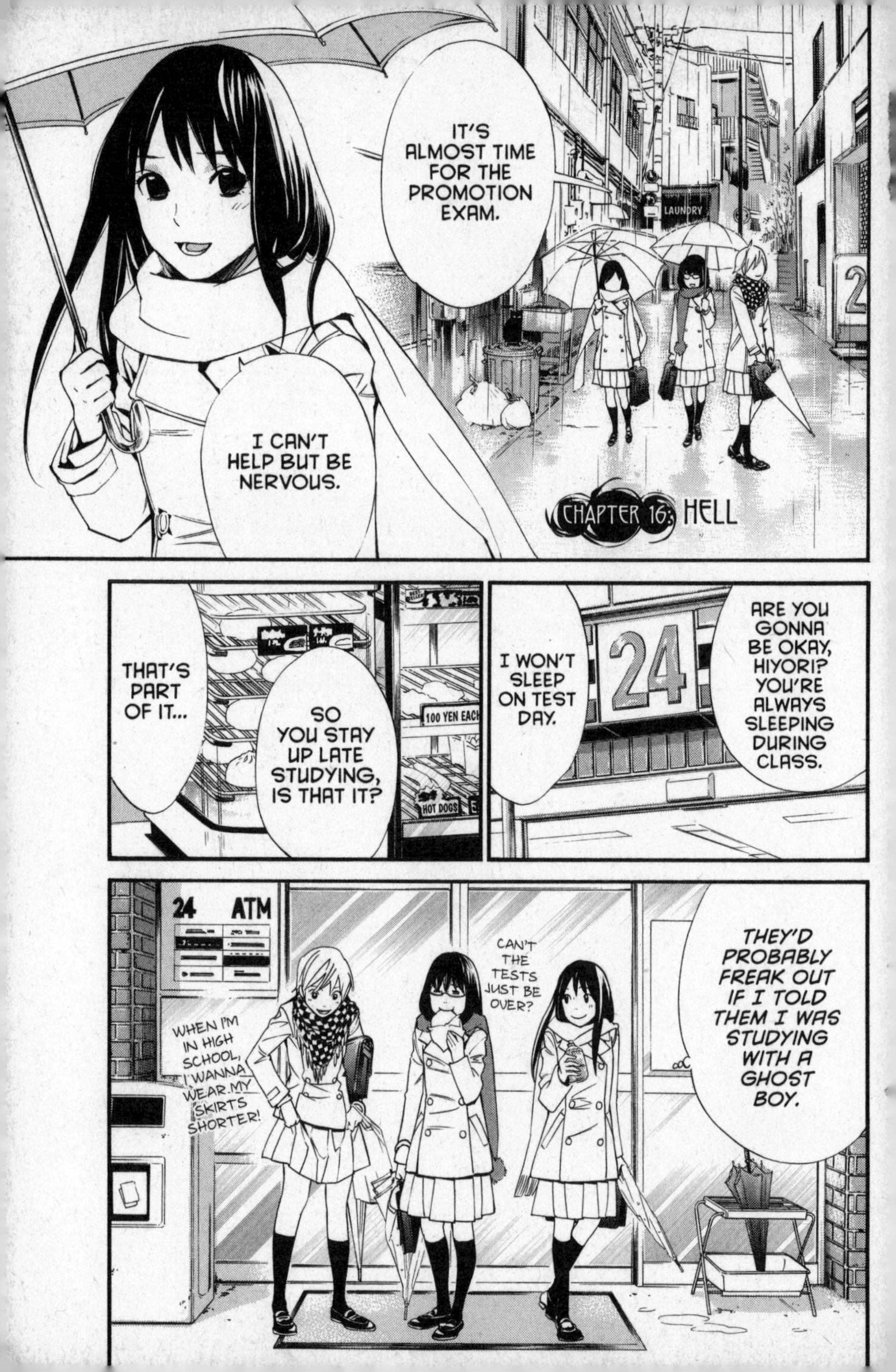
IT'S ALMOST TIME FOR THE PROMOTION EXAM.
LAUNDRY
I CAN'T HELP BUT BE NERVOUS.
CHAPTER 16: HELL
24
ARE YOU GONNA BE OKAY, HIYORI? YOU'RE ALWAYS SLEEPING DURING CLASS.
I WON'T SLEEP ON TEST DAY.
100 YEN EACH
HOT DOGS
SO YOU STAY UP LATE STUDYING, IS THAT IT?
THAT'S PART OF IT...
THEY'D PROBABLY FREAK OUT IF I TOLD THEM I WAS STUDYING WITH A GHOST BOY.
CAN'T THE TESTS JUST BE OVER?
24 ATM
WHEN I'M IN HIGH SCHOOL, I WANNA WEAR MY SKIRTS SHORTER!

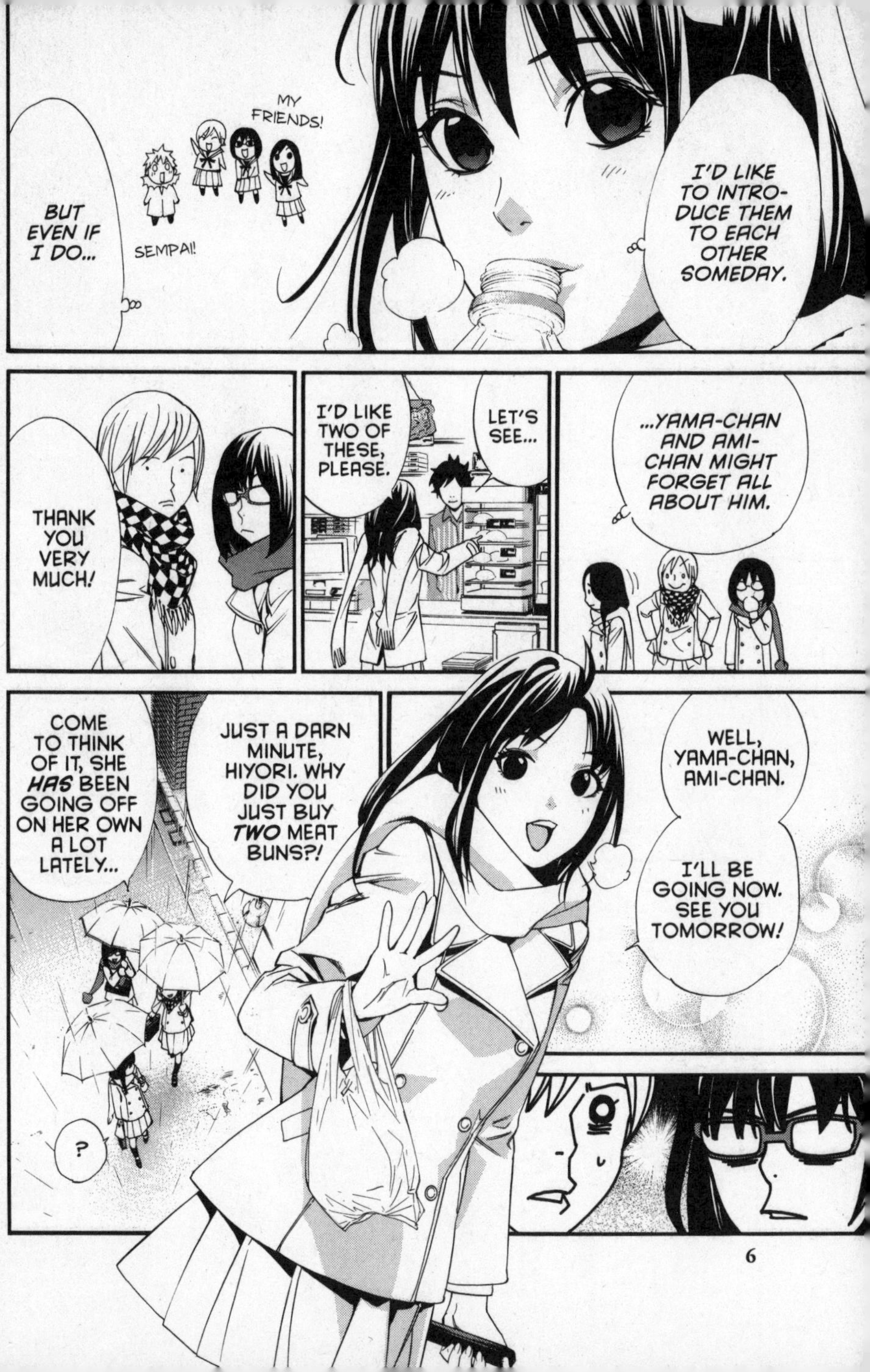
I'D LIKE TO INTRODUCE THEM TO EACH OTHER SOMEDAY.
MY FRIENDS!
SEMPAI!
BUT EVEN IF I DO...
...YAMA-CHAN AND AMI-CHAN MIGHT FORGET ALL ABOUT HIM.
LET'S SEE...
I'D LIKE TWO OF THESE, PLEASE.
THANK YOU VERY MUCH!
WELL, YAMA-CHAN, AMI-CHAN.
I'LL BE GOING NOW. SEE YOU TOMORROW!
JUST A DARN MINUTE, HIYORI. WHY DID YOU JUST BUY *TWO* MEAT BUNS?!
COME TO THINK OF IT, SHE *HAS* BEEN GOING OFF ON HER OWN A LOT LATELY...
?

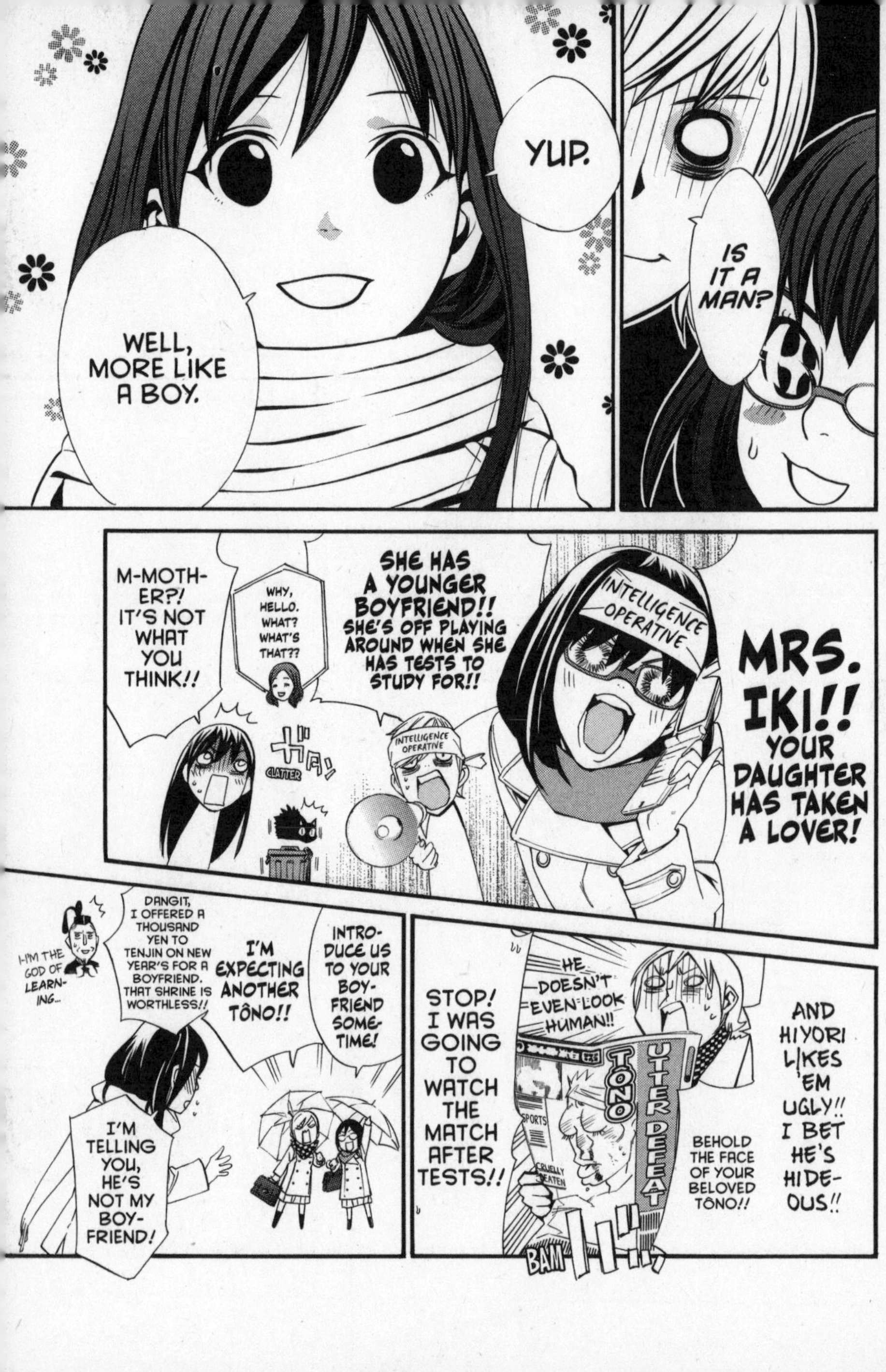
IS IT A MAN?
YUP.
WELL, MORE LIKE A BOY.
MRS. IKI!! YOUR DAUGHTER HAS TAKEN A LOVER!
INTELLIGENCE OPERATIVE
SHE HAS A YOUNGER BOYFRIEND!! SHE'S OFF PLAYING AROUND WHEN SHE HAS TESTS TO STUDY FOR!!
INTELLIGENCE OPERATIVE
WHY, HELLO. WHAT? WHAT'S THAT??
M-MOTHER?! IT'S NOT WHAT YOU THINK!!
CLATTER
AND HIYORI LIKES 'EM UGLY!! I BET HE'S HIDE-OUS!!
HE DOESN'T EVEN LOOK HUMAN!!
BEHOLD THE FACE OF YOUR BELOVED TÔNO!!
TÔNO UTTER DEFEAT
SPORTS
CRUELLY BEATEN
STOP! I WAS GOING TO WATCH THE MATCH AFTER TESTS!!
BAM
INTRO-DUCE US TO YOUR BOY-FRIEND SOME-TIME!
I'M EXPECTING ANOTHER TÔNO!!
DANGIT, I OFFERED A THOUSAND YEN TO TENJIN ON NEW YEAR'S FOR A BOYFRIEND. THAT SHRINE IS WORTHLESS!!
I-I'M THE GOD OF LEARN-ING...
I'M TELLING YOU, HE'S NOT MY BOY-FRIEND!

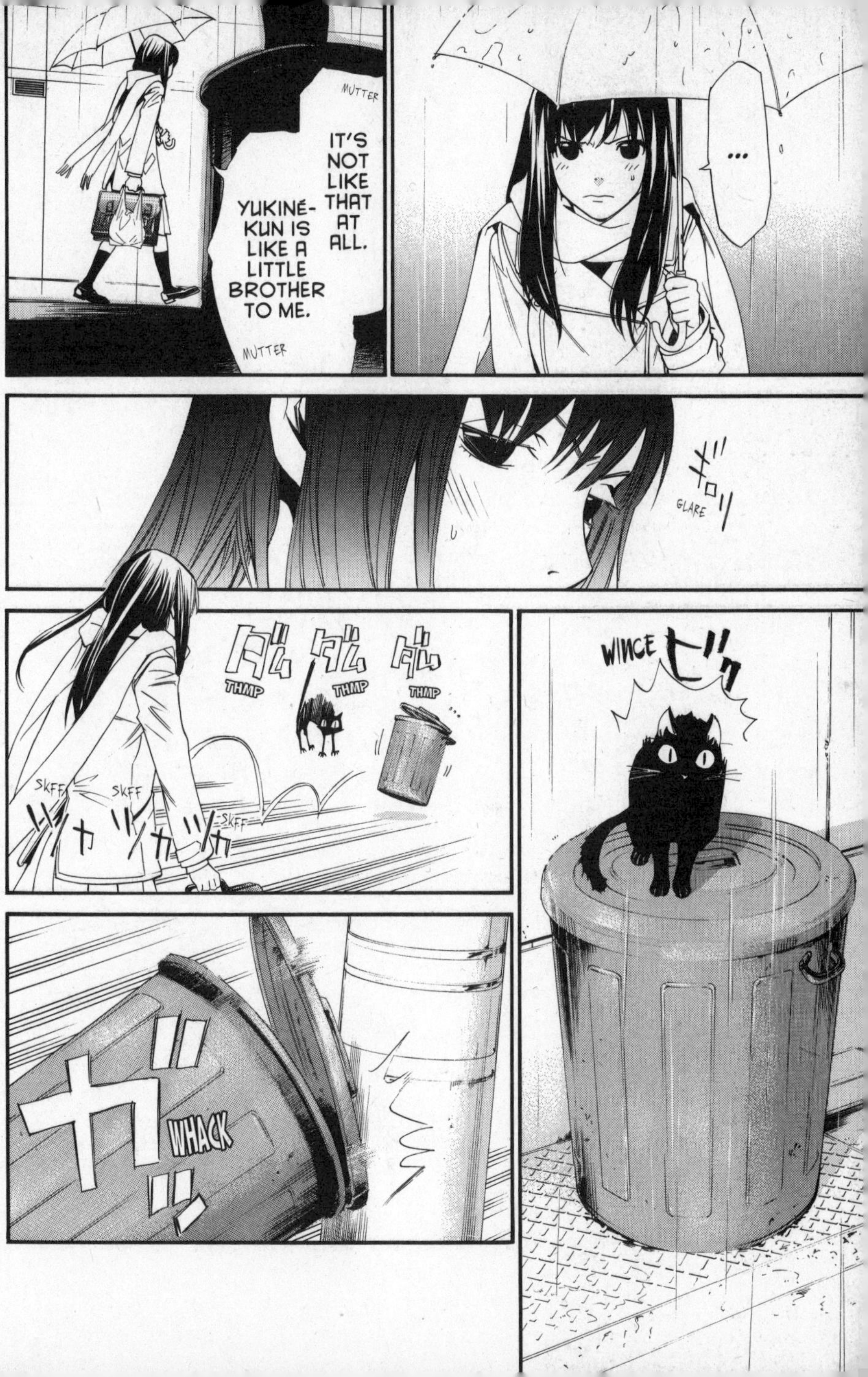
...
MUTTER
IT'S NOT LIKE THAT AT ALL.
YUKINÉ-KUN IS LIKE A LITTLE BROTHER TO ME.
MUTTER
GLARE
WINCE
THMP
THMP
THMP
SKFF
SKFF
SKFF
WHACK

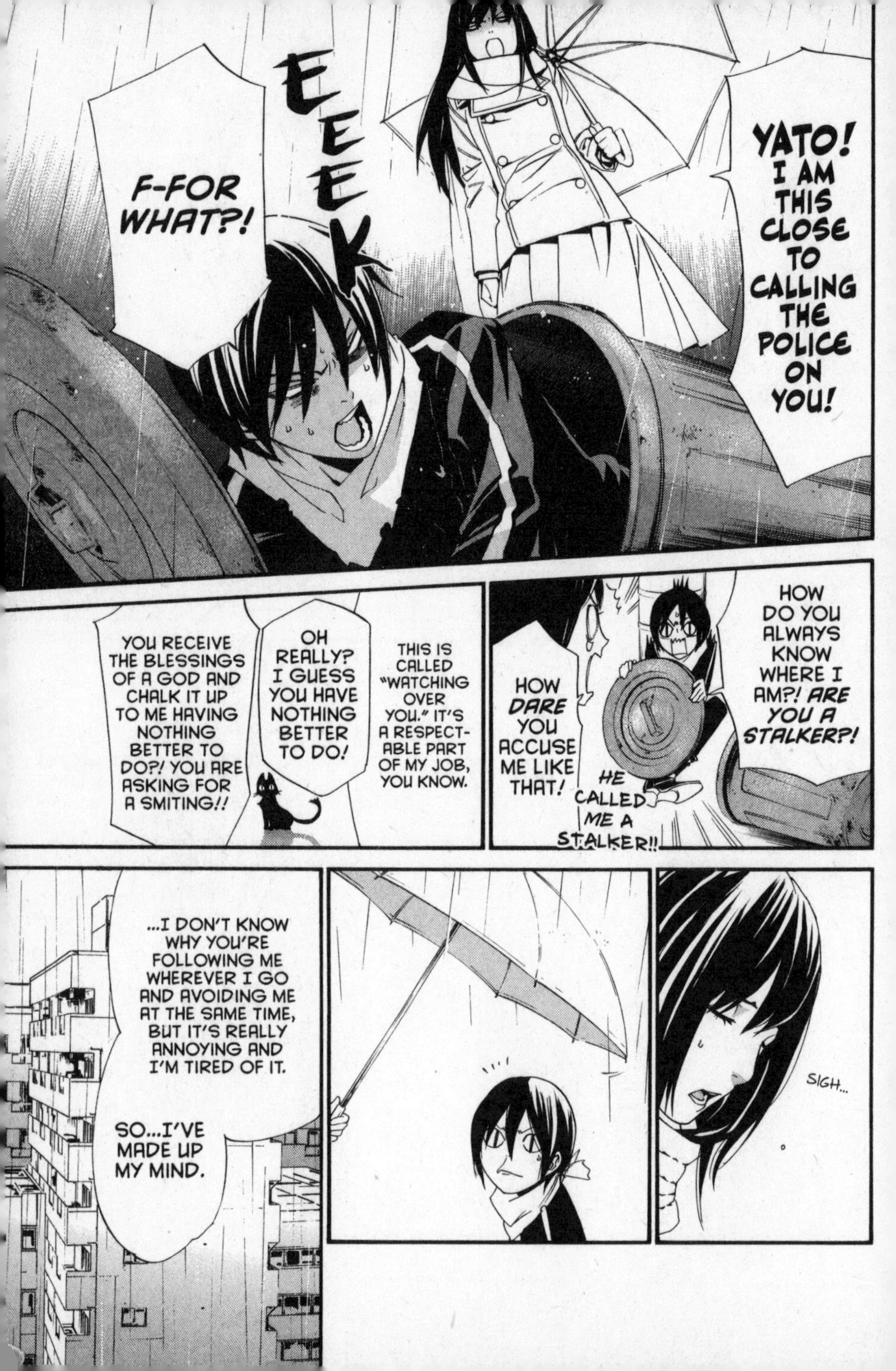
YATO! I AM THIS CLOSE TO CALLING THE POLICE ON YOU!
EEEEK
F-FOR WHAT?!
HOW DO YOU ALWAYS KNOW WHERE I AM?! ARE YOU A STALKER?!
HOW DARE YOU ACCUSE ME LIKE THAT!
HE CALLED ME A STALKER!!
THIS IS CALLED "WATCHING OVER YOU." IT'S A RESPECT-ABLE PART OF MY JOB, YOU KNOW.
OH REALLY? I GUESS YOU HAVE NOTHING BETTER TO DO!
YOU RECEIVE THE BLESSINGS OF A GOD AND CHALK IT UP TO ME HAVING NOTHING BETTER TO DO?! YOU ARE ASKING FOR A SMITING!!
SIGH...
...I DON'T KNOW WHY YOU'RE FOLLOWING ME WHEREVER I GO AND AVOIDING ME AT THE SAME TIME, BUT IT'S REALLY ANNOYING AND I'M TIRED OF IT.
SO...I'VE MADE UP MY MIND.

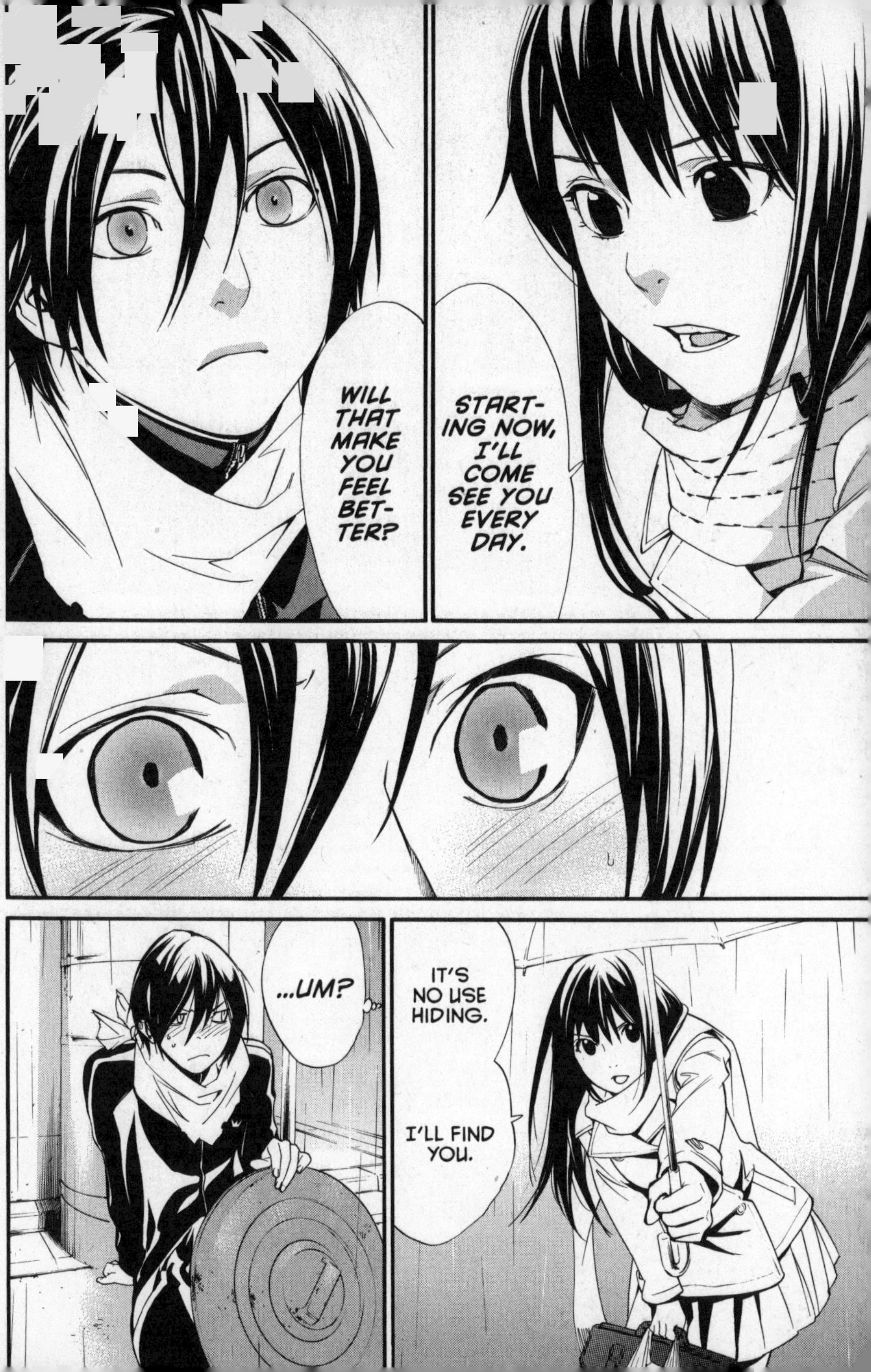
STARTING NOW, I'LL COME SEE YOU EVERY DAY.
WILL THAT MAKE YOU FEEL BETTER?
IT'S NO USE HIDING.
I'LL FIND YOU.
...UM?

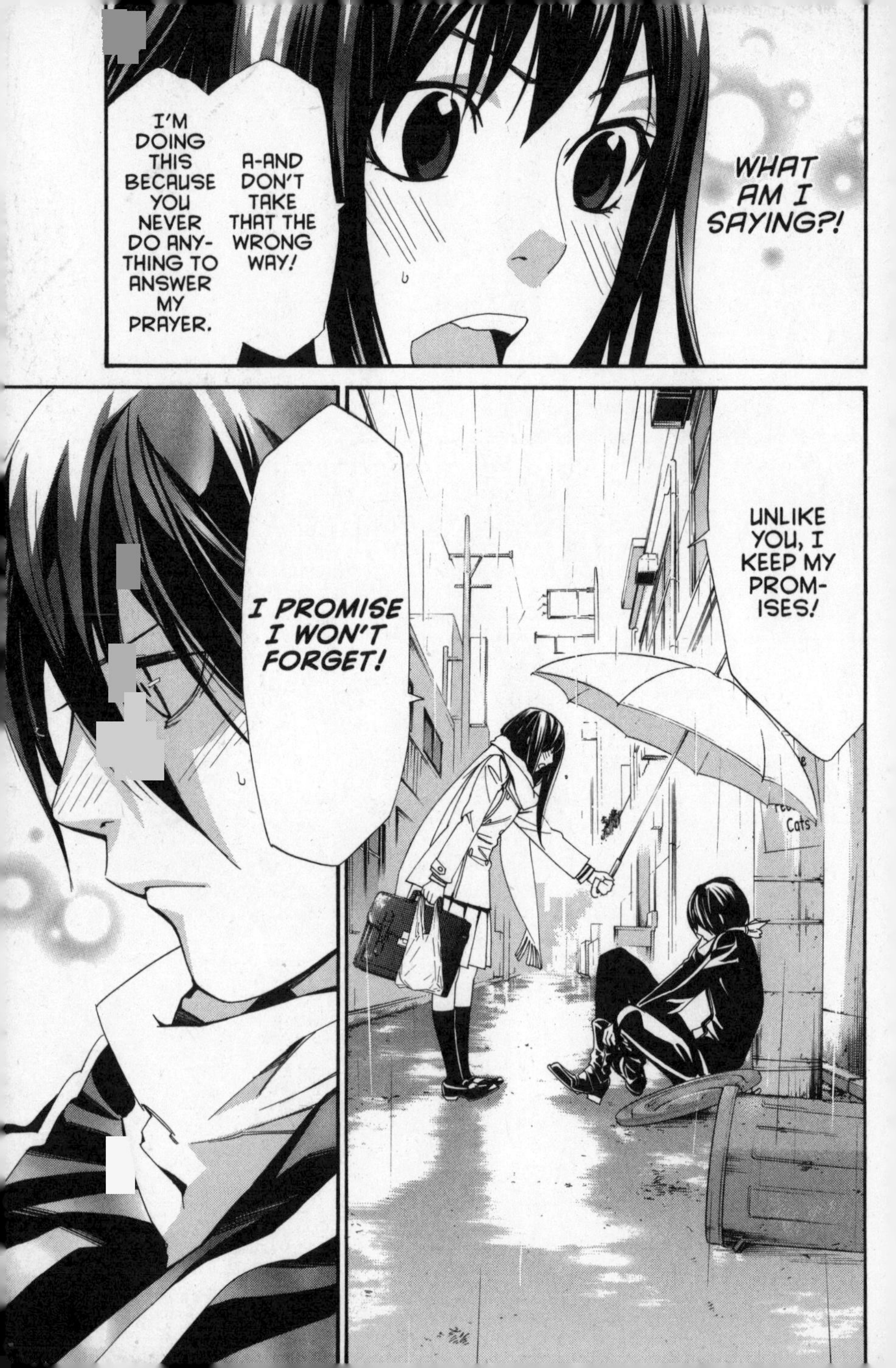
WHAT AM I SAYING?!
A-AND DON'T TAKE THAT THE WRONG WAY!
I'M DOING THIS BECAUSE YOU NEVER DO ANY-THING TO ANSWER MY PRAYER.
UNLIKE YOU, I KEEP MY PROM-ISES!
Cats
I PROMISE I WON'T FORGET!

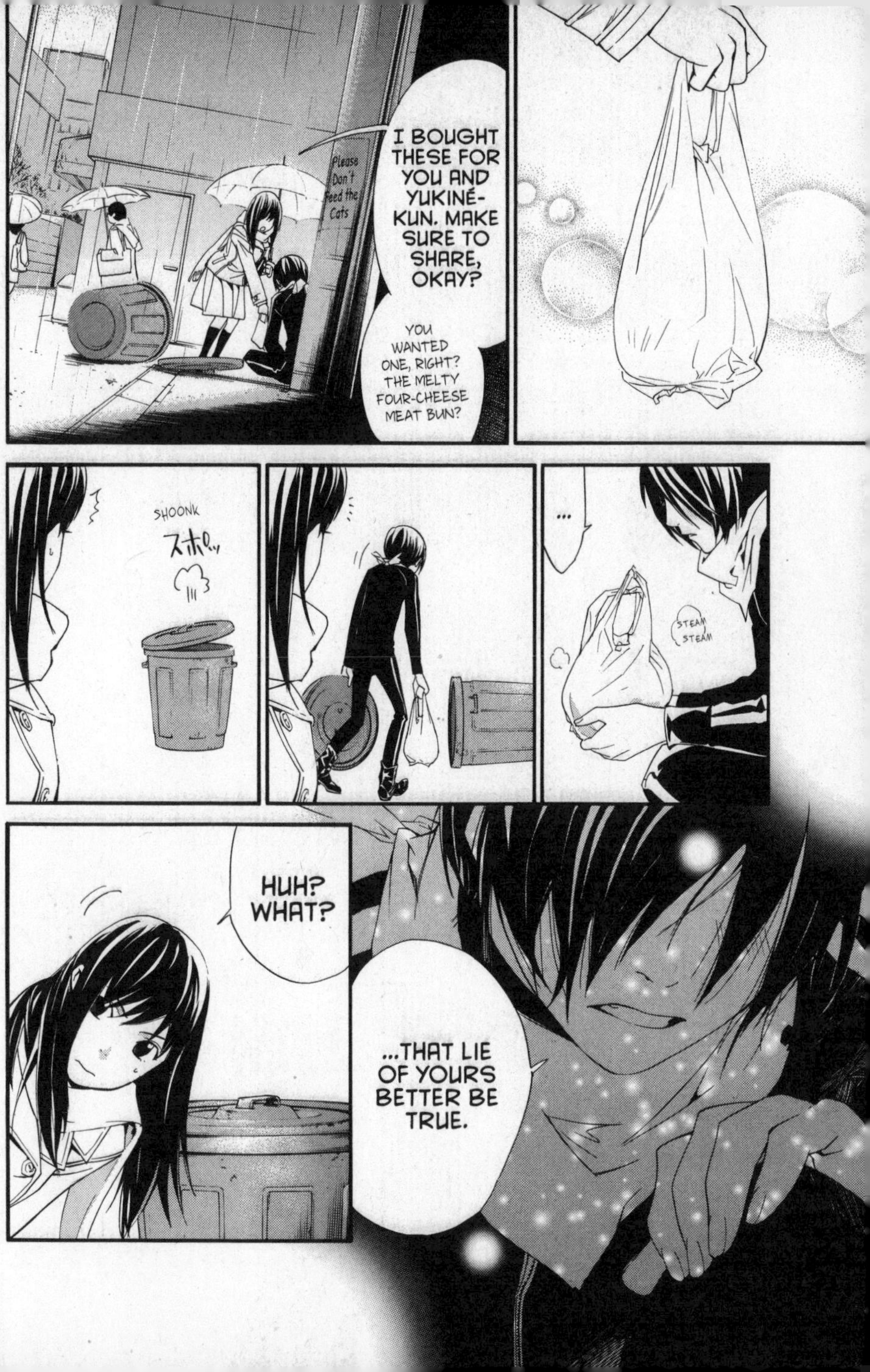
I BOUGHT THESE FOR YOU AND YUKINÉ-KUN. MAKE SURE TO SHARE, OKAY?
YOU WANTED ONE, RIGHT? THE MELTY FOUR-CHEESE MEAT BUN?
Please Don't Feed the Cats
...
STEAM STEAM
SHOONK
スポッ
HUH? WHAT?
...THAT LIE OF YOURS BETTER BE TRUE.

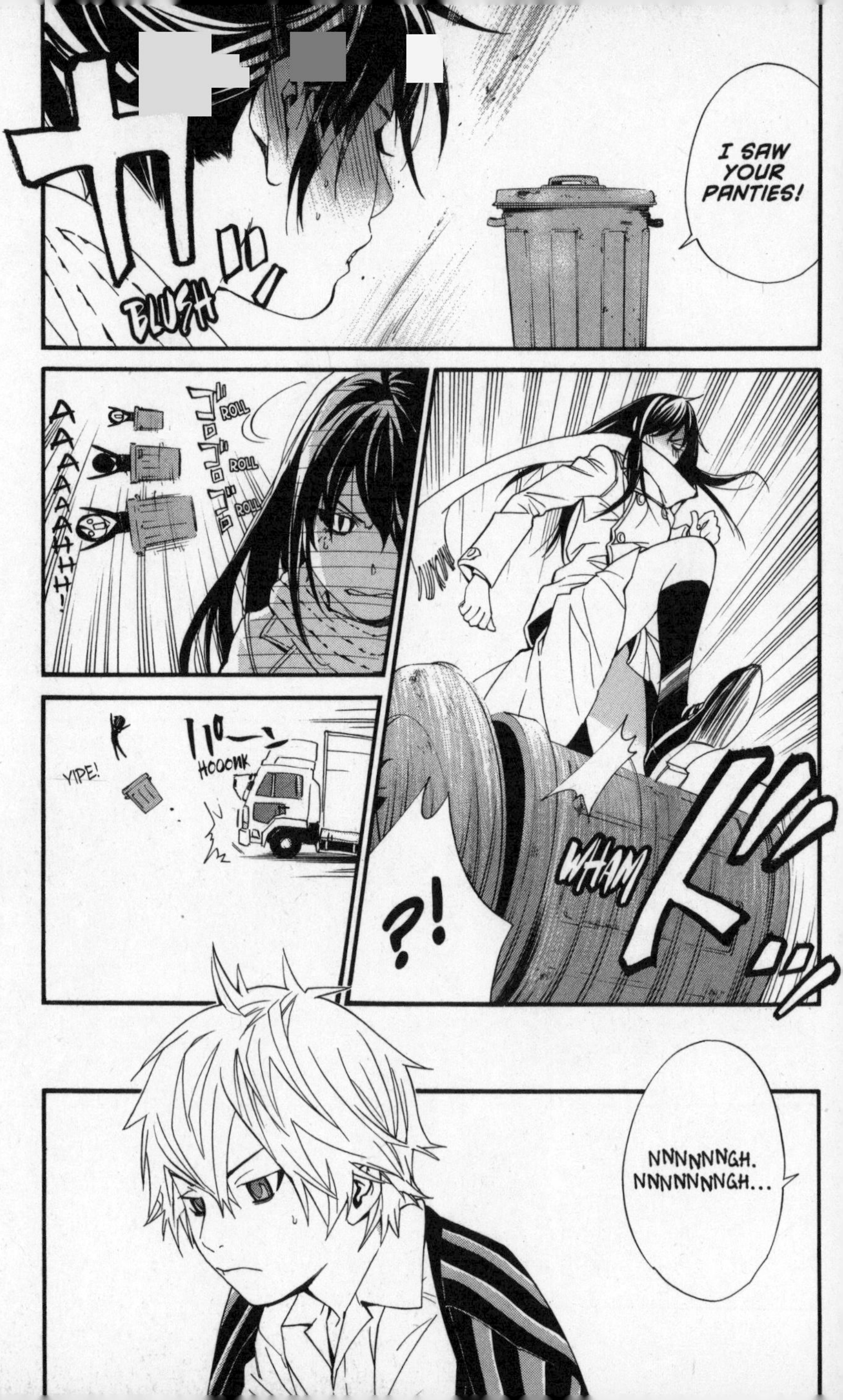
I SAW YOUR PANTIES!
BLUSH
WHAM
?!
ROLL
ROLL
ROLL
AAAAAAHHH!
YIPE!
HOOONK
NNNNNNGH. NNNNNNNGH...

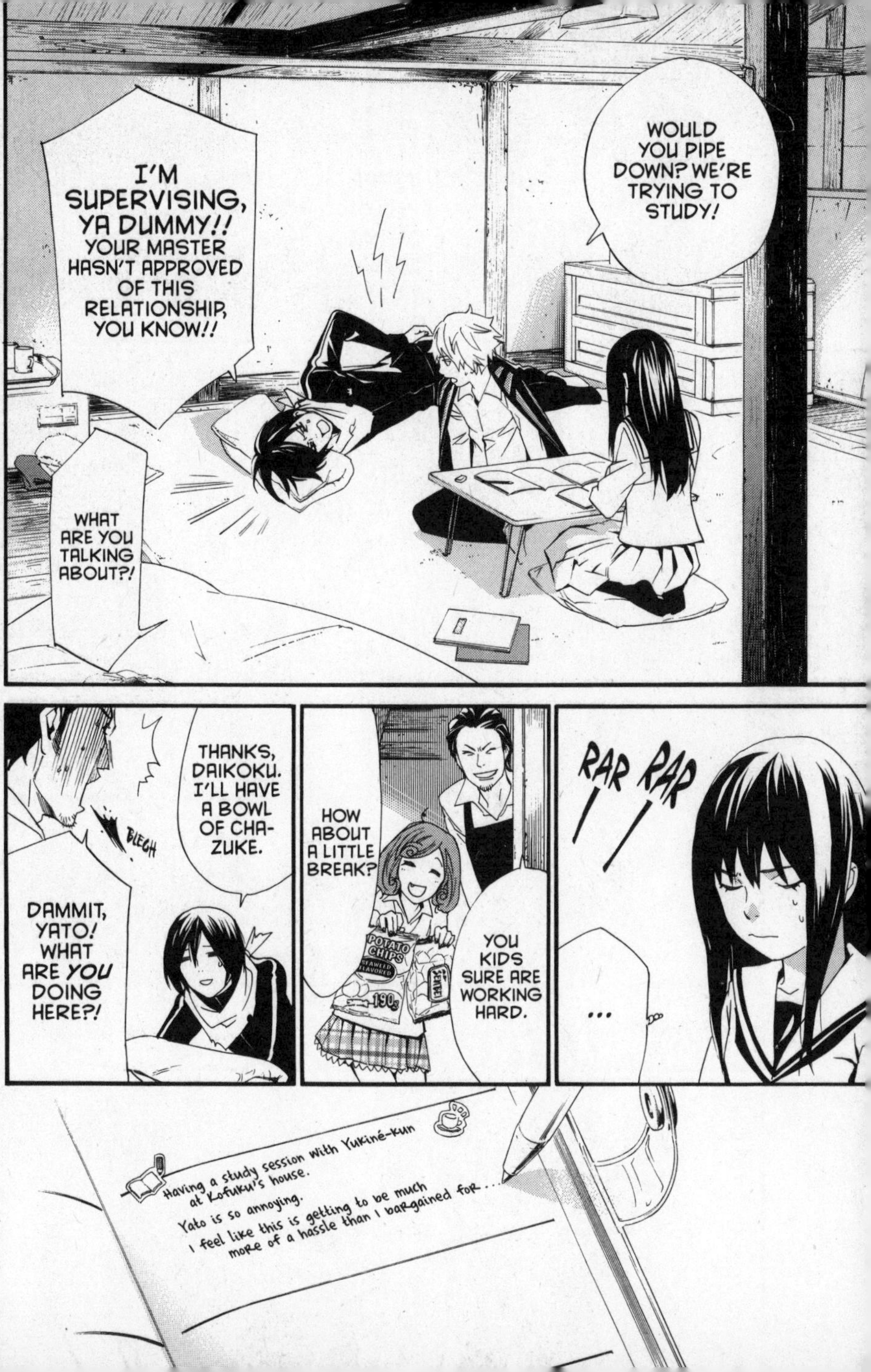
WOULD YOU PIPE DOWN? WE'RE TRYING TO STUDY!
I'M SUPERVISING, YA DUMMY!! YOUR MASTER HASN'T APPROVED OF THIS RELATIONSHIP, YOU KNOW!!
WHAT ARE YOU TALKING ABOUT?!
RAR RAR
...
YOU KIDS SURE ARE WORKING HARD.
HOW ABOUT A LITTLE BREAK?
POTATO CHIPS
SEAWEED FLAVORED
190g
SENBEI
THANKS, DAIKOKU. I'LL HAVE A BOWL OF CHA-ZUKE.
BLEGH
DAMMIT, YATO! WHAT ARE *YOU* DOING HERE?!
Having a study session with Yukiné-kun at Kofuku's house.
Yato is so annoying.
I feel like this is getting to be much more of a hassle than I bargained for...

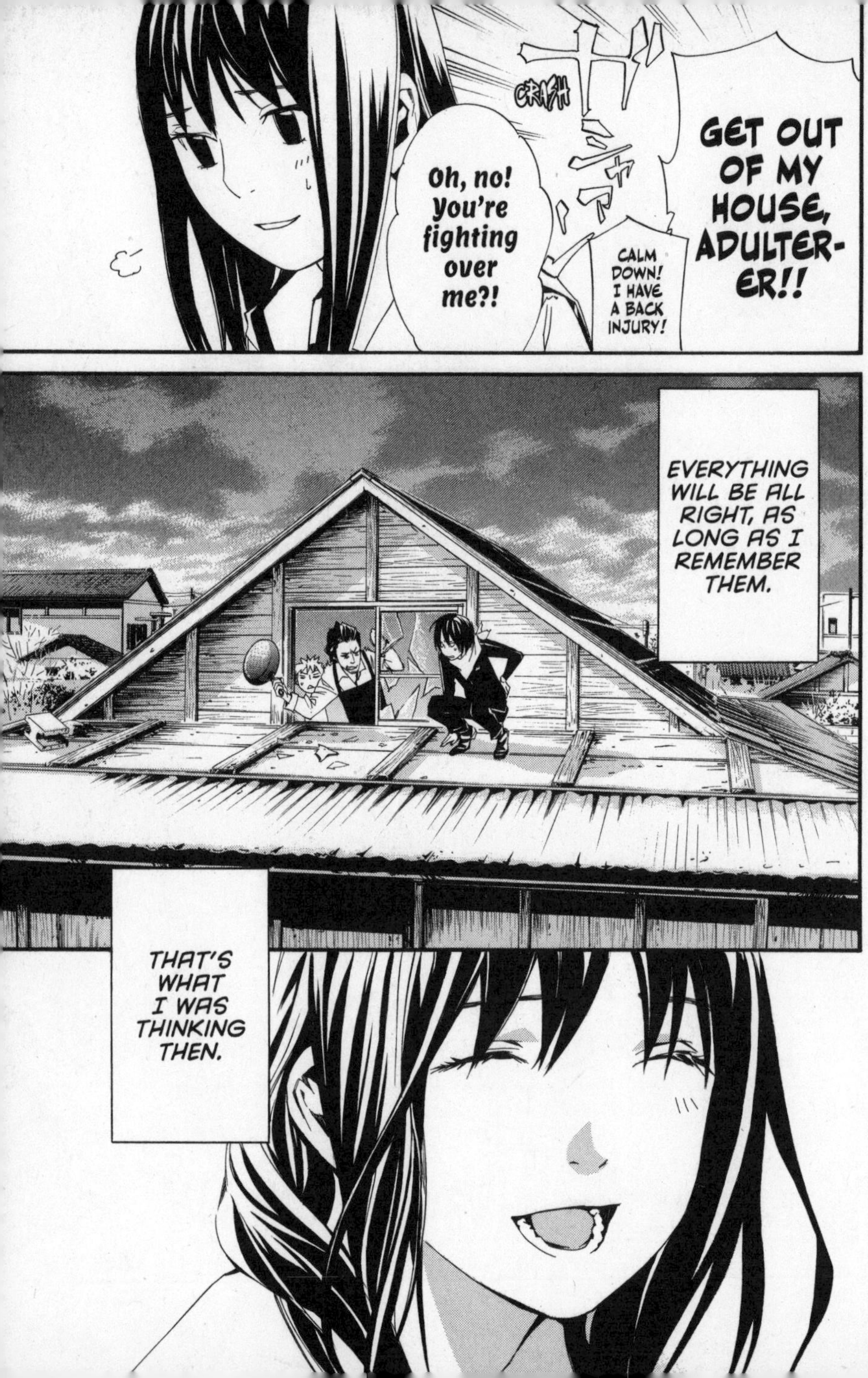
GET OUT OF MY HOUSE, ADULTER-ER!!
CALM DOWN! I HAVE A BACK INJURY!
CRASH
Oh, no! You're fighting over me?!
EVERYTHING WILL BE ALL RIGHT, AS LONG AS I REMEMBER THEM.
THAT'S WHAT I WAS THINKING THEN.

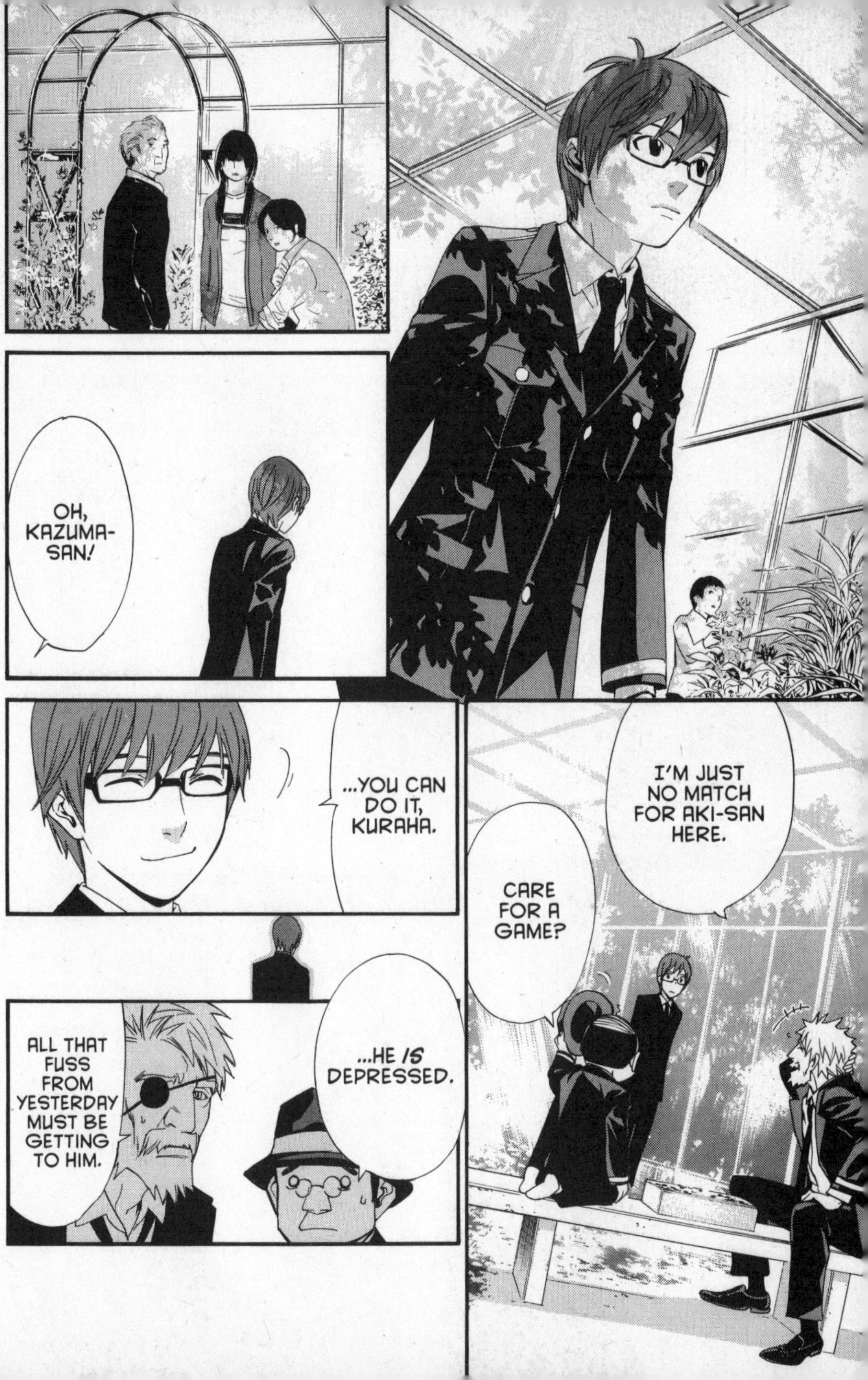
OH, KAZUMA-SAN!
I'M JUST NO MATCH FOR AKI-SAN HERE.
CARE FOR A GAME?
...YOU CAN DO IT, KURAHA.
...HE IS DEPRESSED.
ALL THAT FUSS FROM YESTERDAY MUST BE GETTING TO HIM.

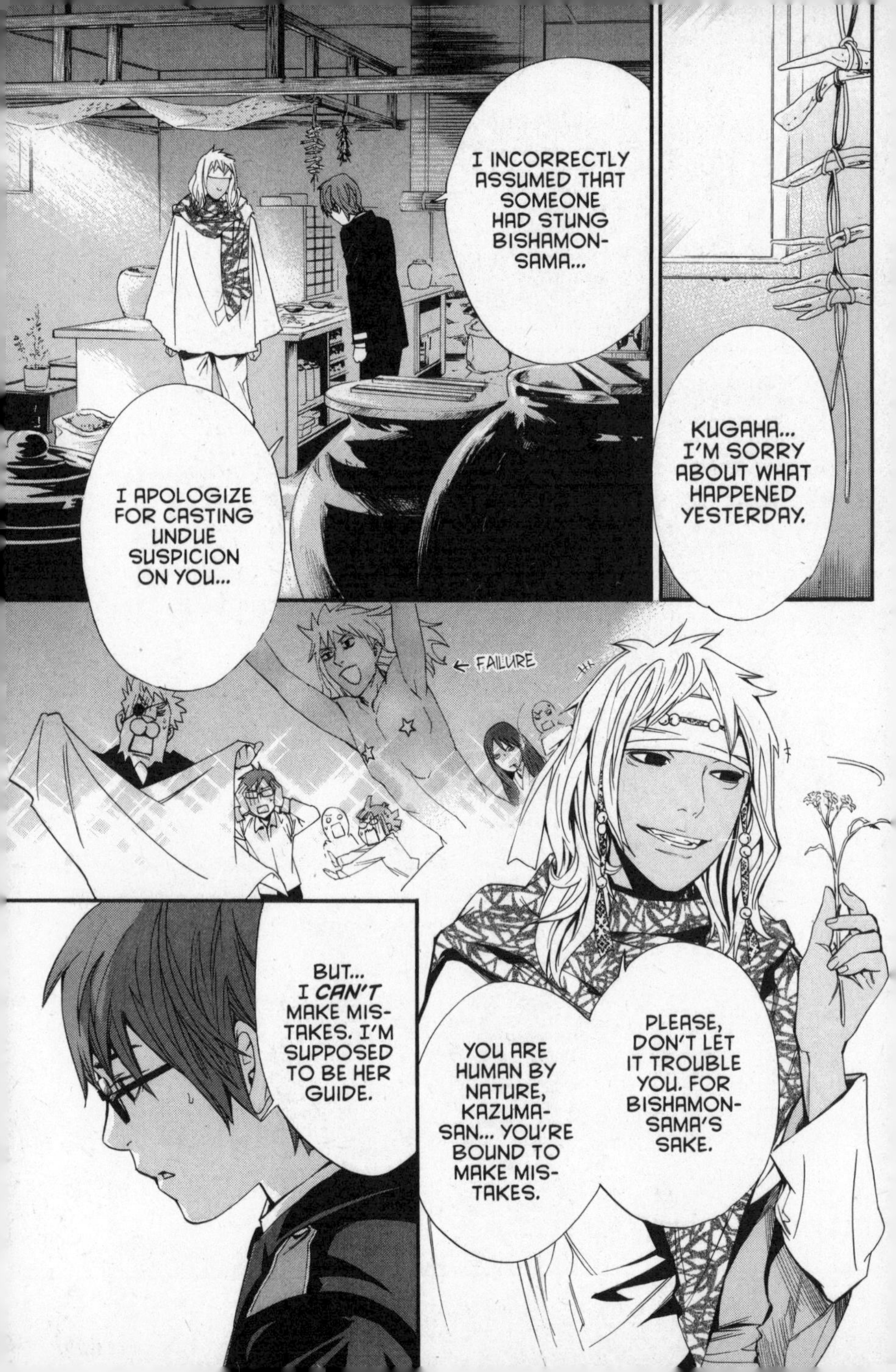

KUGAHA... I'M SORRY ABOUT WHAT HAPPENED YESTERDAY.
I INCORRECTLY ASSUMED THAT SOMEONE HAD STUNG BISHAMON-SAMA...
I APOLOGIZE FOR CASTING UNDUE SUSPICION ON YOU...
← FAILURE
PLEASE, DON'T LET IT TROUBLE YOU. FOR BISHAMON-SAMA'S SAKE.
YOU ARE HUMAN BY NATURE, KAZUMA-SAN... YOU'RE BOUND TO MAKE MIS-TAKES.
BUT... I *CAN'T* MAKE MIS-TAKES. I'M SUPPOSED TO BE HER GUIDE.

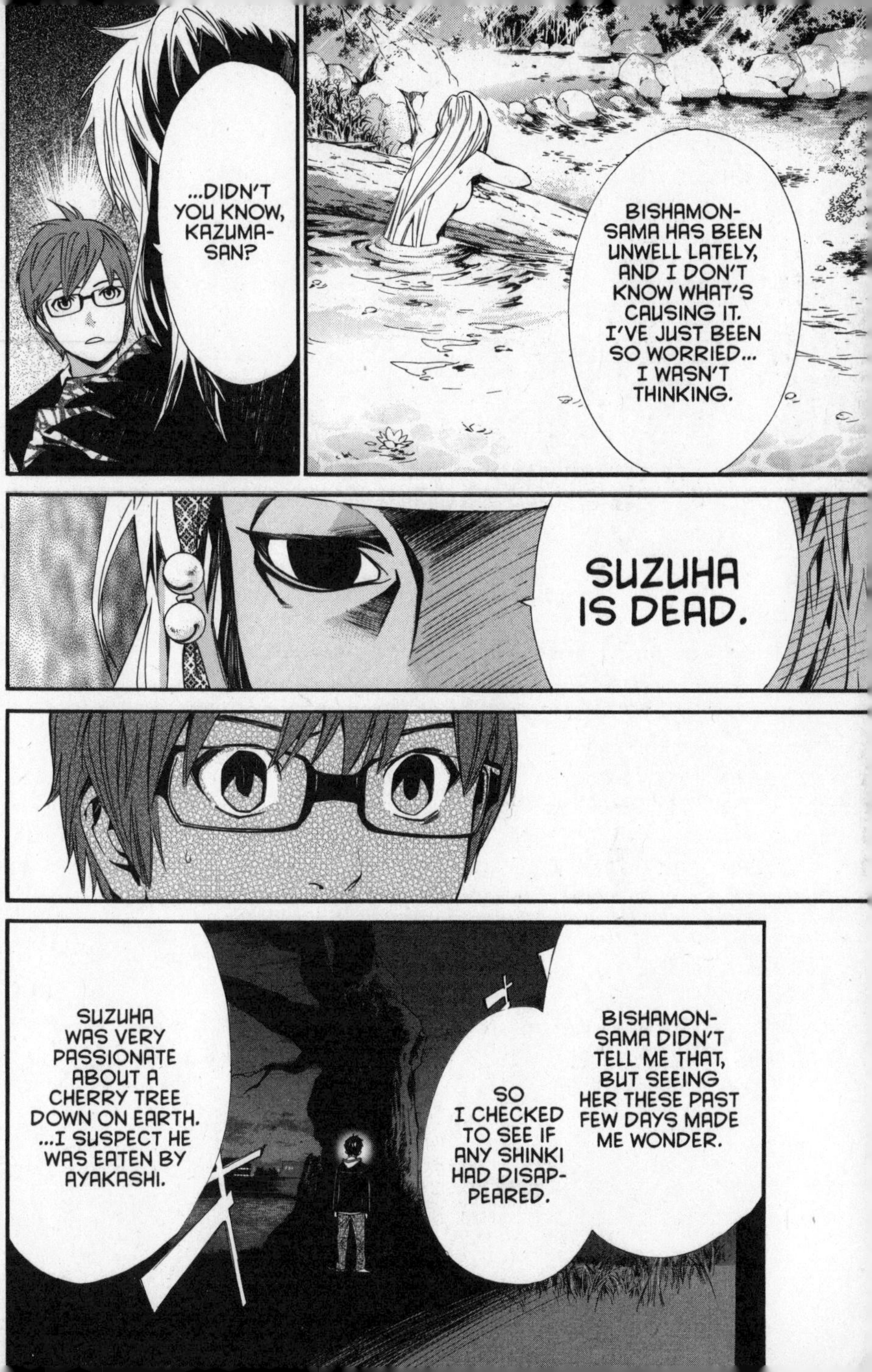
BISHAMON-SAMA HAS BEEN UNWELL LATELY, AND I DON'T KNOW WHAT'S CAUSING IT. I'VE JUST BEEN SO WORRIED... I WASN'T THINKING.
...DIDN'T YOU KNOW, KAZUMA-SAN?
SUZUHA IS DEAD.
BISHAMON-SAMA DIDN'T TELL ME THAT, BUT SEEING HER THESE PAST FEW DAYS MADE ME WONDER.
SO I CHECKED TO SEE IF ANY SHINKI HAD DISAP-PEARED.
SUZUHA WAS VERY PASSIONATE ABOUT A CHERRY TREE DOWN ON EARTH. ...I SUSPECT HE WAS EATEN BY AYAKASHI.

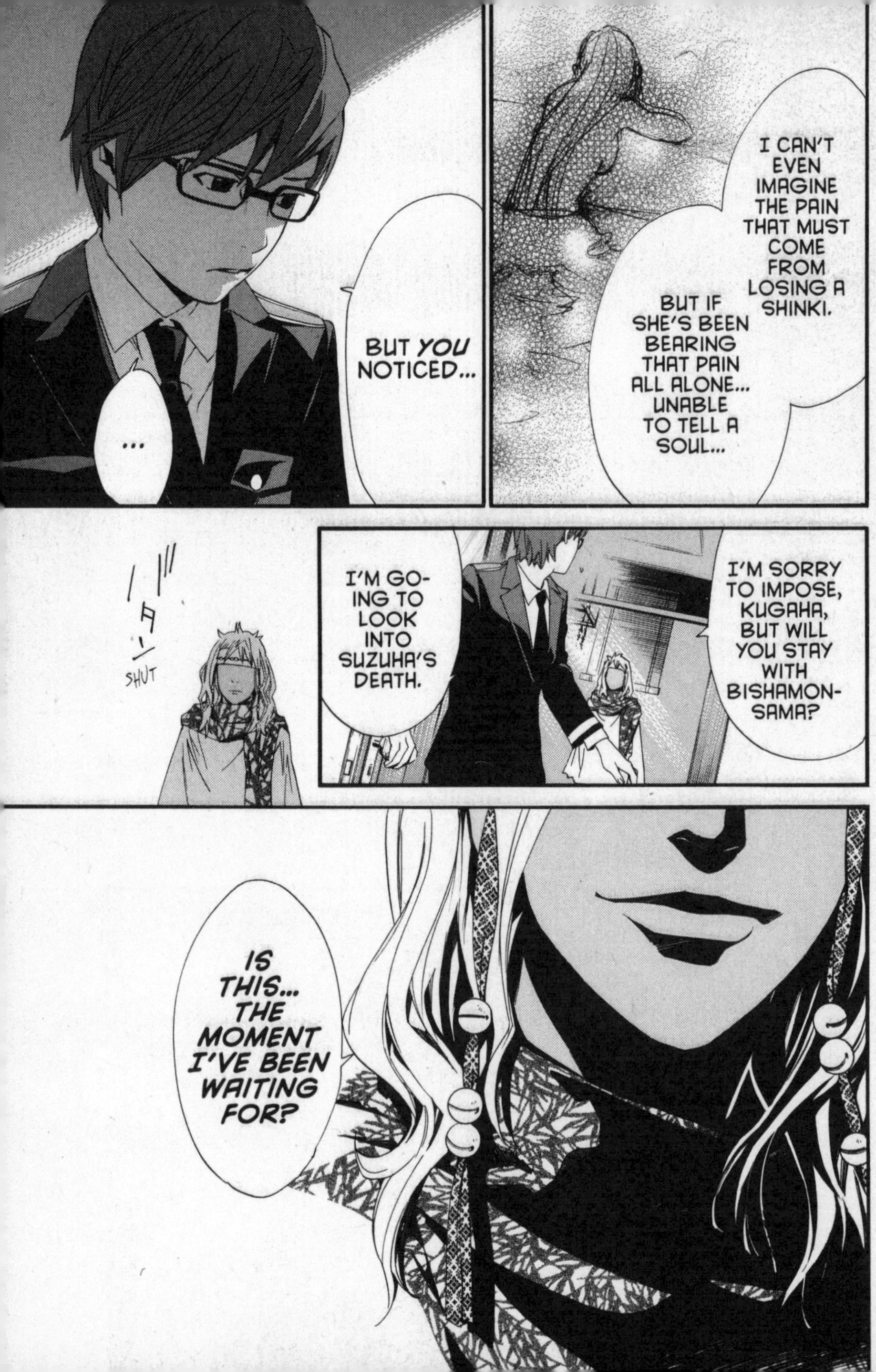
I CAN'T EVEN IMAGINE THE PAIN THAT MUST COME FROM LOSING A SHINKI.
BUT IF SHE'S BEEN BEARING THAT PAIN ALL ALONE... UNABLE TO TELL A SOUL...
BUT *YOU* NOTICED...
...
I'M SORRY TO IMPOSE, KUGAHA, BUT WILL YOU STAY WITH BISHAMON-SAMA?
I'M GO-ING TO LOOK INTO SUZUHA'S DEATH.
バタン
SHUT
IS THIS... THE MOMENT I'VE BEEN WAITING FOR?

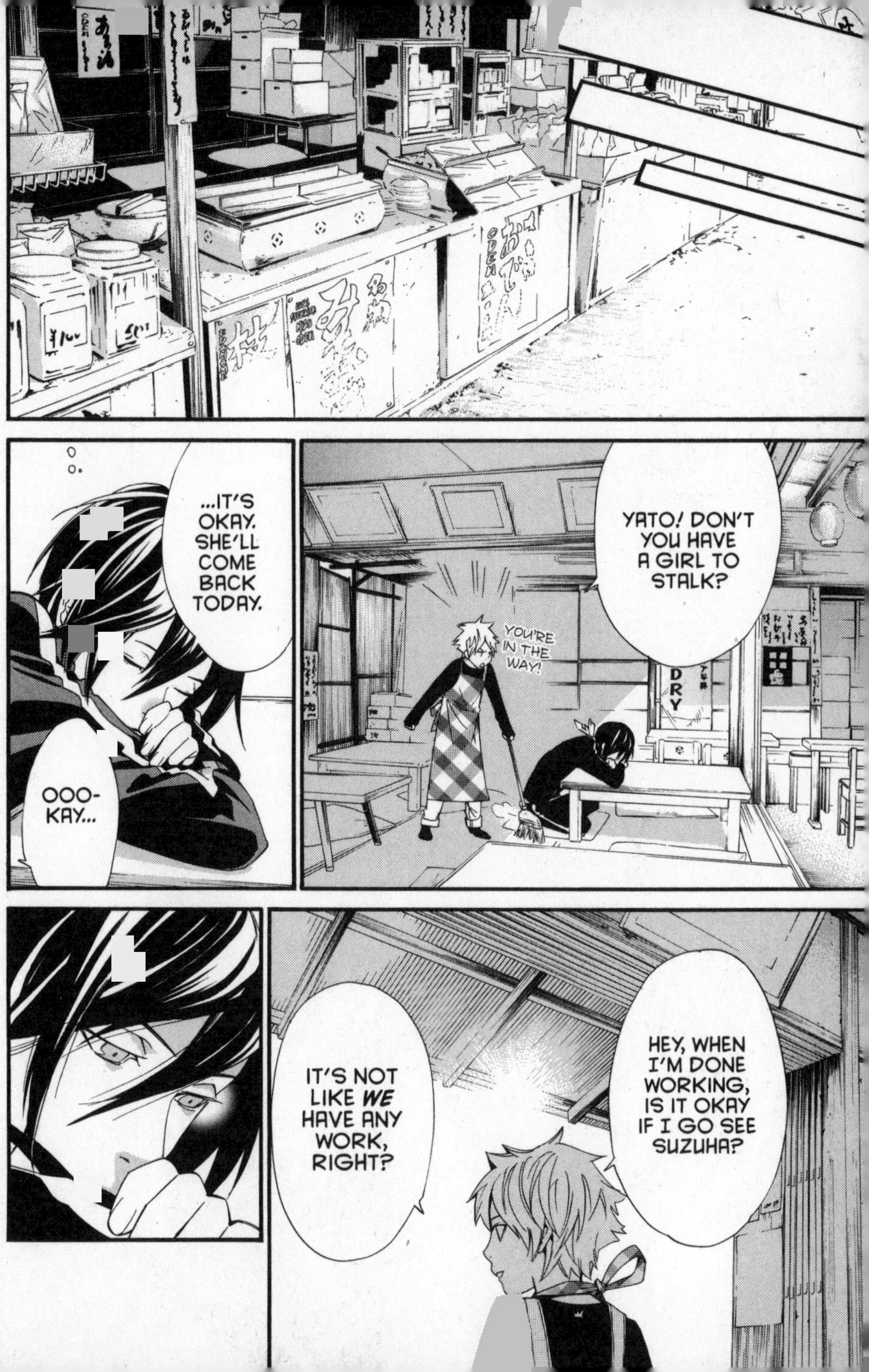
YATO! DON'T YOU HAVE A GIRL TO STALK?
YOU'RE IN THE WAY!
DRY
...IT'S OKAY. SHE'LL COME BACK TODAY.
OOO-KAY...
HEY, WHEN I'M DONE WORKING, IS IT OKAY IF I GO SEE SUZUHA?
IT'S NOT LIKE *WE* HAVE ANY WORK, RIGHT?

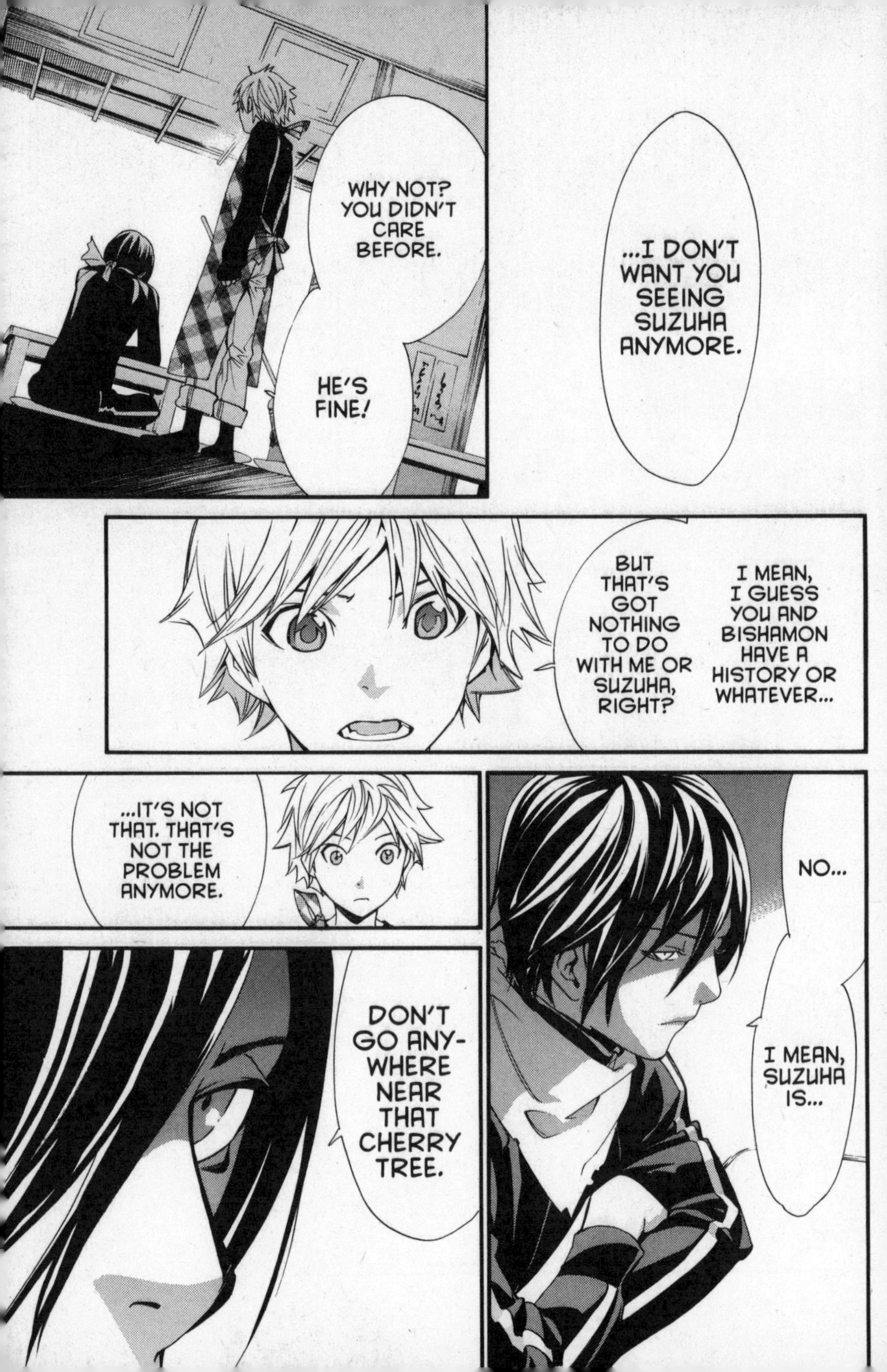
...I DON'T WANT YOU SEEING SUZUHA ANYMORE.
WHY NOT? YOU DIDN'T CARE BEFORE.
HE'S FINE!
I MEAN, I GUESS YOU AND BISHAMON HAVE A HISTORY OR WHATEVER...
BUT THAT'S GOT NOTHING TO DO WITH ME OR SUZUHA, RIGHT?
NO...
I MEAN, SUZUHA IS...
...IT'S NOT THAT. THAT'S NOT THE PROBLEM ANYMORE.
DON'T GO ANY-WHERE NEAR THAT CHERRY TREE.

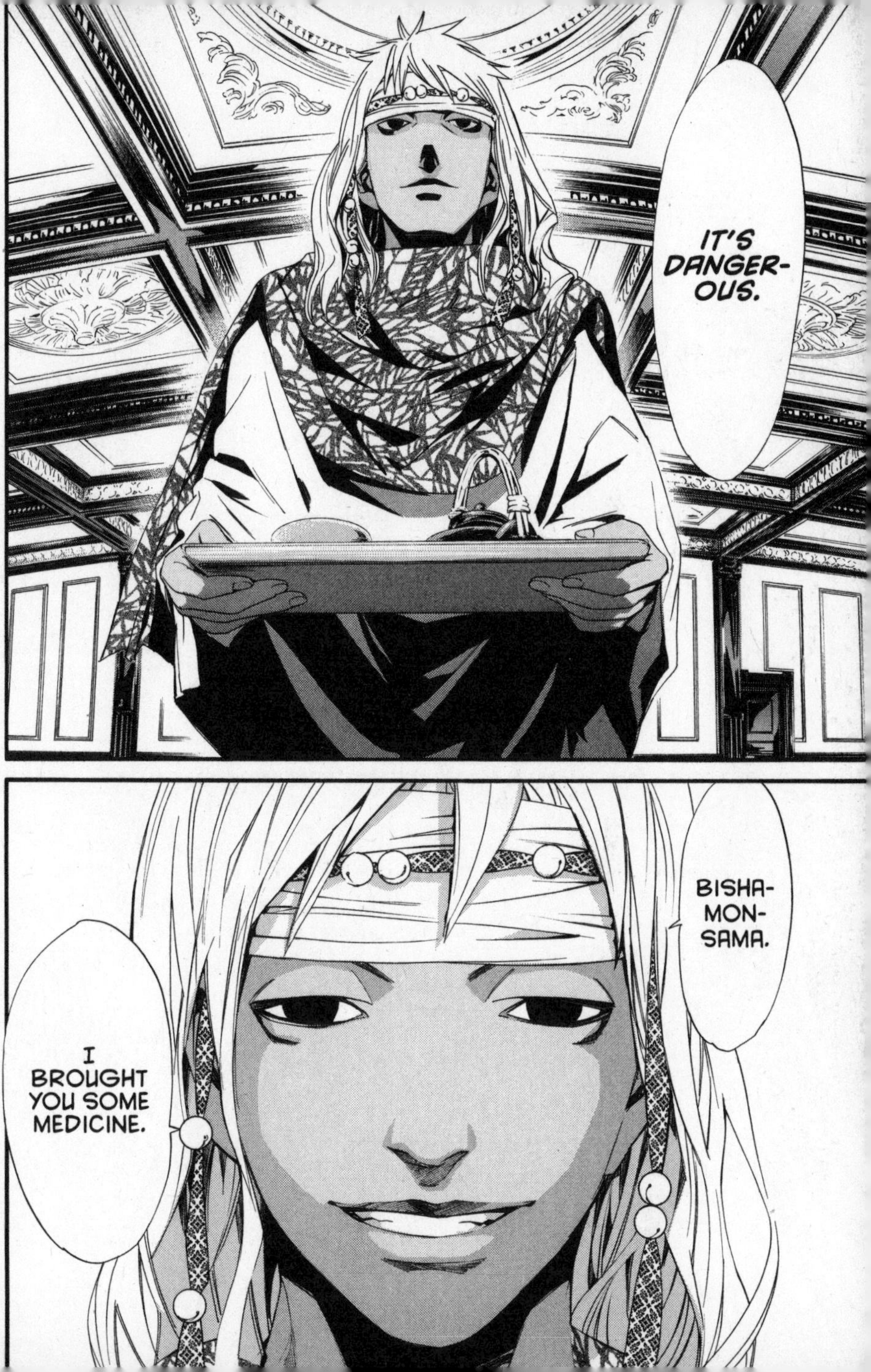
IT'S DANGER-OUS.
BISHA-MON-SAMA.
I BROUGHT YOU SOME MEDICINE.

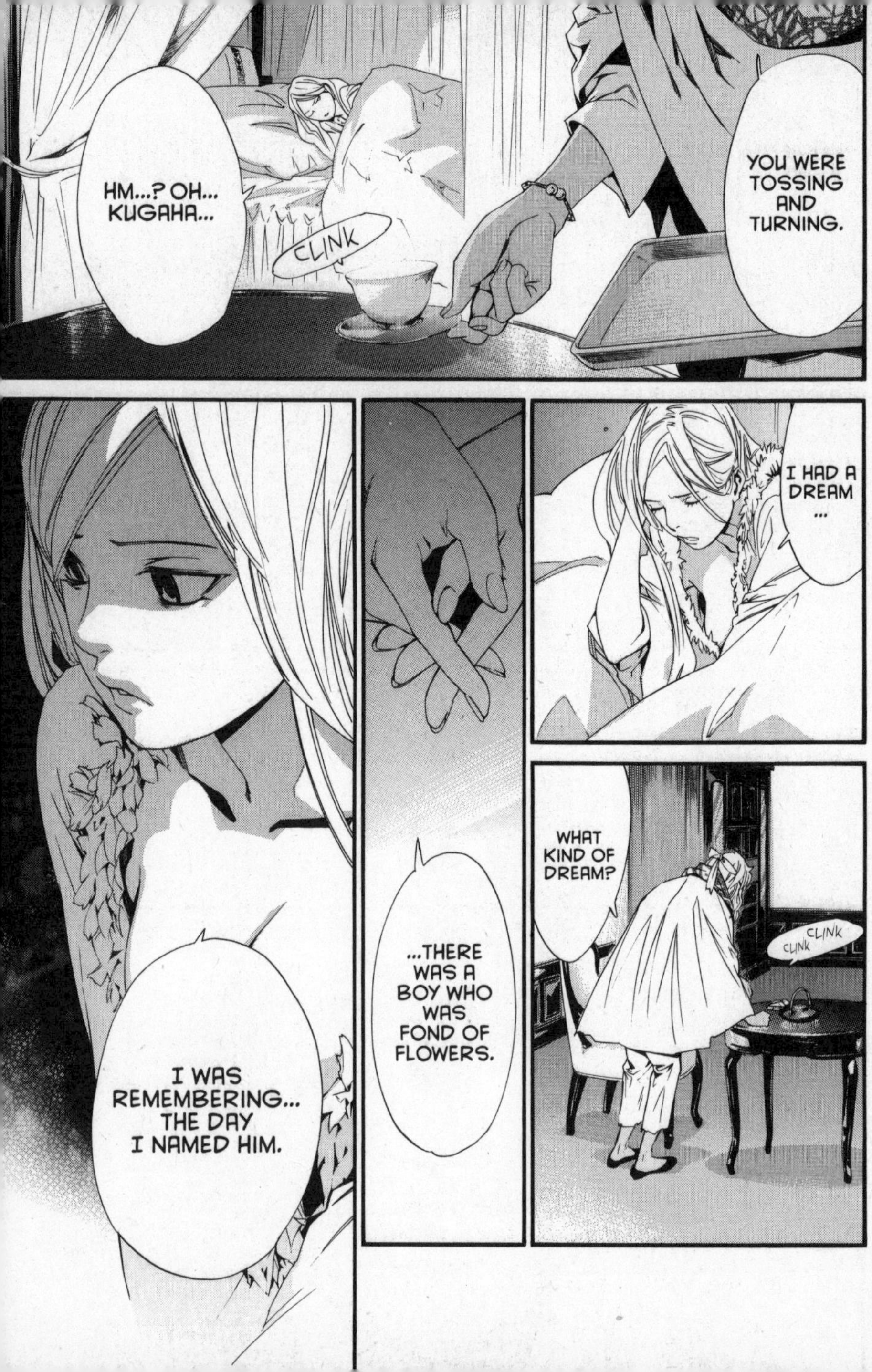
YOU WERE TOSSING AND TURNING.
CLINK
HM...? OH... KUGAHA...
I HAD A DREAM ...
WHAT KIND OF DREAM?
CLINK CLINK
...THERE WAS A BOY WHO WAS FOND OF FLOWERS.
I WAS REMEMBERING... THE DAY I NAMED HIM.

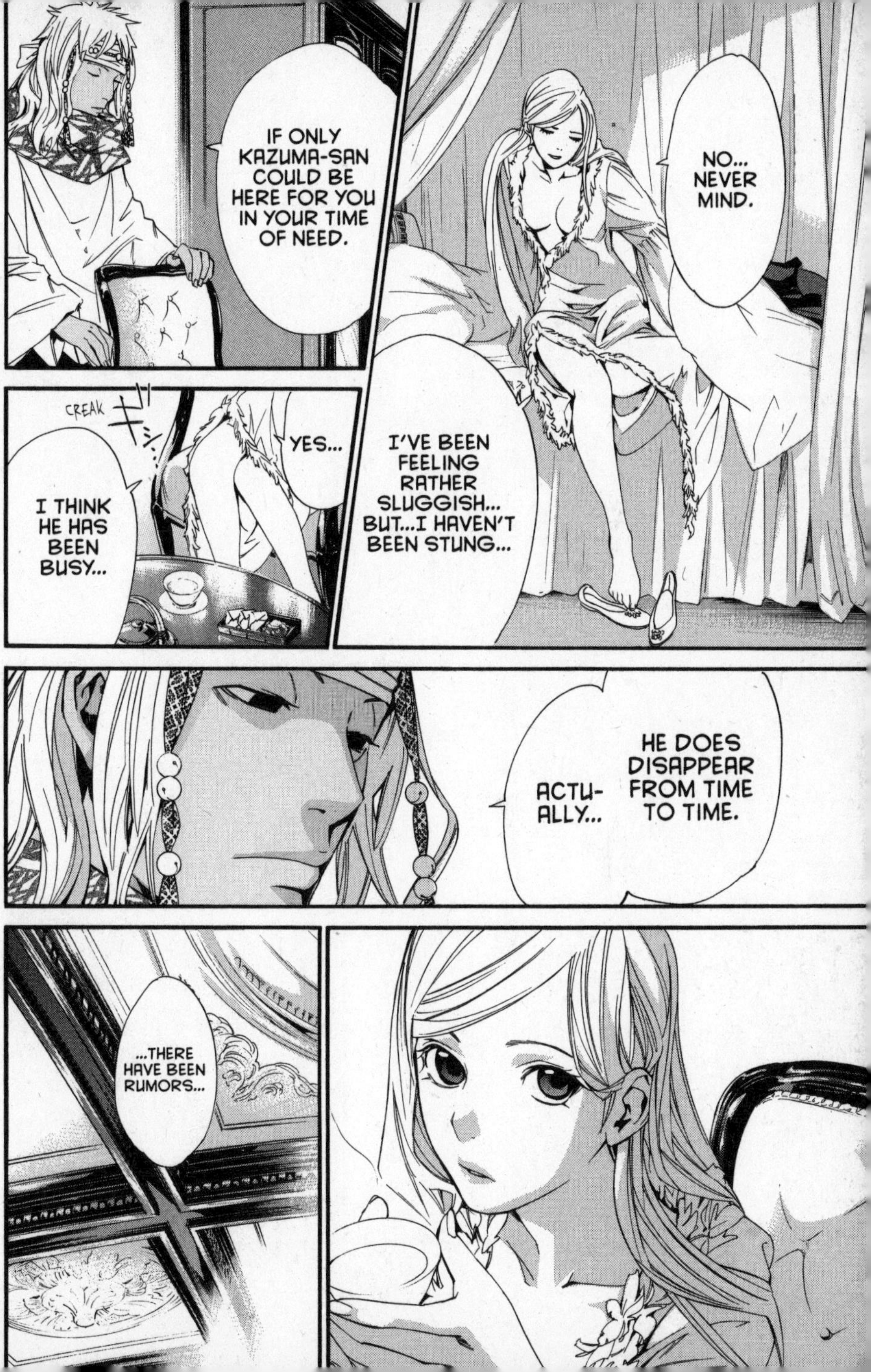
NO... NEVER MIND.
I'VE BEEN FEELING RATHER SLUGGISH... BUT...I HAVEN'T BEEN STUNG...
IF ONLY KAZUMA-SAN COULD BE HERE FOR YOU IN YOUR TIME OF NEED.
YES...
CREAK
I THINK HE HAS BEEN BUSY...
ACTU-ALLY... HE DOES DISAPPEAR FROM TIME TO TIME.
...THERE HAVE BEEN RUMORS...

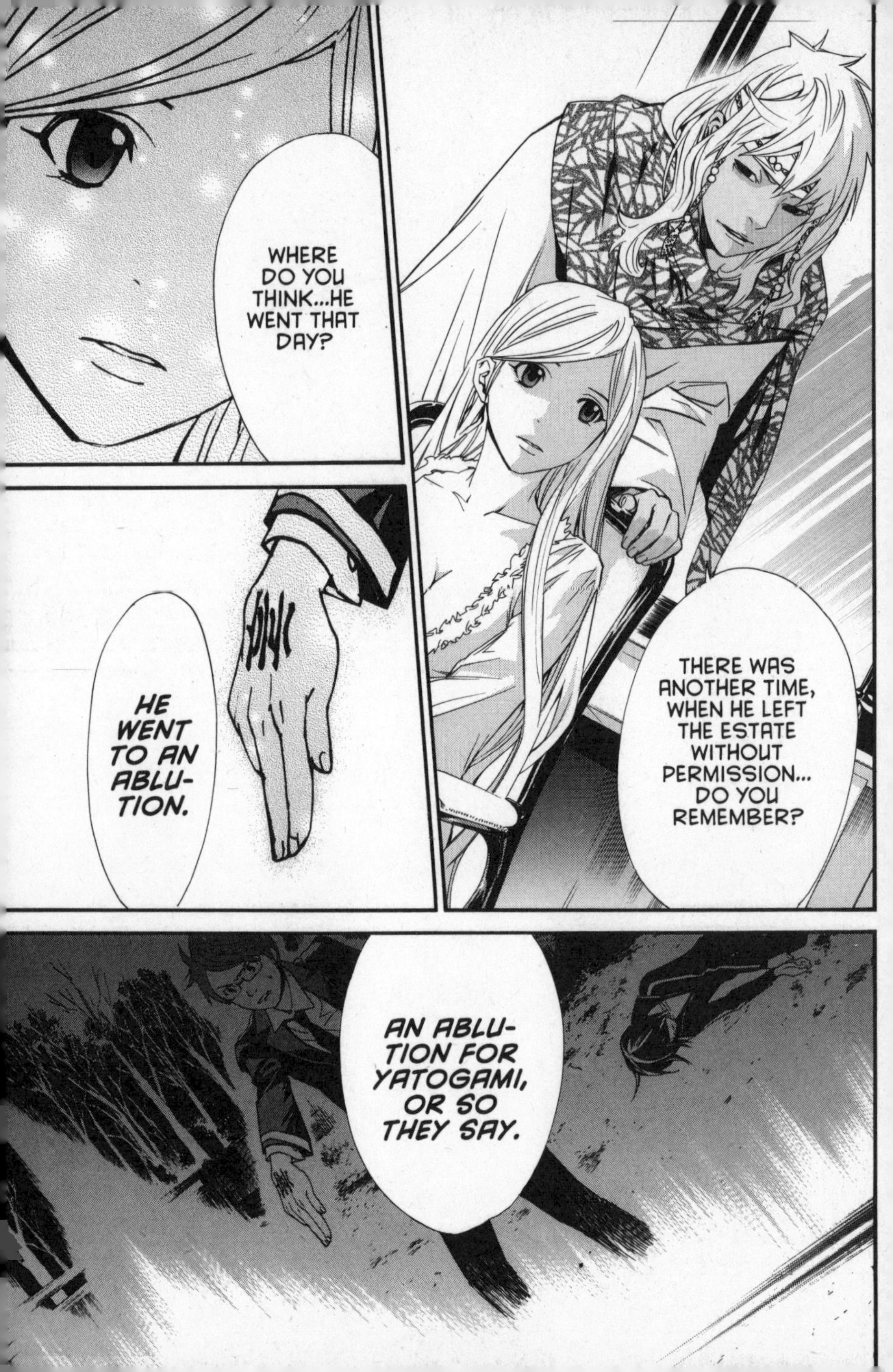
THERE WAS ANOTHER TIME, WHEN HE LEFT THE ESTATE WITHOUT PERMISSION... DO YOU REMEMBER?
WHERE DO YOU THINK...HE WENT THAT DAY?
HE WENT TO AN ABLUTION.
AN ABLUTION FOR YATOGAMI, OR SO THEY SAY.

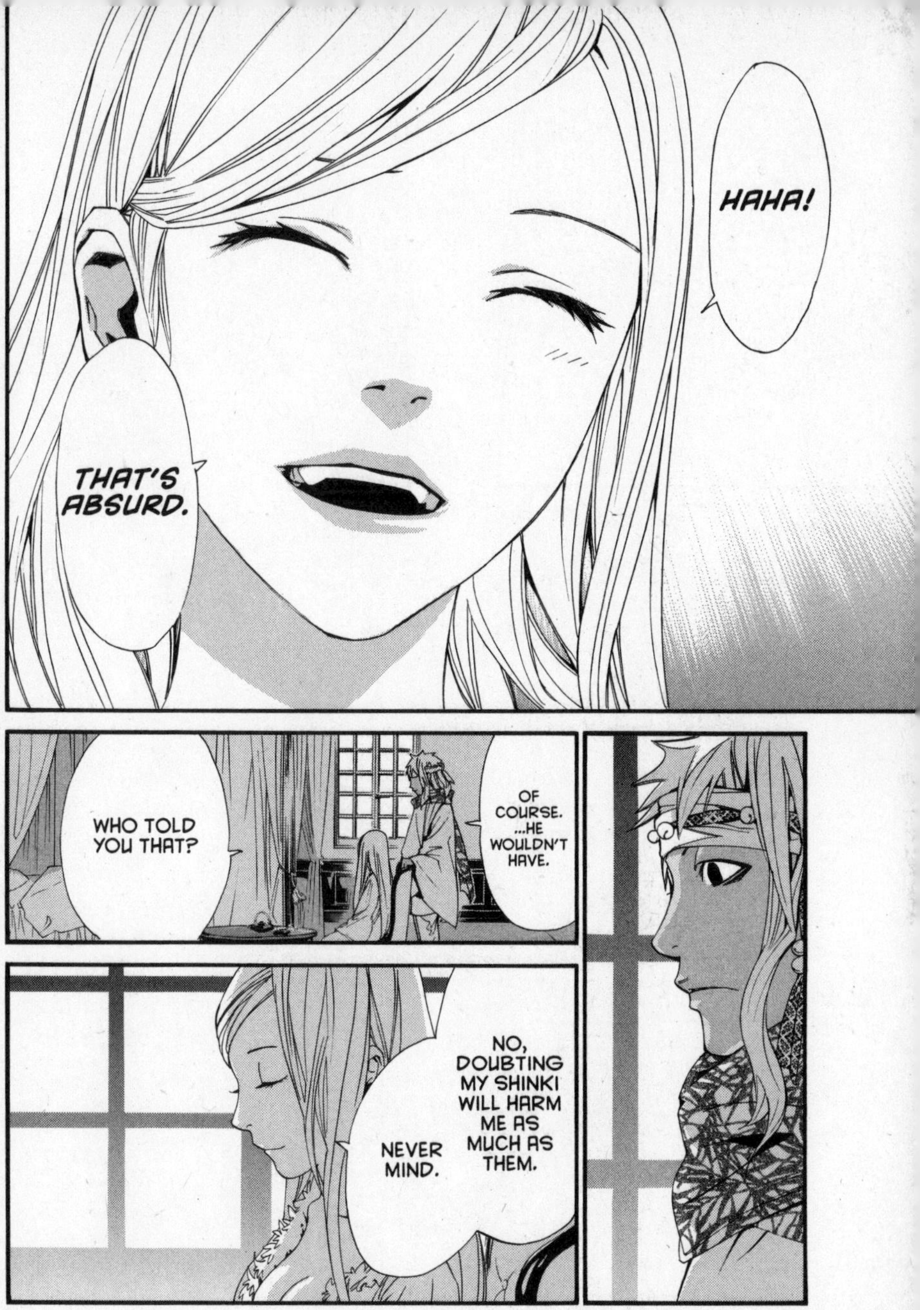
HAHA!
THAT'S ABSURD.
OF COURSE. ...HE WOULDN'T HAVE.
WHO TOLD YOU THAT?
NO, DOUBTING MY SHINKI WILL HARM ME AS MUCH AS THEM.
NEVER MIND.

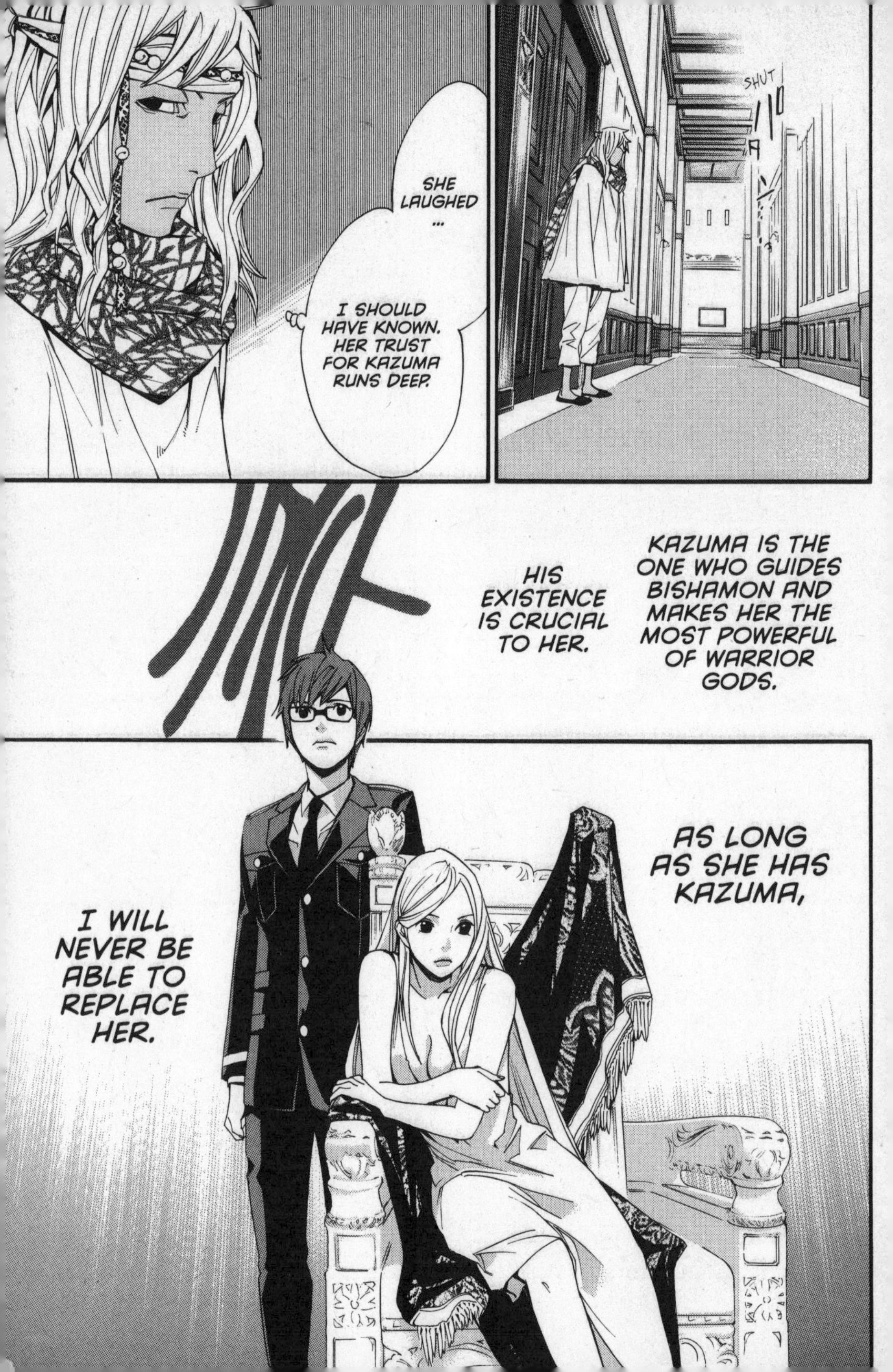
SHUT
SHE LAUGHED...
I SHOULD HAVE KNOWN. HER TRUST FOR KAZUMA RUNS DEEP.
KAZUMA IS THE ONE WHO GUIDES BISHAMON AND MAKES HER THE MOST POWERFUL OF WARRIOR GODS.
HIS EXISTENCE IS CRUCIAL TO HER.
AS LONG AS SHE HAS KAZUMA,
I WILL NEVER BE ABLE TO REPLACE HER.

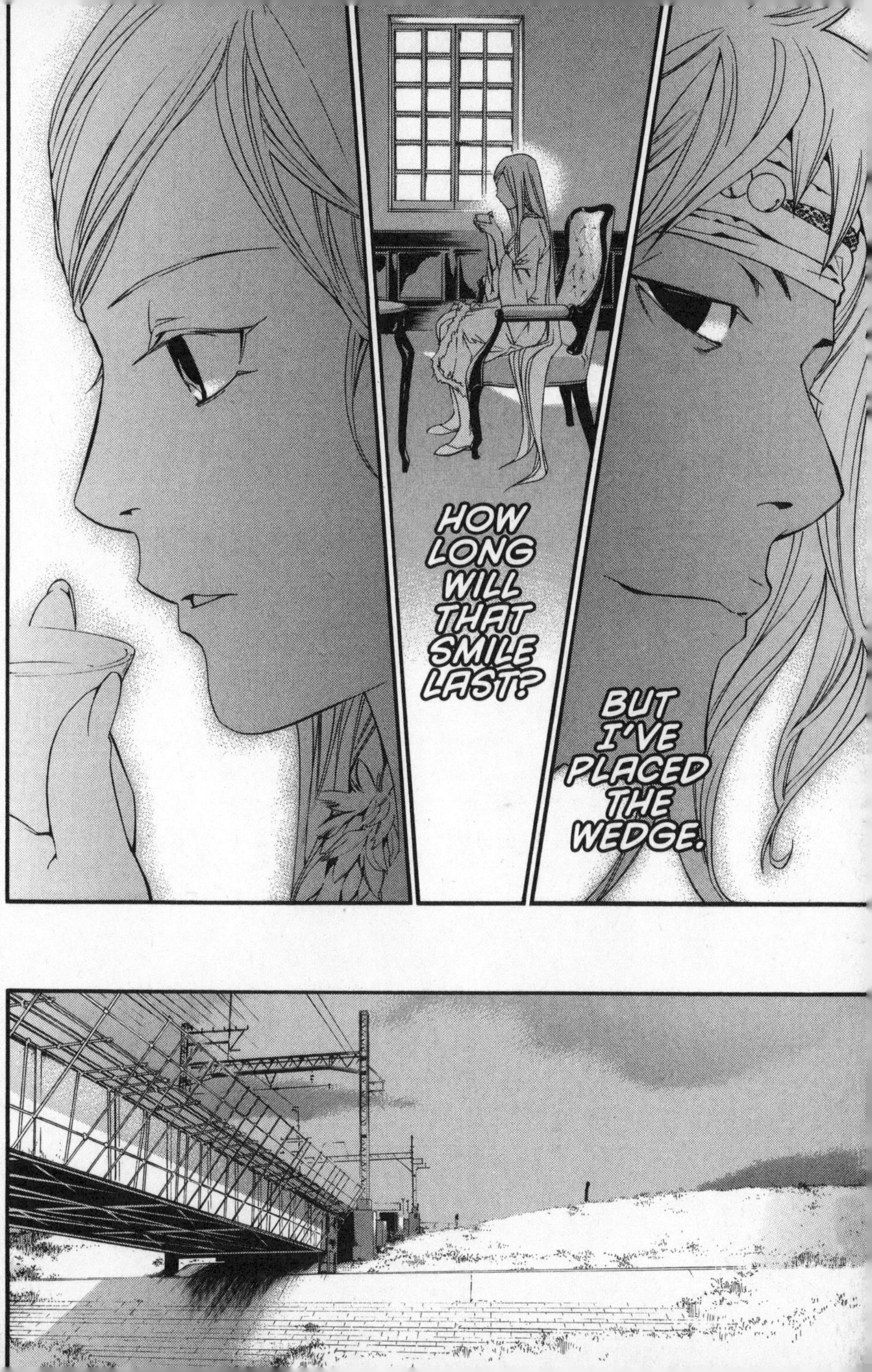
HOW LONG WILL THAT SMILE LAST?
BUT I'VE PLACED THE WEDGE.

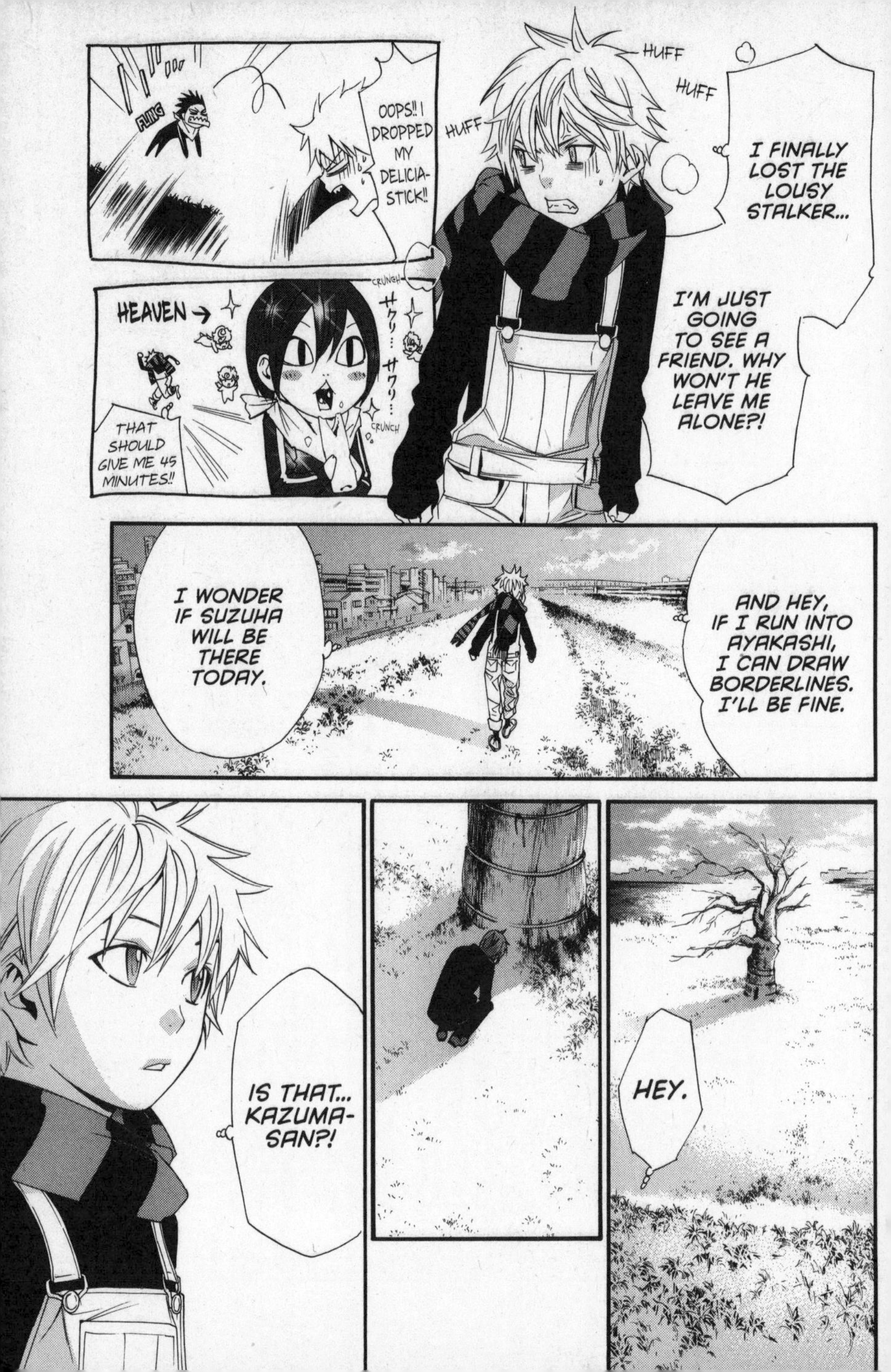
HUFF
HUFF
HUFF
I FINALLY LOST THE LOUSY STALKER...
I'M JUST GOING TO SEE A FRIEND. WHY WON'T HE LEAVE ME ALONE?!
FLING
OOPS!! I DROPPED MY DELICIA-STICK!!
CRUNCH
サクリ… サワリ…
CRUNCH
HEAVEN →
THAT SHOULD GIVE ME 45 MINUTES!!
AND HEY, IF I RUN INTO AYAKASHI, I CAN DRAW BORDERLINES. I'LL BE FINE.
I WONDER IF SUZUHA WILL BE THERE TODAY.
HEY.
IS THAT... KAZUMA-SAN?!

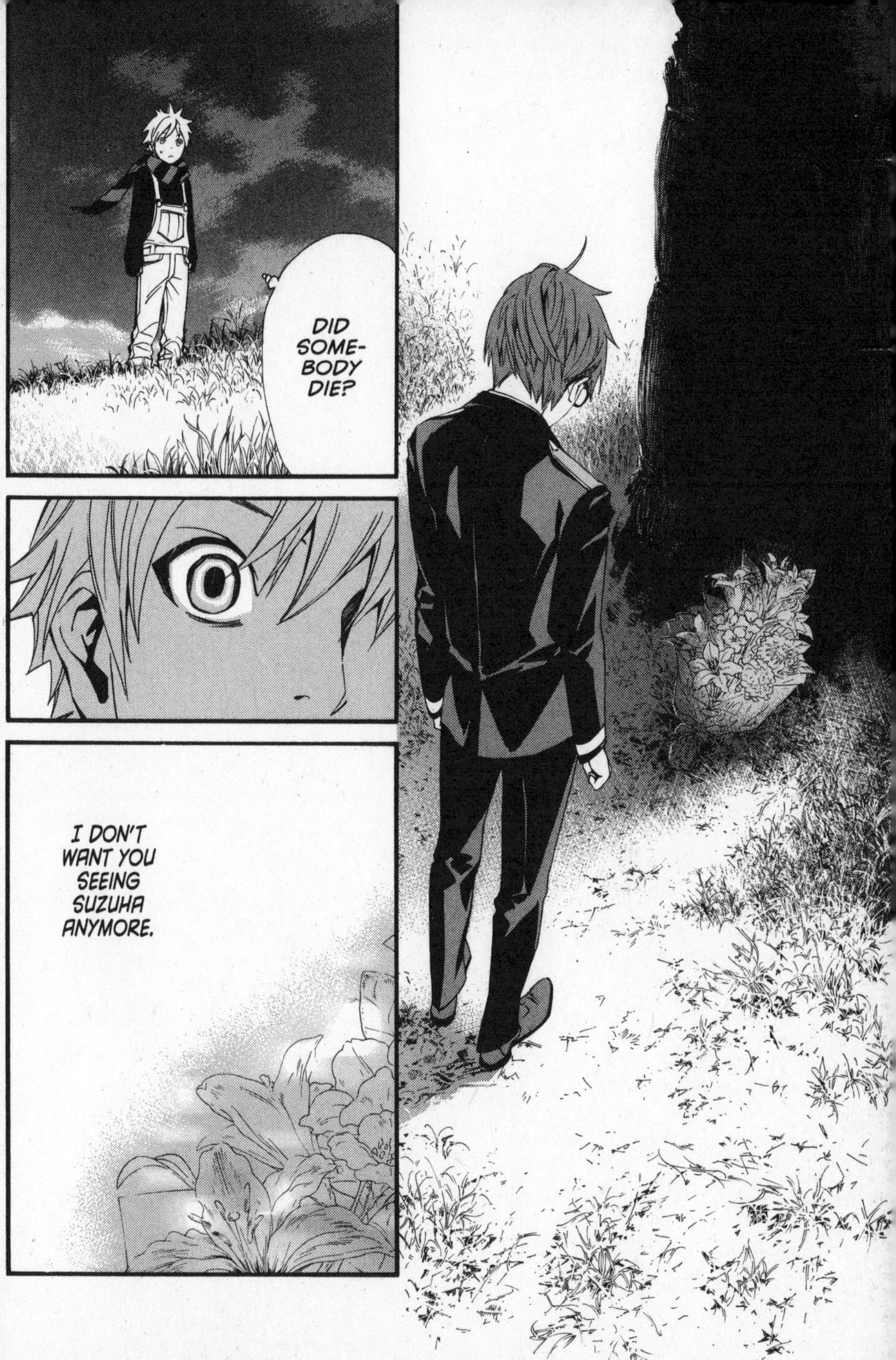
DID SOMEBODY DIE?
I DON'T WANT YOU SEEING SUZUHA ANYMORE.

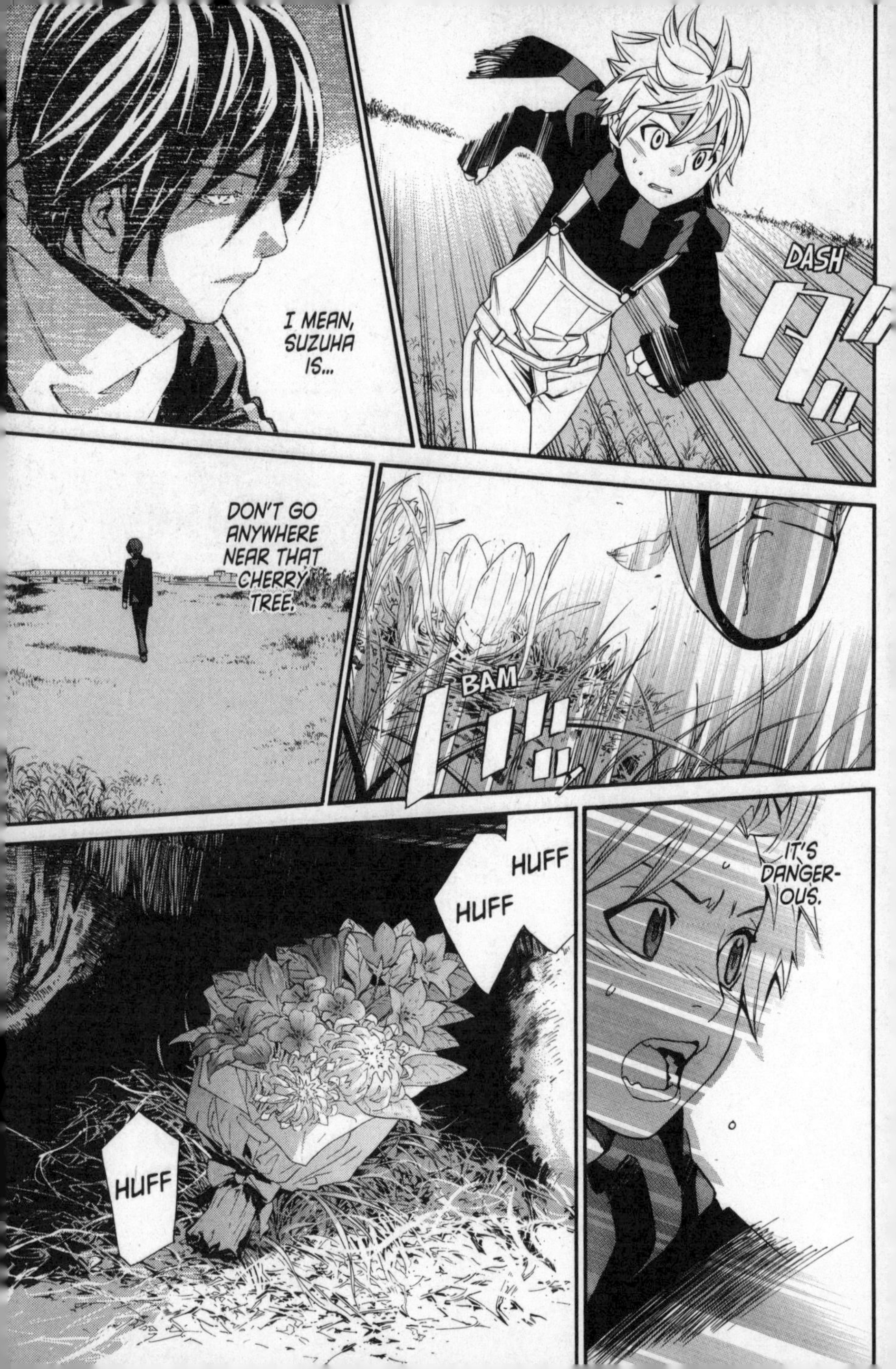
DASH
ダッ
I MEAN, SUZUHA IS...
BAM
ドッ
DON'T GO ANYWHERE NEAR THAT CHERRY TREE.
IT'S DANGER-OUS.
HUFF
HUFF
HUFF

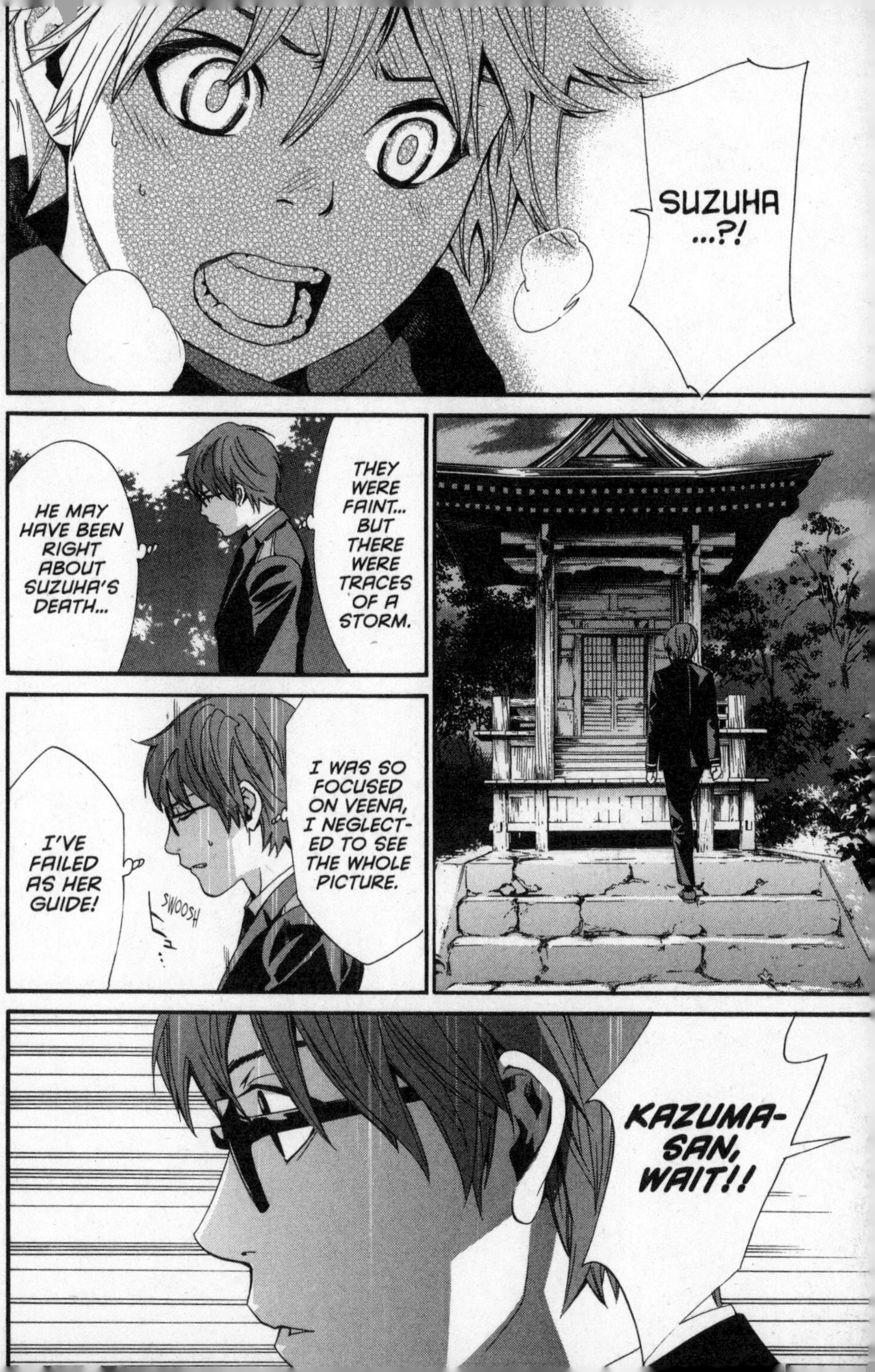
SUZUHA ...?!
THEY WERE FAINT... BUT THERE WERE TRACES OF A STORM.
HE MAY HAVE BEEN RIGHT ABOUT SUZUHA'S DEATH...
I WAS SO FOCUSED ON VEENA, I NEGLECT-ED TO SEE THE WHOLE PICTURE.
SWOOSH
I'VE FAILED AS HER GUIDE!
KAZUMA-SAN, WAIT!!

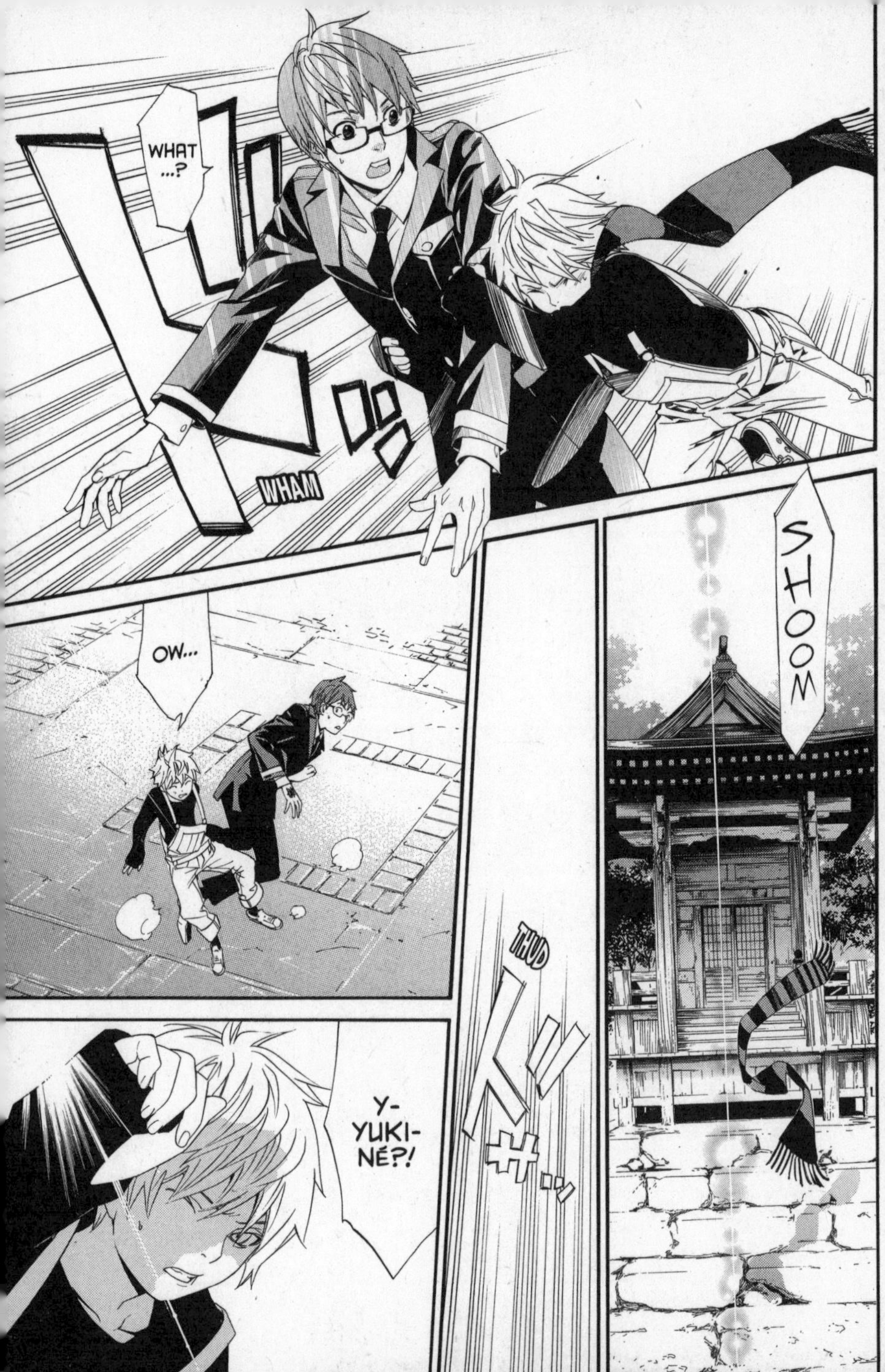
WHAT ...?
WHAM
SHOOM
THUD
OW...
Y-YUKINÉ?!

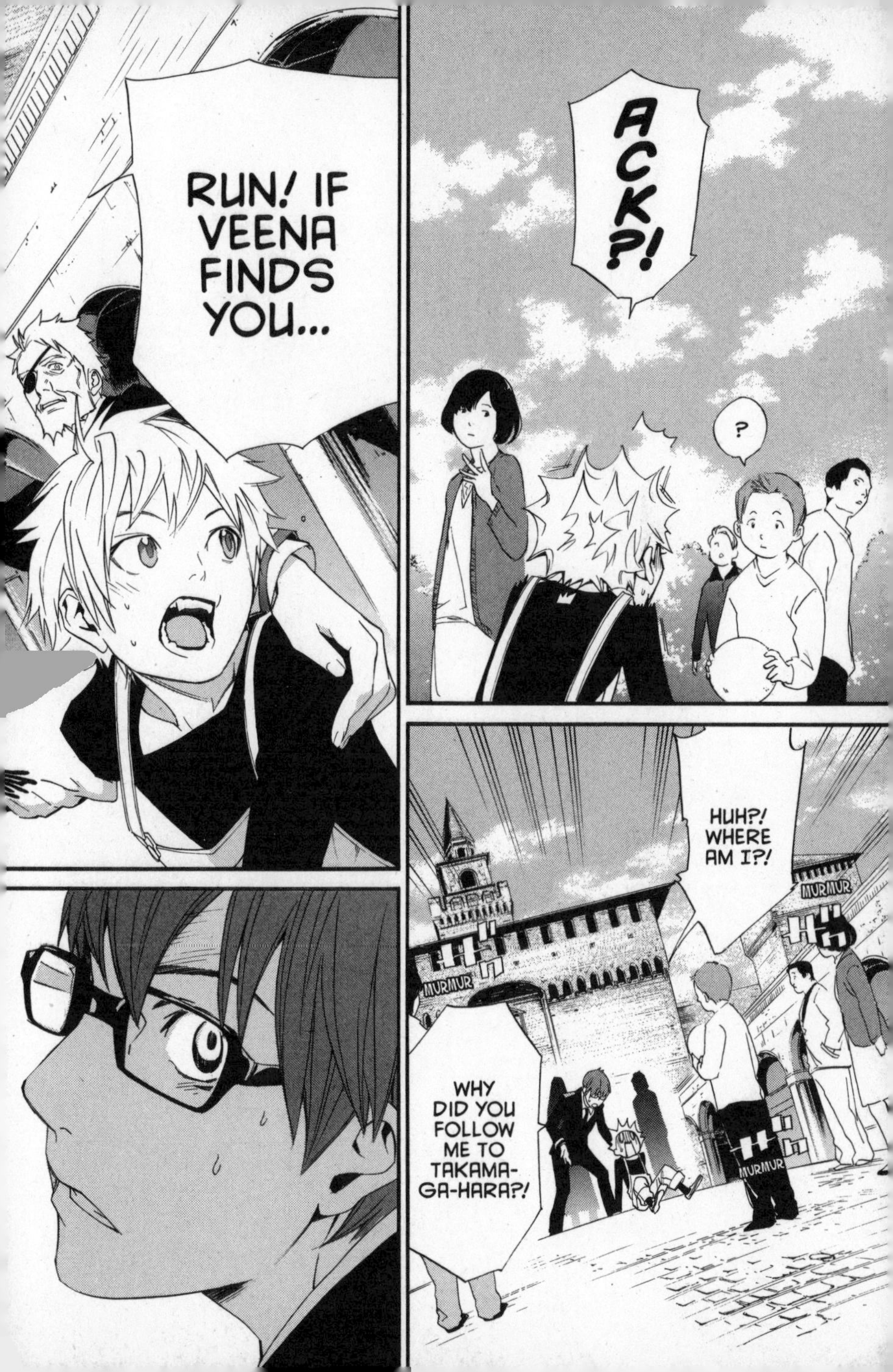
ACK?!
?
RUN! IF VEENA FINDS YOU...
HUH?! WHERE AM I?!
MURMUR
MURMUR
WHY DID YOU FOLLOW ME TO TAKAMA-GA-HARA?!
MURMUR

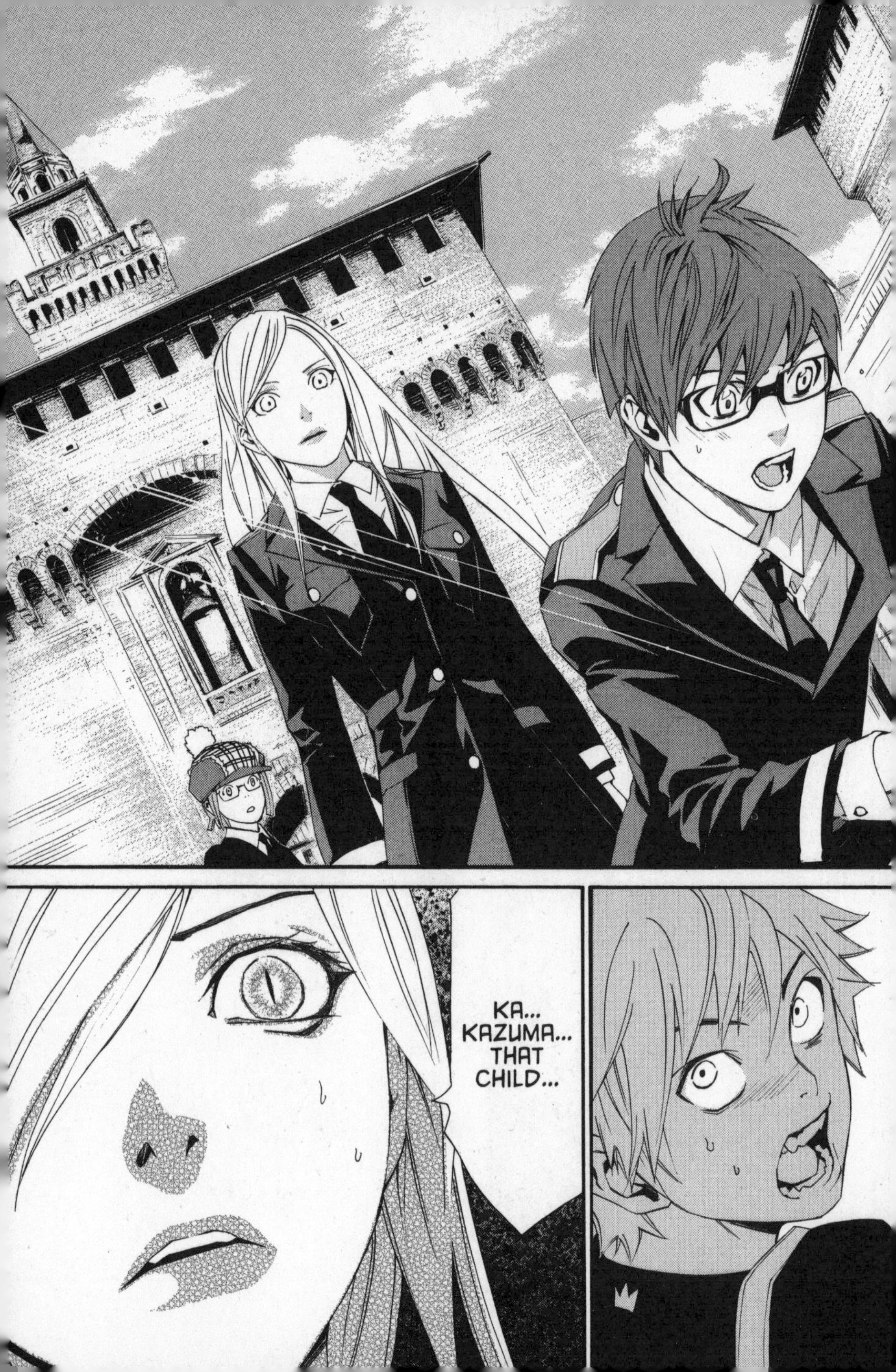
KA... KAZUMA... THAT CHILD...

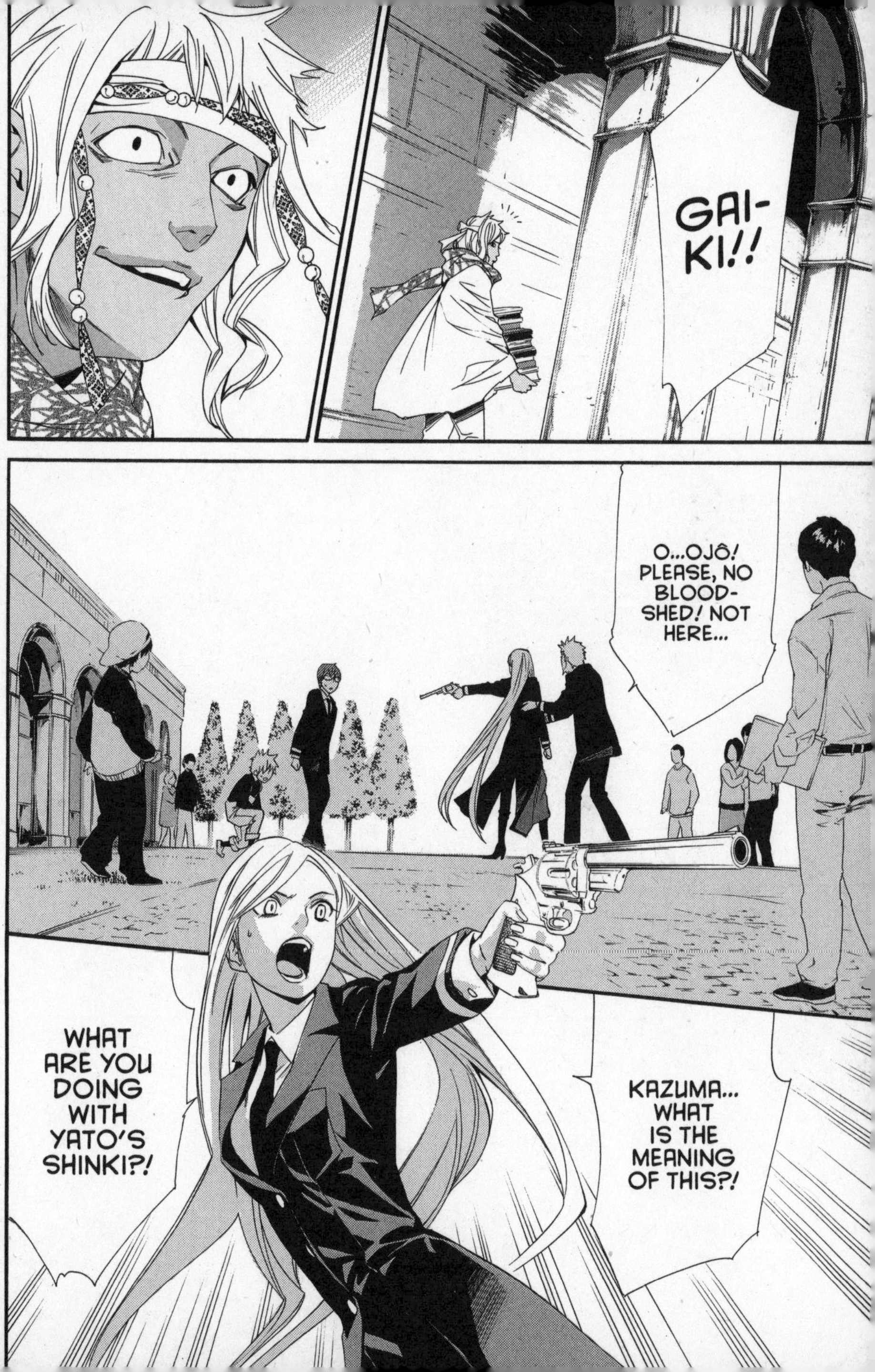
GAI-KI!!
O...OJÔ! PLEASE, NO BLOOD-SHED! NOT HERE...
KAZUMA... WHAT IS THE MEANING OF THIS?!
WHAT ARE YOU DOING WITH YATO'S SHINKI?!

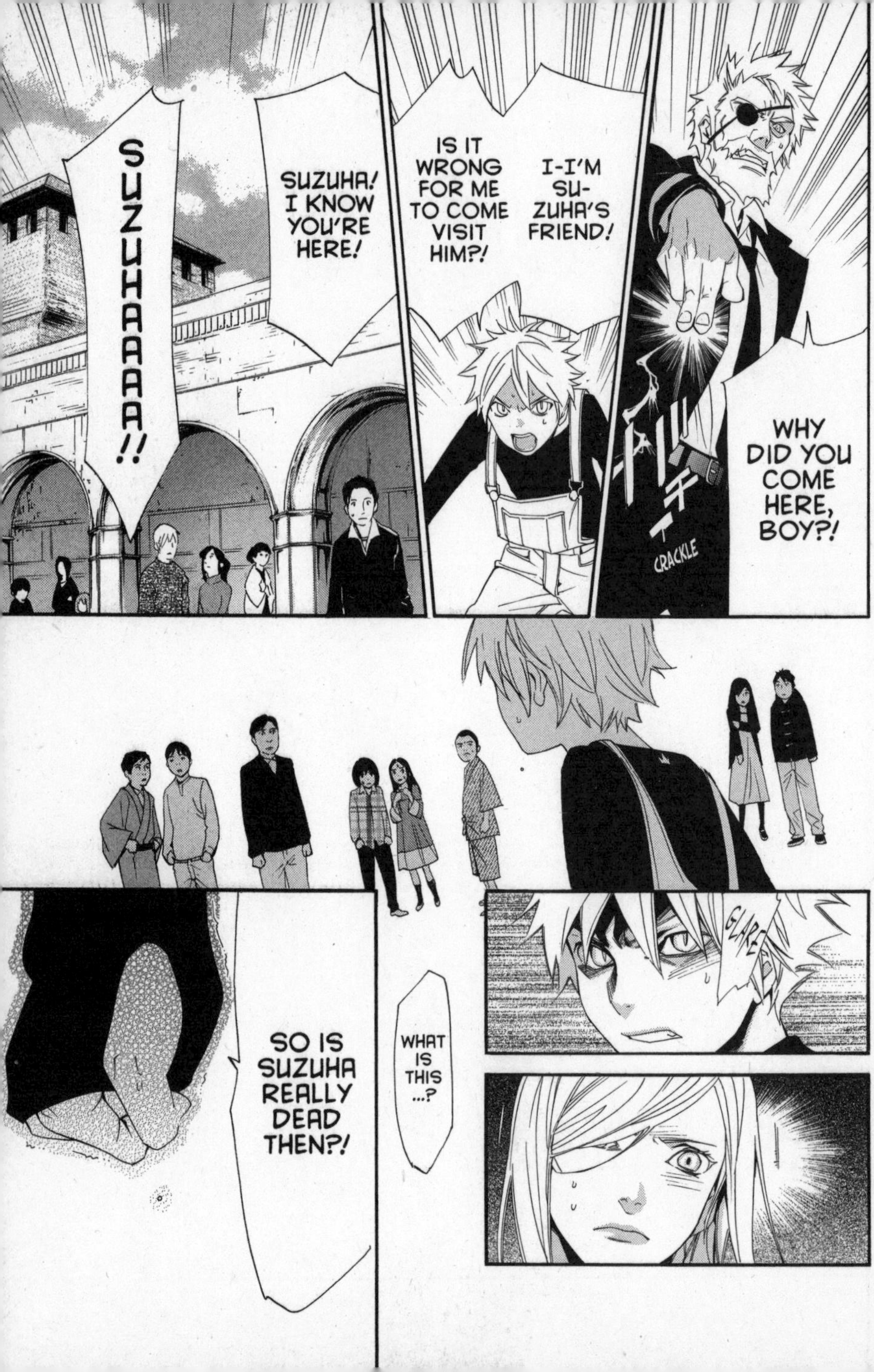
WHY DID YOU COME HERE, BOY?!
CRACKLE
I-I'M SU-ZUHA'S FRIEND!
IS IT WRONG FOR ME TO COME VISIT HIM?!
SUZUHA! I KNOW YOU'RE HERE!
SUZUHAAAAAA!!
GLARE
WHAT IS THIS ...?
SO IS SUZUHA REALLY DEAD THEN?!

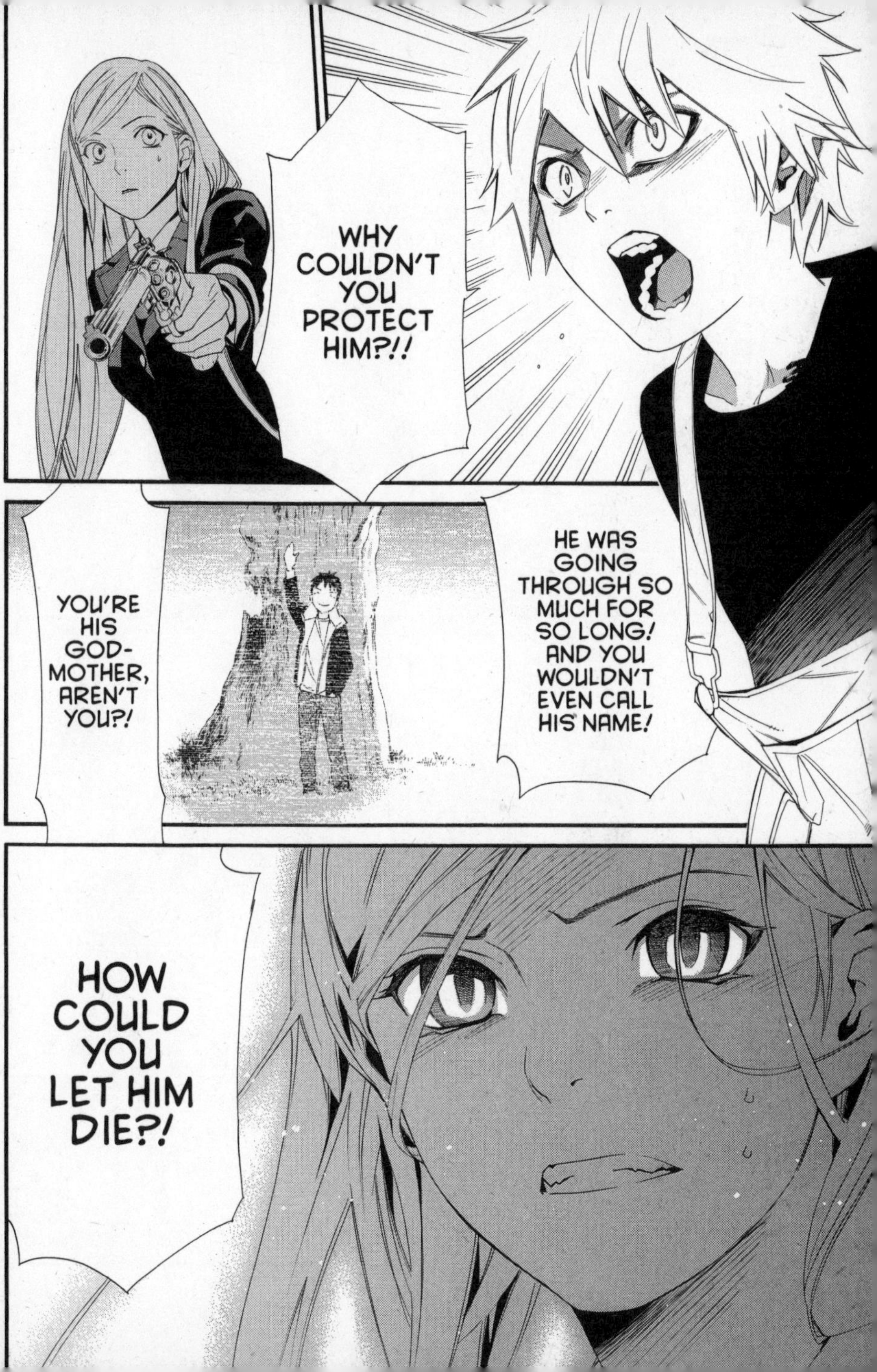
WHY COULDN'T YOU PROTECT HIM?!!
HE WAS GOING THROUGH SO MUCH FOR SO LONG! AND YOU WOULDN'T EVEN CALL HIS NAME!
YOU'RE HIS GOD-MOTHER, AREN'T YOU?!
HOW COULD YOU LET HIM DIE?!

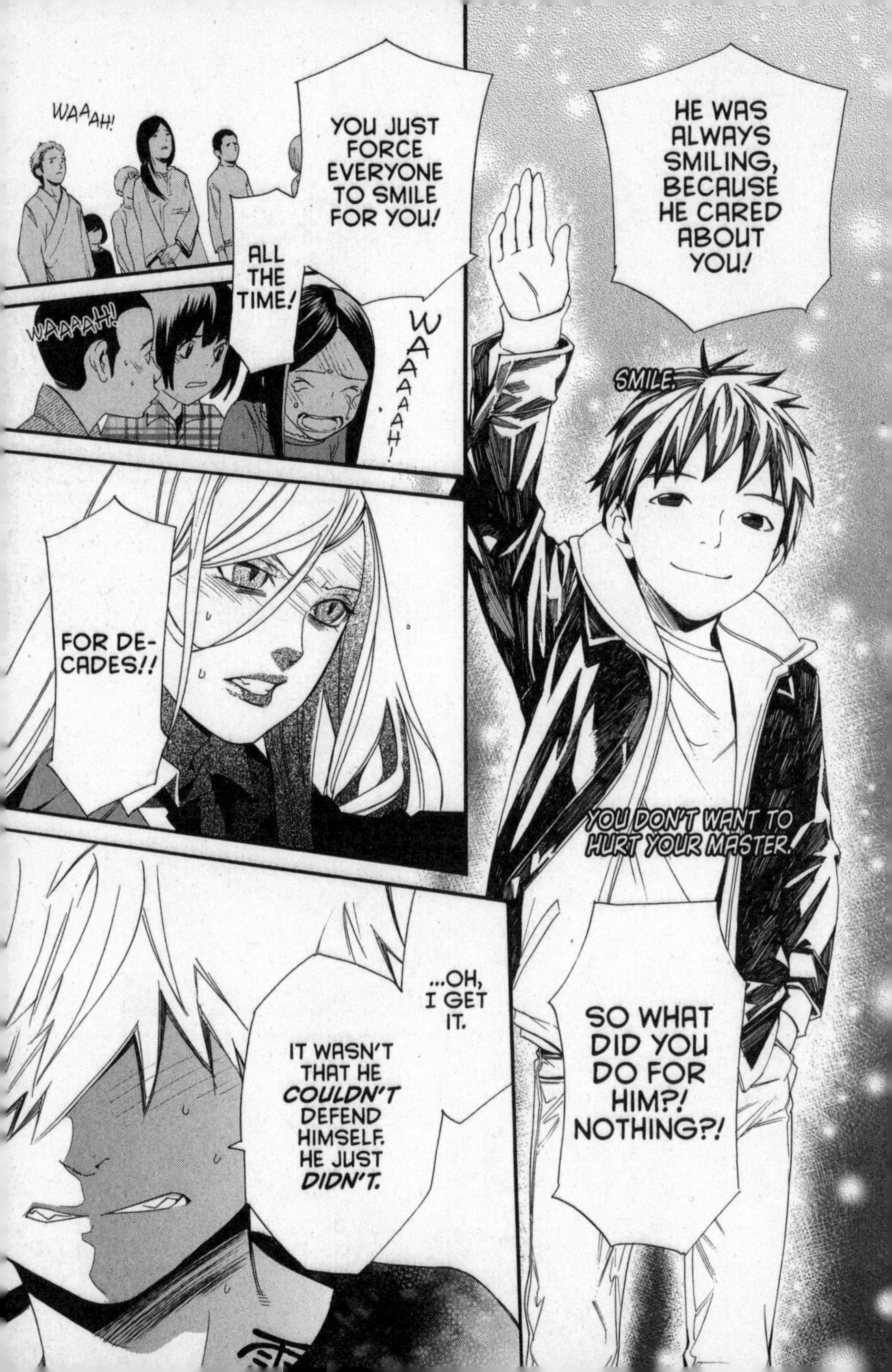
HE WAS ALWAYS SMILING, BECAUSE HE CARED ABOUT YOU!
SMILE.
YOU DON'T WANT TO HURT YOUR MASTER.
SO WHAT DID YOU DO FOR HIM?! NOTHING?!
YOU JUST FORCE EVERYONE TO SMILE FOR YOU!
WAAAH!
ALL THE TIME!
WAAAAAH!
WAAAAH!
FOR DE-CADES!!
...OH, I GET IT.
IT WASN'T THAT HE *COULDN'T* DEFEND HIMSELF. HE JUST *DIDN'T*.

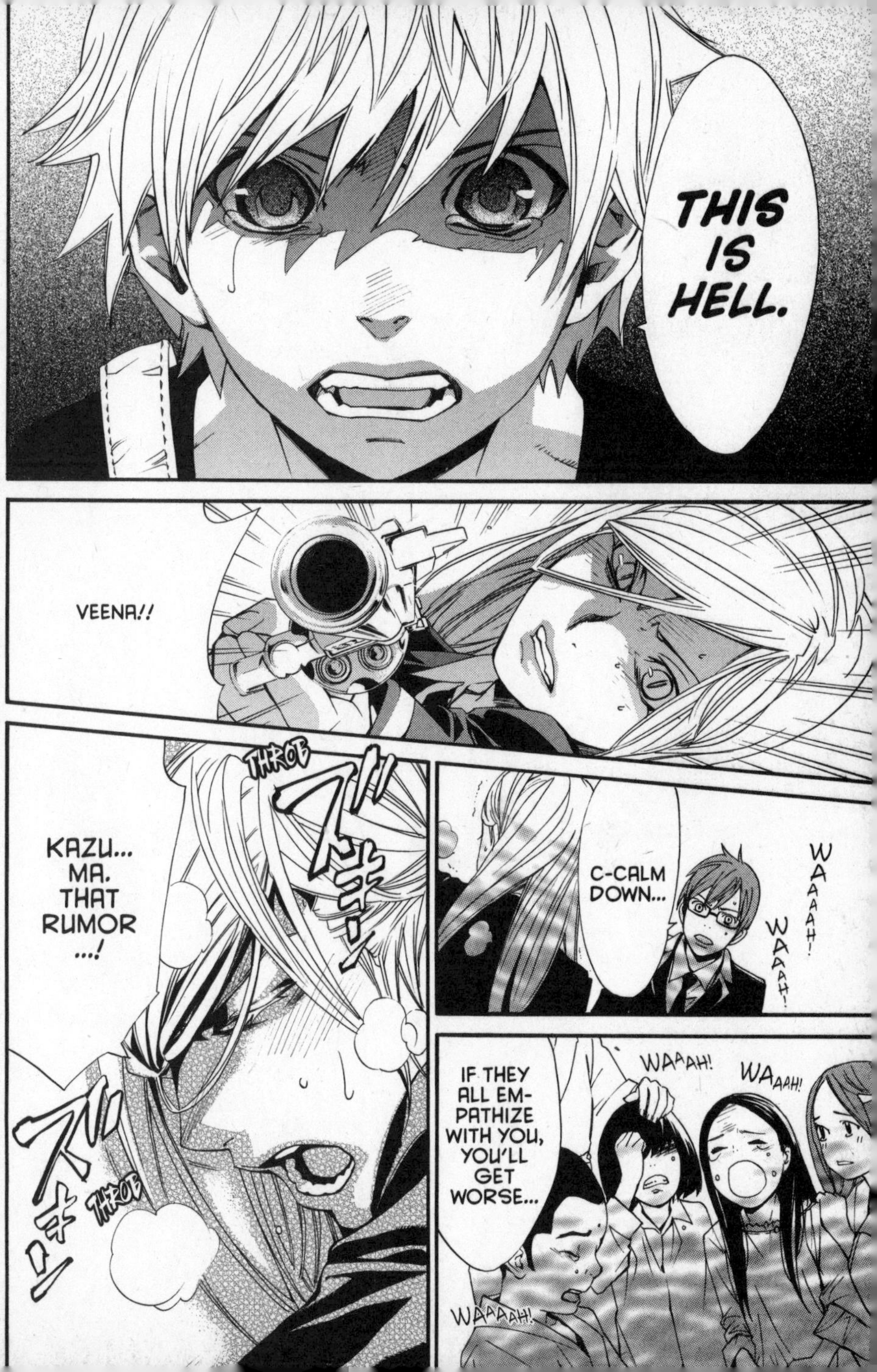
THIS IS HELL.
VEENA!!
WAAAAH!
WAAAH!
C-CALM DOWN...
WAAAH!
WAAAH!
IF THEY ALL EM-PATHIZE WITH YOU, YOU'LL GET WORSE...
WAAAAH!
THROB
KAZU... MA. THAT RUMOR ...!
THROB

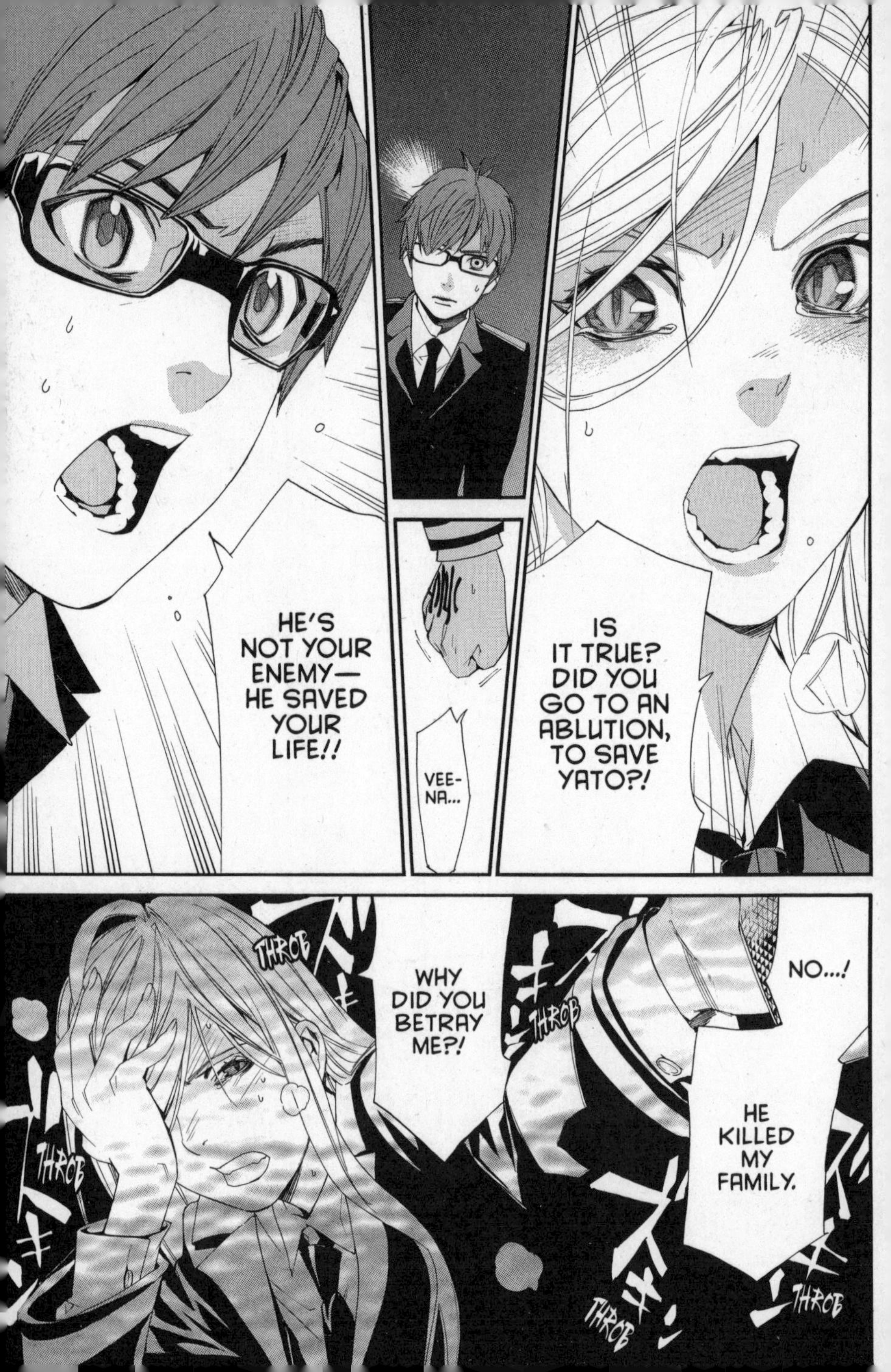
IS IT TRUE? DID YOU GO TO AN ABLUTION, TO SAVE YATO?!
VEE-NA...
HE'S NOT YOUR ENEMY— HE SAVED YOUR LIFE!!
NO...!
HE KILLED MY FAMILY.
THROB
THROB
THROB
WHY DID YOU BETRAY ME?!
THROB
THROB
THROB

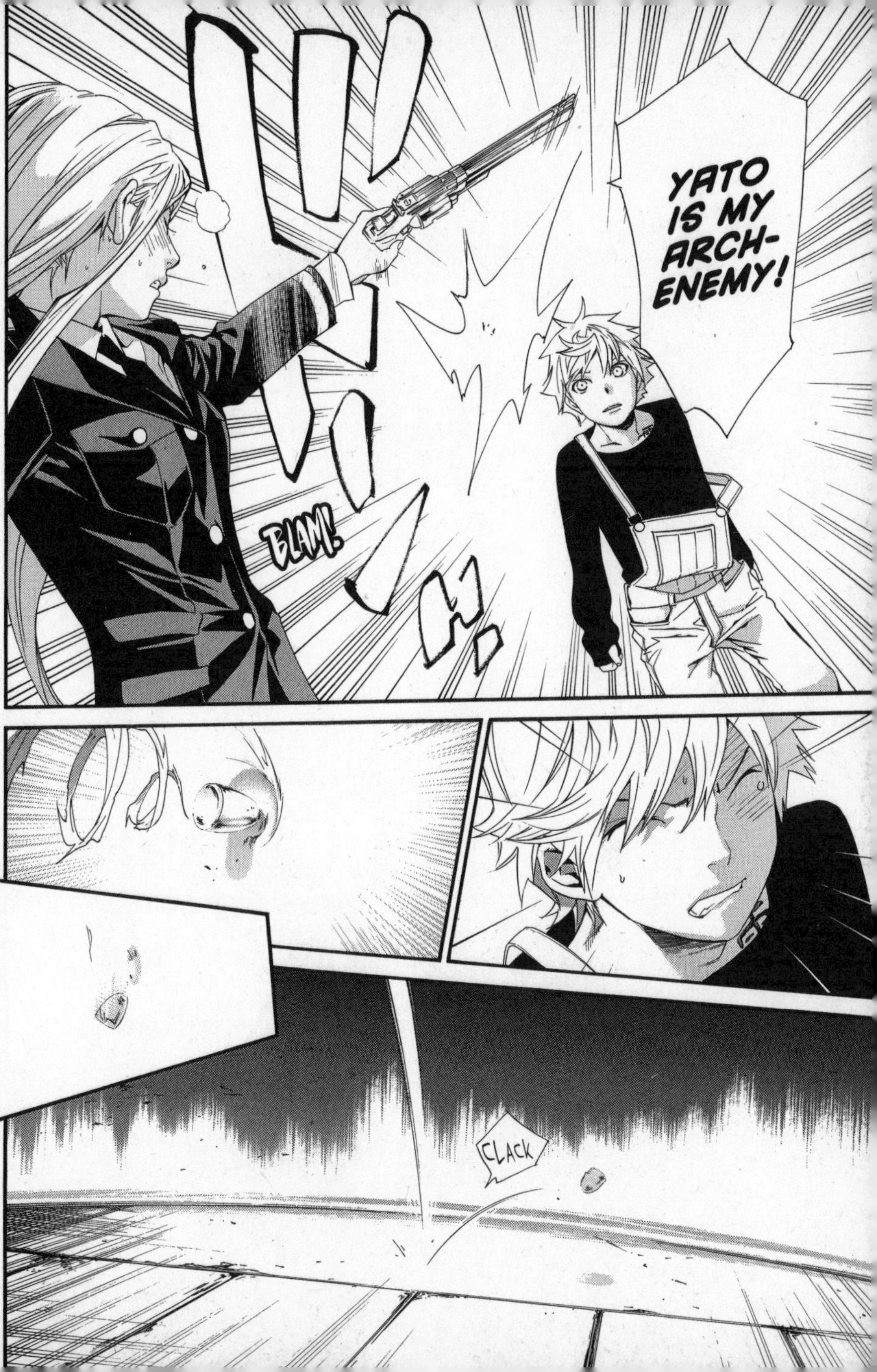
YATO IS MY ARCH-ENEMY!
BLAM!
CLACK

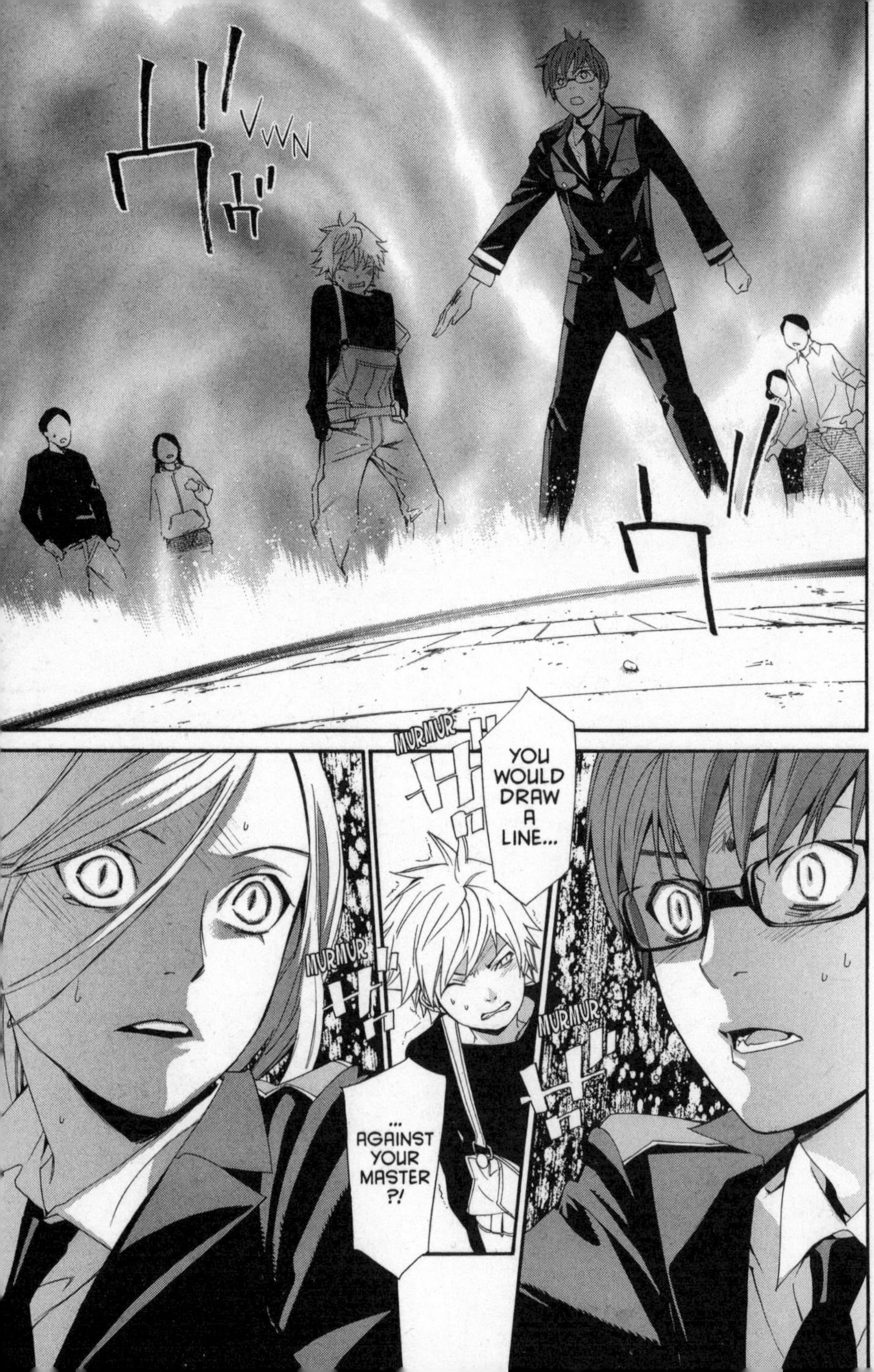
VVVN
YOU WOULD DRAW A LINE...
MURMUR
MURMUR
MURMUR
...AGAINST YOUR MASTER ?!

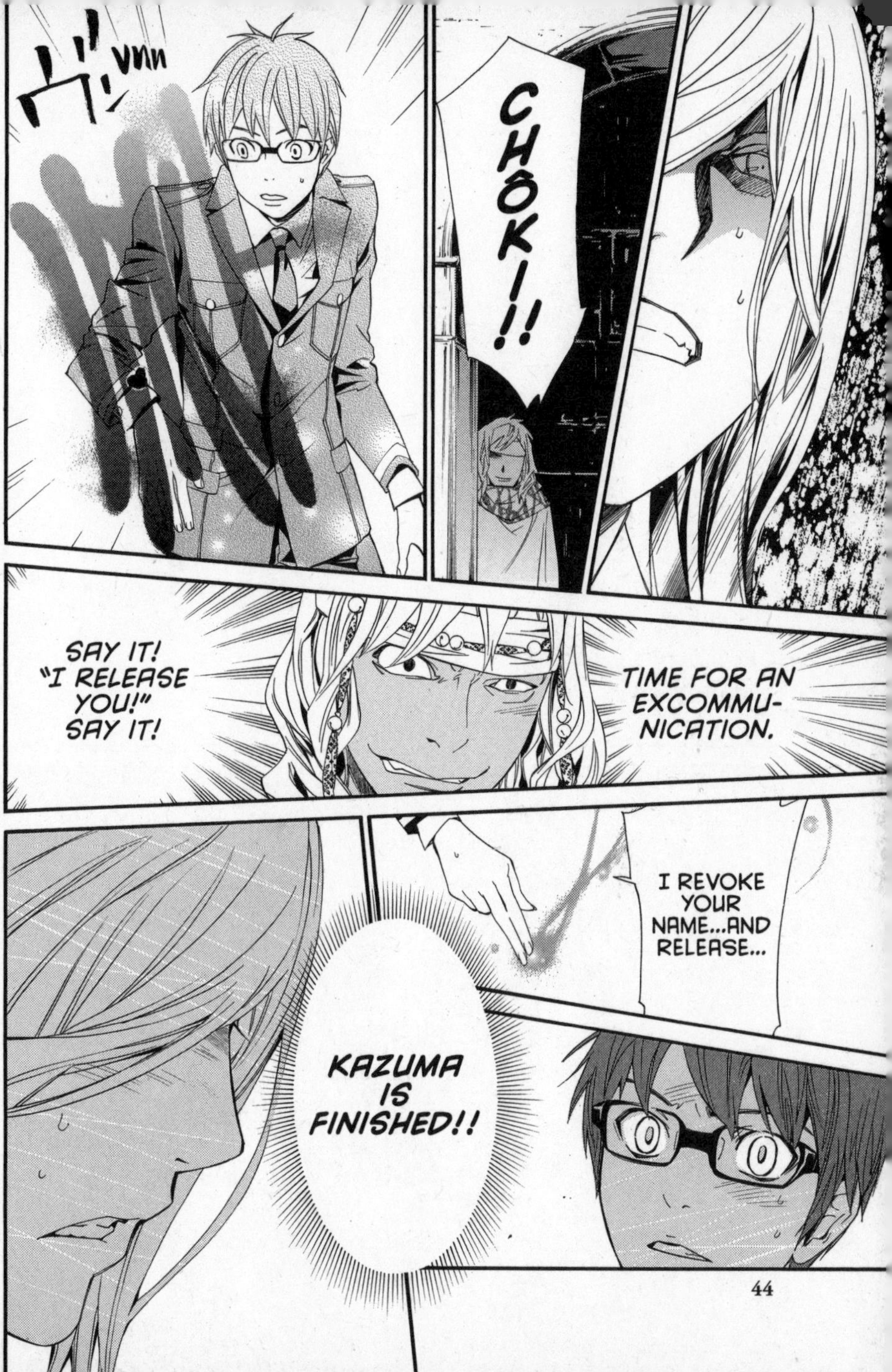
CHŌKI!!
VNNN
TIME FOR AN EXCOMMUNICATION.
SAY IT! "I RELEASE YOU!" SAY IT!
I REVOKE YOUR NAME...AND RELEASE...
KAZUMA IS FINISHED!!

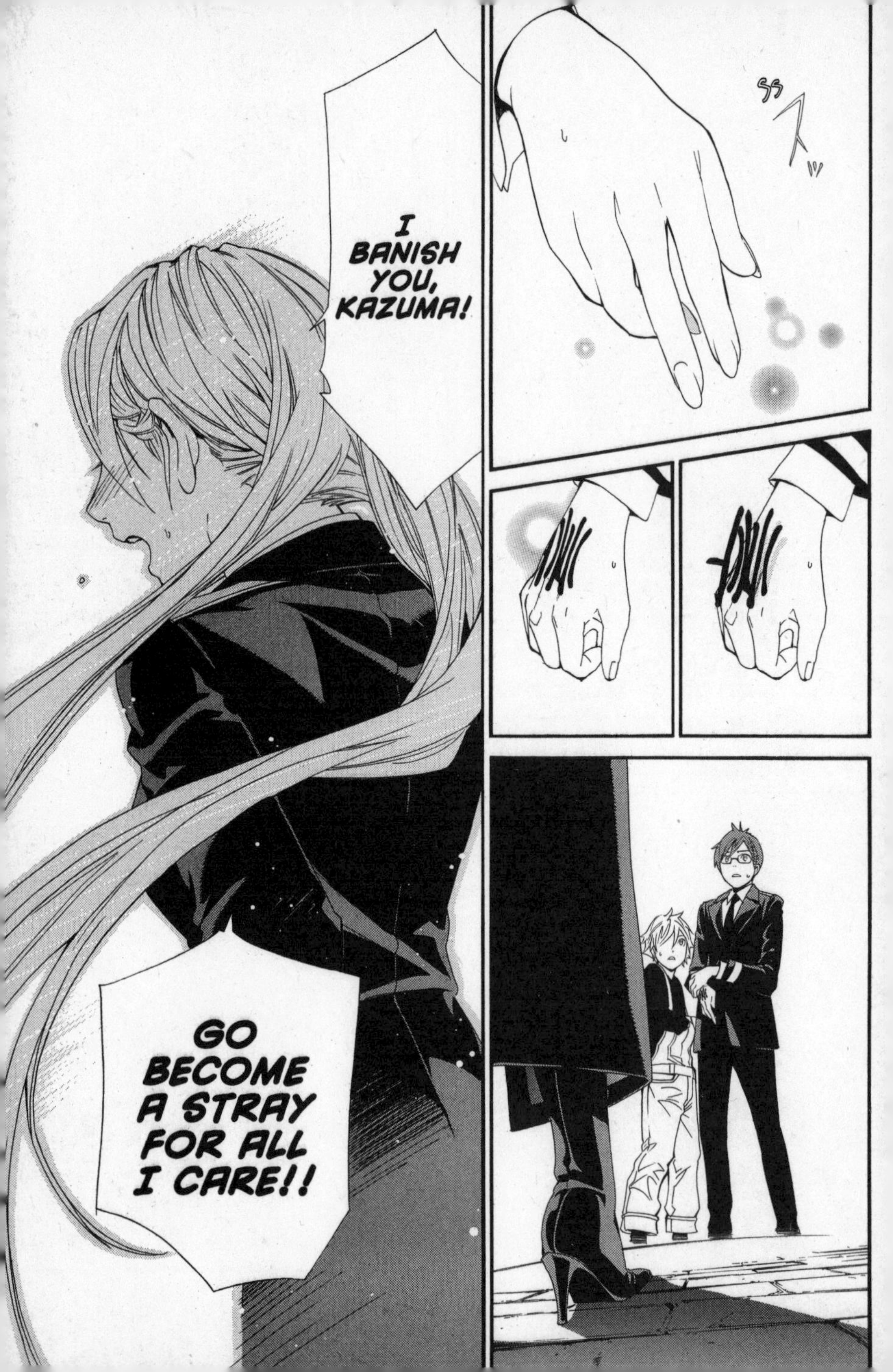
SS
I BANISH YOU, KAZUMA!
GO BECOME A STRAY FOR ALL I CARE!!

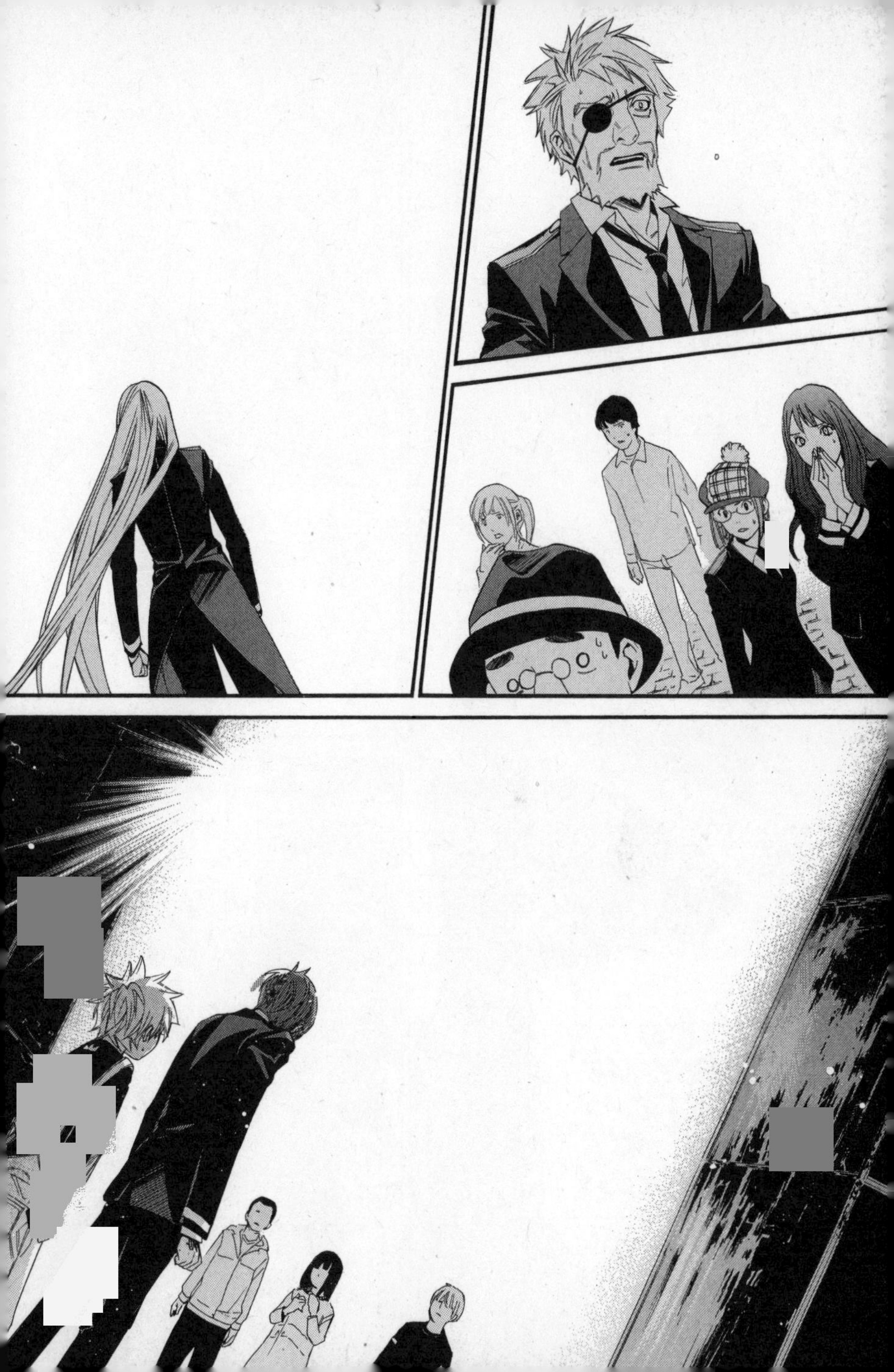

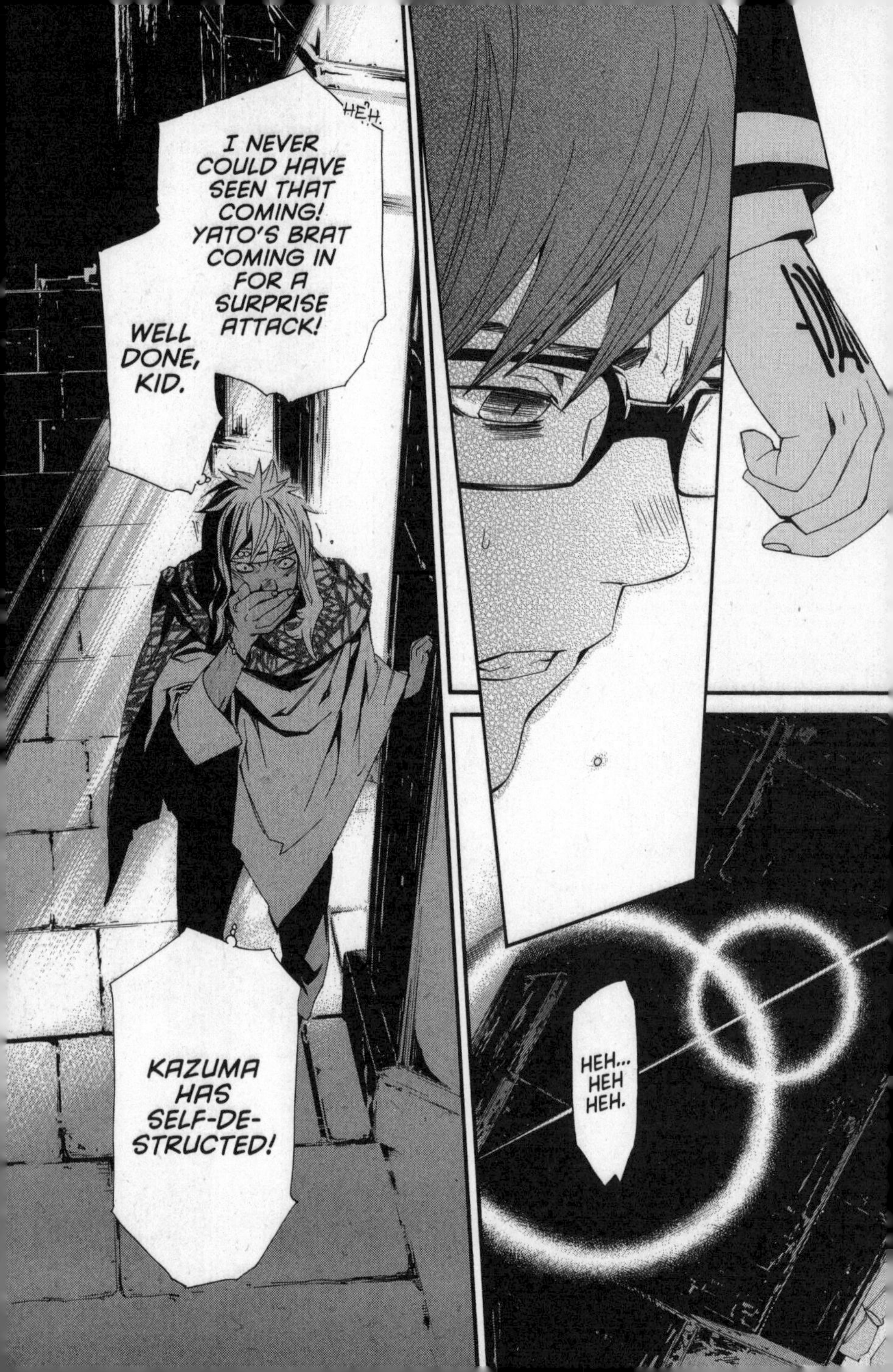
HEH... HEH HEH.
HEH.
I NEVER COULD HAVE SEEN THAT COMING! YATO'S BRAT COMING IN FOR A SURPRISE ATTACK!
WELL DONE, KID.
KAZUMA HAS SELF-DE-STRUCTED!

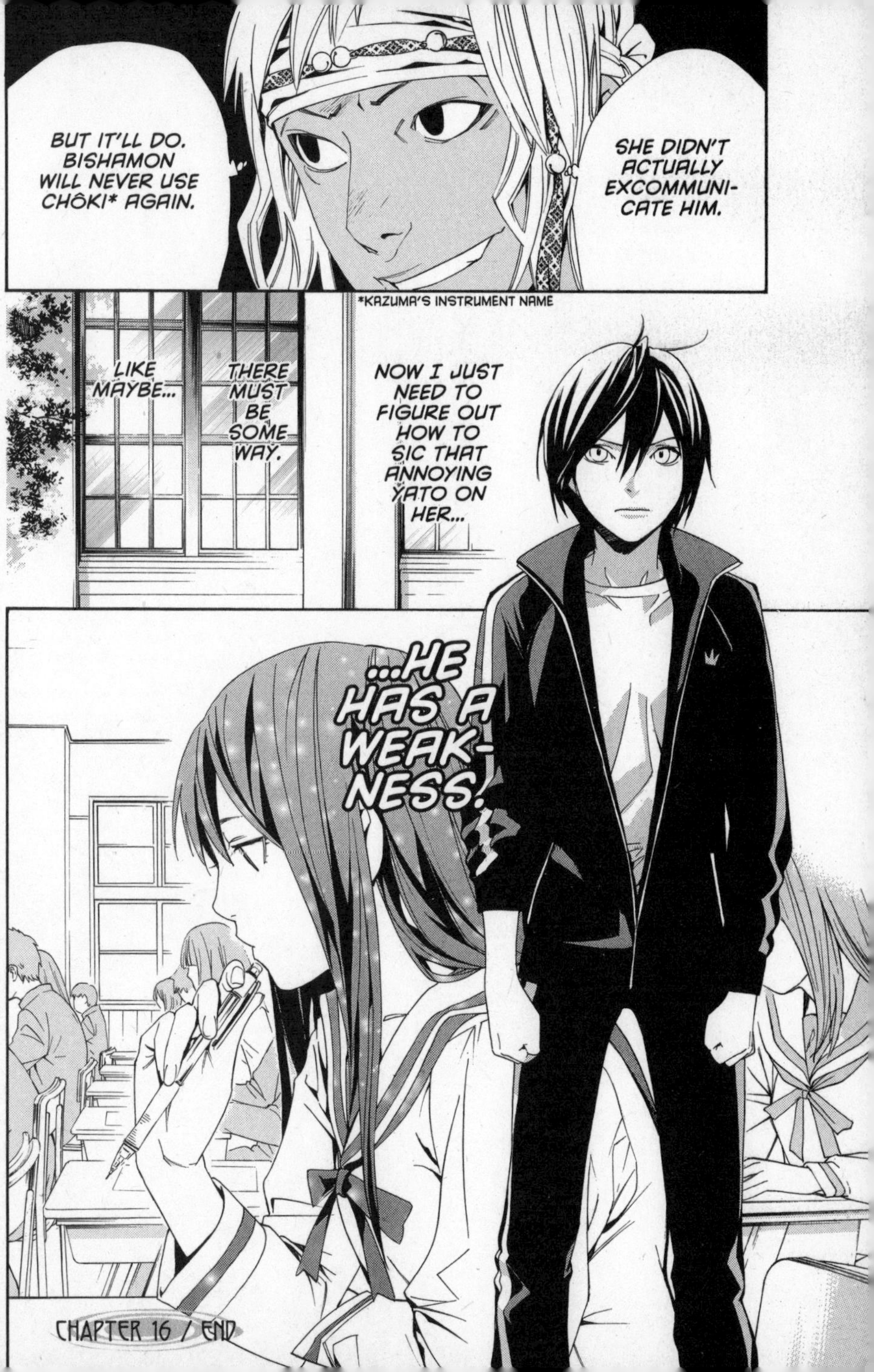
SHE DIDN'T ACTUALLY EXCOMMUNICATE HIM.
BUT IT'LL DO. BISHAMON WILL NEVER USE CHÔKI* AGAIN.
*KAZUMA'S INSTRUMENT NAME
NOW I JUST NEED TO FIGURE OUT HOW TO SIC THAT ANNOYING YATO ON HER...
THERE MUST BE SOME WAY.
LIKE MAYBE...
...HE HAS A WEAK-NESS!
CHAPTER 16 / END

野

曽

神

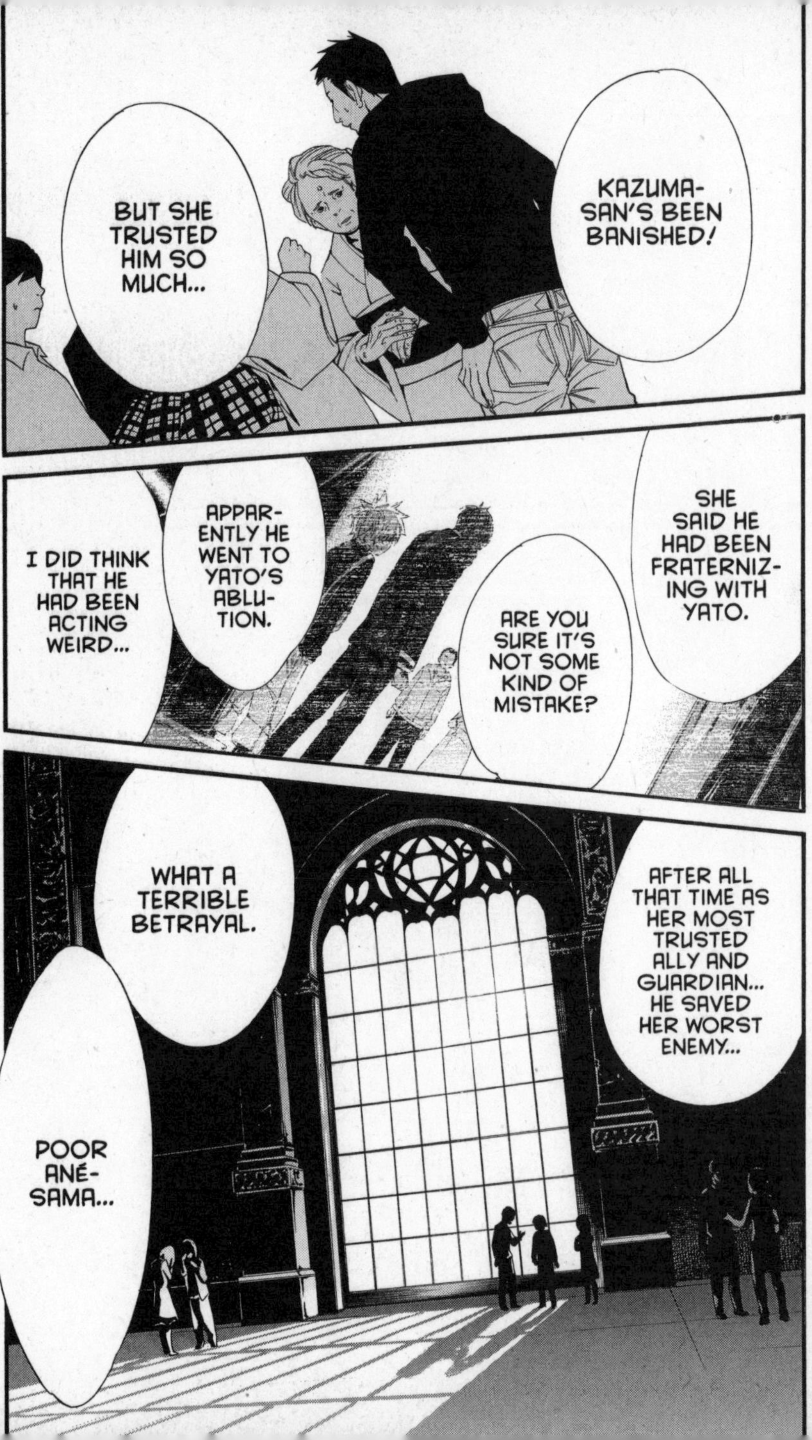
KAZUMA-SAN'S BEEN BANISHED!
BUT SHE TRUSTED HIM SO MUCH...
SHE SAID HE HAD BEEN FRATERNIZING WITH YATO.
ARE YOU SURE IT'S NOT SOME KIND OF MISTAKE?
APPARENTLY HE WENT TO YATO'S ABLUTION.
I DID THINK THAT HE HAD BEEN ACTING WEIRD...
AFTER ALL THAT TIME AS HER MOST TRUSTED ALLY AND GUARDIAN... HE SAVED HER WORST ENEMY...
WHAT A TERRIBLE BETRAYAL.
POOR ANÉ-SAMA...

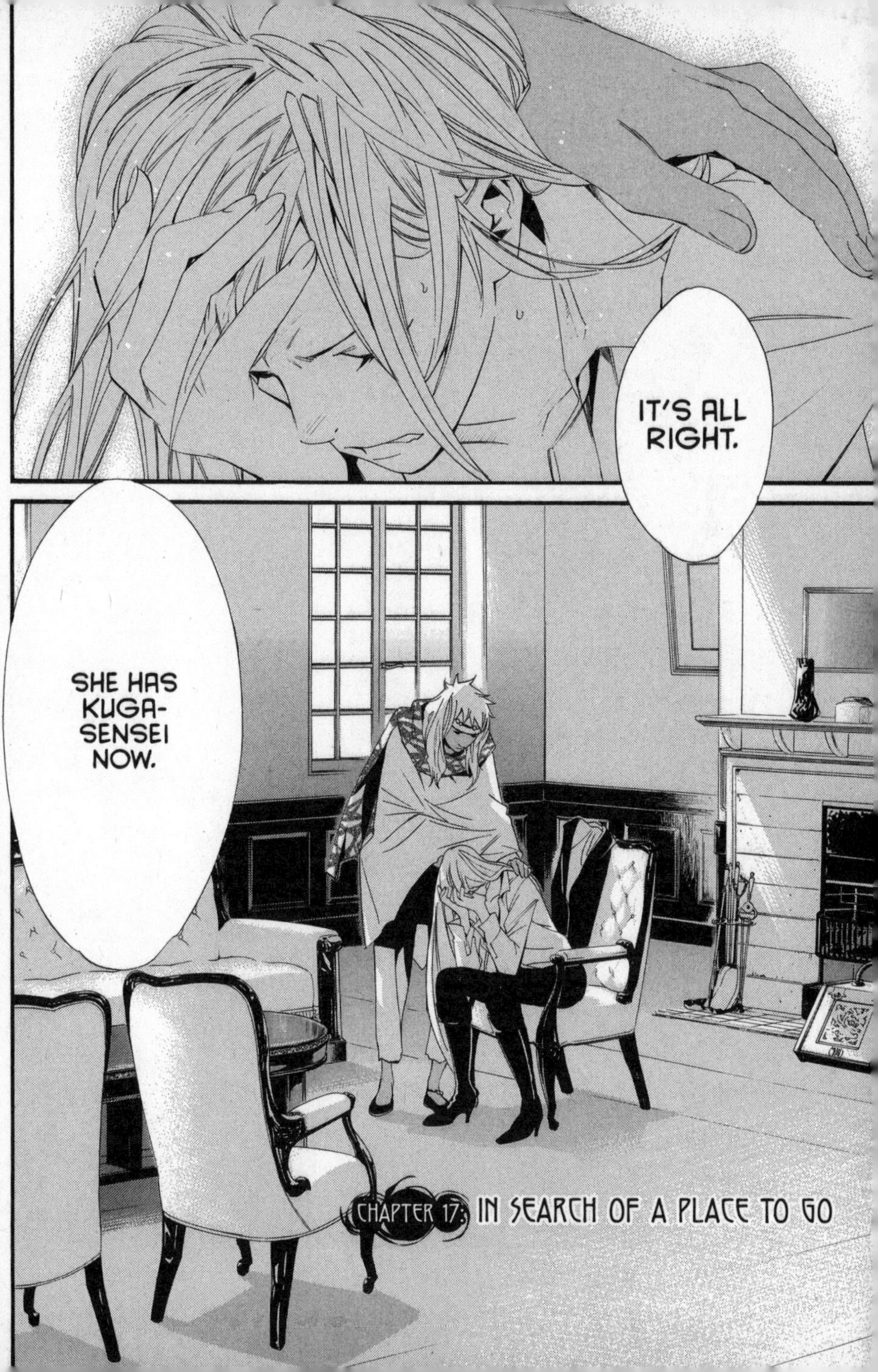
IT'S ALL RIGHT.
SHE HAS KUGA-SENSEI NOW.
CHAPTER 17: IN SEARCH OF A PLACE TO GO

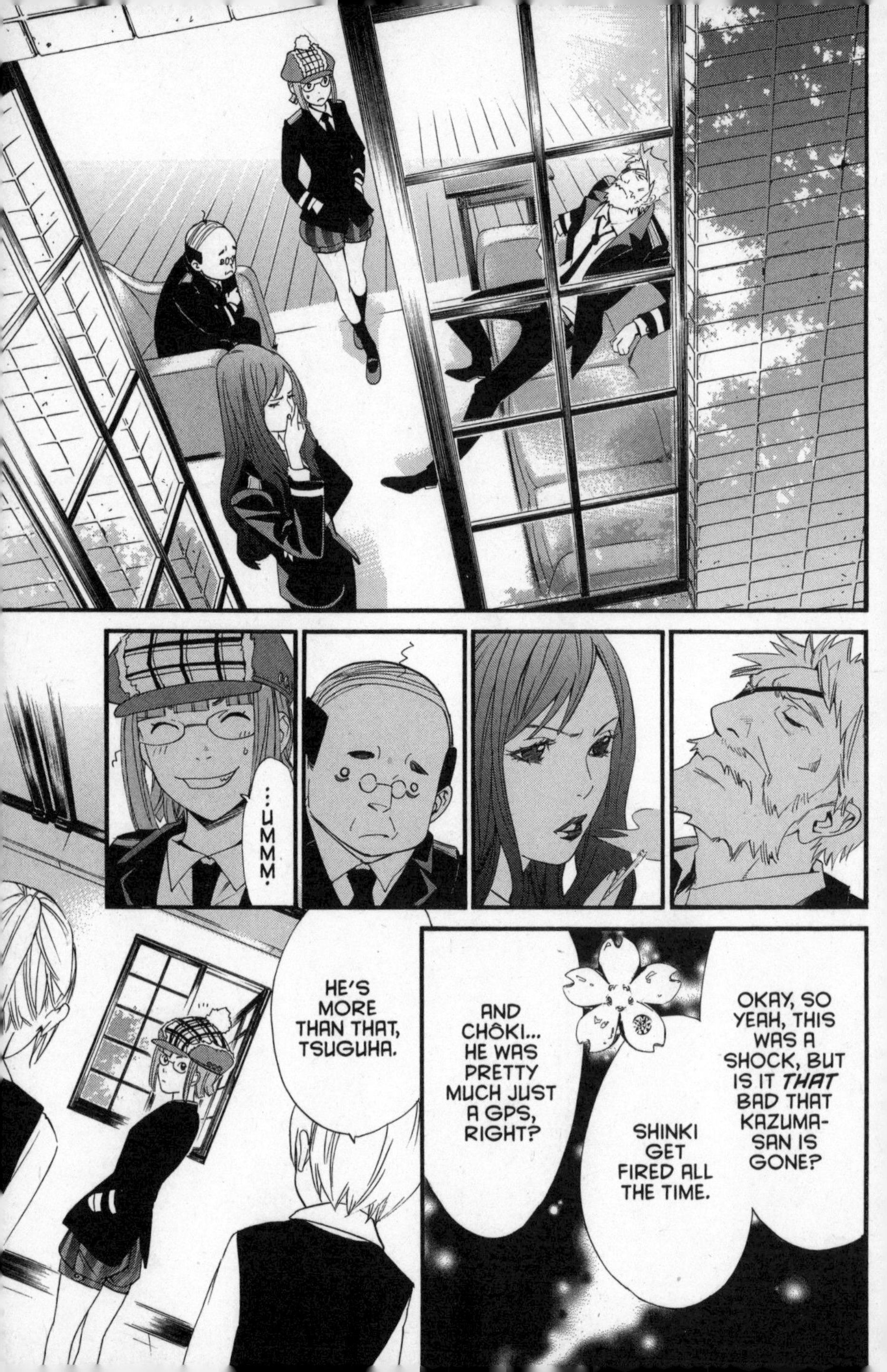
...UMMM.
OKAY, SO YEAH, THIS WAS A SHOCK, BUT IS IT *THAT* BAD THAT KAZUMA-SAN IS GONE?
SHINKI GET FIRED ALL THE TIME.
AND CHÔKI... HE WAS PRETTY MUCH JUST A GPS, RIGHT?
HE'S MORE THAN THAT, TSUGUHA.

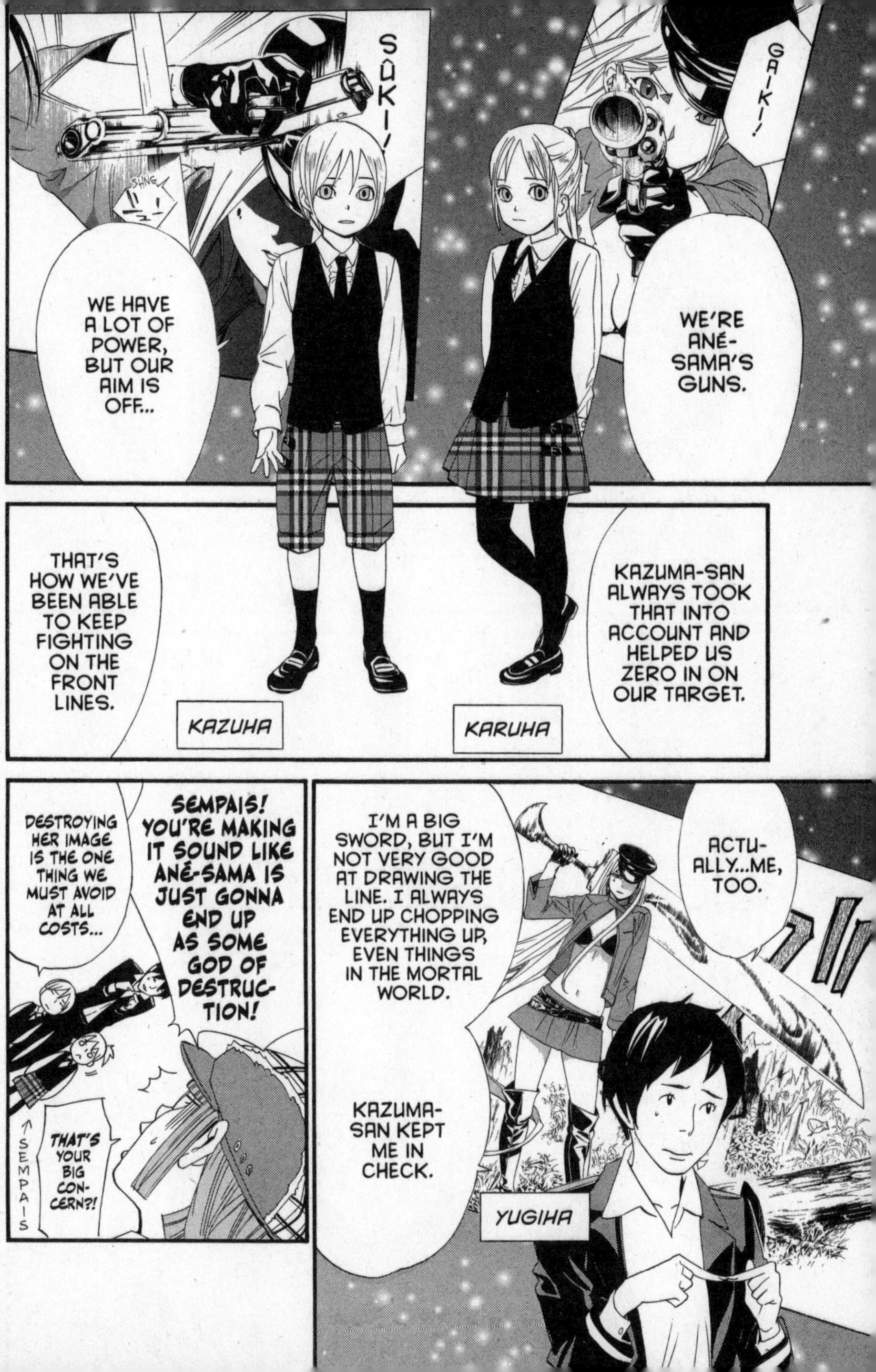
GAIKI!
WE'RE ANÉ-SAMA'S GUNS.
SÛKI!
SHNG
WE HAVE A LOT OF POWER, BUT OUR AIM IS OFF...
KAZUMA-SAN ALWAYS TOOK THAT INTO ACCOUNT AND HELPED US ZERO IN ON OUR TARGET.
KARUHA
KAZUHA
THAT'S HOW WE'VE BEEN ABLE TO KEEP FIGHTING ON THE FRONT LINES.
ACTU-ALLY...ME, TOO.
I'M A BIG SWORD, BUT I'M NOT VERY GOOD AT DRAWING THE LINE. I ALWAYS END UP CHOPPING EVERYTHING UP, EVEN THINGS IN THE MORTAL WORLD.
KAZUMA-SAN KEPT ME IN CHECK.
YUGIHA
SEMPAIS! YOU'RE MAKING IT SOUND LIKE ANÉ-SAMA IS JUST GONNA END UP AS SOME GOD OF DESTRUC-TION!
DESTROYING HER IMAGE IS THE ONE THING WE MUST AVOID AT ALL COSTS...
THAT'S YOUR BIG CON-CERN?!
↑SEMPAIS

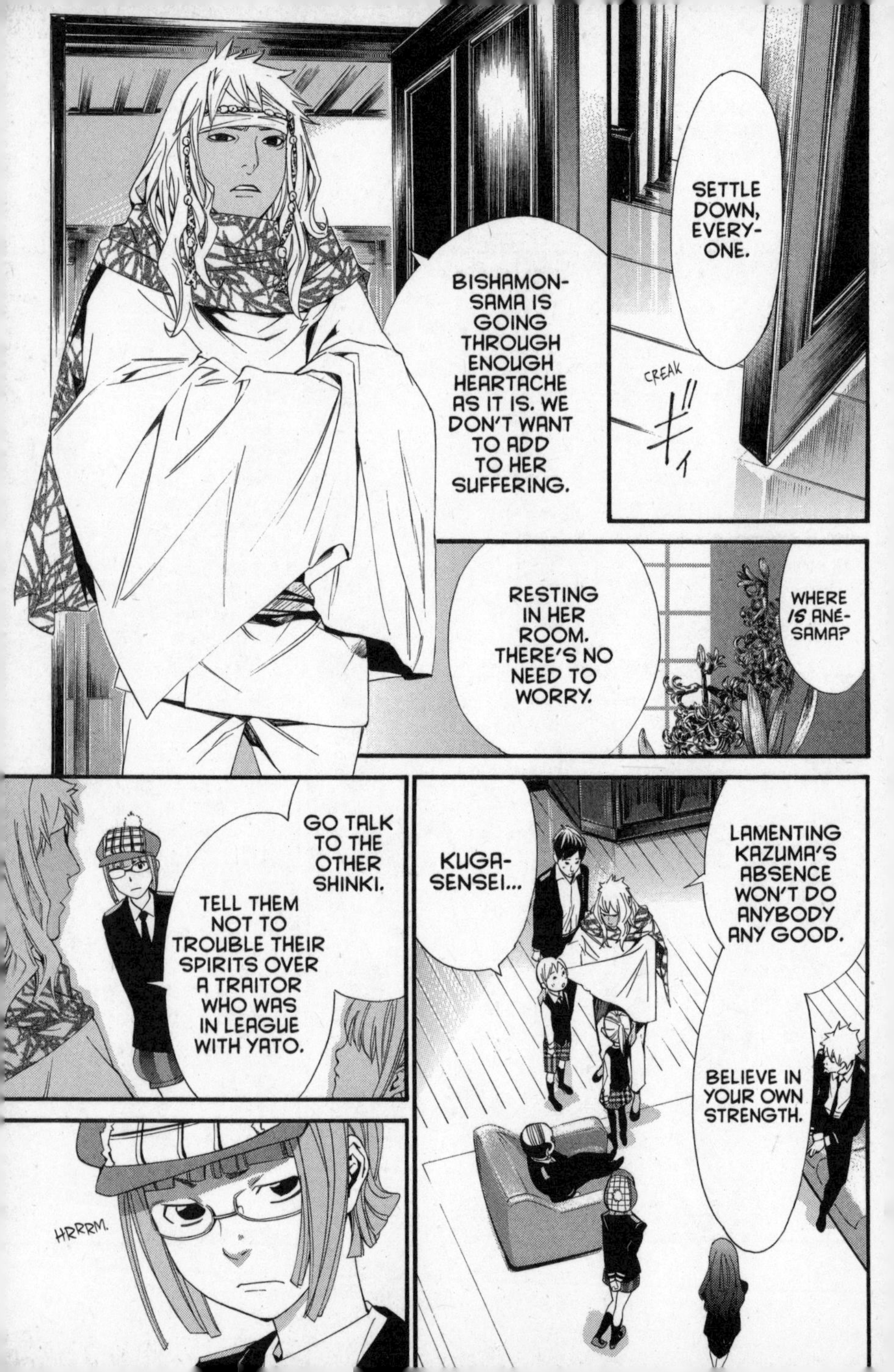
SETTLE DOWN, EVERY-ONE.
CREAK
WHERE IS ANÉ-SAMA?
RESTING IN HER ROOM. THERE'S NO NEED TO WORRY.
BISHAMON-SAMA IS GOING THROUGH ENOUGH HEARTACHE AS IT IS. WE DON'T WANT TO ADD TO HER SUFFERING.
LAMENTING KAZUMA'S ABSENCE WON'T DO ANYBODY ANY GOOD.
KUGA-SENSEI...
BELIEVE IN YOUR OWN STRENGTH.
GO TALK TO THE OTHER SHINKI.
TELL THEM NOT TO TROUBLE THEIR SPIRITS OVER A TRAITOR WHO WAS IN LEAGUE WITH YATO.
HRRRM.

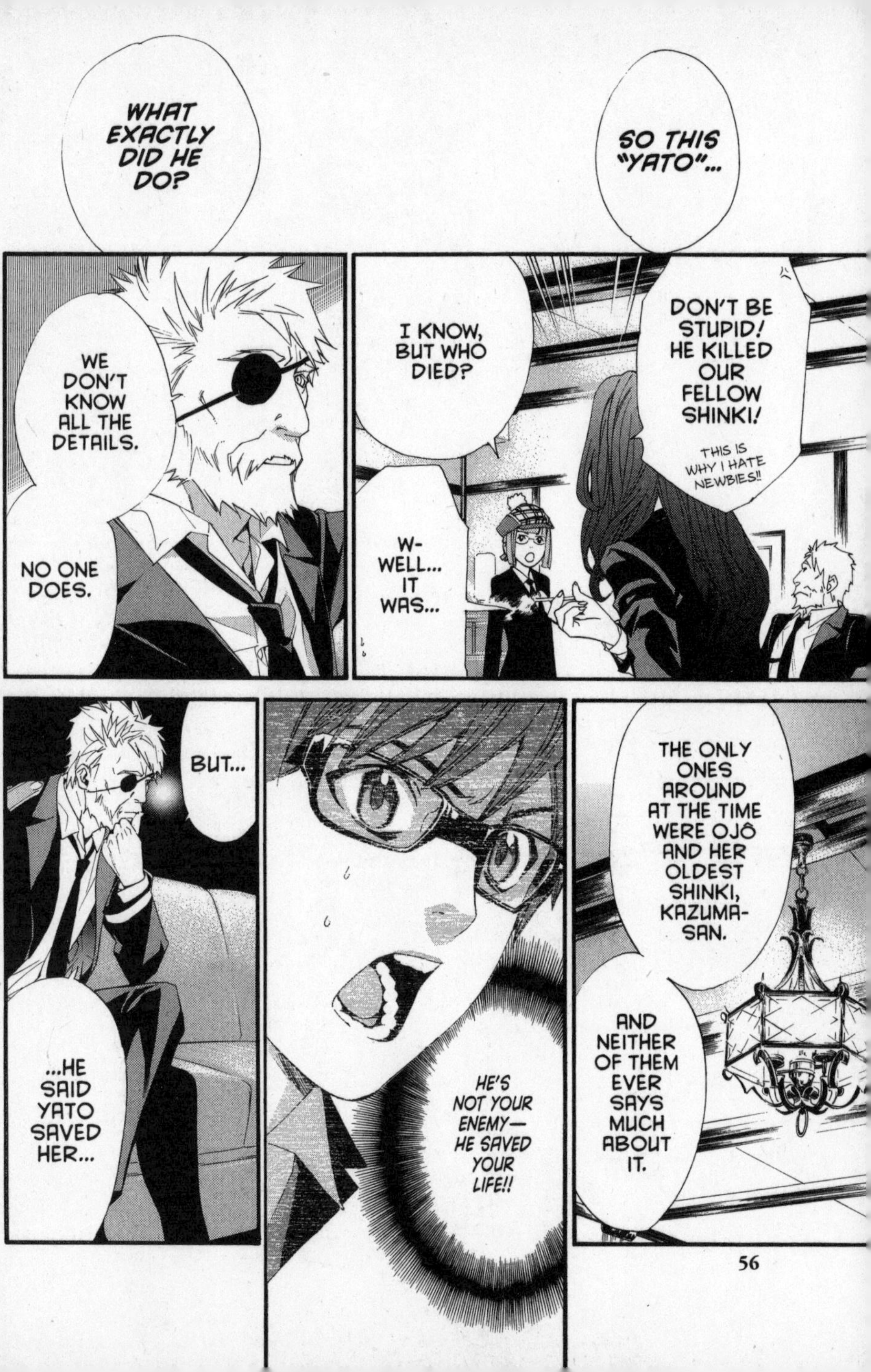
SO THIS "YATO"...
WHAT EXACTLY DID HE DO?
DON'T BE STUPID! HE KILLED OUR FELLOW SHINKI!
THIS IS WHY I HATE NEWBIES!!
I KNOW, BUT WHO DIED?
W-WELL... IT WAS...
WE DON'T KNOW ALL THE DETAILS.
NO ONE DOES.
THE ONLY ONES AROUND AT THE TIME WERE OJÔ AND HER OLDEST SHINKI, KAZUMA-SAN.
AND NEITHER OF THEM EVER SAYS MUCH ABOUT IT.
HE'S NOT YOUR ENEMY—HE SAVED YOUR LIFE!!
BUT...
...HE SAID YATO SAVED HER...

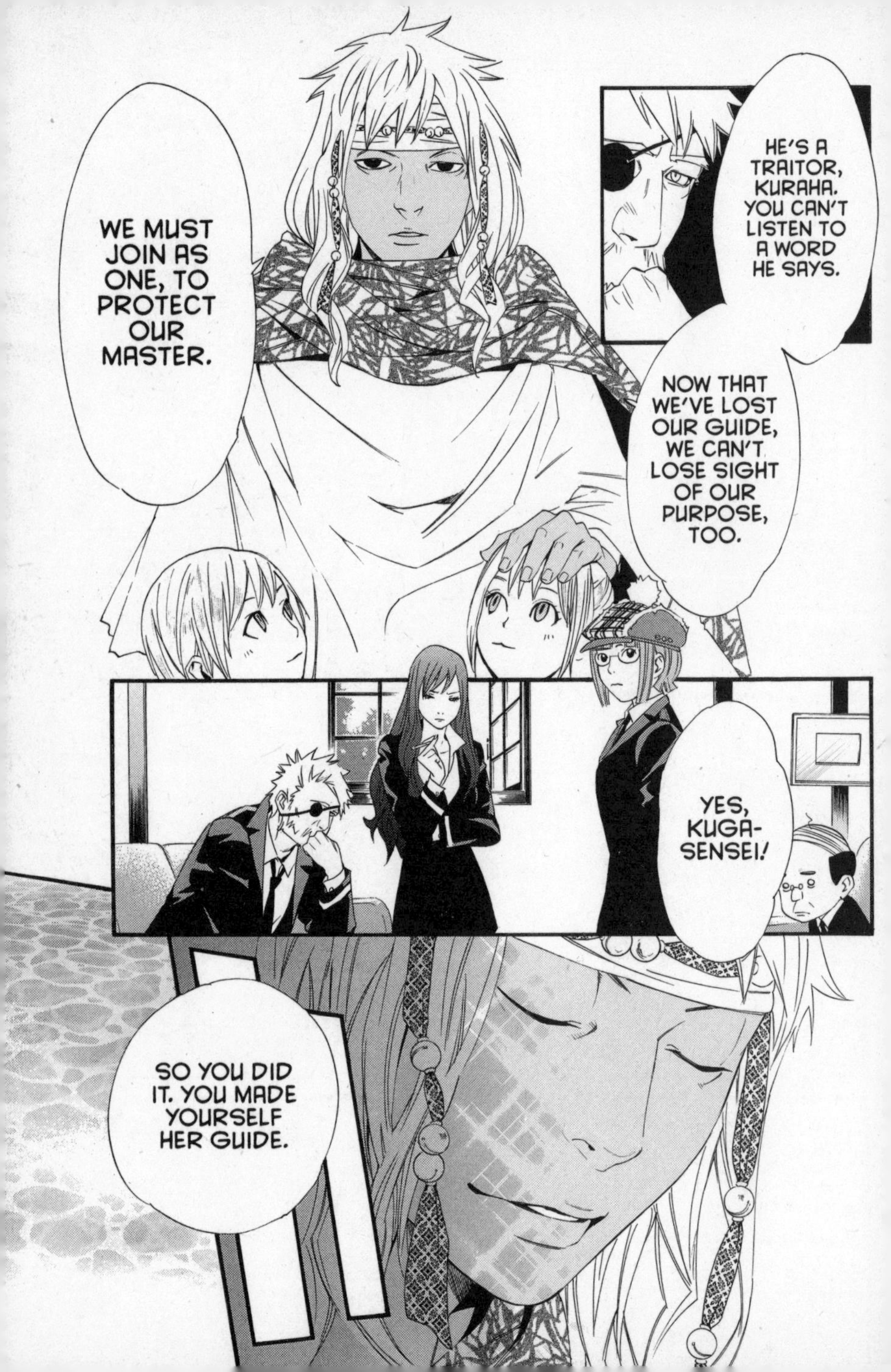
HE'S A TRAITOR, KURAHA. YOU CAN'T LISTEN TO A WORD HE SAYS.
WE MUST JOIN AS ONE, TO PROTECT OUR MASTER.
NOW THAT WE'VE LOST OUR GUIDE, WE CAN'T LOSE SIGHT OF OUR PURPOSE, TOO.
YES, KUGA-SENSEI!
SO YOU DID IT. YOU MADE YOURSELF HER GUIDE.

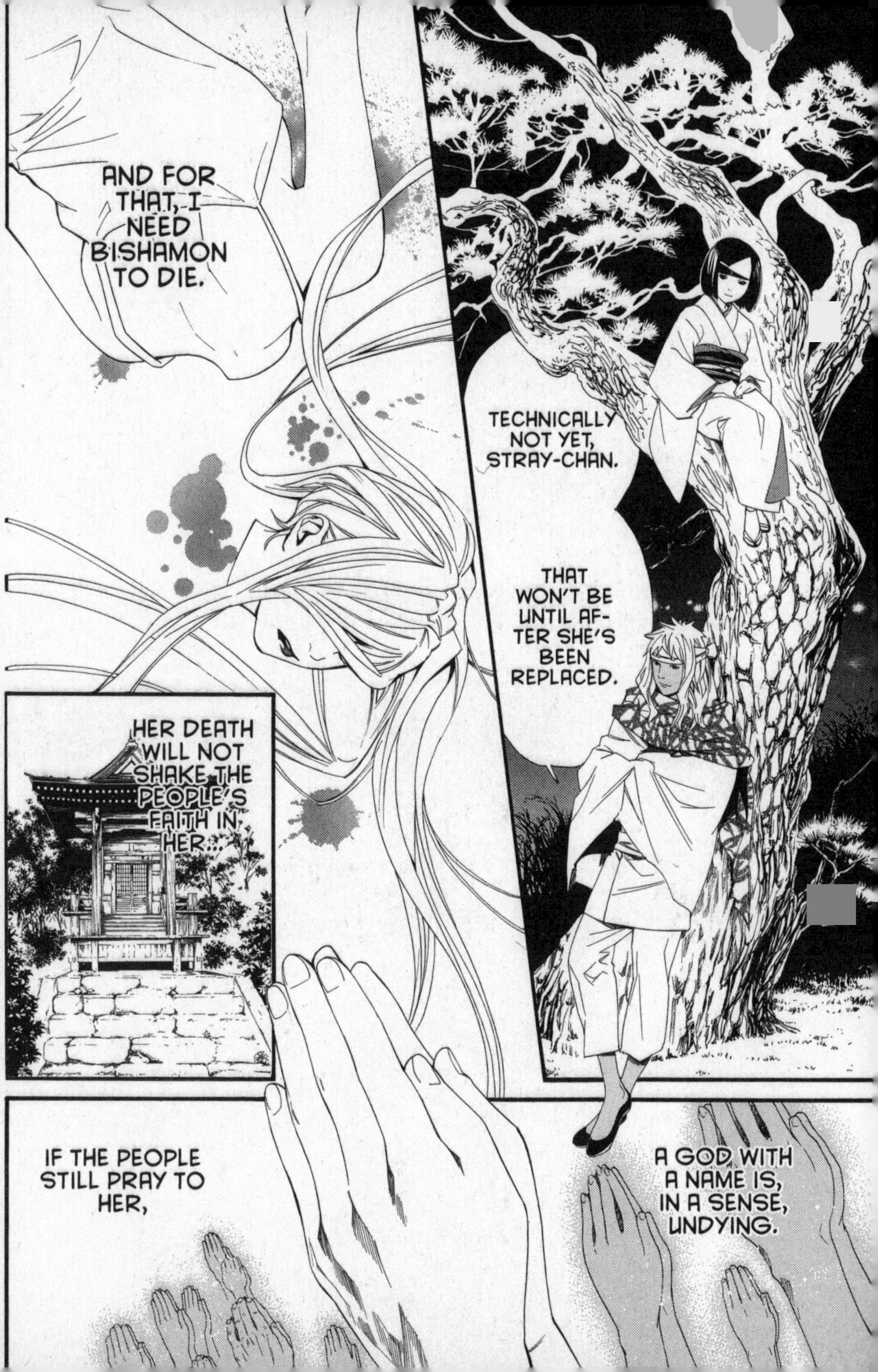
TECHNICALLY NOT YET, STRAY-CHAN.
THAT WON'T BE UNTIL AF-TER SHE'S BEEN REPLACED.
AND FOR THAT, I NEED BISHAMON TO DIE.
HER DEATH WILL NOT SHAKE THE PEOPLE'S FAITH IN HER...
A GOD WITH A NAME IS, IN A SENSE, UNDYING.
IF THE PEOPLE STILL PRAY TO HER,

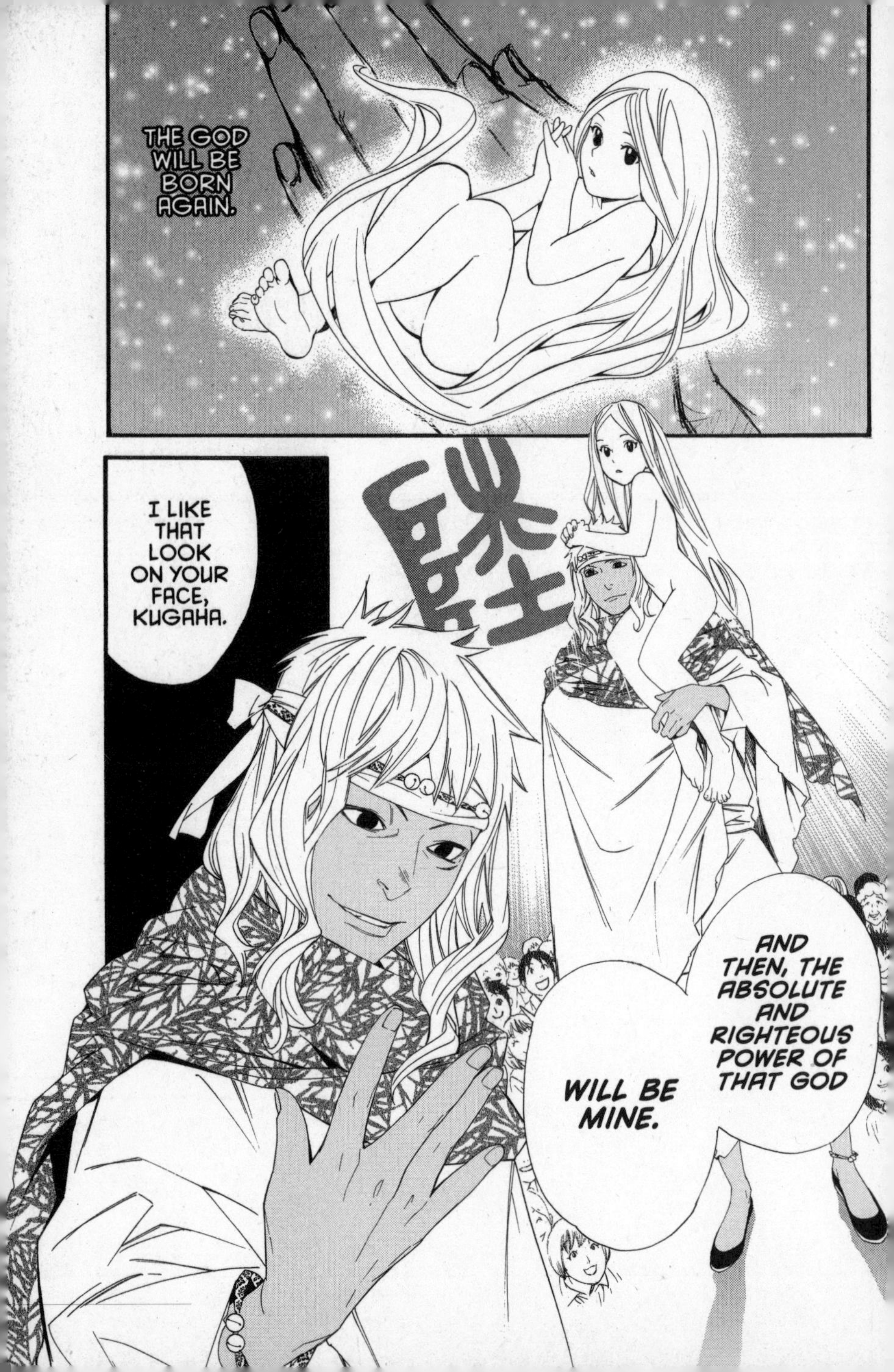
THE GOD WILL BE BORN AGAIN.
I LIKE THAT LOOK ON YOUR FACE, KUGAHA.
AND THEN, THE ABSOLUTE AND RIGHTEOUS POWER OF THAT GOD
WILL BE MINE.

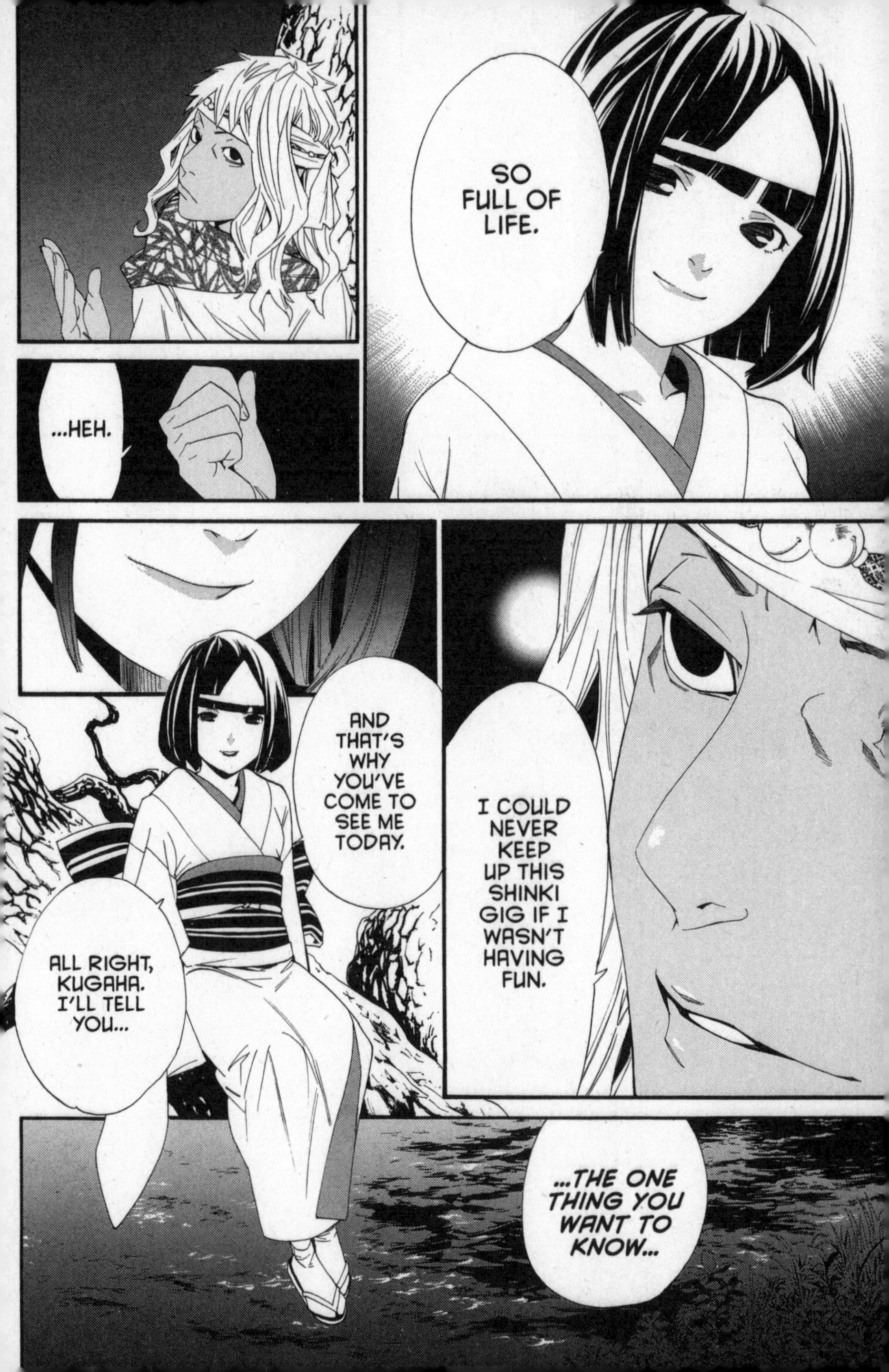
SO FULL OF LIFE.
...HEH.
I COULD NEVER KEEP UP THIS SHINKI GIG IF I WASN'T HAVING FUN.
AND THAT'S WHY YOU'VE COME TO SEE ME TODAY.
ALL RIGHT, KUGAHA. I'LL TELL YOU...
...THE ONE THING YOU WANT TO KNOW...

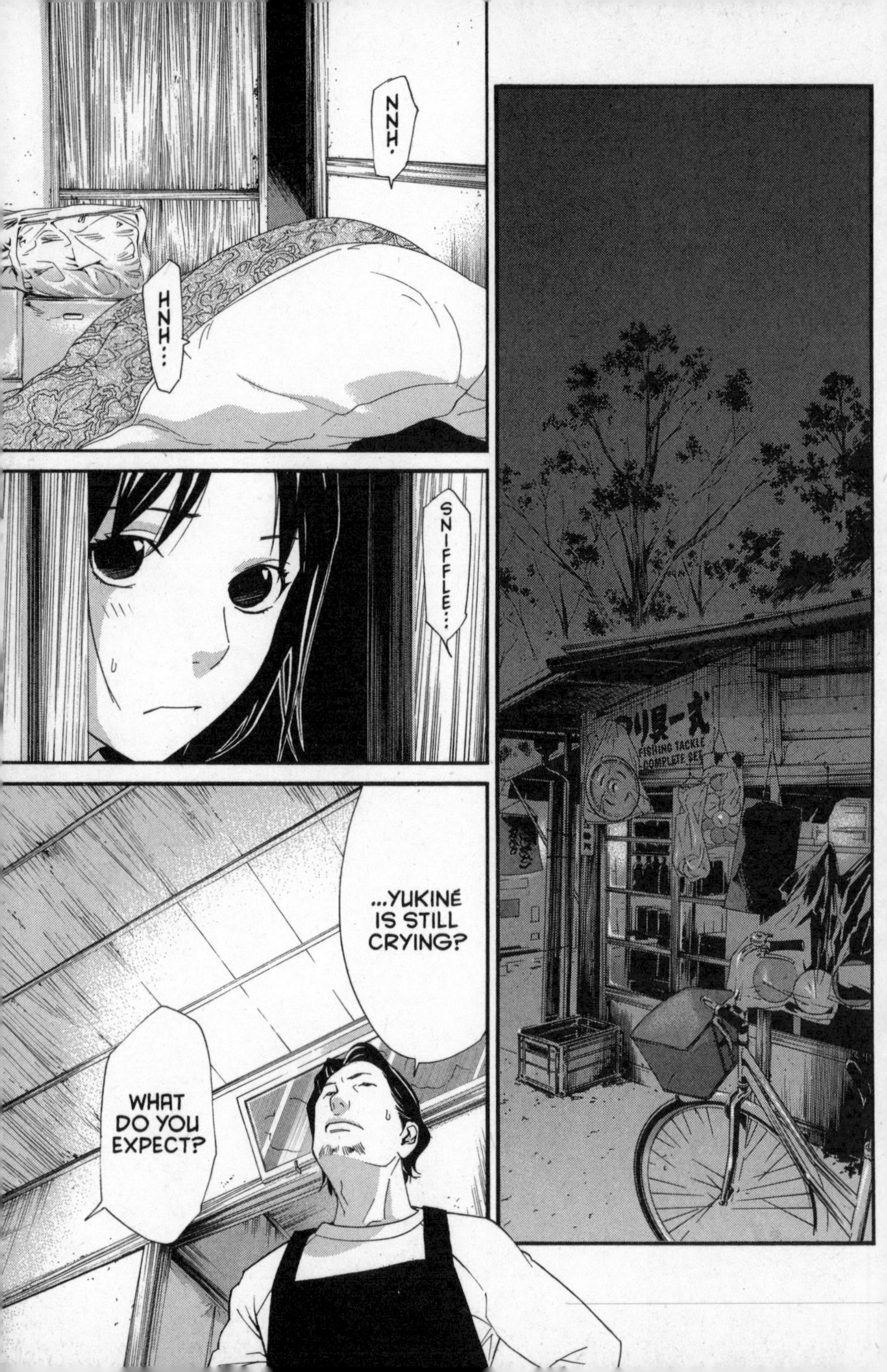
NNH.
HNH...
SNIFFLE...
...YUKINÉ IS STILL CRYING?
WHAT DO YOU EXPECT?

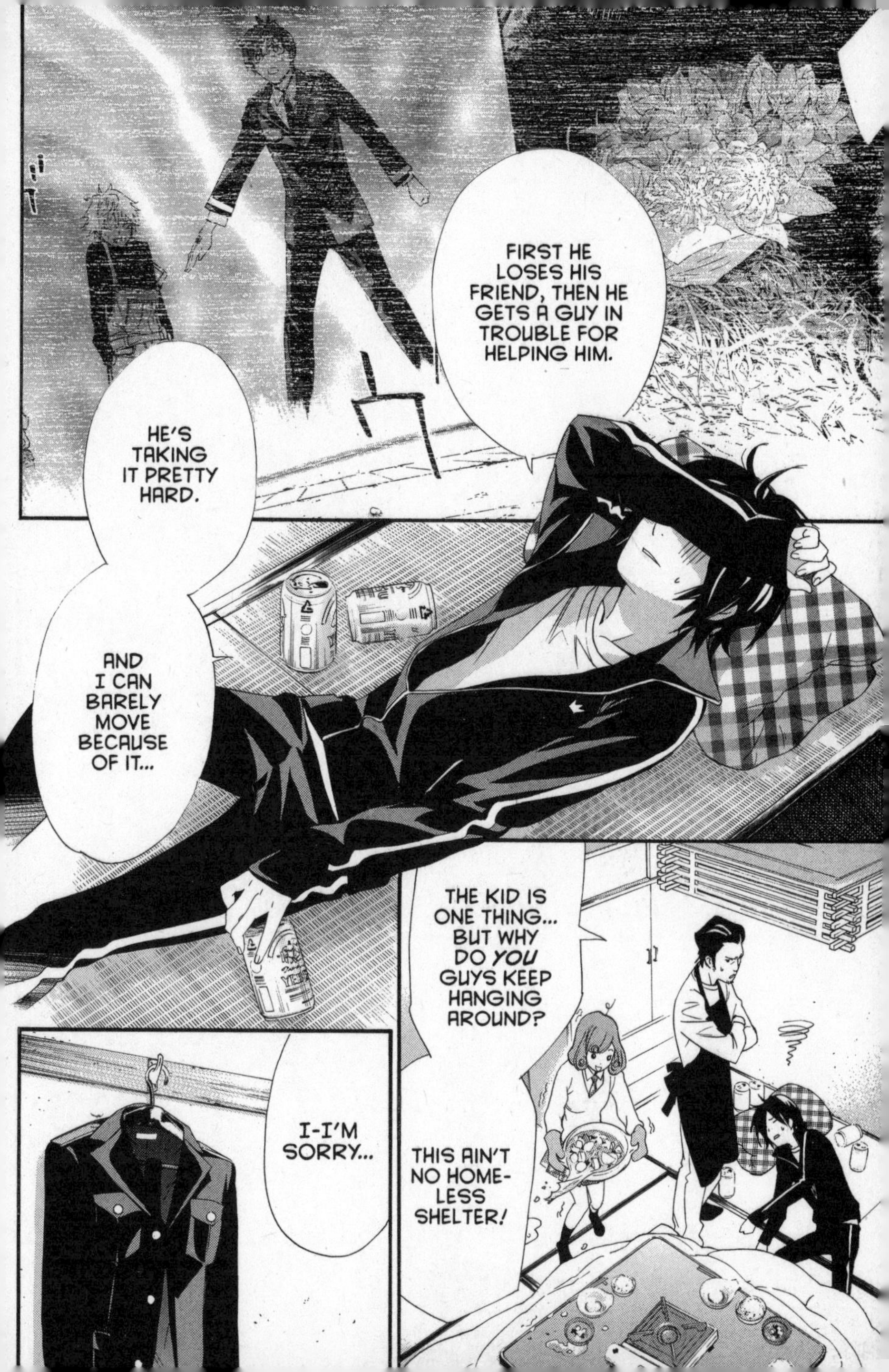

FIRST HE LOSES HIS FRIEND, THEN HE GETS A GUY IN TROUBLE FOR HELPING HIM.
HE'S TAKING IT PRETTY HARD.
AND I CAN BARELY MOVE BECAUSE OF IT...
THE KID IS ONE THING... BUT WHY DO *YOU* GUYS KEEP HANGING AROUND?
THIS AIN'T NO HOME-LESS SHELTER!
I-I'M SORRY...

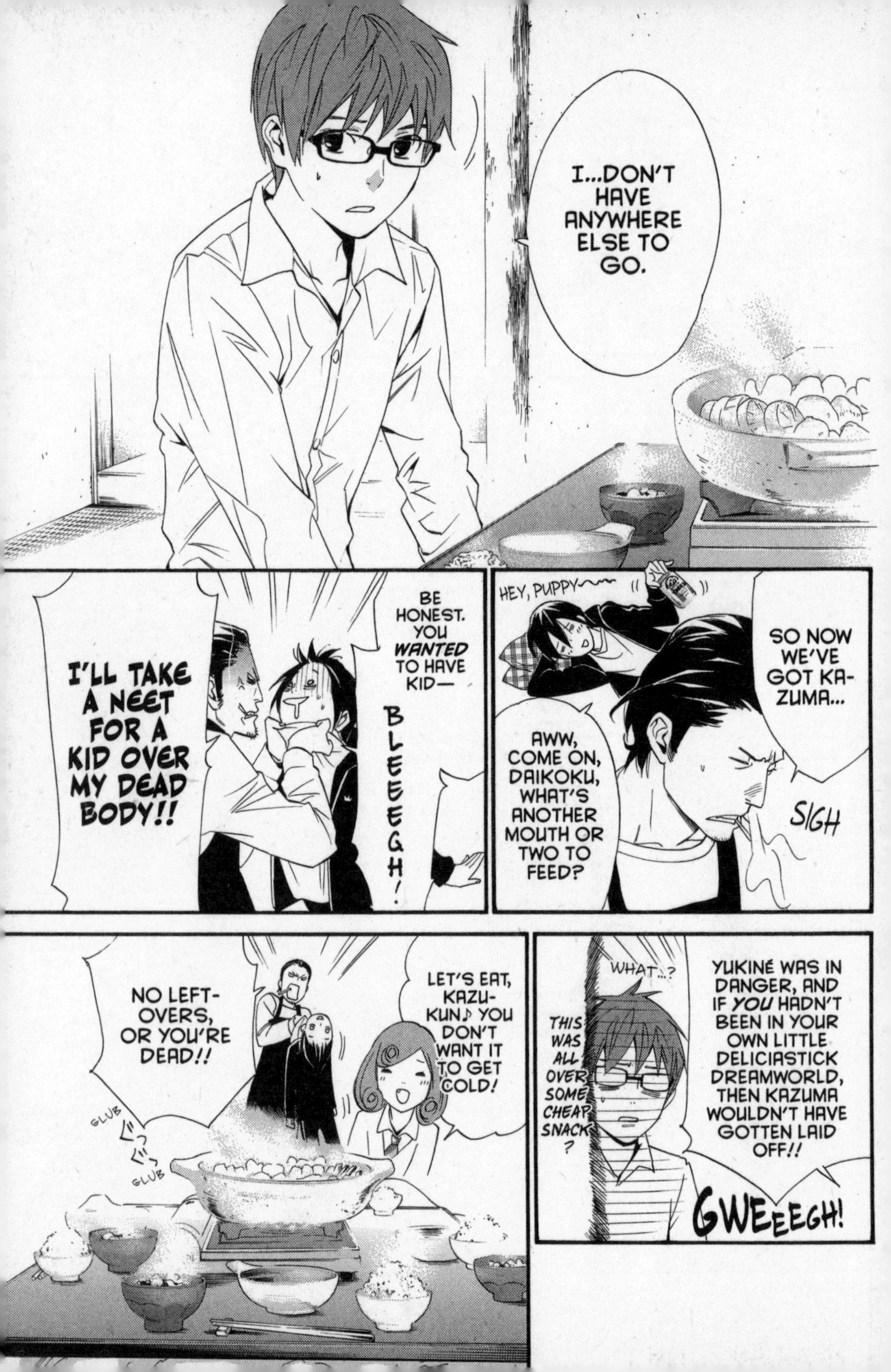
I...DON'T HAVE ANYWHERE ELSE TO GO.
SO NOW WE'VE GOT KA-ZUMA...
HEY, PUPPY~~
SIGH
AWW, COME ON, DAIKOKU, WHAT'S ANOTHER MOUTH OR TWO TO FEED?
BE HONEST. YOU *WANTED* TO HAVE KID—
BLEEEGH!
I'LL TAKE A NEET FOR A KID OVER MY DEAD BODY!!
YUKINÉ WAS IN DANGER, AND IF *YOU* HADN'T BEEN IN YOUR OWN LITTLE DELICIASTICK DREAMWORLD, THEN KAZUMA WOULDN'T HAVE GOTTEN LAID OFF!!
WHAT...?
THIS WAS ALL OVER SOME CHEAP SNACK?
GWEEEGH!
LET'S EAT, KAZU-KUN♪ YOU DON'T WANT IT TO GET COLD!
NO LEFT-OVERS, OR YOU'RE DEAD!!
GLUB
GLUB

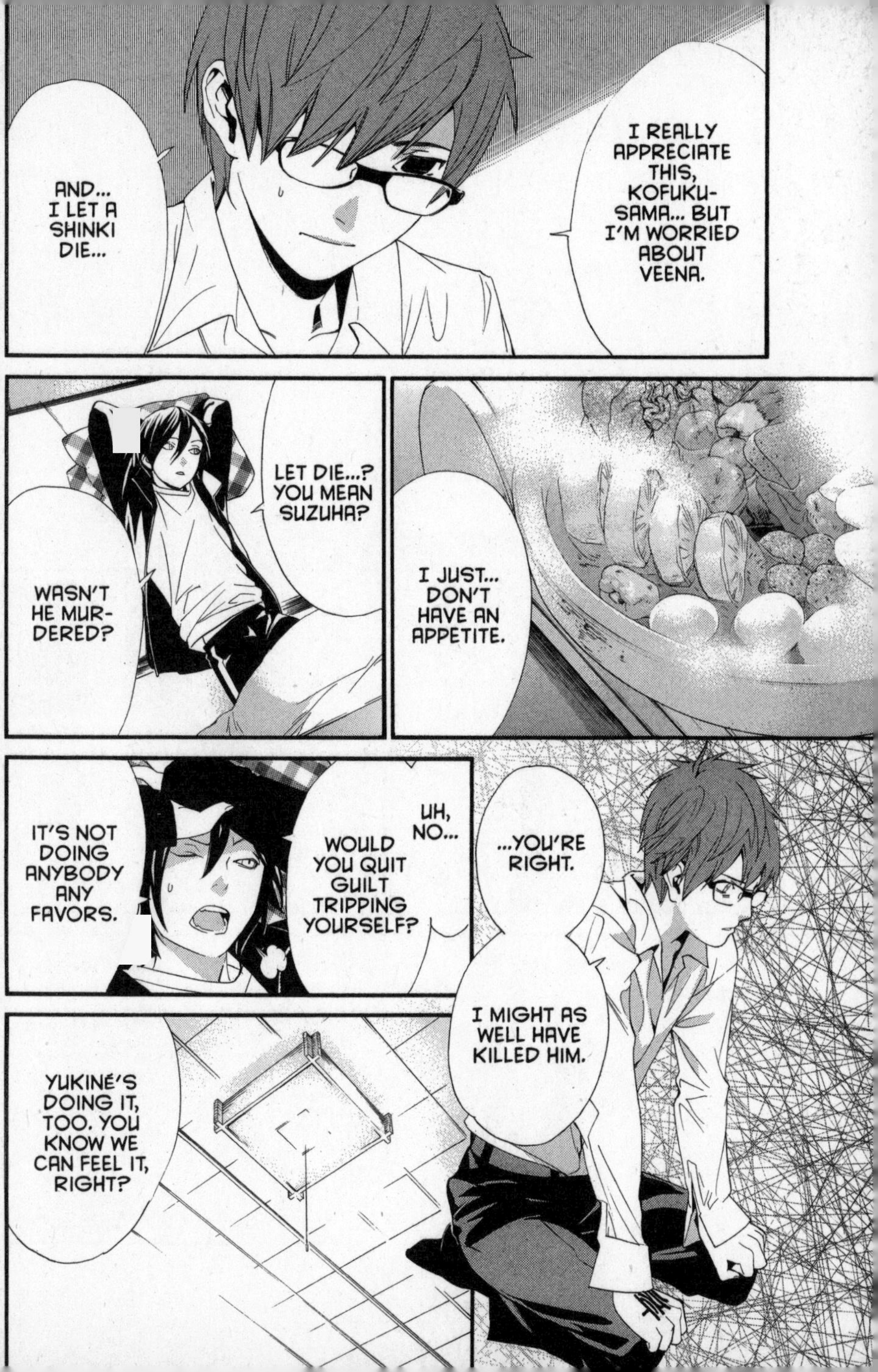

I REALLY APPRECIATE THIS, KOFUKU-SAMA... BUT I'M WORRIED ABOUT VEENA.
AND... I LET A SHINKI DIE...
I JUST... DON'T HAVE AN APPETITE.
LET DIE...? YOU MEAN SUZUHA?
WASN'T HE MURDERED?
...YOU'RE RIGHT.
I MIGHT AS WELL HAVE KILLED HIM.
UH, NO...
WOULD YOU QUIT GUILT TRIPPING YOURSELF?
IT'S NOT DOING ANYBODY ANY FAVORS.
YUKINÉ'S DOING IT, TOO. YOU KNOW WE CAN FEEL IT, RIGHT?

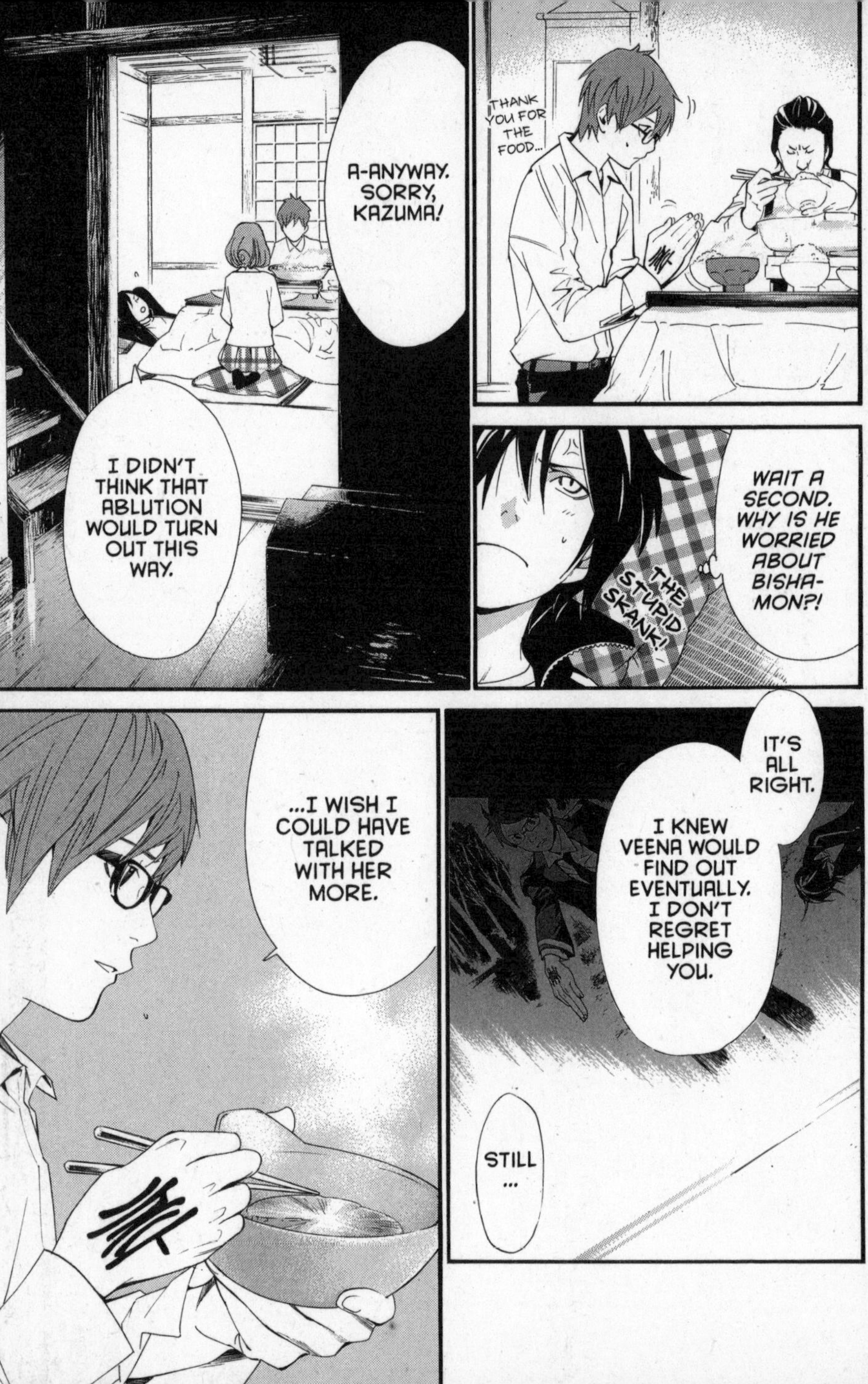
THANK YOU FOR THE FOOD...
WAIT A SECOND. WHY IS HE WORRIED ABOUT BISHA-MON?!
THE STUPID SKANK!
A-ANYWAY. SORRY, KAZUMA!
I DIDN'T THINK THAT ABLUTION WOULD TURN OUT THIS WAY.
IT'S ALL RIGHT.
I KNEW VEENA WOULD FIND OUT EVENTUALLY. I DON'T REGRET HELPING YOU.
STILL ...
...I WISH I COULD HAVE TALKED WITH HER MORE.

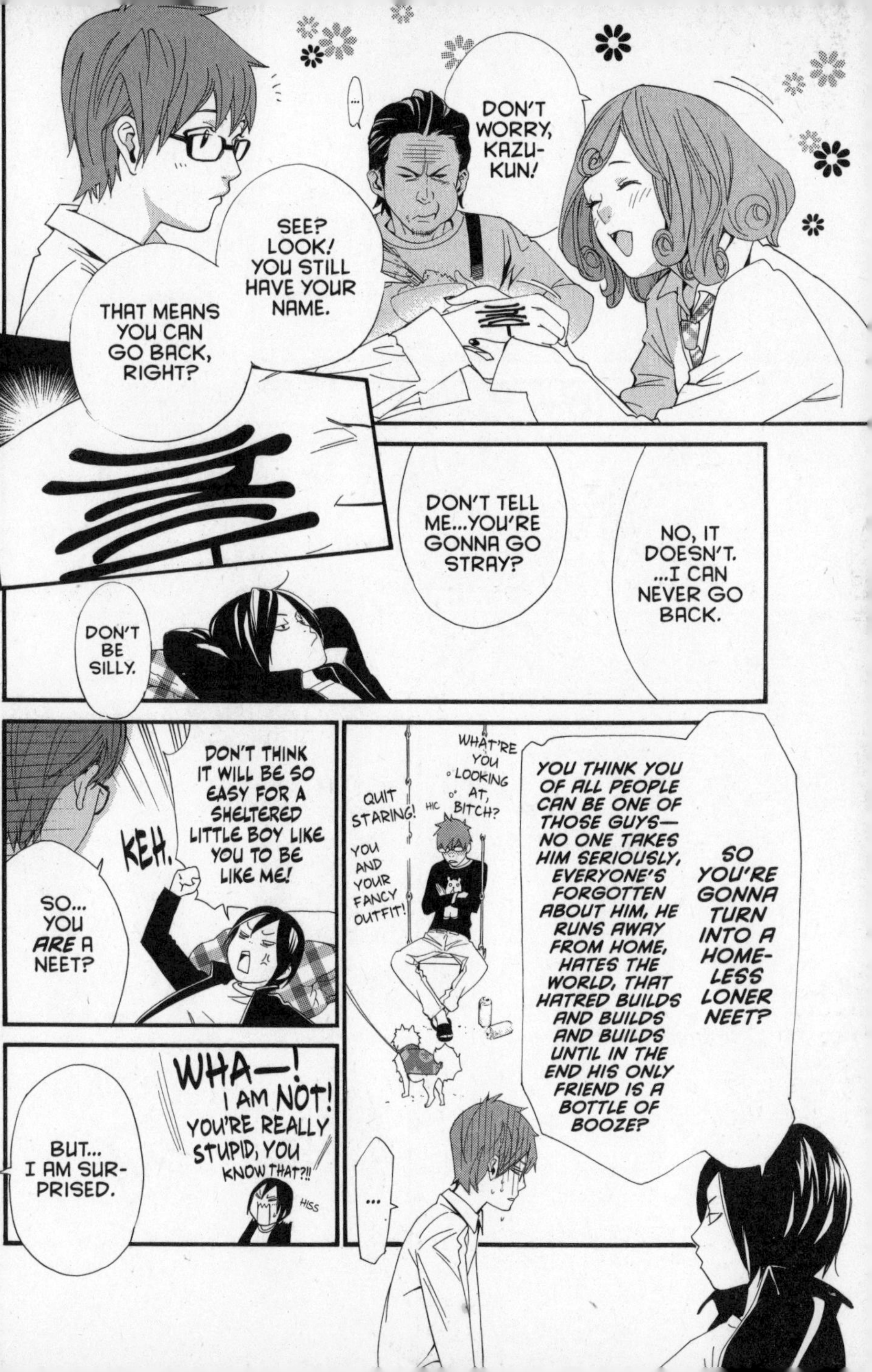
DON'T WORRY, KAZU-KUN!
...
SEE? LOOK! YOU STILL HAVE YOUR NAME.
THAT MEANS YOU CAN GO BACK, RIGHT?
NO, IT DOESN'T. ...I CAN NEVER GO BACK.
DON'T TELL ME...YOU'RE GONNA GO STRAY?
DON'T BE SILLY.
SO YOU'RE GONNA TURN INTO A HOME-LESS LONER NEET?
YOU THINK YOU OF ALL PEOPLE CAN BE ONE OF THOSE GUYS— NO ONE TAKES HIM SERIOUSLY, EVERYONE'S FORGOTTEN ABOUT HIM, HE RUNS AWAY FROM HOME, HATES THE WORLD, THAT HATRED BUILDS AND BUILDS AND BUILDS UNTIL IN THE END HIS ONLY FRIEND IS A BOTTLE OF BOOZE?
WHAT'RE YOU LOOKING AT, BITCH?
HIC
QUIT STARING!
YOU AND YOUR FANCY OUTFIT!
...
DON'T THINK IT WILL BE SO EASY FOR A SHELTERED LITTLE BOY LIKE YOU TO BE LIKE ME!
KEH.
SO... YOU ARE A NEET?
WHA—! I AM NOT! YOU'RE REALLY STUPID, YOU KNOW THAT?!!
HISS
BUT... I AM SUR-PRISED.

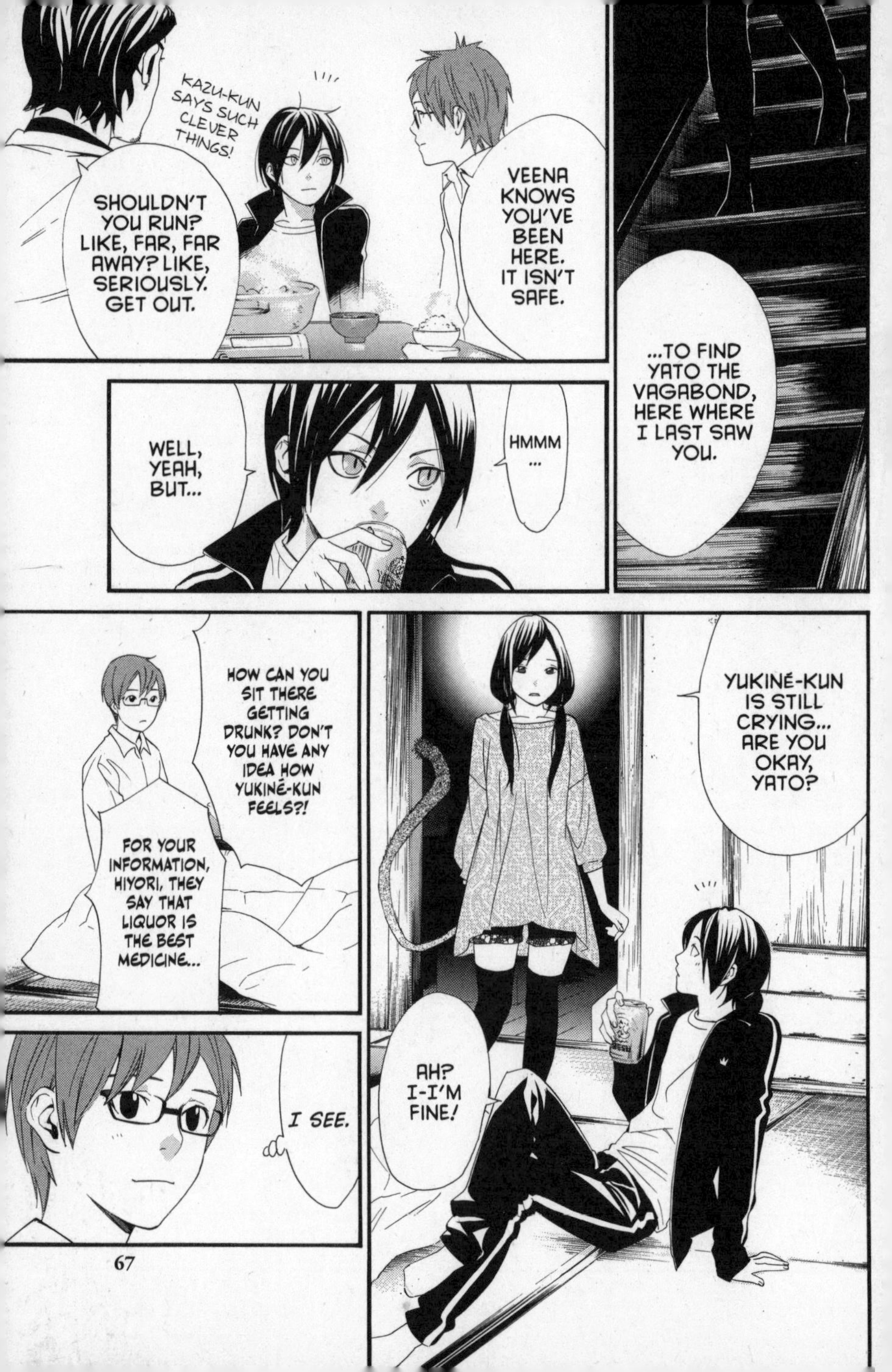
...TO FIND YATO THE VAGABOND, HERE WHERE I LAST SAW YOU.
VEENA KNOWS YOU'VE BEEN HERE. IT ISN'T SAFE.
KAZU-KUN SAYS SUCH CLEVER THINGS!
SHOULDN'T YOU RUN? LIKE, FAR, FAR AWAY? LIKE, SERIOUSLY. GET OUT.
HMMM ...
WELL, YEAH, BUT...
YUKINÉ-KUN IS STILL CRYING... ARE YOU OKAY, YATO?
AH? I-I'M FINE!
HOW CAN YOU SIT THERE GETTING DRUNK? DON'T YOU HAVE ANY IDEA HOW YUKINÉ-KUN FEELS?!
FOR YOUR INFORMATION, HIYORI, THEY SAY THAT LIQUOR IS THE BEST MEDICINE...
I SEE.

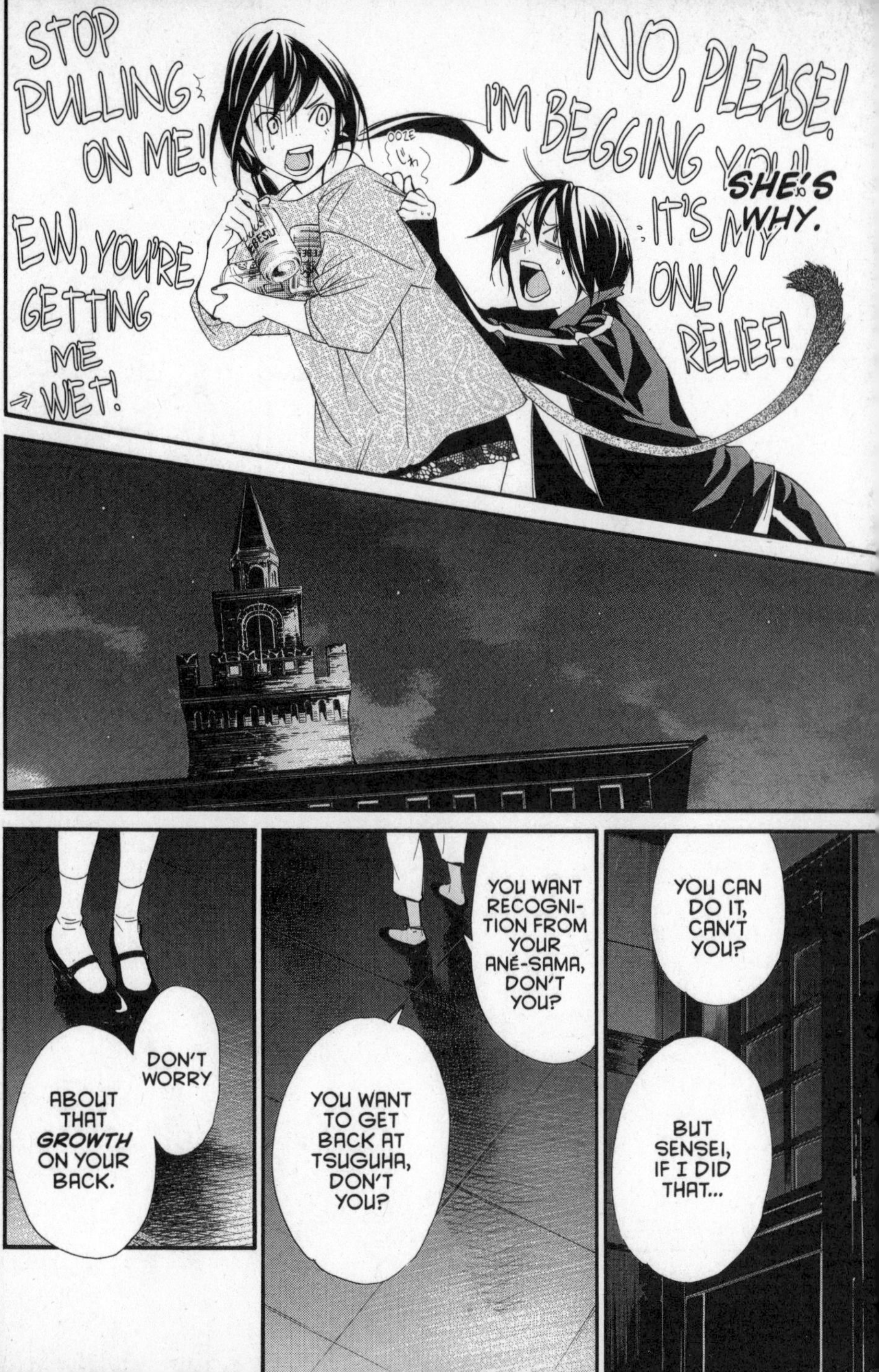
NO, PLEASE! I'M BEGGING YOU! IT'S MY ONLY RELIEF!
SHE'S WHY.
OOZE
STOP PULLING ON ME!
EW, YOU'RE GETTING ME WET!
YOU CAN DO IT, CAN'T YOU?
BUT SENSEI, IF I DID THAT...
YOU WANT RECOGNITION FROM YOUR ANÉ-SAMA, DON'T YOU?
YOU WANT TO GET BACK AT TSUGUHA, DON'T YOU?
DON'T WORRY
ABOUT THAT GROWTH ON YOUR BACK.

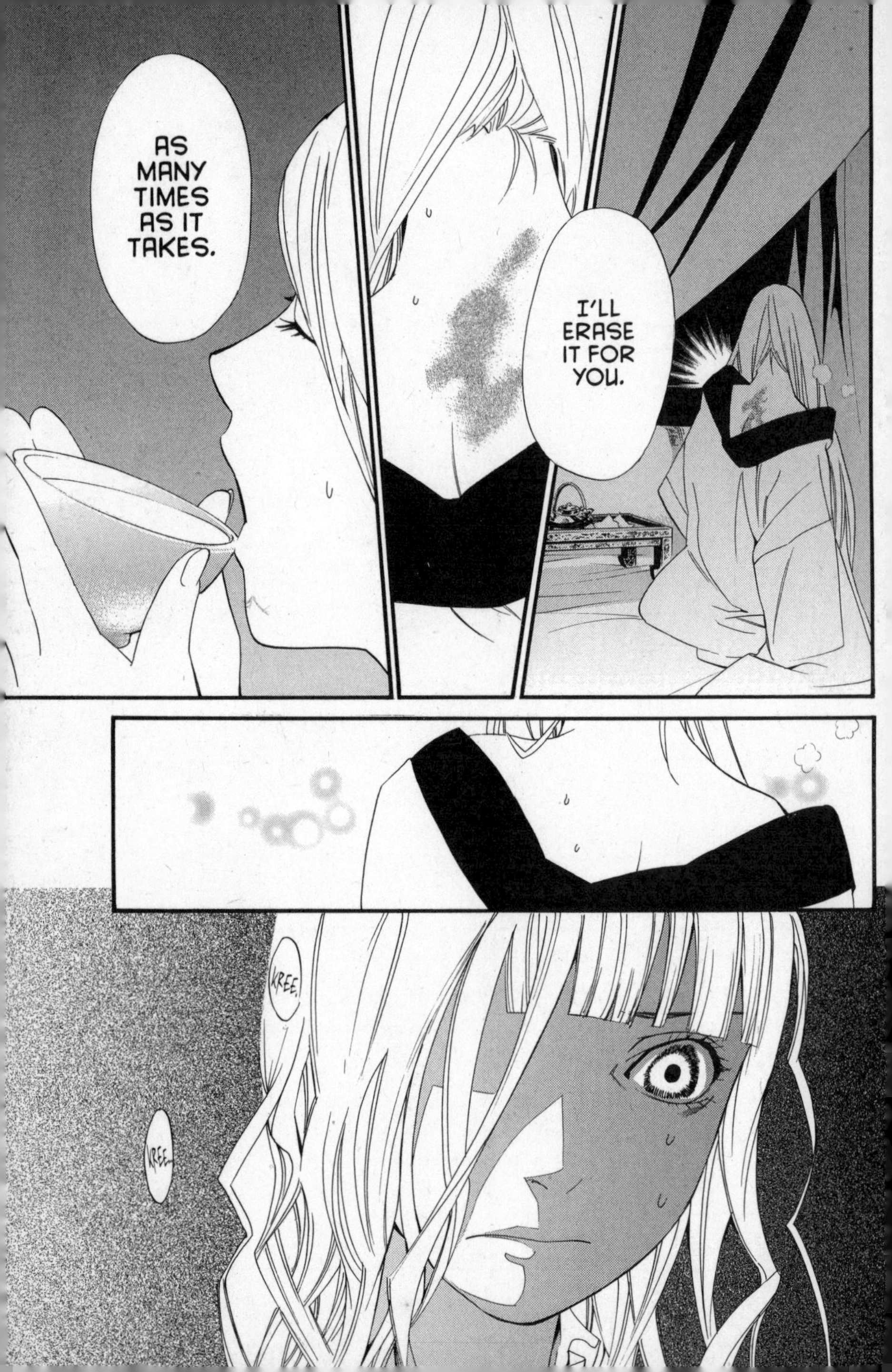
I'LL ERASE IT FOR YOU.
AS MANY TIMES AS IT TAKES.
KREE.
KREE...

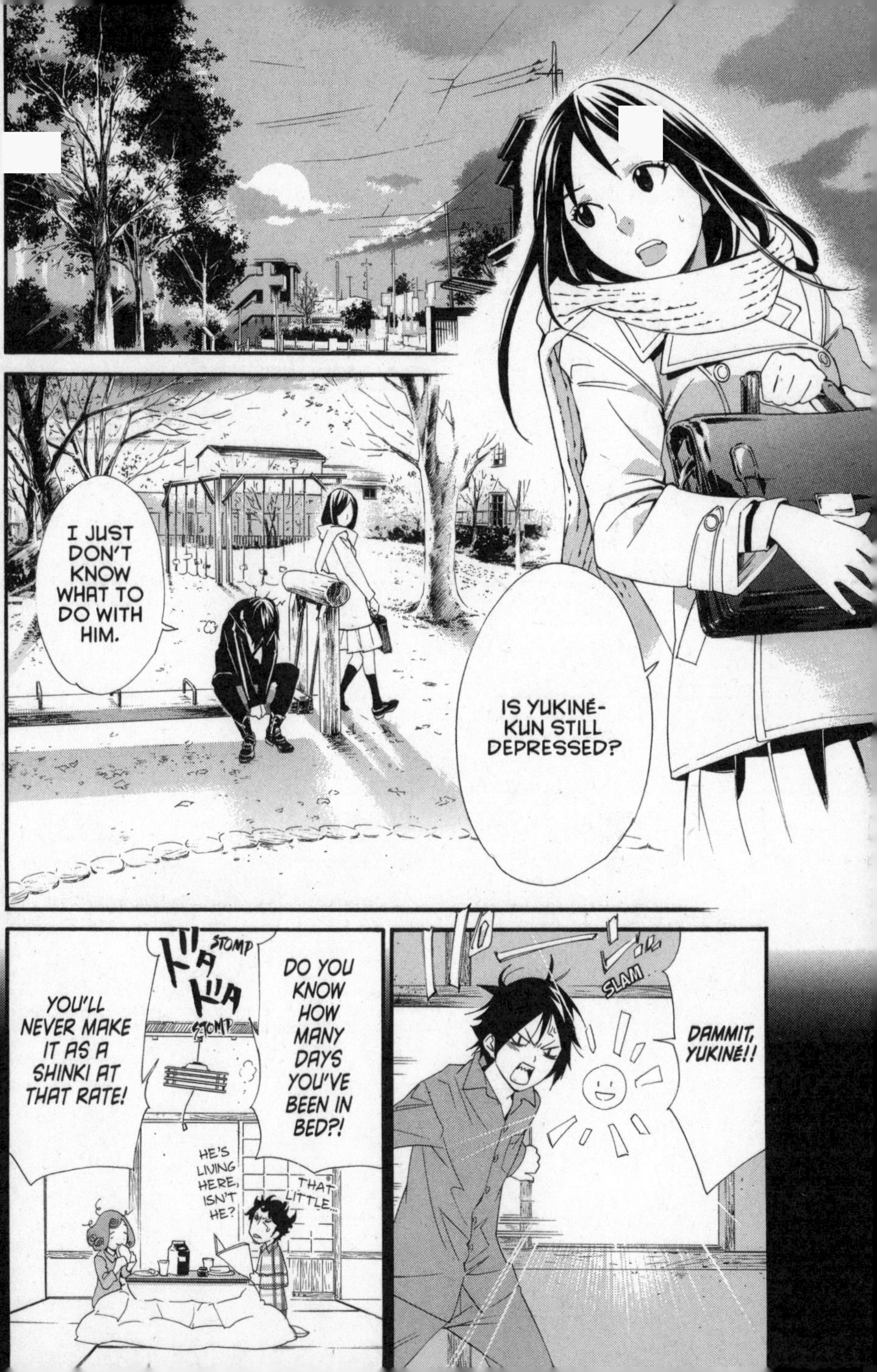
IS YUKINÉ-KUN STILL DEPRESSED?
I JUST DON'T KNOW WHAT TO DO WITH HIM.
SLAM
DAMMIT, YUKINÉ!!
STOMP
DO YOU KNOW HOW MANY DAYS YOU'VE BEEN IN BED?!
STOMP
YOU'LL NEVER MAKE IT AS A SHINKI AT THAT RATE!
THAT LITTLE...
HE'S LIVING HERE, ISN'T HE?

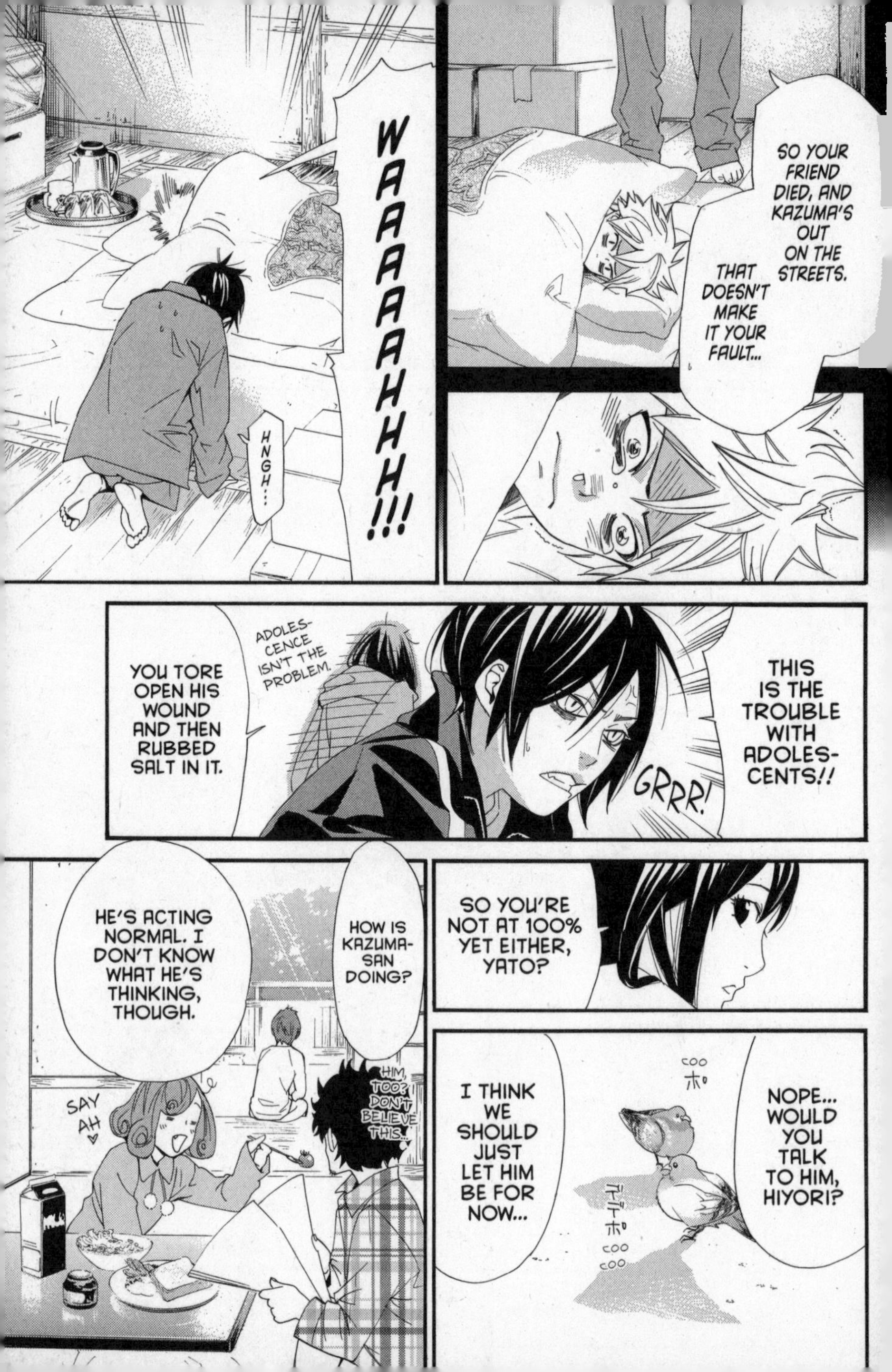

SO YOUR FRIEND DIED, AND KAZUMA'S OUT ON THE STREETS.
THAT DOESN'T MAKE IT YOUR FAULT...
WAAAAAAHHH!!!
HNGH...
THIS IS THE TROUBLE WITH ADOLESCENTS!!
GRRR!
ADOLESCENCE ISN'T THE PROBLEM.
YOU TORE OPEN HIS WOUND AND THEN RUBBED SALT IN IT.
SO YOU'RE NOT AT 100% YET EITHER, YATO?
NOPE... WOULD YOU TALK TO HIM, HIYORI?
COO ポ
I THINK WE SHOULD JUST LET HIM BE FOR NOW...
デデポ COO COO
HOW IS KAZUMA-SAN DOING?
HE'S ACTING NORMAL. I DON'T KNOW WHAT HE'S THINKING, THOUGH.
HIM, TOO? DON'T BELIEVE THIS...
SAY AH ♥

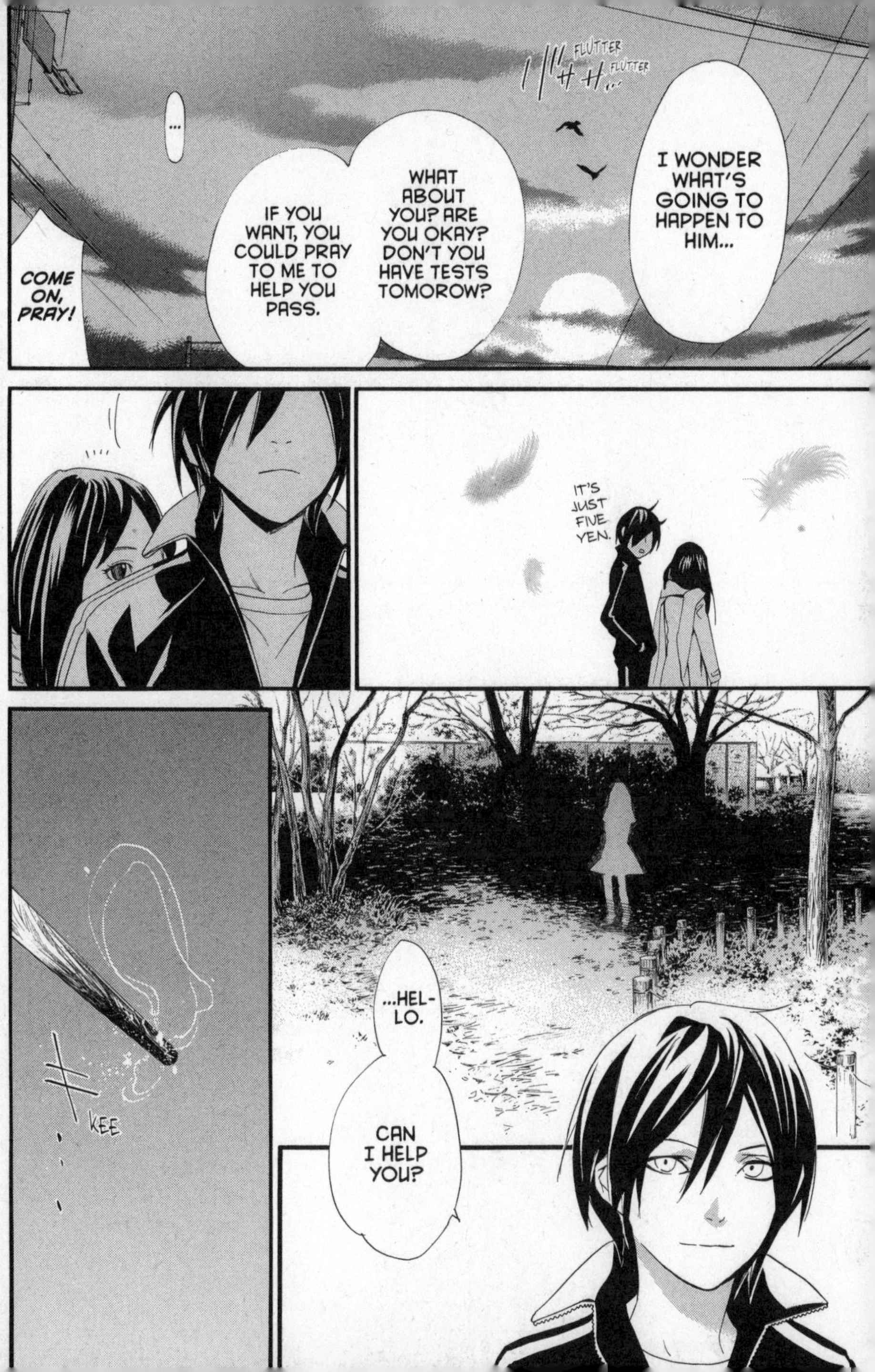
FLUTTER
FLUTTER...
I WONDER WHAT'S GOING TO HAPPEN TO HIM...
WHAT ABOUT YOU? ARE YOU OKAY? DON'T YOU HAVE TESTS TOMORROW?
IF YOU WANT, YOU COULD PRAY TO ME TO HELP YOU PASS.
...
COME ON, PRAY!
IT'S JUST FIVE YEN.
...HEL-LO.
CAN I HELP YOU?
KEE

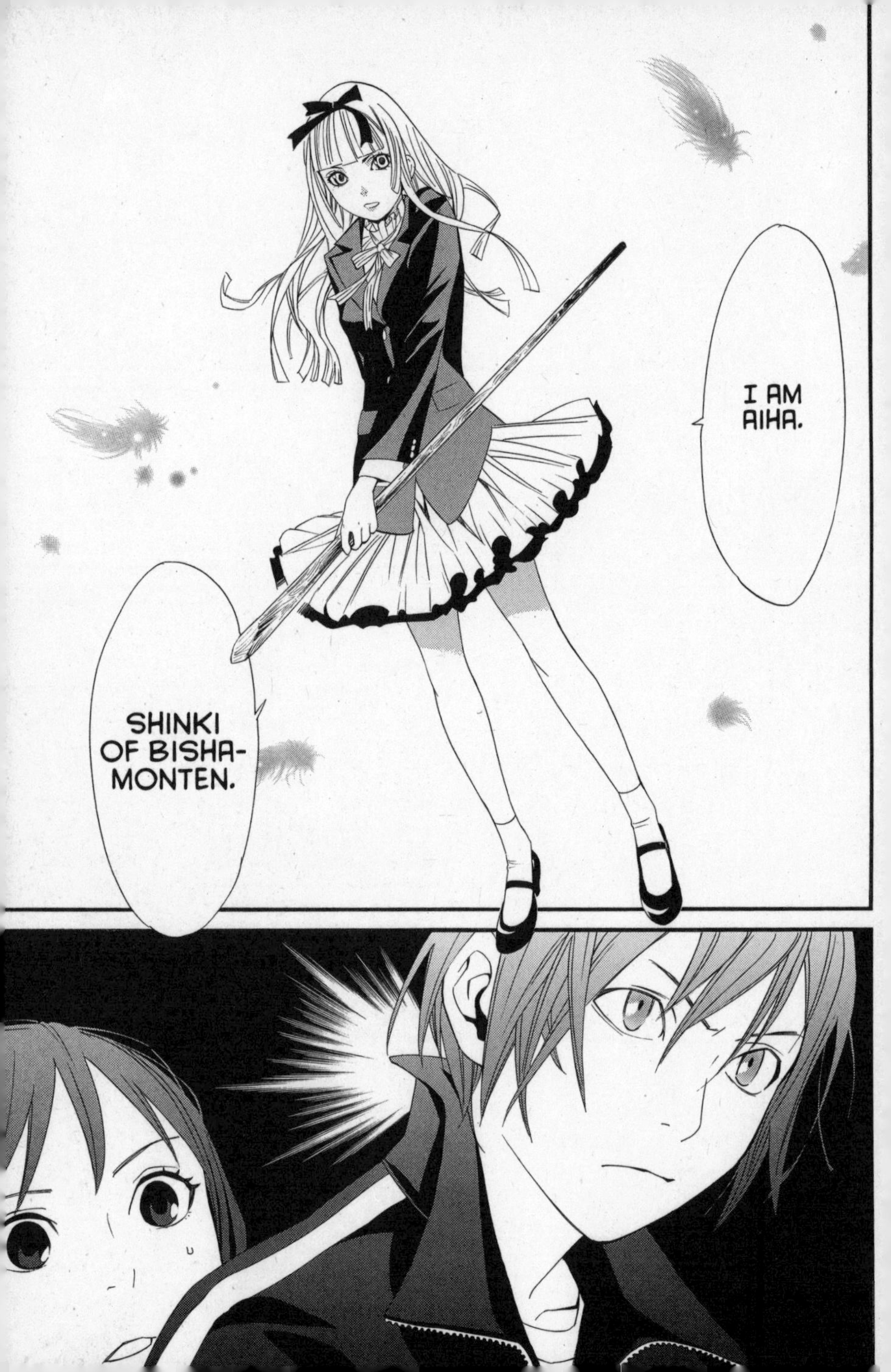
I AM AIHA.
SHINKI OF BISHA-MONTEN.

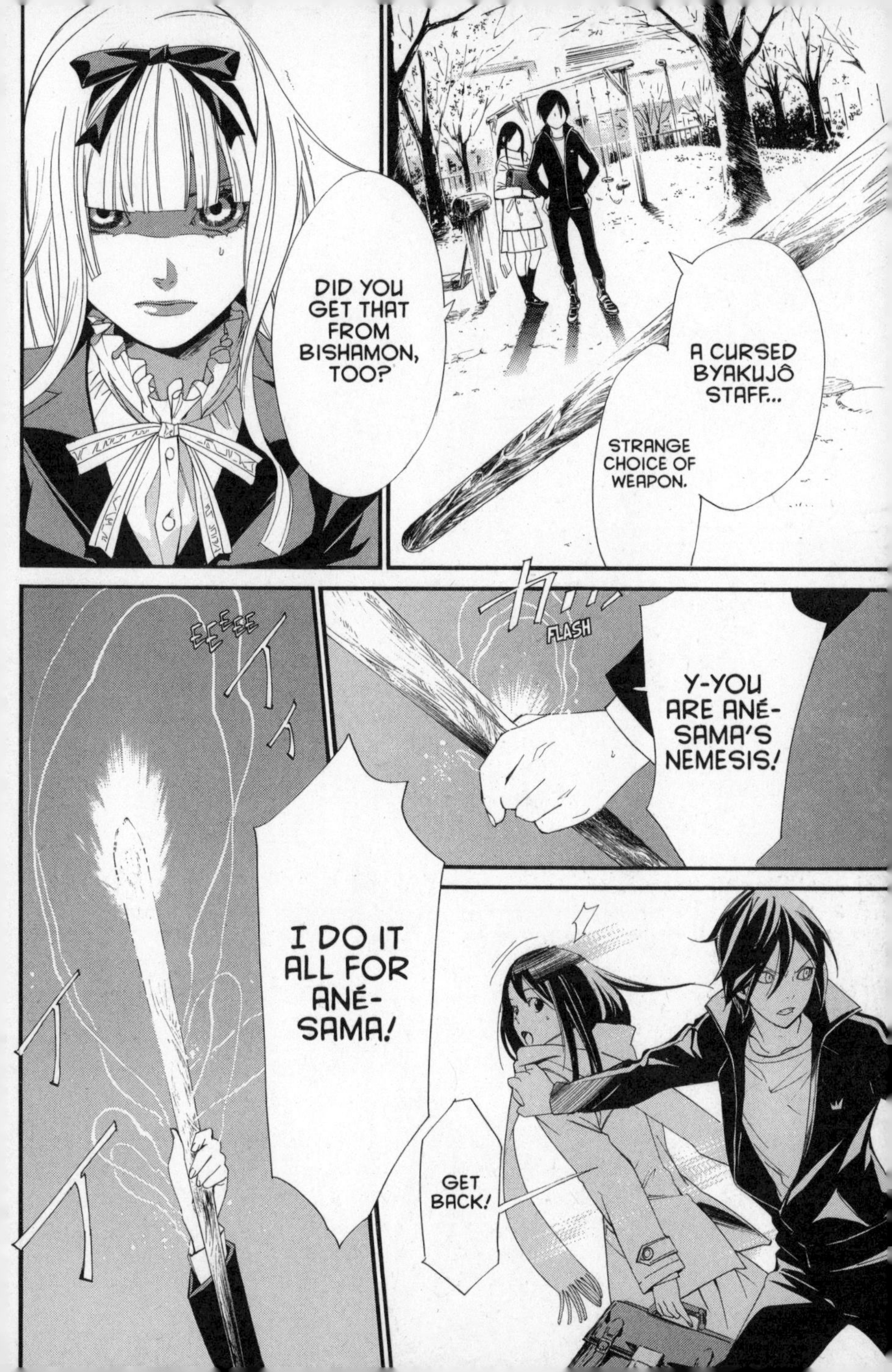
A CURSED BYAKUJÔ STAFF...
STRANGE CHOICE OF WEAPON.
DID YOU GET THAT FROM BISHAMON, TOO?
FLASH
Y-YOU ARE ANÉ-SAMA'S NEMESIS!
GET BACK!
I DO IT ALL FOR ANÉ-SAMA!

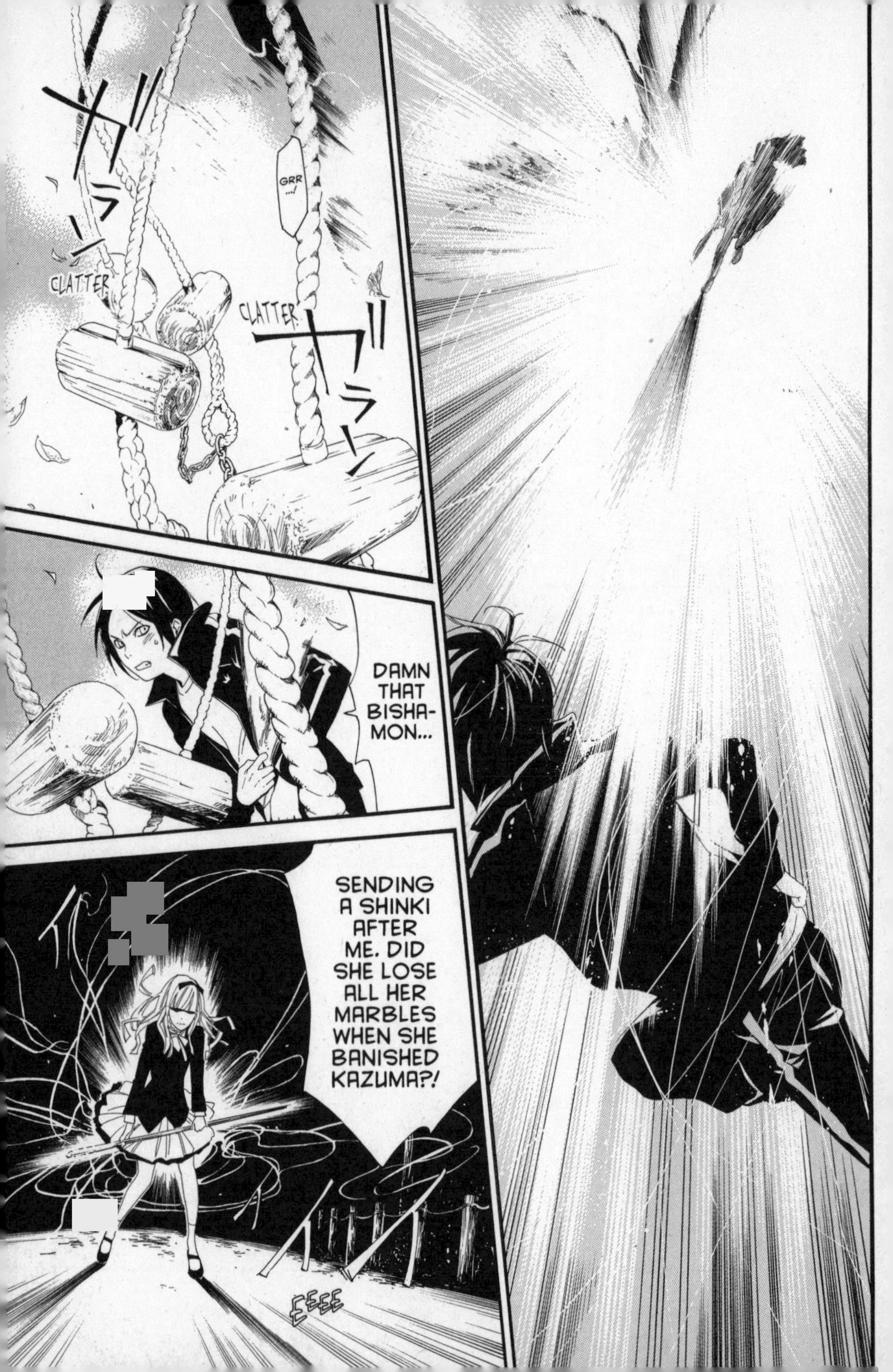
GRR ...!
CLATTER
CLATTER
DAMN THAT BISHAMON...
SENDING A SHINKI AFTER ME. DID SHE LOSE ALL HER MARBLES WHEN SHE BANISHED KAZUMA?!
EEEE

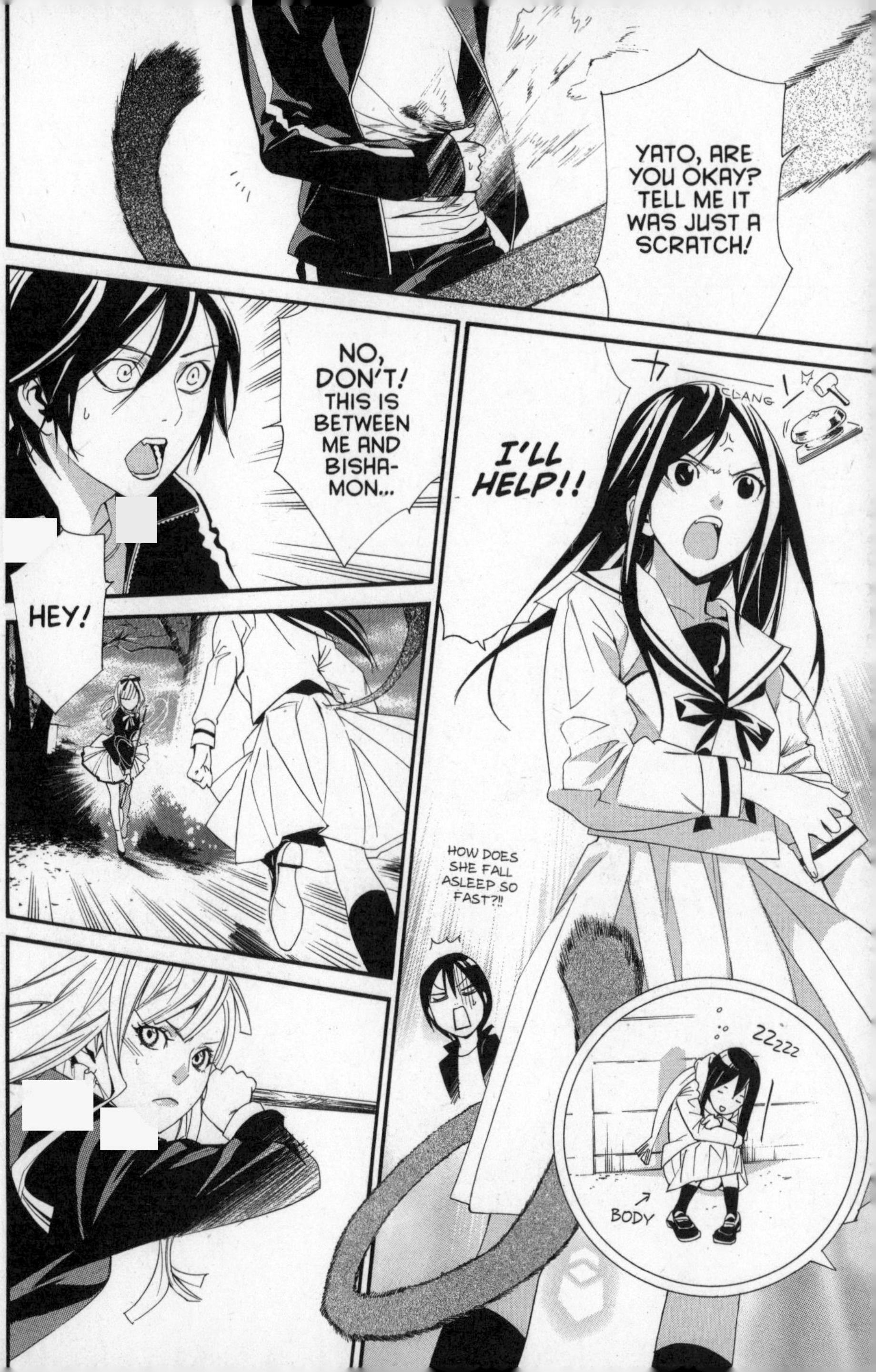
YATO, ARE YOU OKAY? TELL ME IT WAS JUST A SCRATCH!
CLANG
I'LL HELP!!
HOW DOES SHE FALL ASLEEP SO FAST?!!
ZZZZZ
BODY
NO, DON'T! THIS IS BETWEEN ME AND BISHAMON...
HEY!

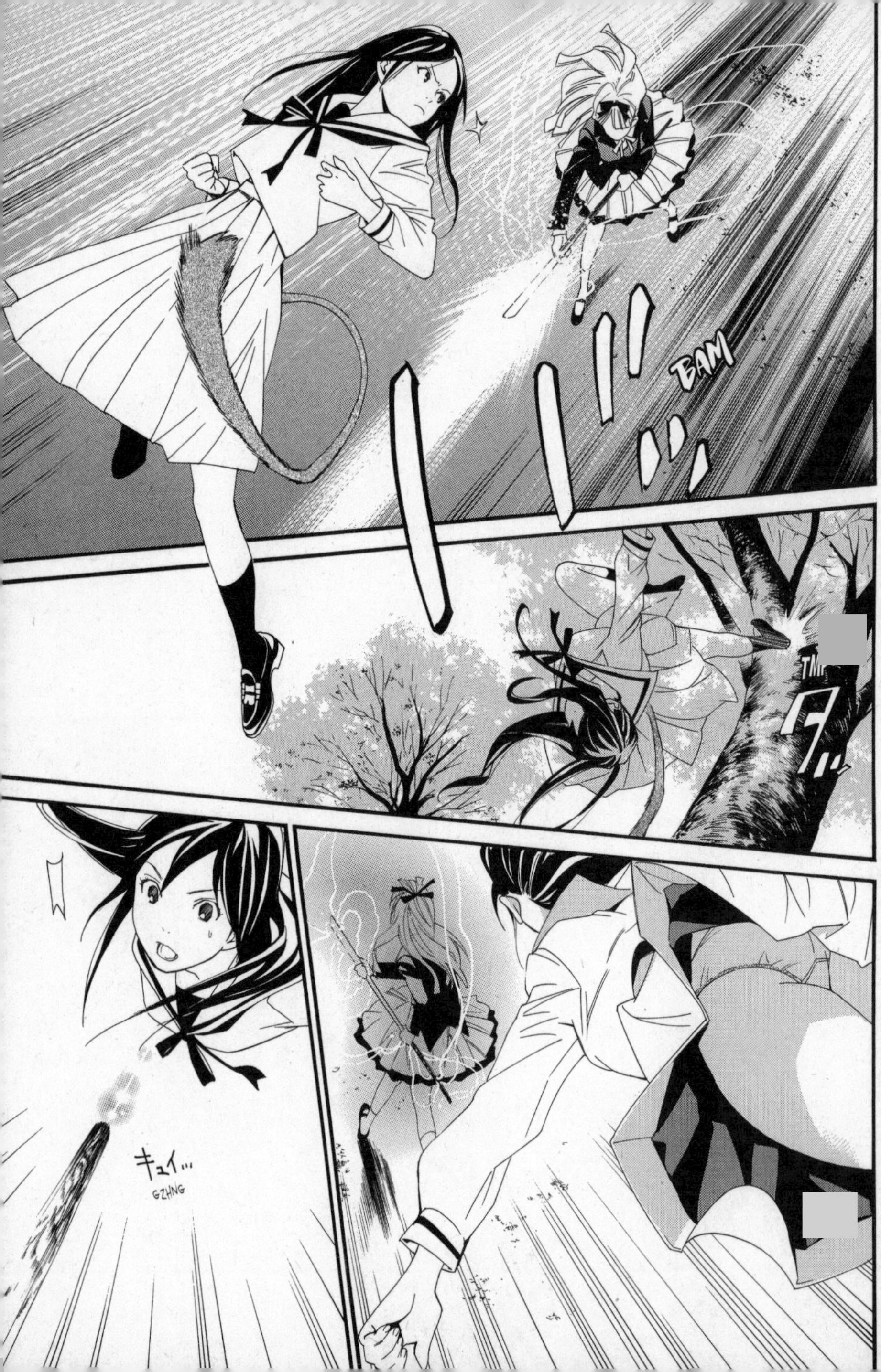
BAM
キュイッ
GZHNG

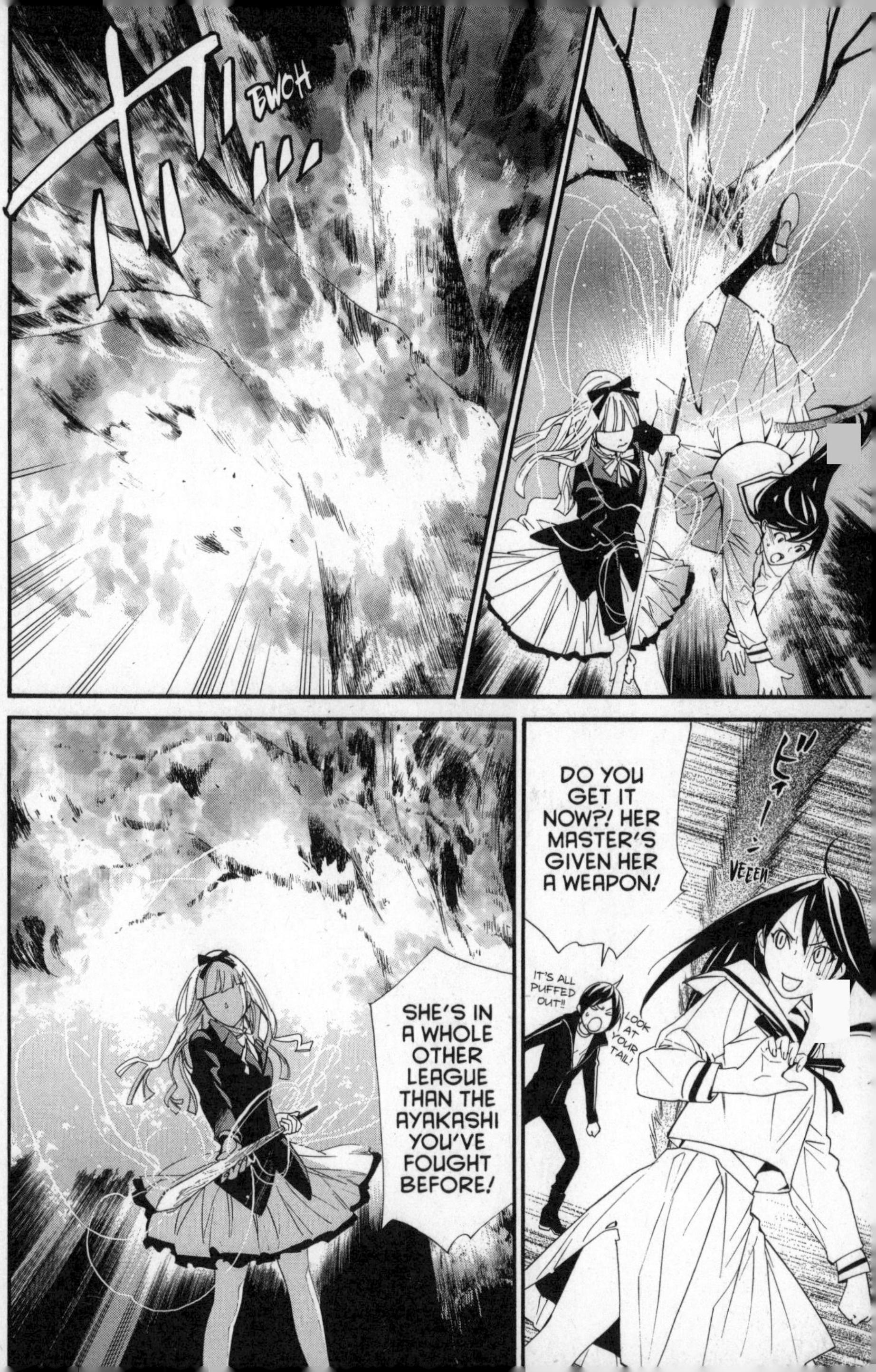
BWOH
DO YOU GET IT NOW?! HER MASTER'S GIVEN HER A WEAPON!
VEEEN
IT'S ALL PUFFED OUT!!
LOOK AT YOUR TAIL!
SHE'S IN A WHOLE OTHER LEAGUE THAN THE AYAKASHI YOU'VE FOUGHT BEFORE!

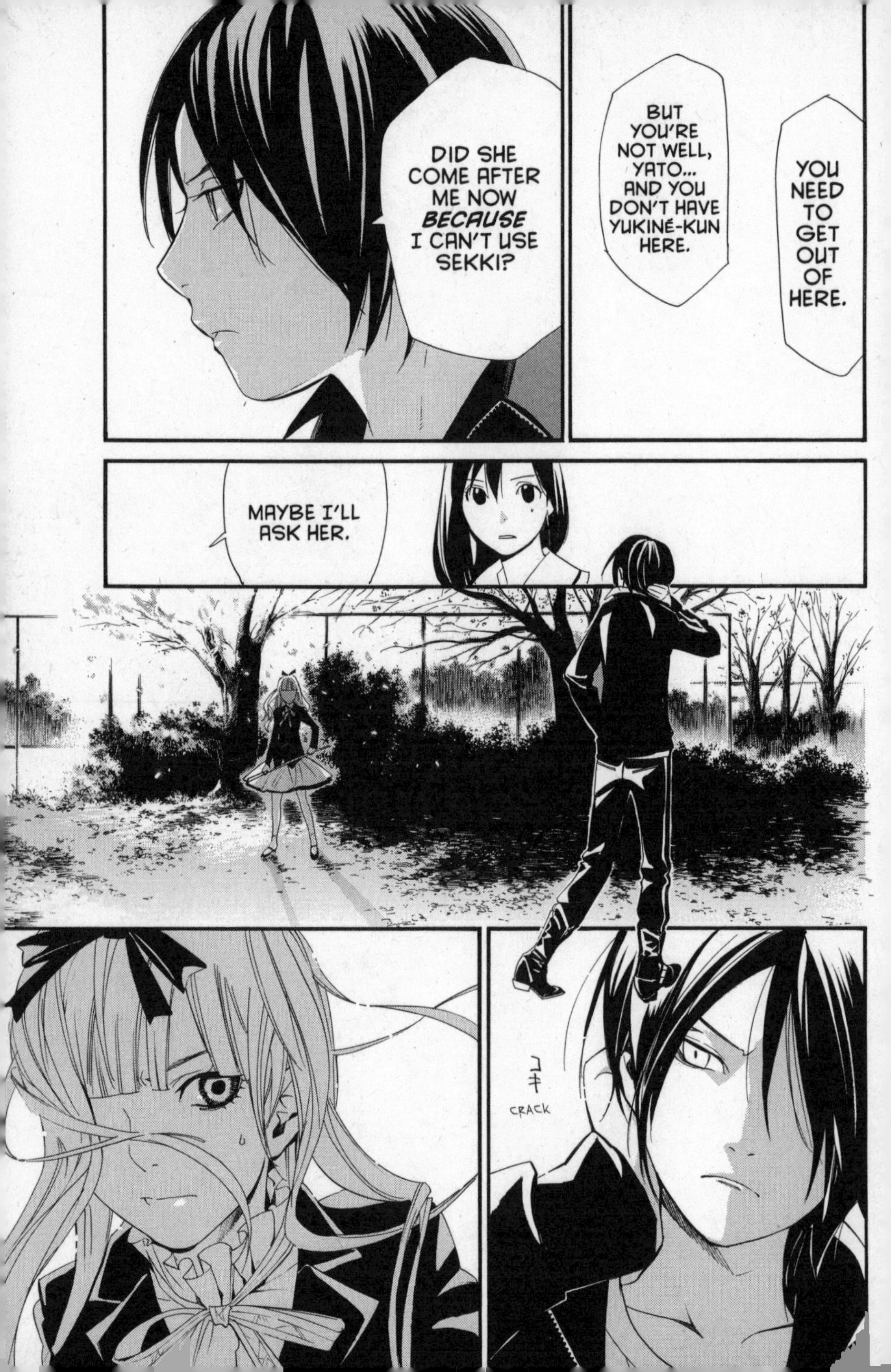
YOU NEED TO GET OUT OF HERE.
BUT YOU'RE NOT WELL, YATO... AND YOU DON'T HAVE YUKINÉ-KUN HERE.
DID SHE COME AFTER ME NOW *BECAUSE* I CAN'T USE SEKKI?
MAYBE I'LL ASK HER.
コキ
CRACK

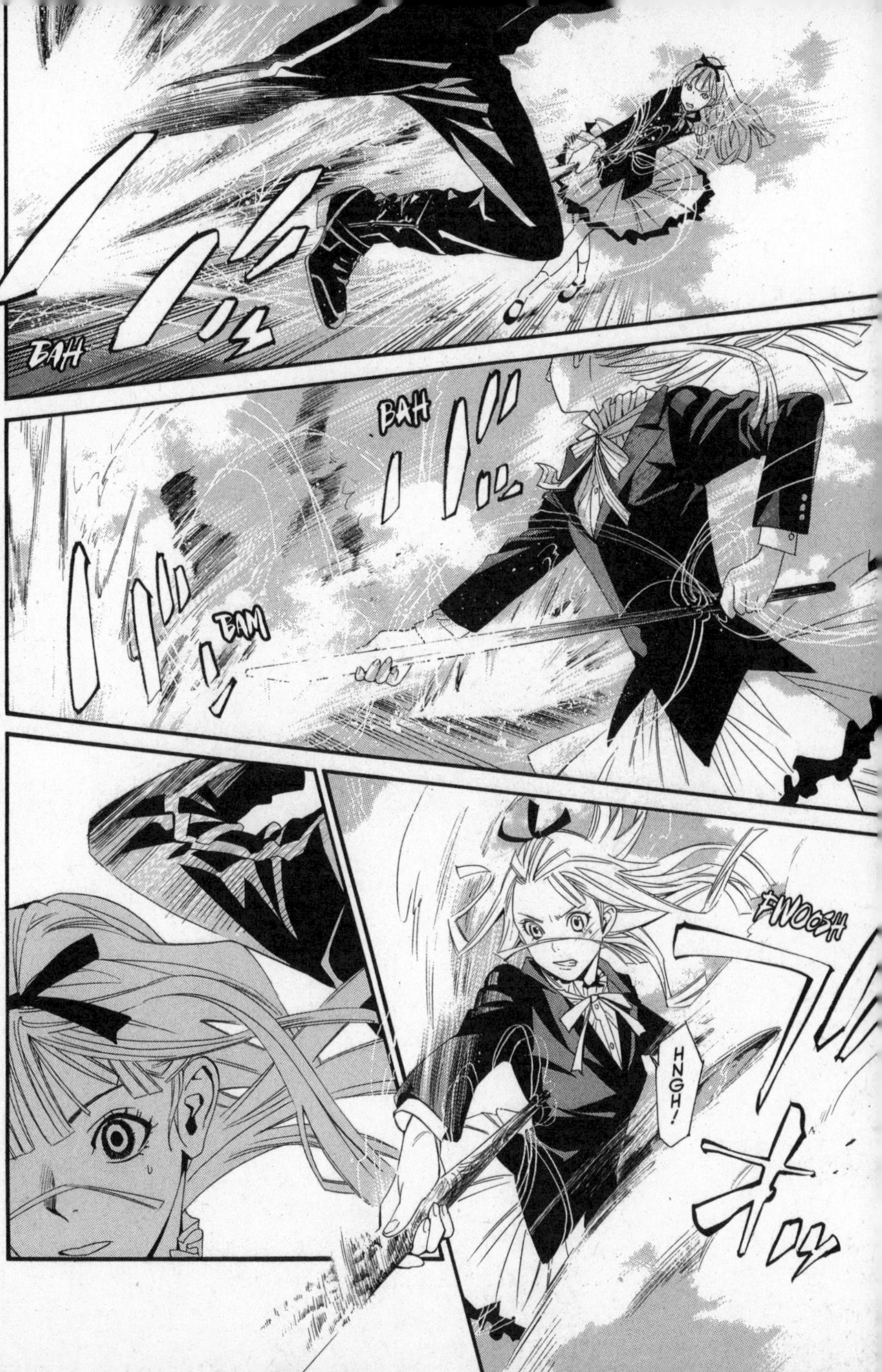
BAH
BAH
BAM
FWOOSH
HNGH!

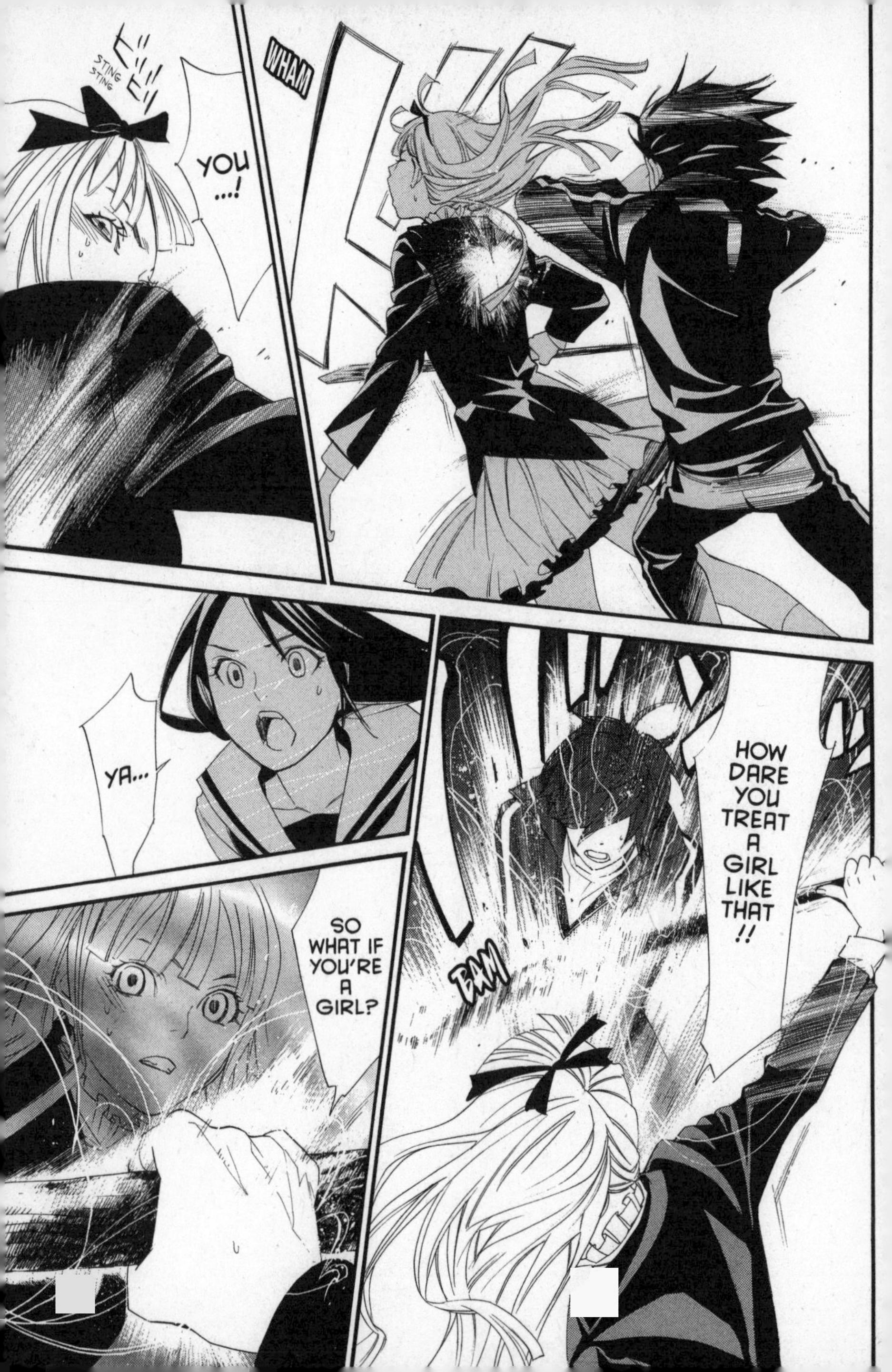

WHAM
...
ビリビリ
STING STING
YOU ...!
HOW DARE YOU TREAT A GIRL LIKE THAT!!
BAM
YA...
SO WHAT IF YOU'RE A GIRL?

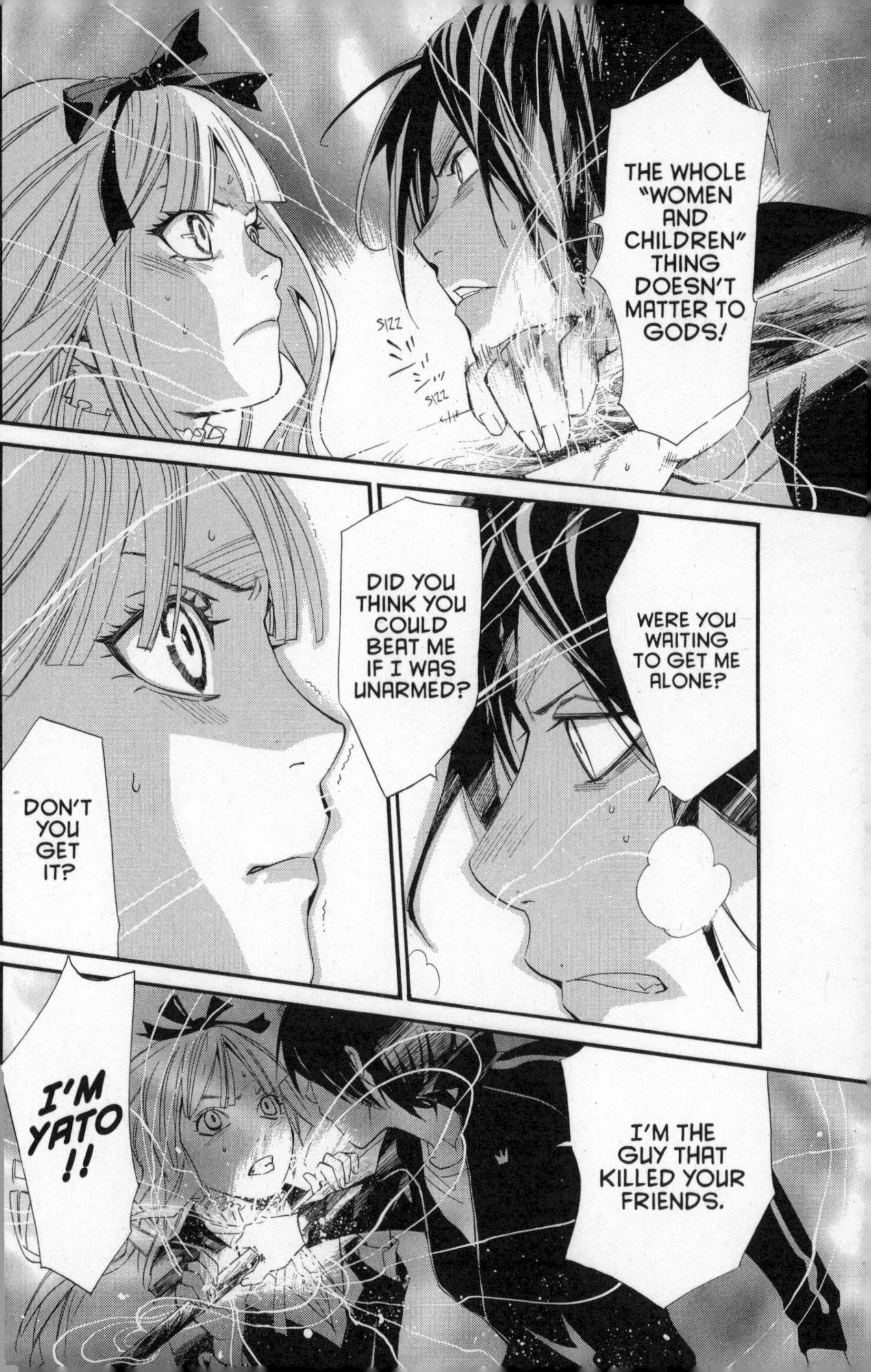
THE WHOLE "WOMEN AND CHILDREN" THING DOESN'T MATTER TO GODS!
SIZZ
SIZZ
WERE YOU WAITING TO GET ME ALONE?
DID YOU THINK YOU COULD BEAT ME IF I WAS UNARMED?
DON'T YOU GET IT?
I'M THE GUY THAT KILLED YOUR FRIENDS.
I'M YATO!!

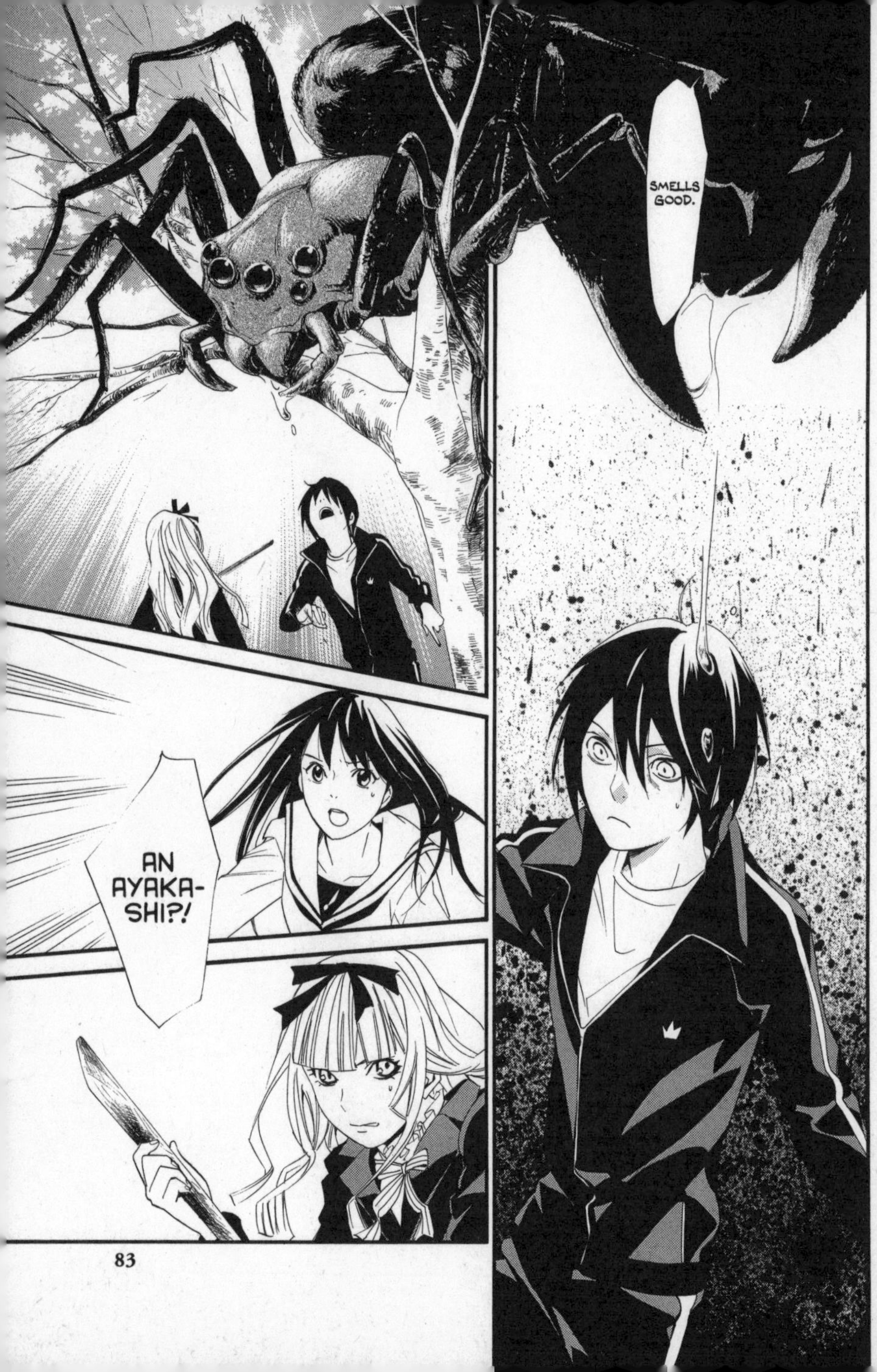
SMELLS GOOD.
AN AYAKA-SHI?!

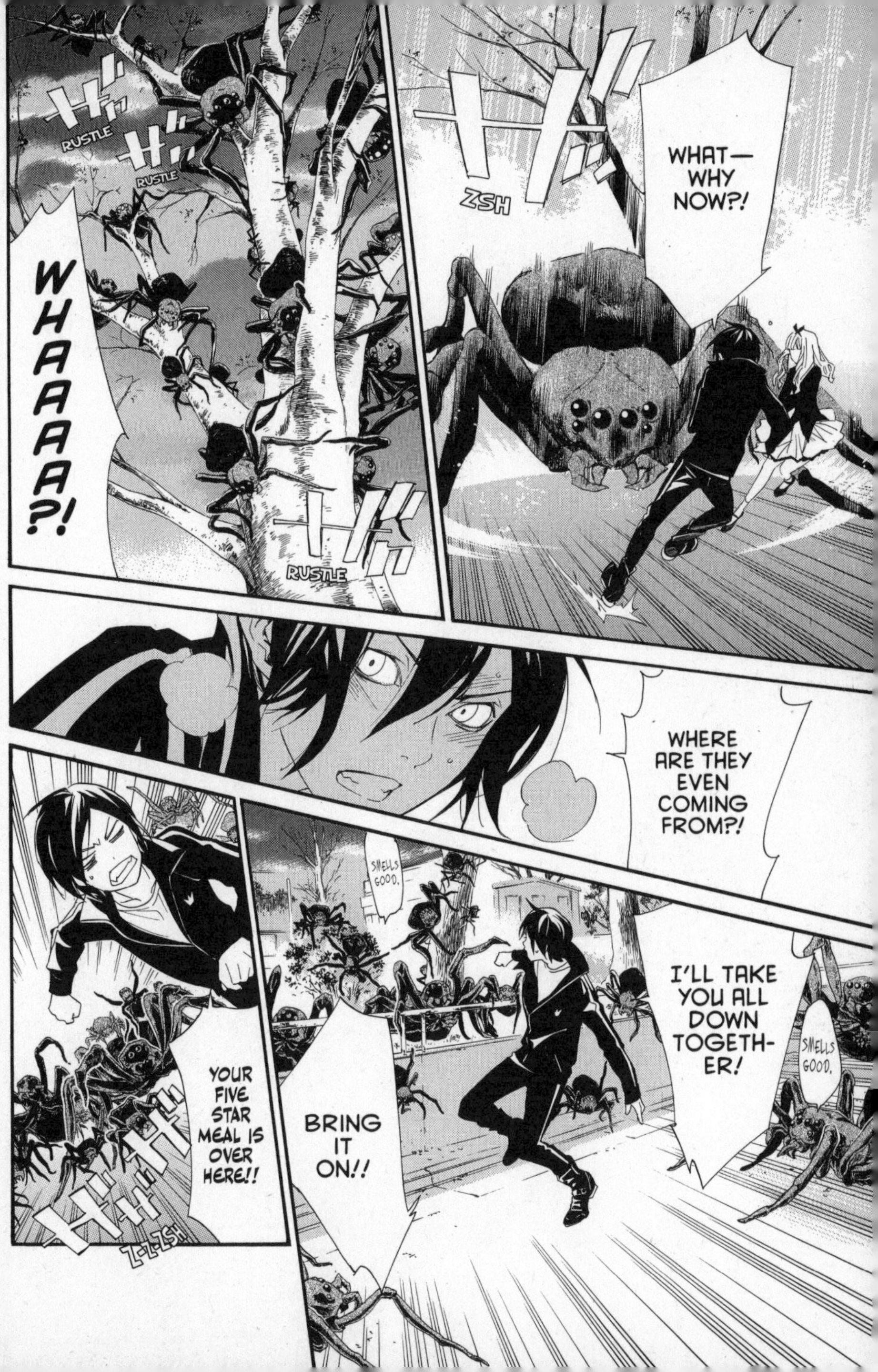
ZSH
WHAT— WHY NOW?!
RUSTLE
RUSTLE
WHAAAAAA?!
RUSTLE
WHERE ARE THEY EVEN COMING FROM?!
SMELLS GOOD.
I'LL TAKE YOU ALL DOWN TOGETH-ER!
SMELLS GOOD.
BRING IT ON!!
YOUR FIVE STAR MEAL IS OVER HERE!!
Z-Z-ZSH

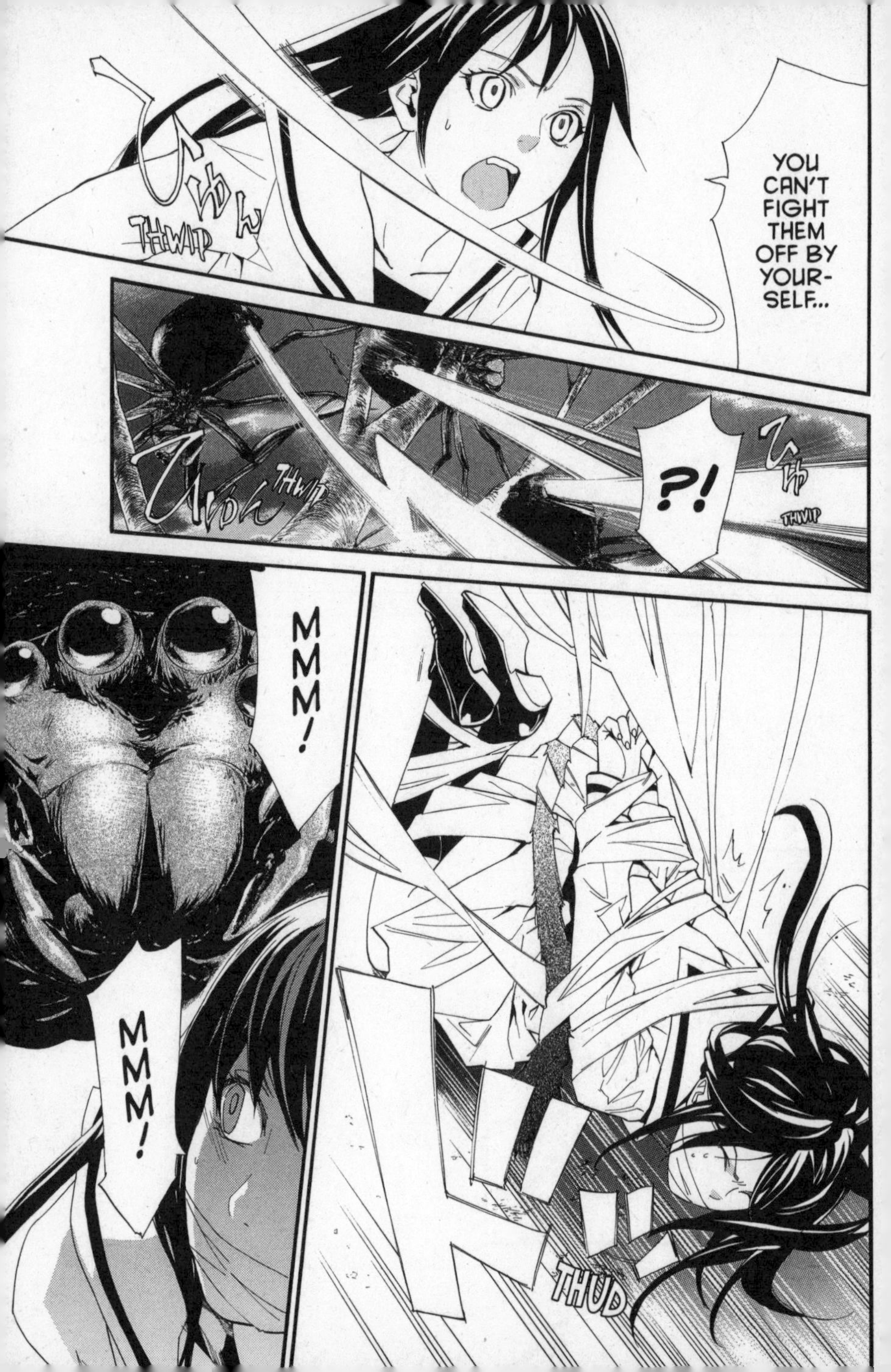
YOU CAN'T FIGHT THEM OFF BY YOUR-SELF...
ひゅん
THWIP
ひゅ
THWIP
?!
ひゅん
THWIP
THUD
MMM!
MMM!

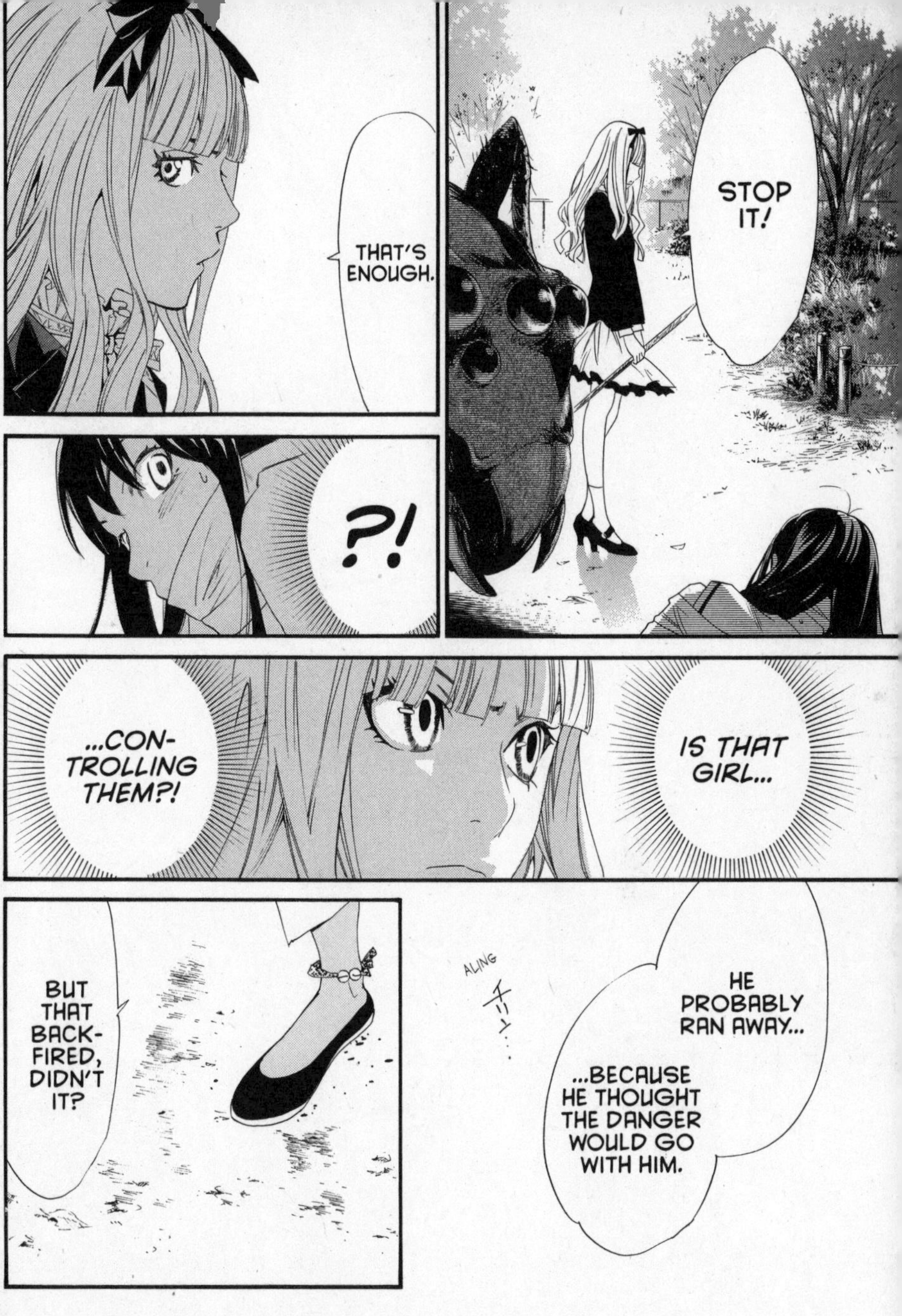
STOP IT!
THAT'S ENOUGH.
?!
IS THAT GIRL...
...CONTROLLING THEM?!
HE PROBABLY RAN AWAY...
...BECAUSE HE THOUGHT THE DANGER WOULD GO WITH HIM.
ALING
チリン...
BUT THAT BACKFIRED, DIDN'T IT?

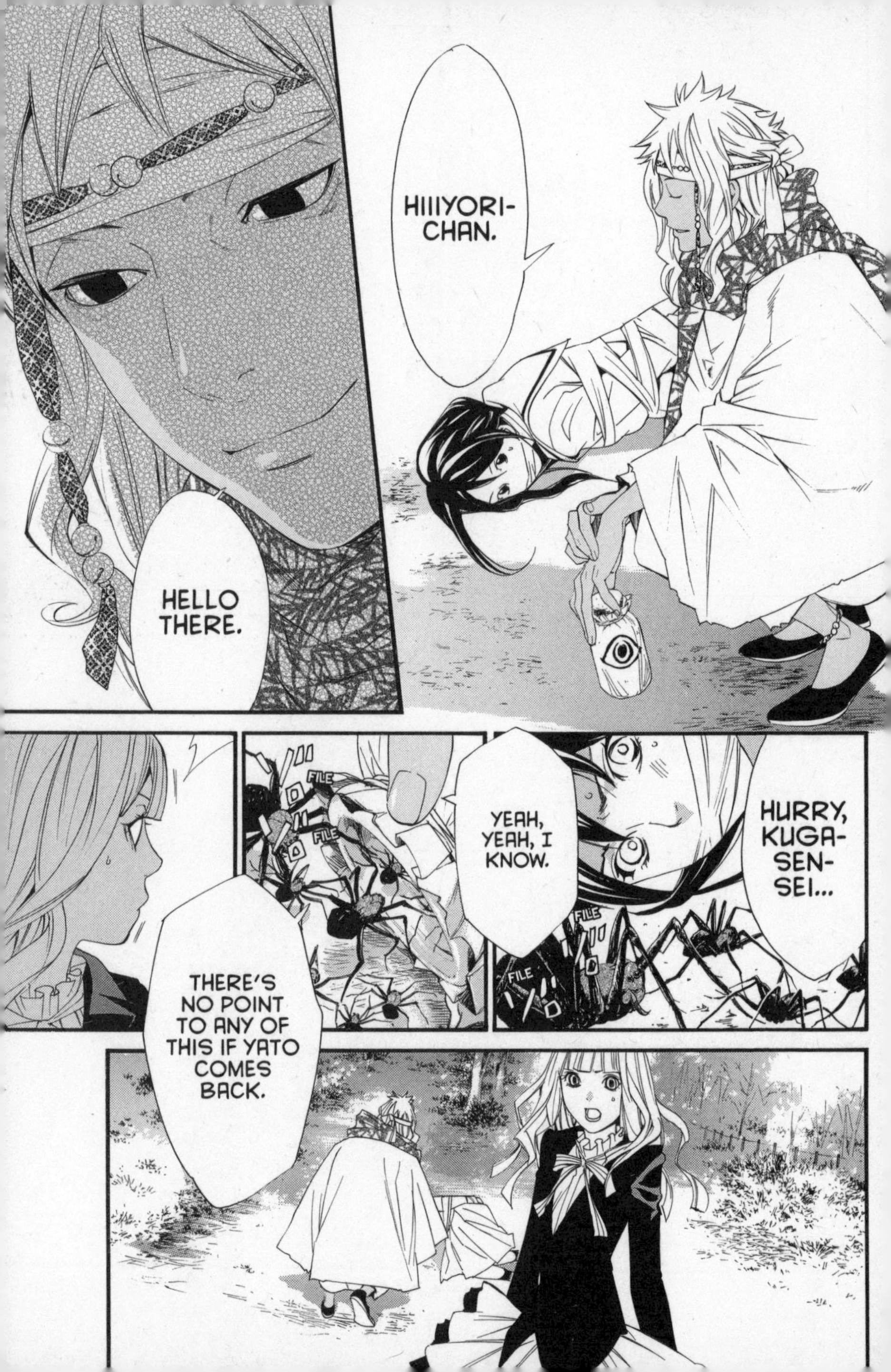
HIIIYORI-CHAN.
HELLO THERE.
HURRY, KUGA-SEN-SEI...
YEAH, YEAH, I KNOW.
FILE
FILE
FILE
FILE
FILE
THERE'S NO POINT TO ANY OF THIS IF YATO COMES BACK.

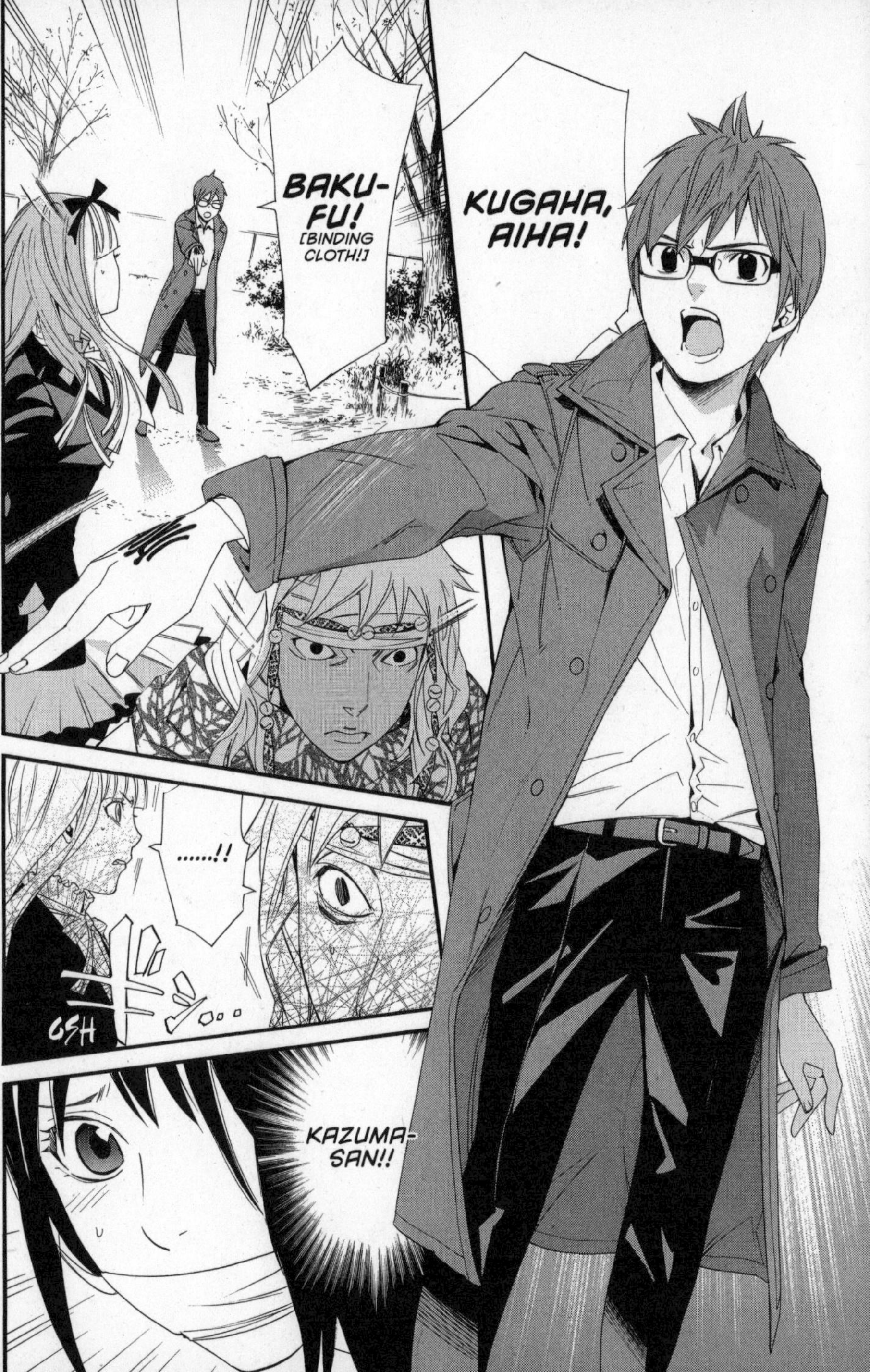
KUGAHA, AIHA!
BAKU-FU! [BINDING CLOTH!]
......!!
GSH
KAZUMA-SAN!!

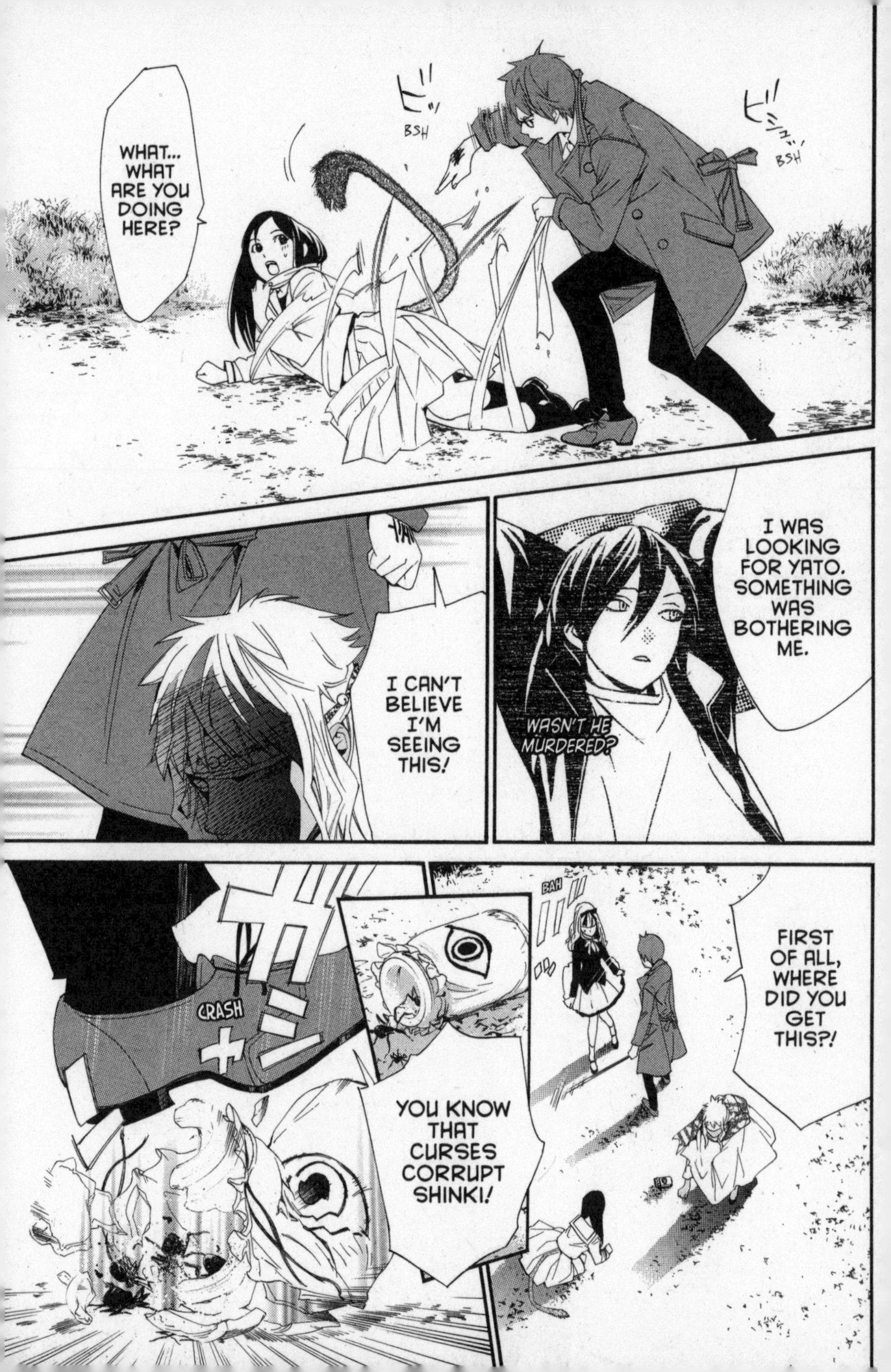
BSH
BSH
WHAT... WHAT ARE YOU DOING HERE?
I WAS LOOKING FOR YATO. SOMETHING WAS BOTHERING ME.
WASN'T HE MURDERED?
I CAN'T BELIEVE I'M SEEING THIS!
BAH
FIRST OF ALL, WHERE DID YOU GET THIS?!
CRASH
YOU KNOW THAT CURSES CORRUPT SHINKI!

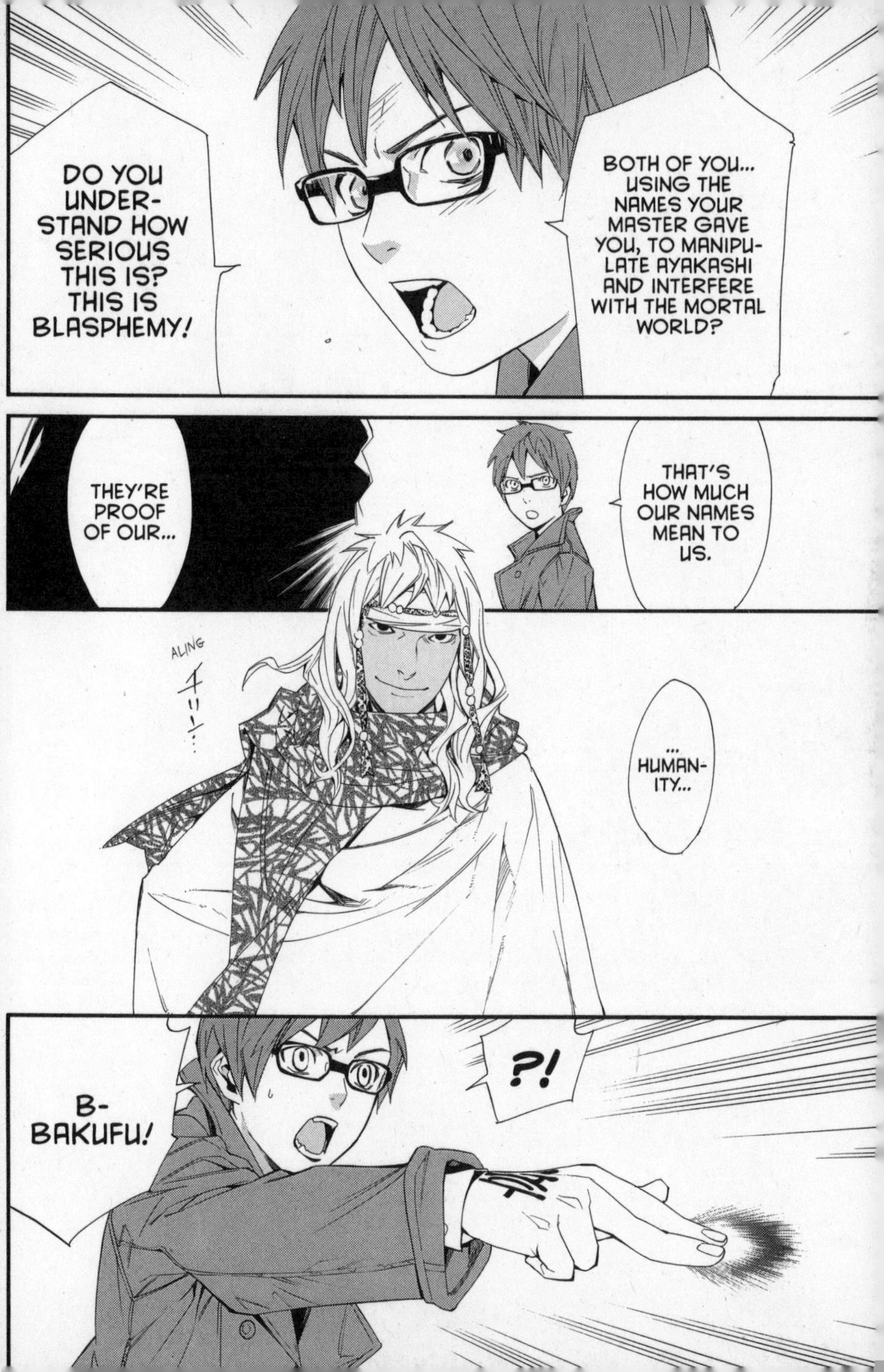
BOTH OF YOU... USING THE NAMES YOUR MASTER GAVE YOU, TO MANIPU-LATE AYAKASHI AND INTERFERE WITH THE MORTAL WORLD?
DO YOU UNDER-STAND HOW SERIOUS THIS IS? THIS IS BLASPHEMY!
THAT'S HOW MUCH OUR NAMES MEAN TO US.
THEY'RE PROOF OF OUR...
... HUMAN-ITY...
ALING
?!
B-BAKUFU!

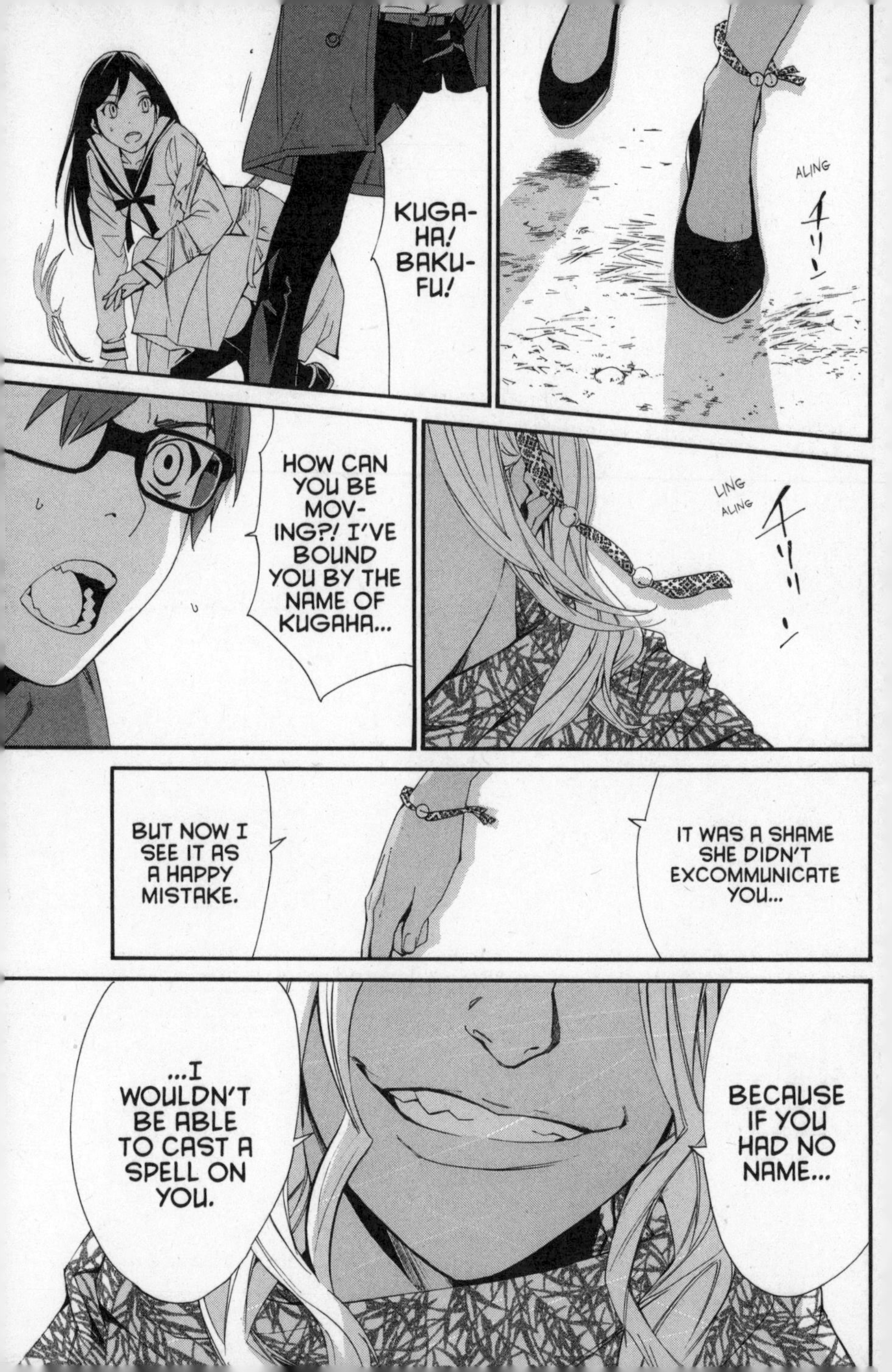
ALING
KUGA-HA! BAKU-FU!
LING ALING
HOW CAN YOU BE MOV-ING?! I'VE BOUND YOU BY THE NAME OF KUGAHA...
IT WAS A SHAME SHE DIDN'T EXCOMMUNICATE YOU...
BUT NOW I SEE IT AS A HAPPY MISTAKE.
BECAUSE IF YOU HAD NO NAME...
...I WOULDN'T BE ABLE TO CAST A SPELL ON YOU.

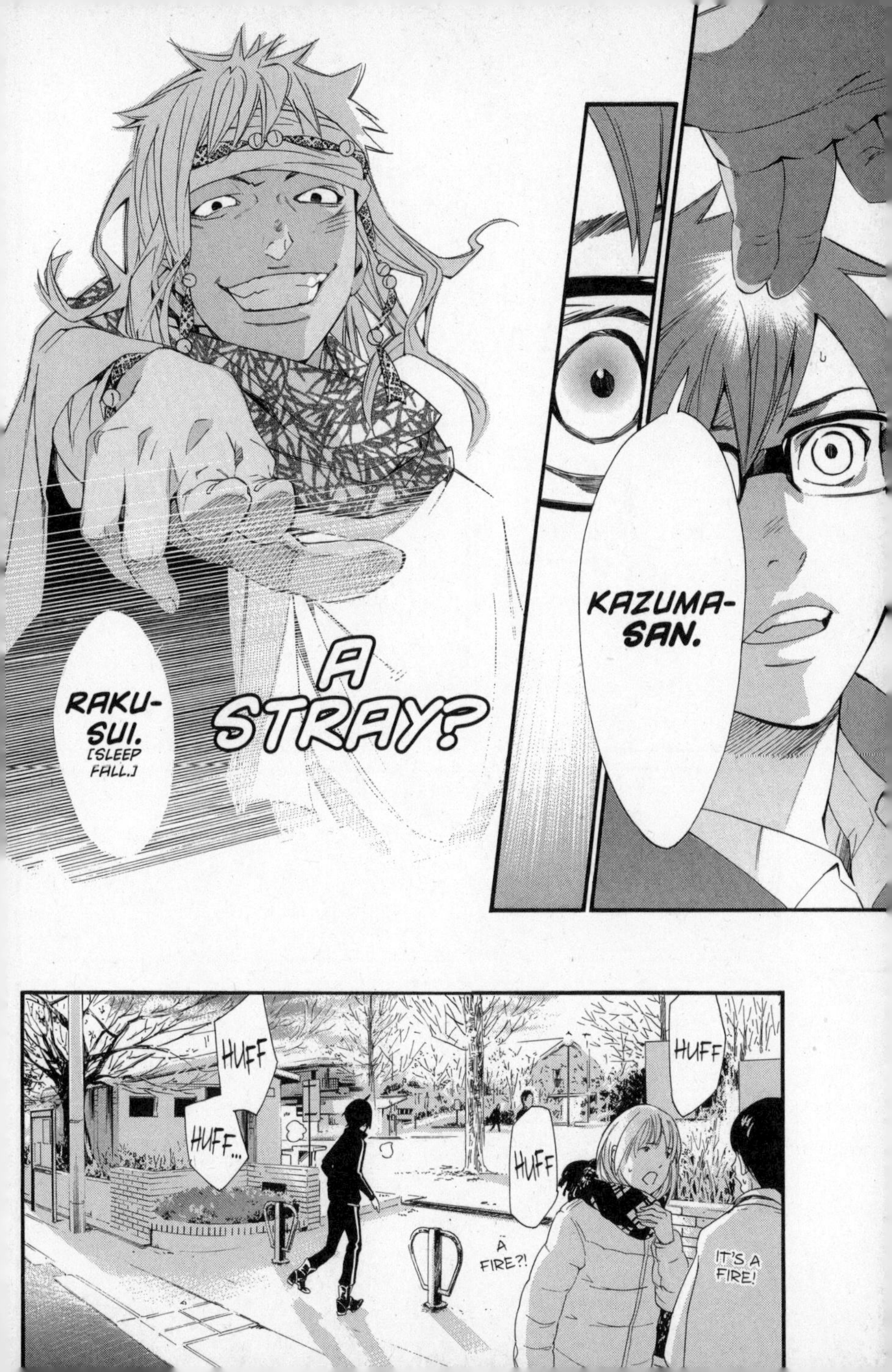
KAZUMA-SAN.
RAKU-SUI. [SLEEP FALL.]
A STRAY?
HUFF
IT'S A FIRE!
A FIRE?!
HUFF
HUFF
HUFF...

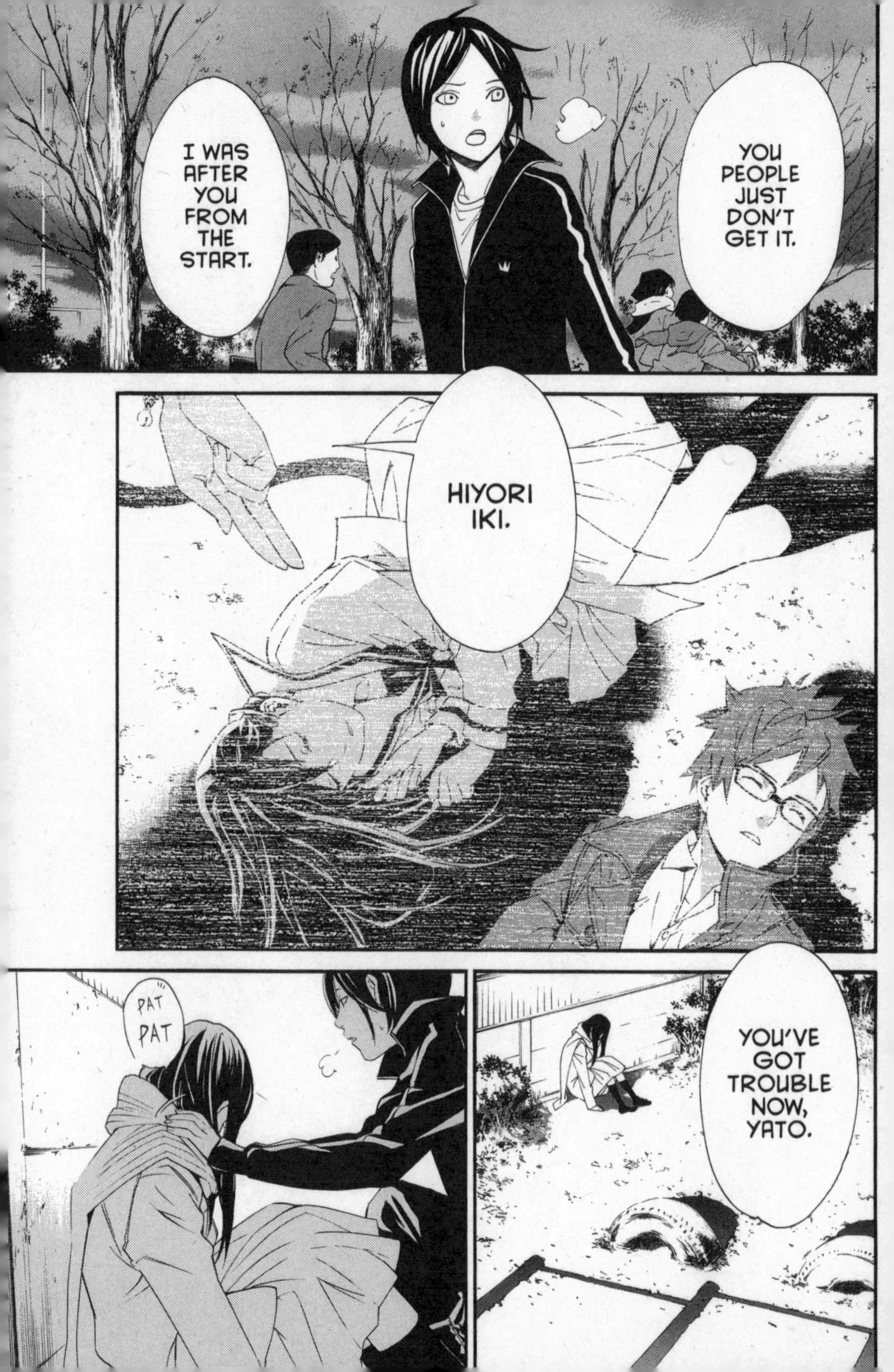

YOU PEOPLE JUST DON'T GET IT.
I WAS AFTER YOU FROM THE START.
HIYORI IKI.
YOU'VE GOT TROUBLE NOW, YATO.
PAT PAT

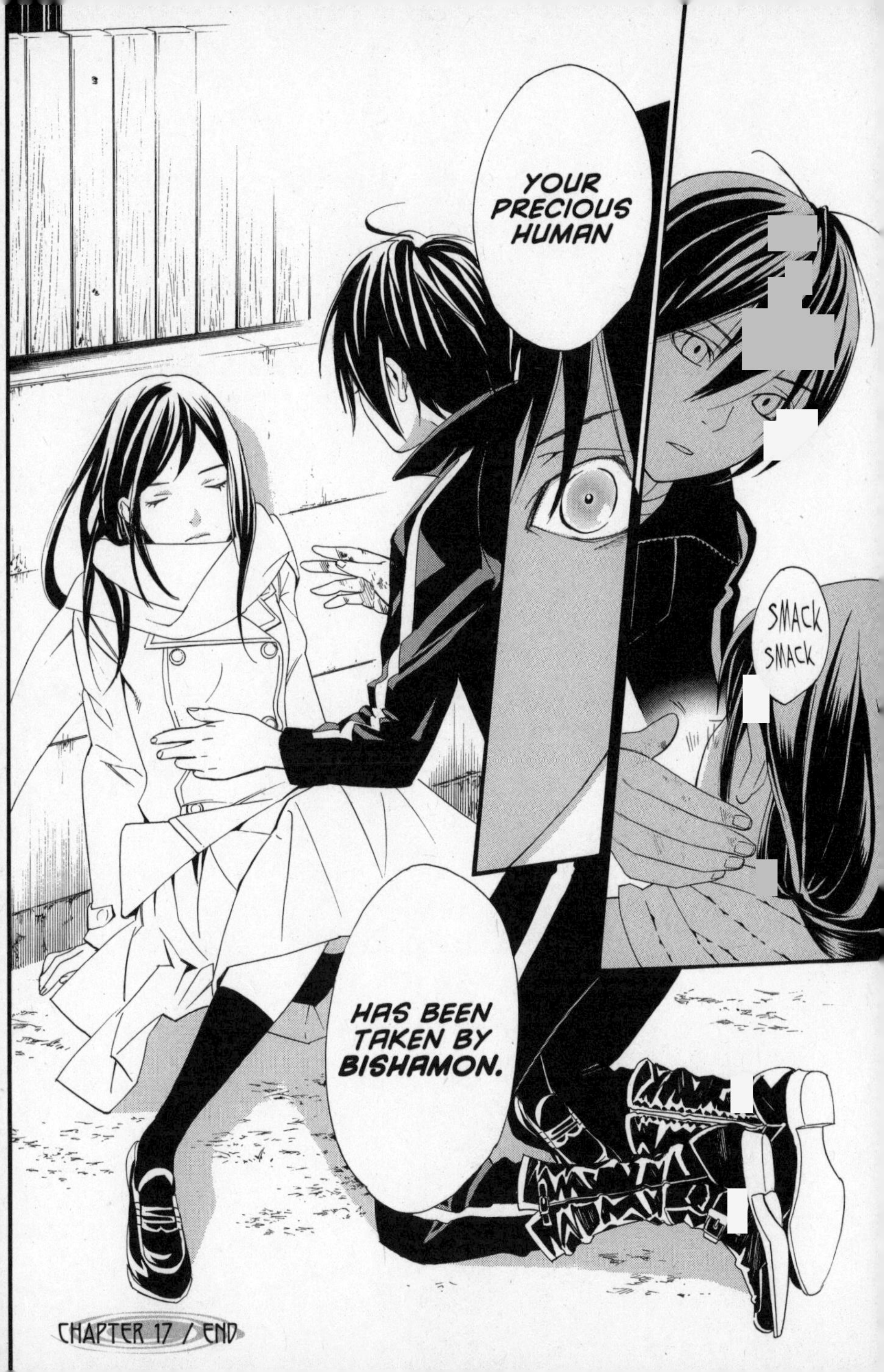
YOUR PRECIOUS HUMAN
SMACK SMACK
HAS BEEN TAKEN BY BISHAMON.

CHAPTER 17 / END

野

兔

禪

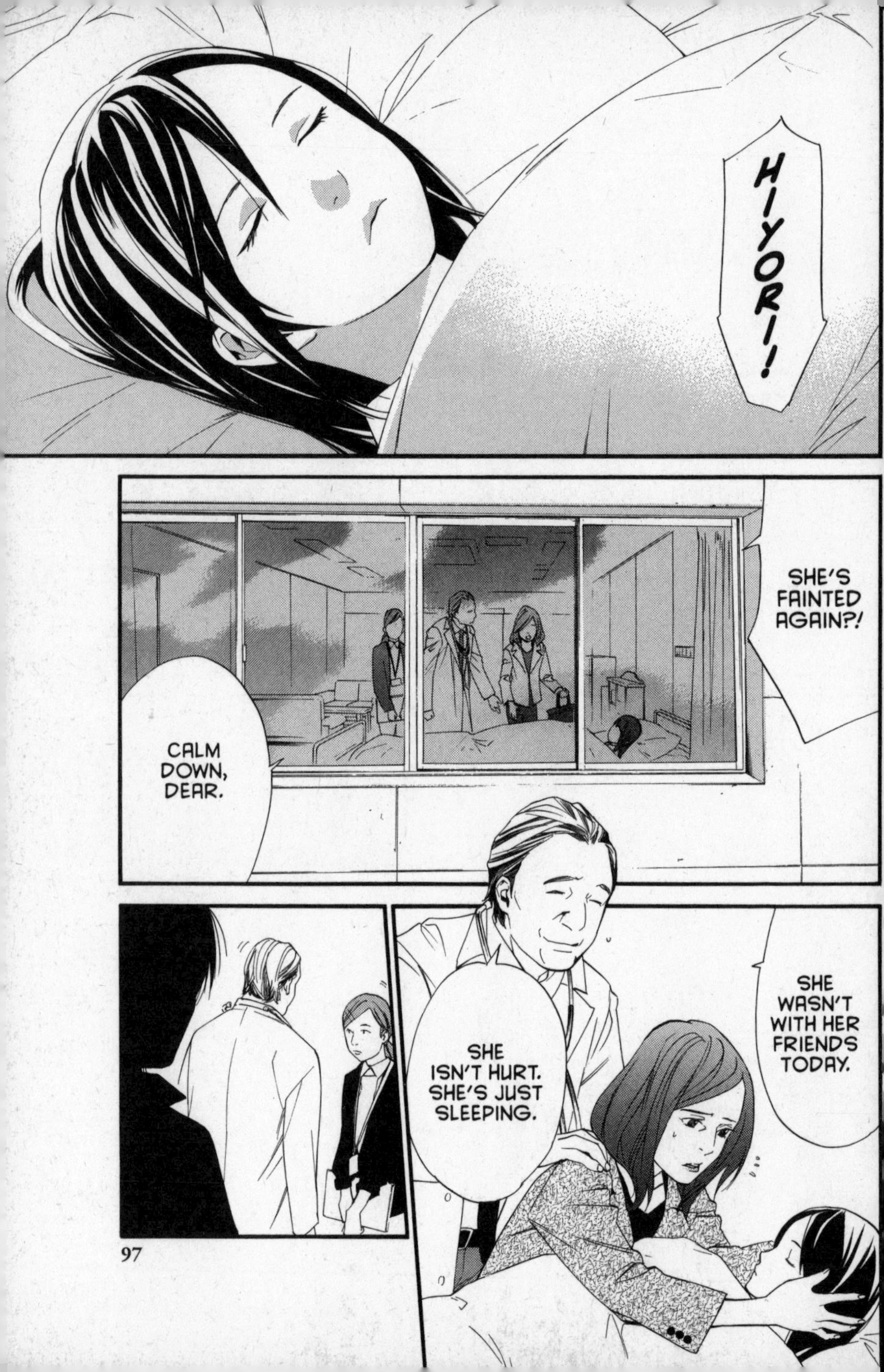
HIYORI!!
SHE'S FAINTED AGAIN?!
CALM DOWN, DEAR.
SHE WASN'T WITH HER FRIENDS TODAY.
SHE ISN'T HURT. SHE'S JUST SLEEPING.

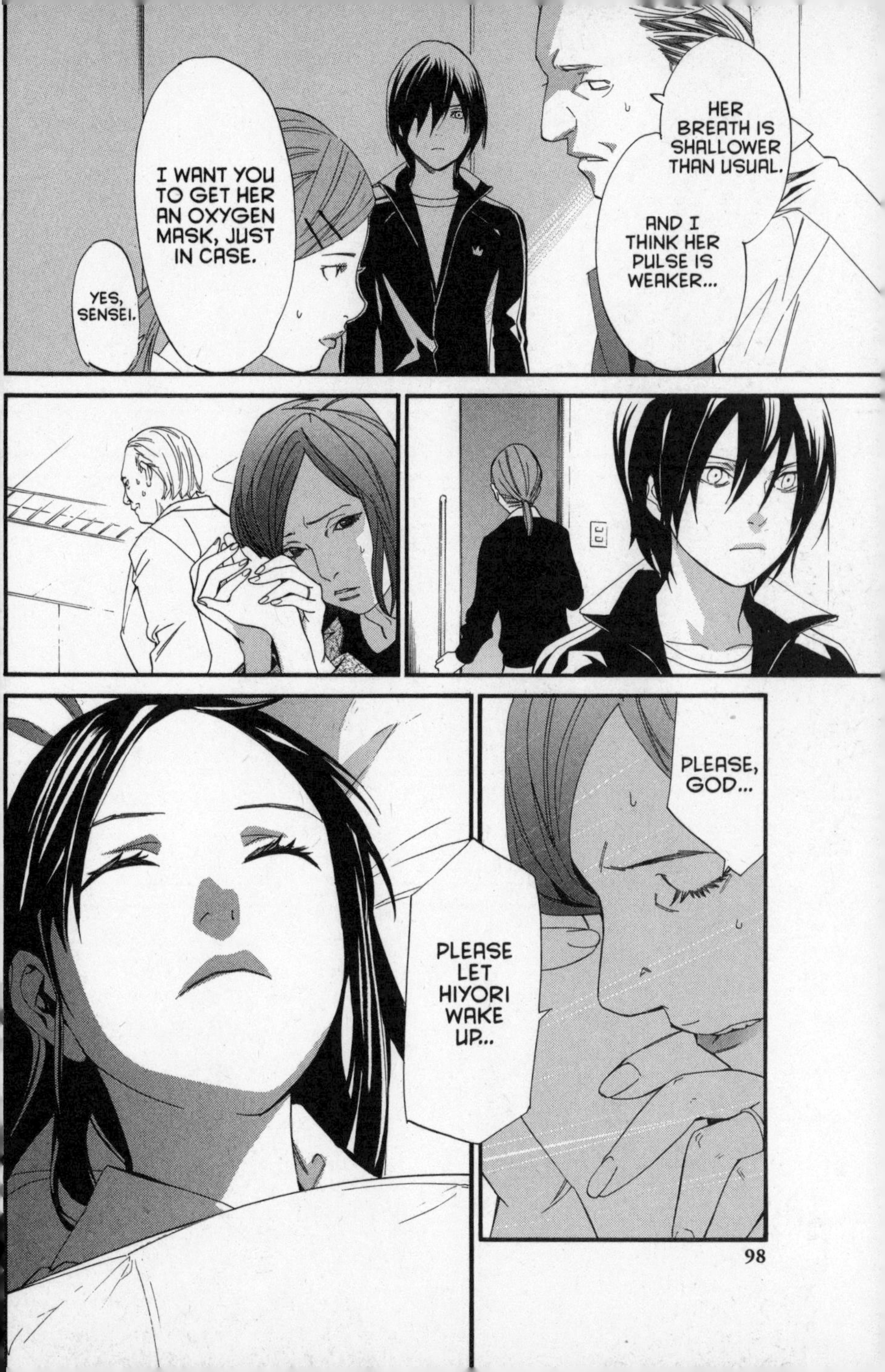
HER BREATH IS SHALLOWER THAN USUAL.
AND I THINK HER PULSE IS WEAKER...
I WANT YOU TO GET HER AN OXYGEN MASK, JUST IN CASE.
YES, SENSEI.
PLEASE, GOD...
PLEASE LET HIYORI WAKE UP...

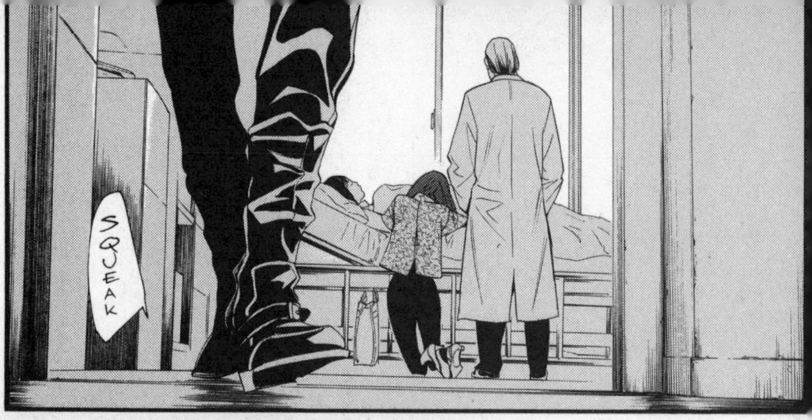
SQUEAK

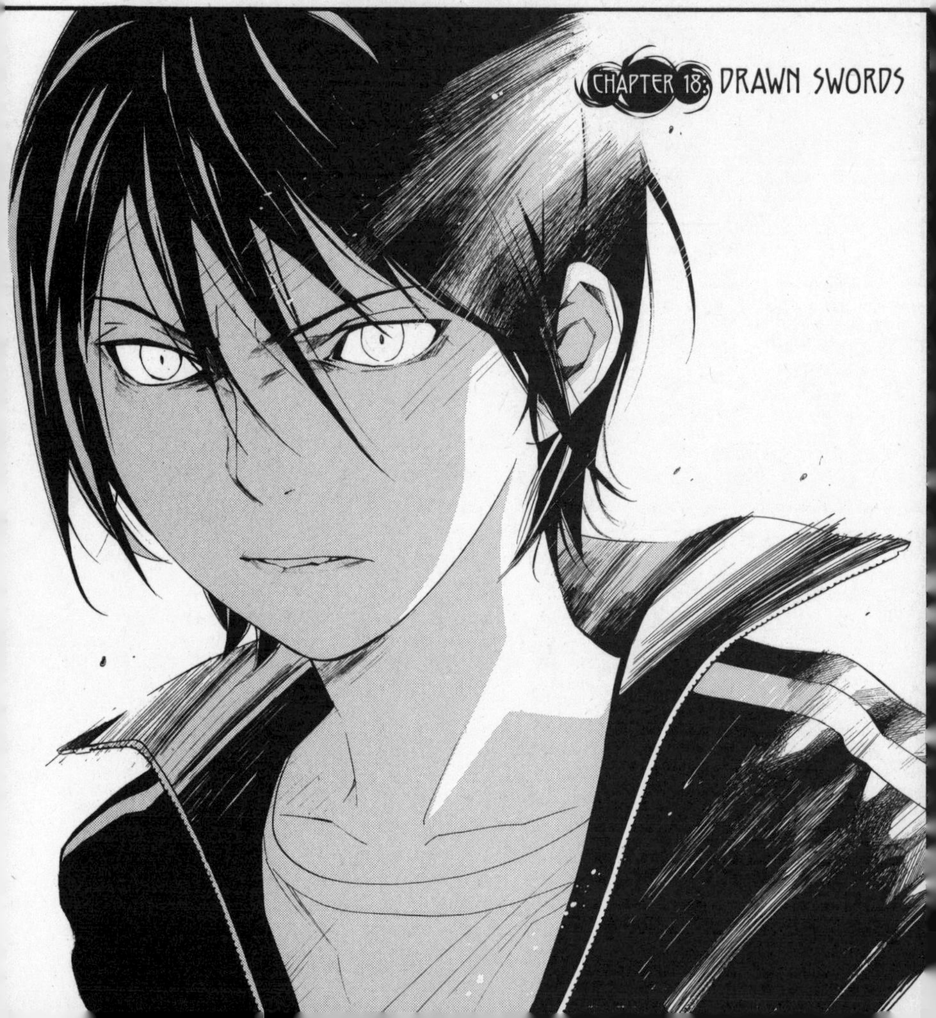
CHAPTER 18: DRAWN SWORDS

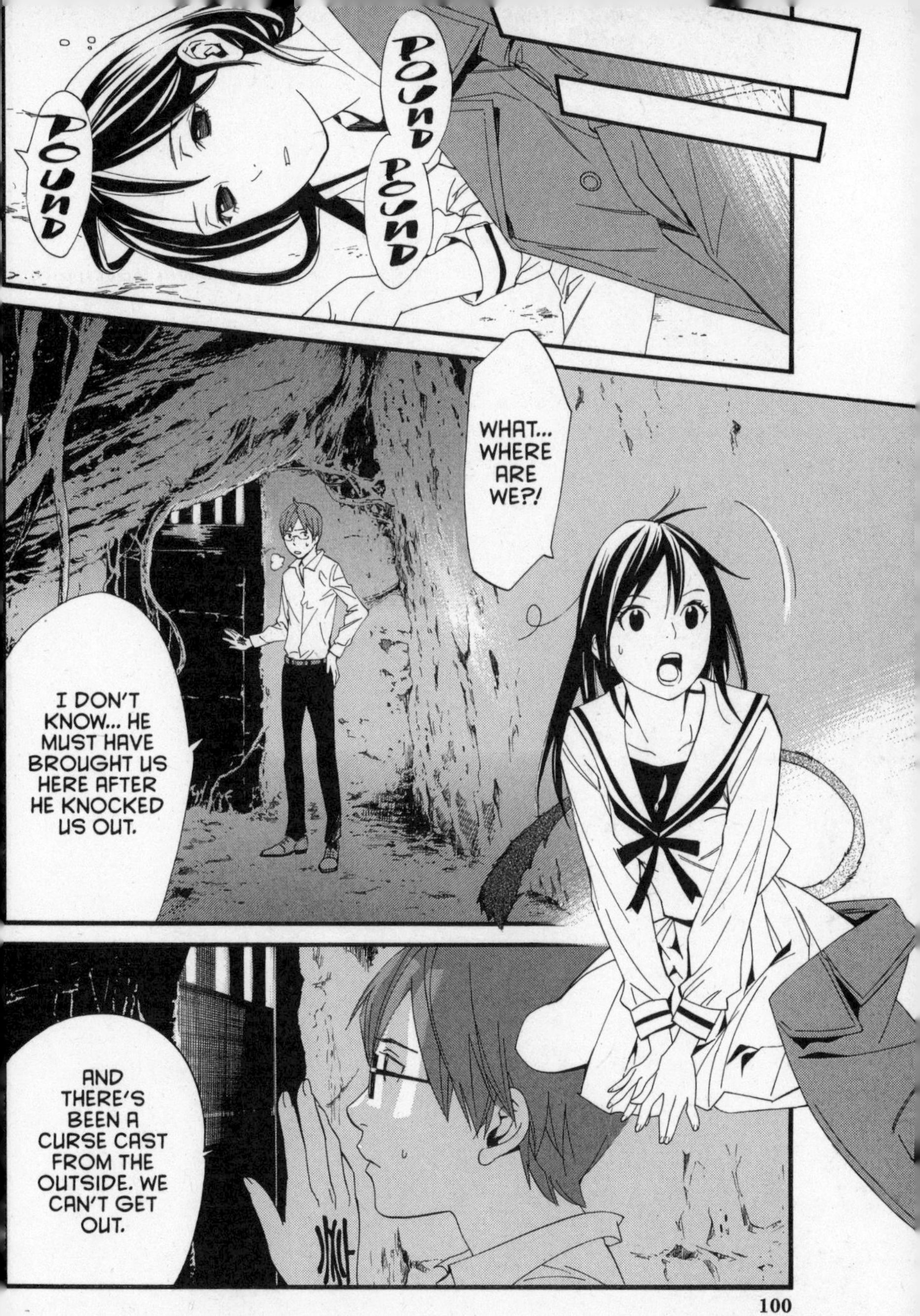
POUND
POUND
POUND
WHAT... WHERE ARE WE?!
I DON'T KNOW... HE MUST HAVE BROUGHT US HERE AFTER HE KNOCKED US OUT.
AND THERE'S BEEN A CURSE CAST FROM THE OUTSIDE. WE CAN'T GET OUT.

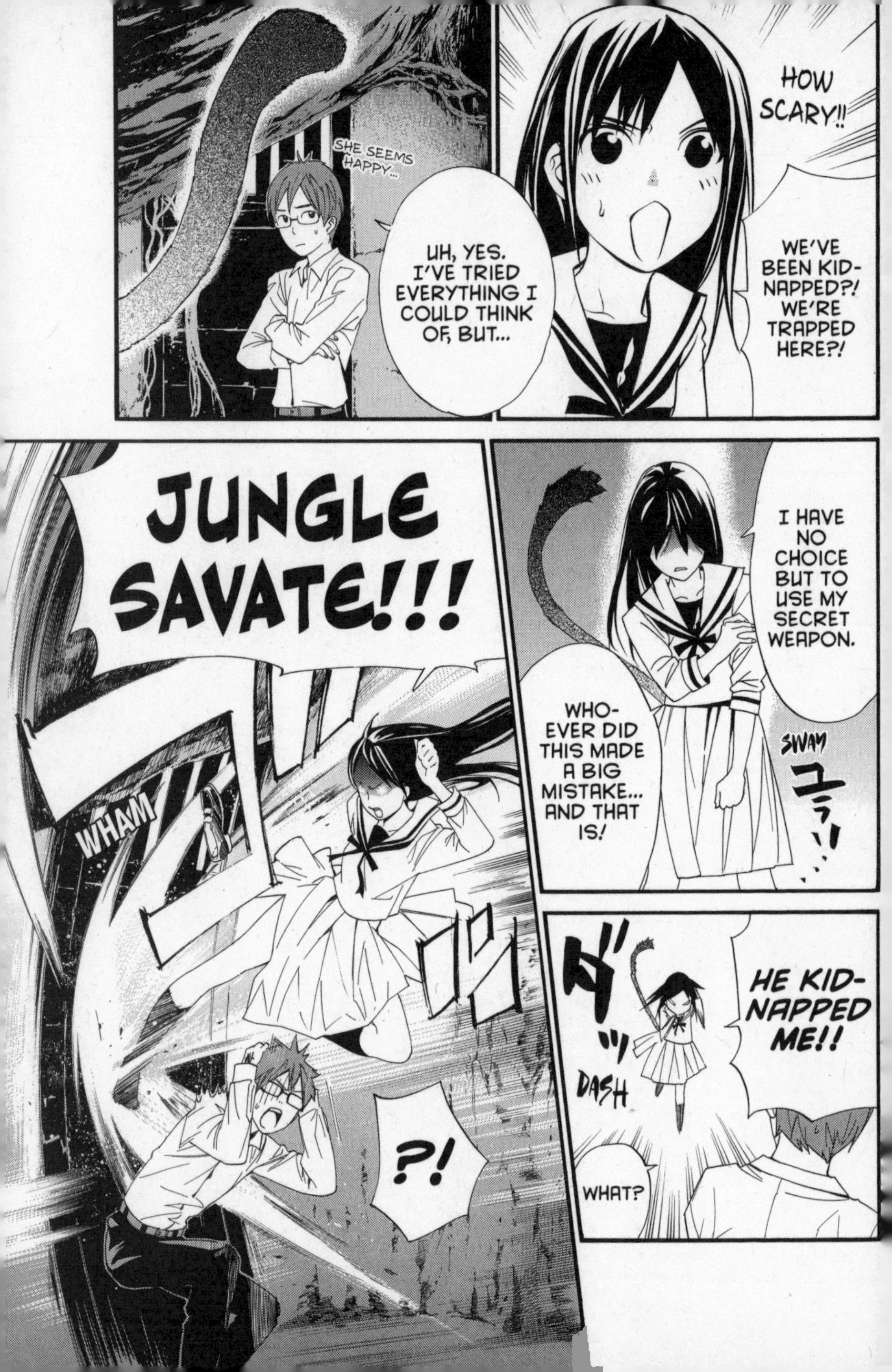
HOW SCARY!!
WE'VE BEEN KID-NAPPED?! WE'RE TRAPPED HERE?!
UH, YES. I'VE TRIED EVERYTHING I COULD THINK OF, BUT...
SHE SEEMS HAPPY...
I HAVE NO CHOICE BUT TO USE MY SECRET WEAPON.
WHO-EVER DID THIS MADE A BIG MISTAKE... AND THAT IS!
SWAY
HE KID-NAPPED ME!!
DASH
WHAT?
JUNGLE SAVATE!!!
WHAM
?!

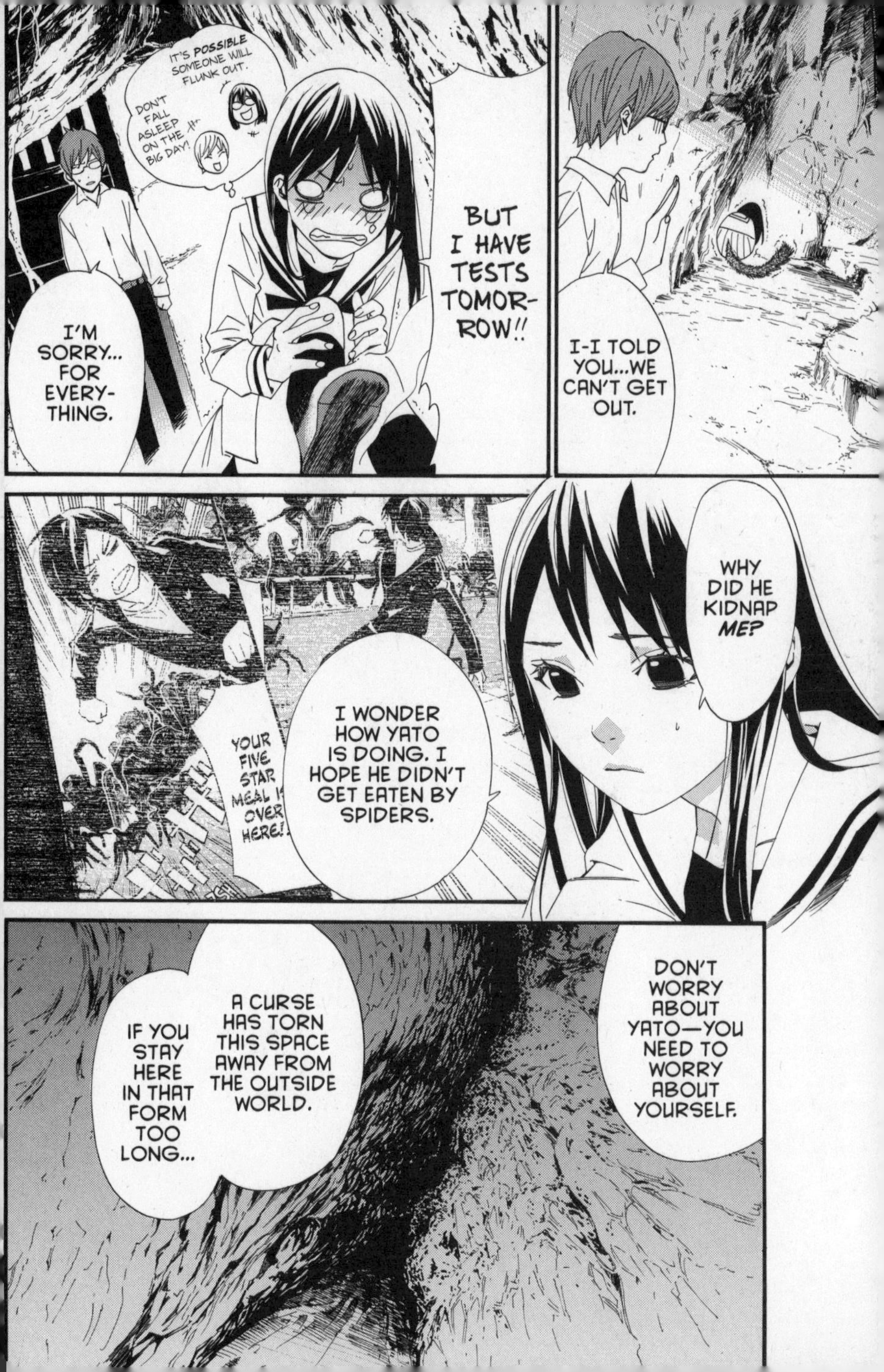
I-I TOLD YOU...WE CAN'T GET OUT.
BUT I HAVE TESTS TOMORROW!!
IT'S POSSIBLE SOMEONE WILL FLUNK OUT.
DON'T FALL ASLEEP ON THE BIG DAY!
I'M SORRY... FOR EVERYTHING.
WHY DID HE KIDNAP ME?
I WONDER HOW YATO IS DOING. I HOPE HE DIDN'T GET EATEN BY SPIDERS.
YOUR FIVE STAR MEAL IS OVER HERE!!
DON'T WORRY ABOUT YATO—YOU NEED TO WORRY ABOUT YOURSELF.
A CURSE HAS TORN THIS SPACE AWAY FROM THE OUTSIDE WORLD.
IF YOU STAY HERE IN THAT FORM TOO LONG...

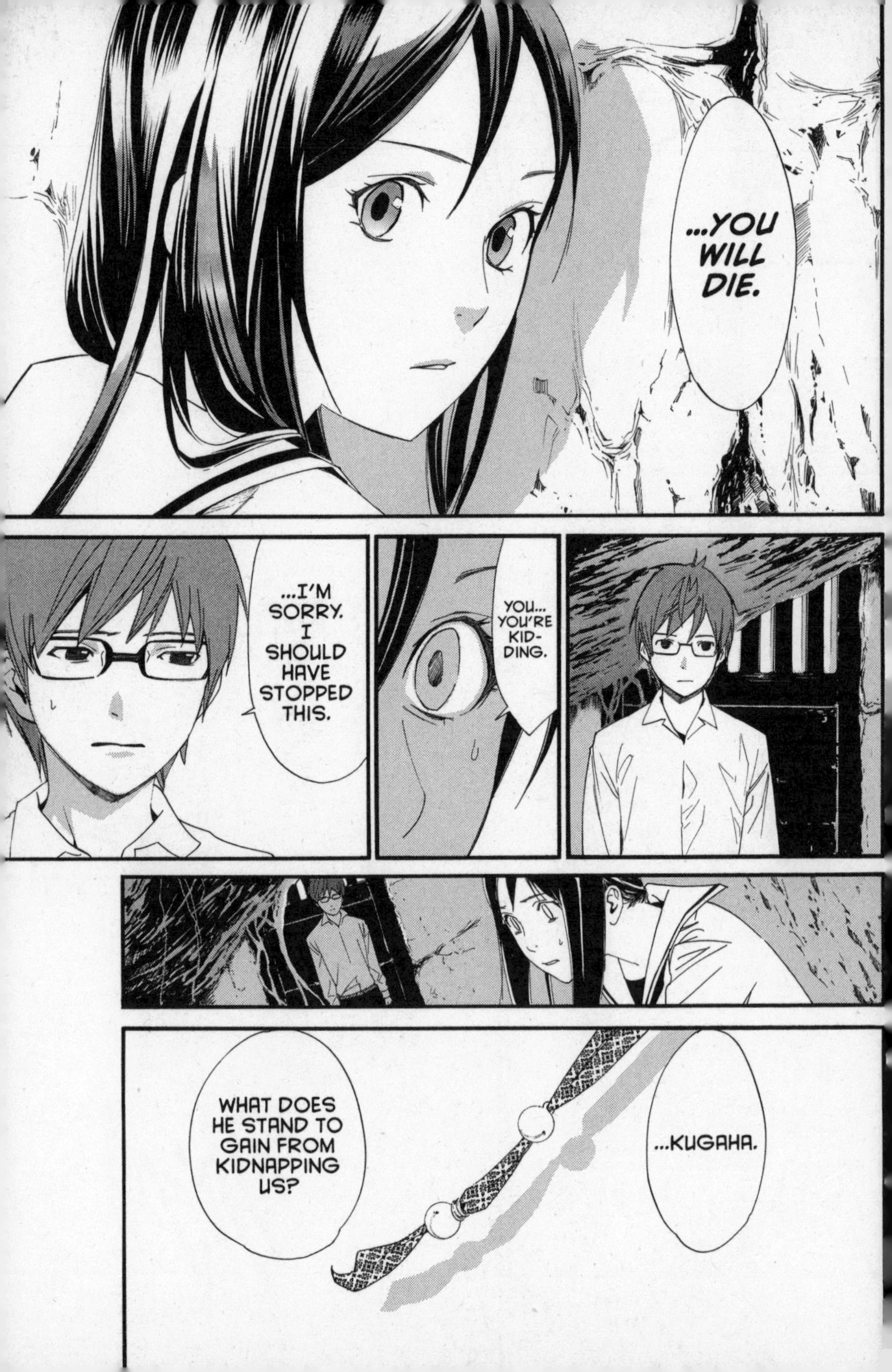
...YOU WILL DIE.
YOU... YOU'RE KID-DING.
...I'M SORRY. I SHOULD HAVE STOPPED THIS.
...KUGAHA.
WHAT DOES HE STAND TO GAIN FROM KIDNAPPING US?

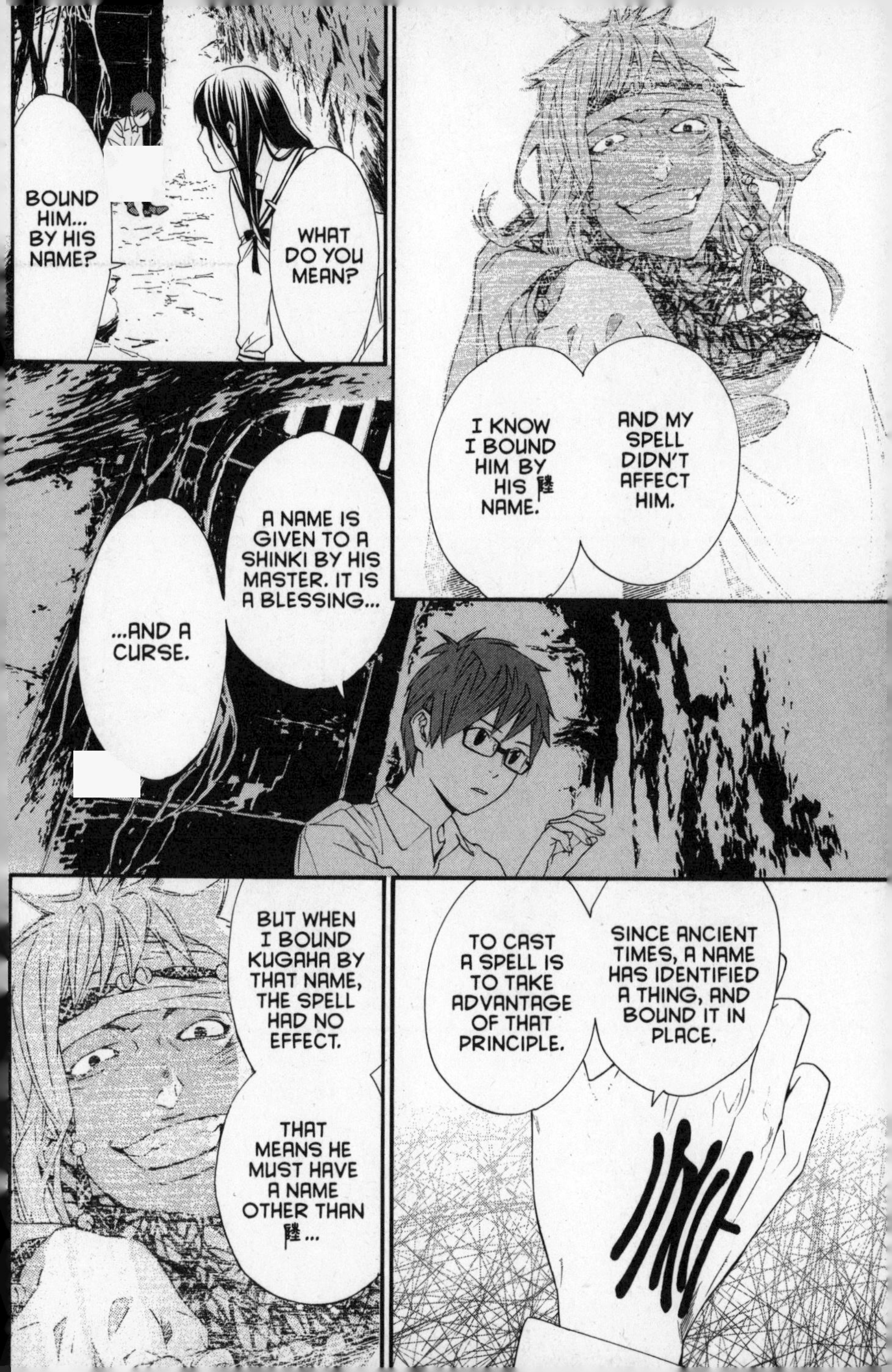
AND MY SPELL DIDN'T AFFECT HIM.
I KNOW I BOUND HIM BY HIS 陸 NAME.
WHAT DO YOU MEAN?
BOUND HIM... BY HIS NAME?
A NAME IS GIVEN TO A SHINKI BY HIS MASTER. IT IS A BLESSING...
...AND A CURSE.
SINCE ANCIENT TIMES, A NAME HAS IDENTIFIED A THING, AND BOUND IT IN PLACE.
TO CAST A SPELL IS TO TAKE ADVANTAGE OF THAT PRINCIPLE.
BUT WHEN I BOUND KUGAHA BY THAT NAME, THE SPELL HAD NO EFFECT.
THAT MEANS HE MUST HAVE A NAME OTHER THAN 陸...

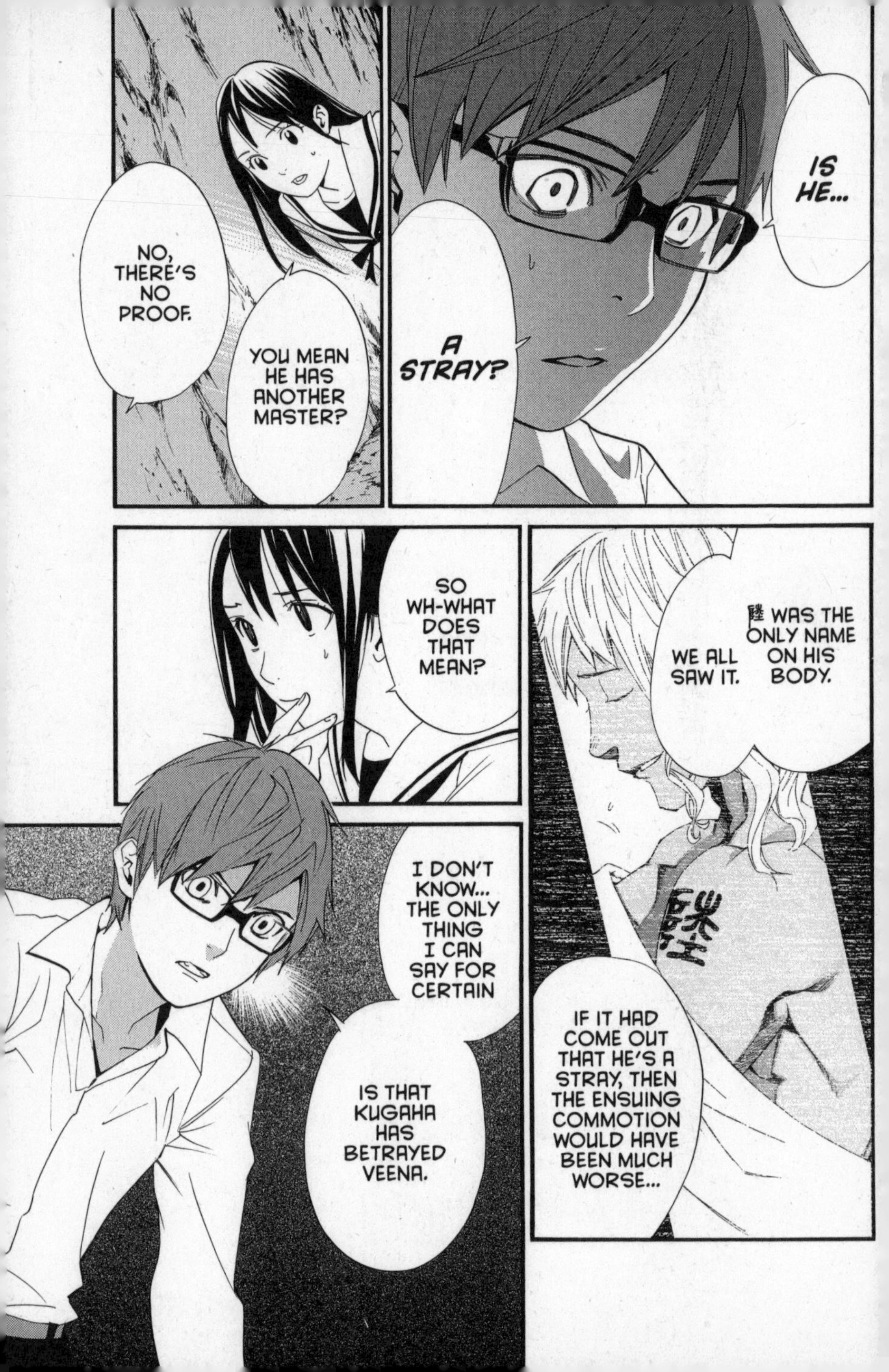
IS HE...
A STRAY?
YOU MEAN HE HAS ANOTHER MASTER?
NO, THERE'S NO PROOF.
陸 WAS THE ONLY NAME ON HIS BODY.
WE ALL SAW IT.
IF IT HAD COME OUT THAT HE'S A STRAY, THEN THE ENSUING COMMOTION WOULD HAVE BEEN MUCH WORSE...
SO WH-WHAT DOES THAT MEAN?
I DON'T KNOW... THE ONLY THING I CAN SAY FOR CERTAIN
IS THAT KUGAHA HAS BETRAYED VEENA.

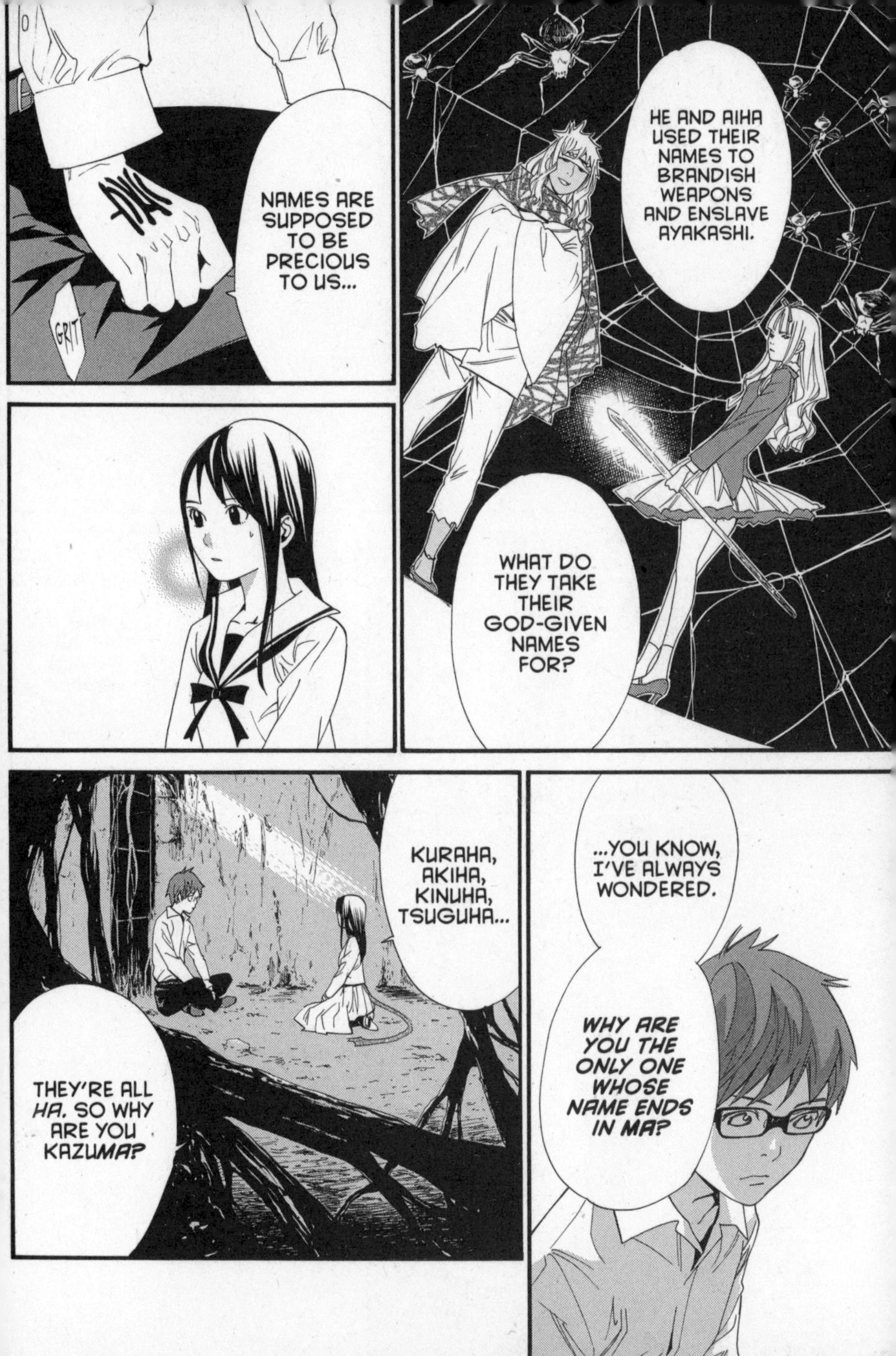
HE AND AIHA USED THEIR NAMES TO BRANDISH WEAPONS AND ENSLAVE AYAKASHI.
WHAT DO THEY TAKE THEIR GOD-GIVEN NAMES FOR?
NAMES ARE SUPPOSED TO BE PRECIOUS TO US...
GRIT
...YOU KNOW, I'VE ALWAYS WONDERED.
WHY ARE YOU THE ONLY ONE WHOSE NAME ENDS IN MA?
KURAHA, AKIHA, KINUHA, TSUGUHA...
THEY'RE ALL HA. SO WHY ARE YOU KAZUMA?

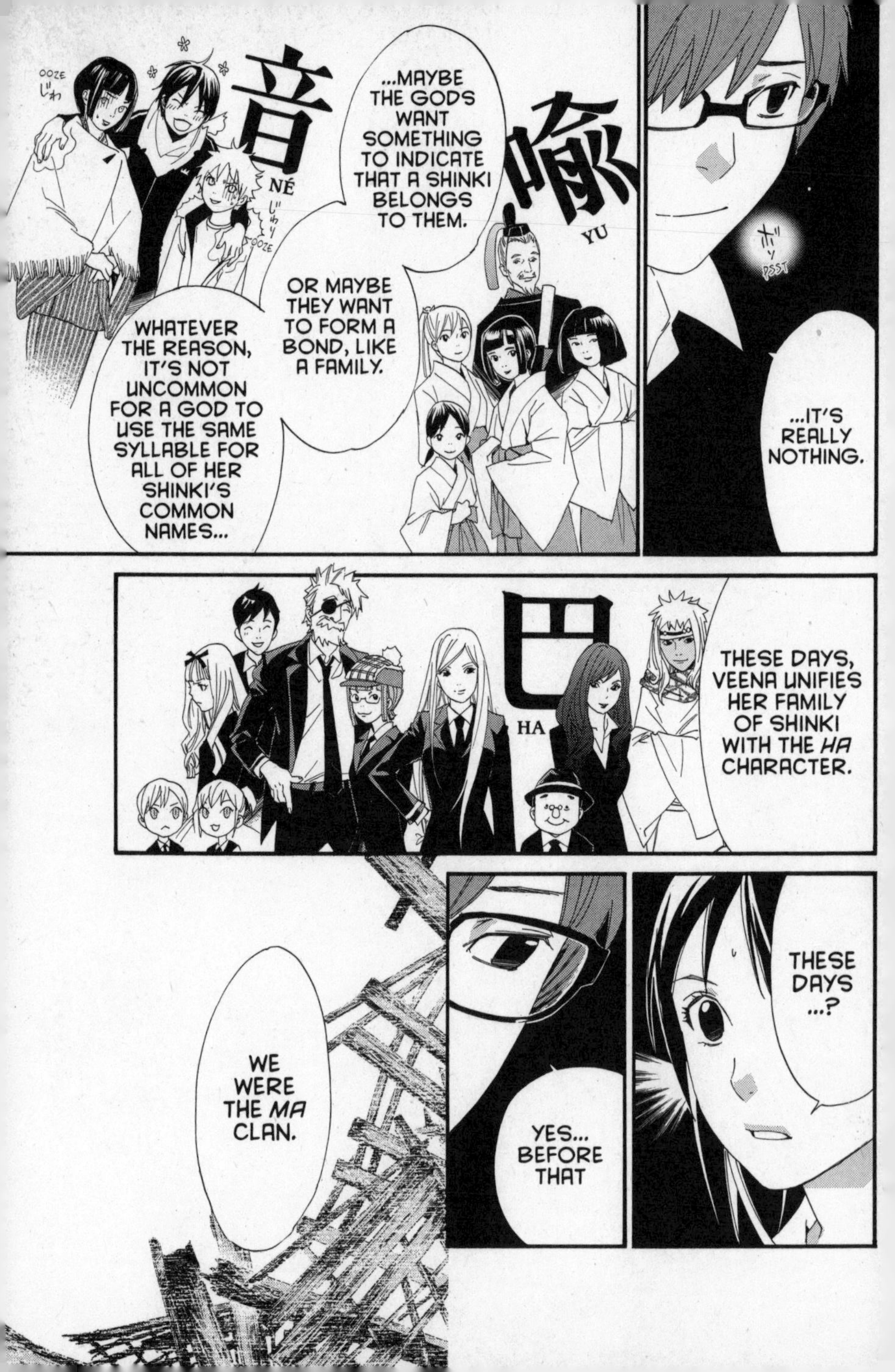
ボソッ
PSST
...IT'S REALLY NOTHING.
喩
YU
...MAYBE THE GODS WANT SOMETHING TO INDICATE THAT A SHINKI BELONGS TO THEM.
音
NÉ
OOZE
じわ
じゅり
OOZE
OR MAYBE THEY WANT TO FORM A BOND, LIKE A FAMILY.
WHATEVER THE REASON, IT'S NOT UNCOMMON FOR A GOD TO USE THE SAME SYLLABLE FOR ALL OF HER SHINKI'S COMMON NAMES...
THESE DAYS, VEENA UNIFIES HER FAMILY OF SHINKI WITH THE *HA* CHARACTER.
巴
HA
THESE DAYS ...?
YES... BEFORE THAT
WE WERE THE *MA* CLAN.

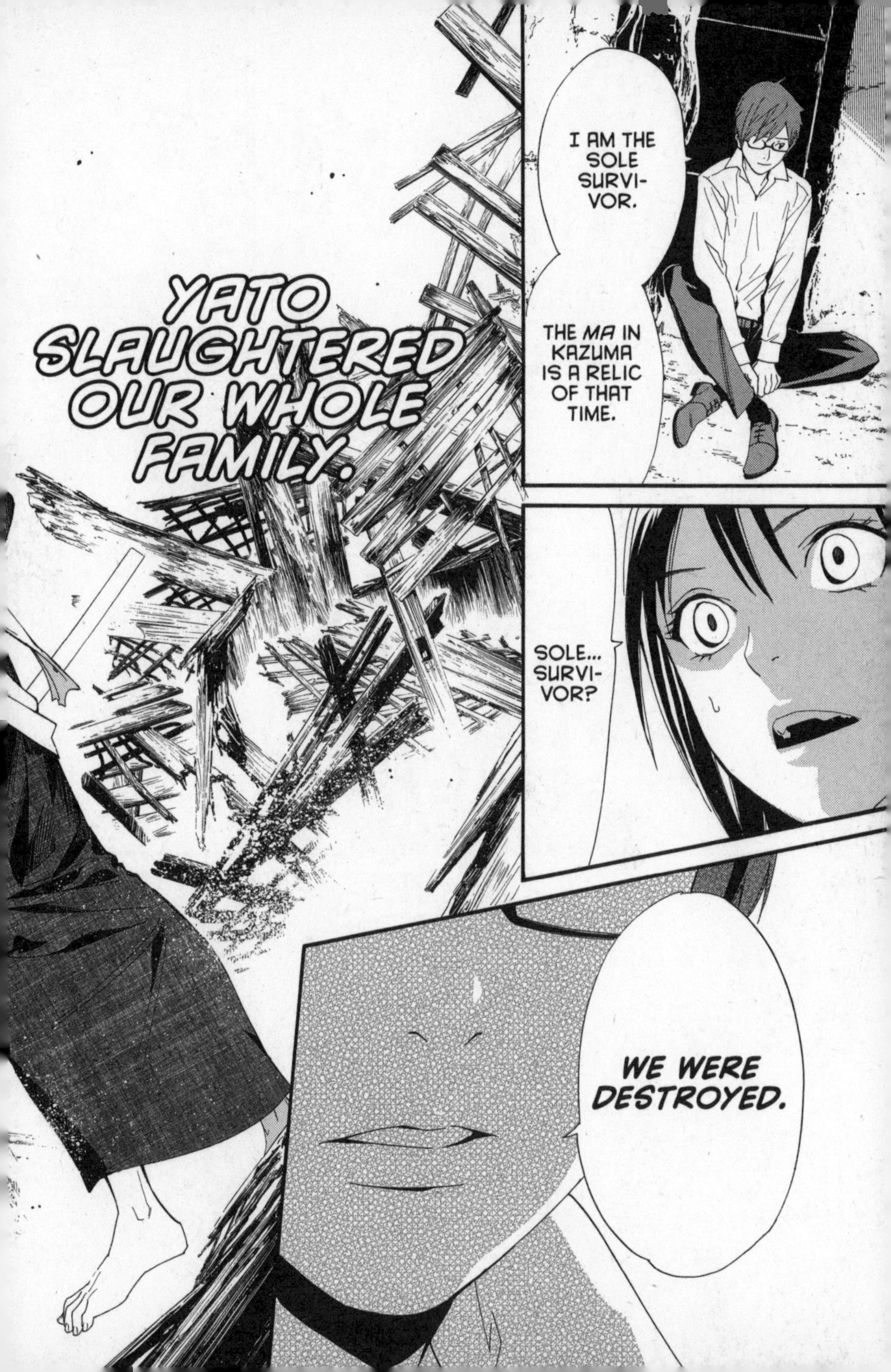
I AM THE SOLE SURVIVOR.
THE *MA* IN KAZUMA IS A RELIC OF THAT TIME.
SOLE... SURVIVOR?
YATO SLAUGHTERED OUR WHOLE FAMILY.
WE WERE DESTROYED.

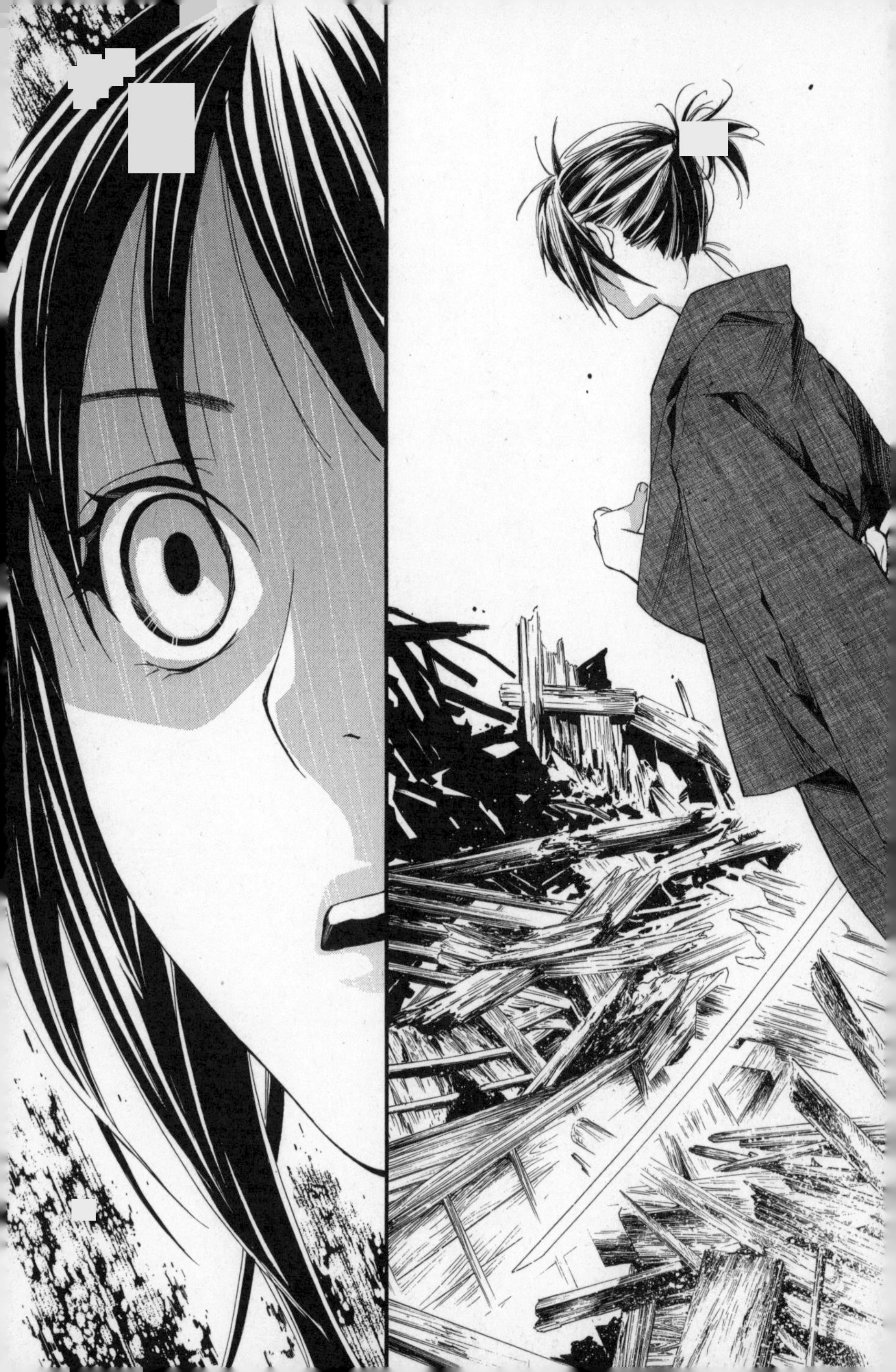

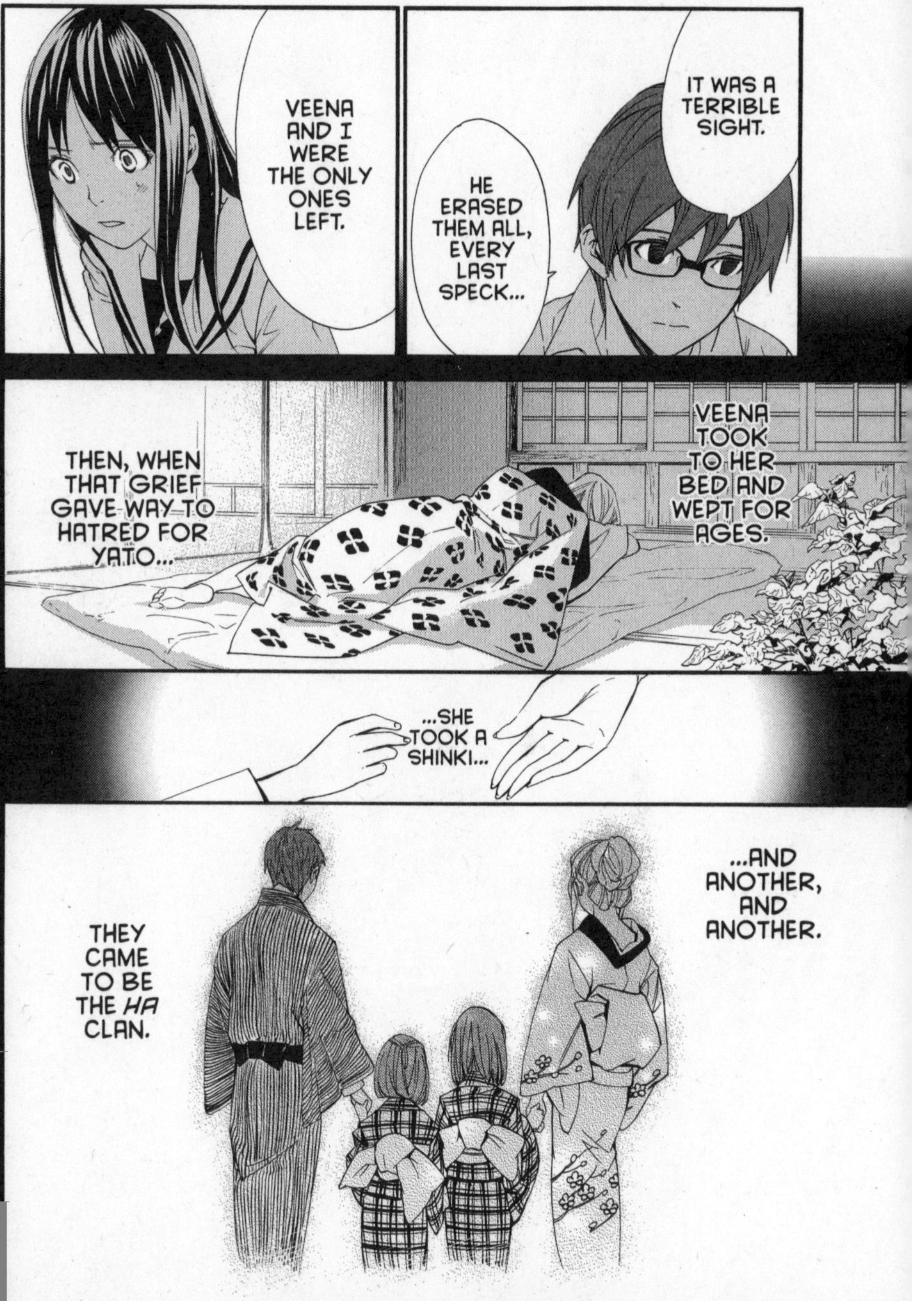
IT WAS A TERRIBLE SIGHT.
HE ERASED THEM ALL, EVERY LAST SPECK...
VEENA AND I WERE THE ONLY ONES LEFT.
VEENA TOOK TO HER BED AND WEPT FOR AGES.
THEN, WHEN THAT GRIEF GAVE WAY TO HATRED FOR YATO...
...SHE TOOK A SHINKI...
...AND ANOTHER, AND ANOTHER.
THEY CAME TO BE THE *HA* CLAN.

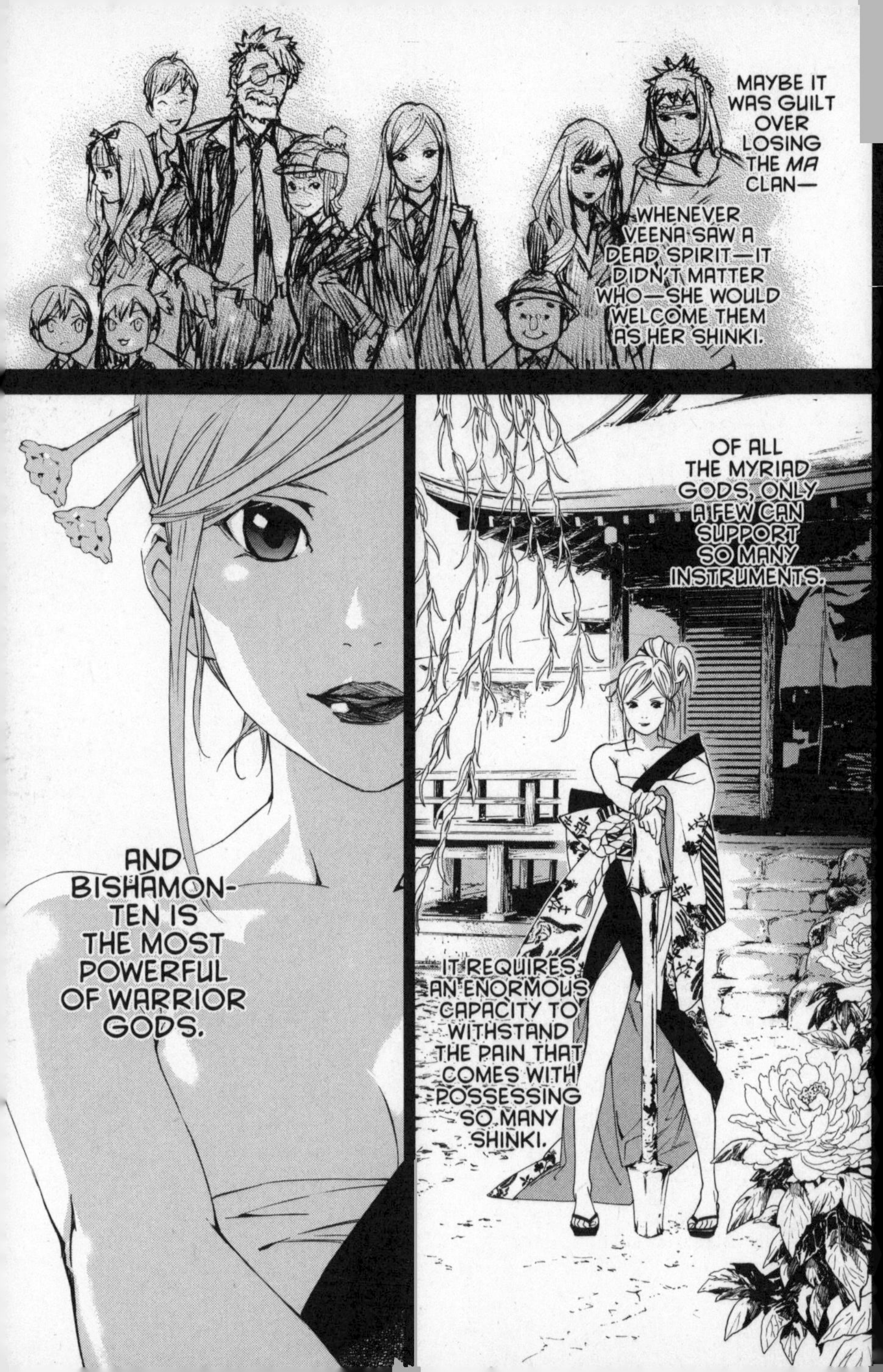
MAYBE IT WAS GUILT OVER LOSING THE *MA* CLAN—
WHENEVER VEENA SAW A DEAD SPIRIT—IT DIDN'T MATTER WHO—SHE WOULD WELCOME THEM AS HER SHINKI.
OF ALL THE MYRIAD GODS, ONLY A FEW CAN SUPPORT SO MANY INSTRUMENTS.
IT REQUIRES AN ENORMOUS CAPACITY TO WITHSTAND THE PAIN THAT COMES WITH POSSESSING SO MANY SHINKI.
AND BISHAMON-TEN IS THE MOST POWERFUL OF WARRIOR GODS.

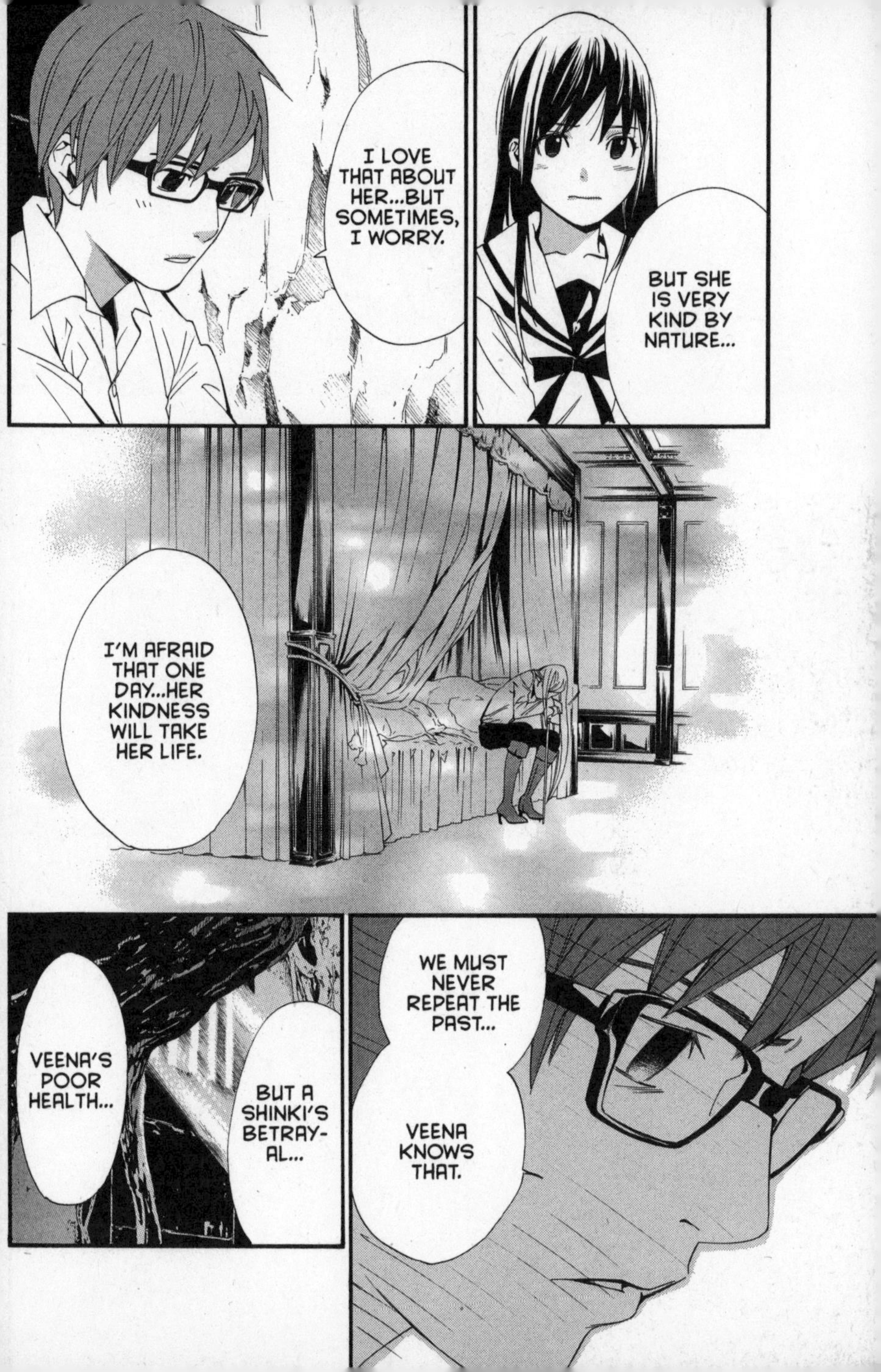

BUT SHE IS VERY KIND BY NATURE...
I LOVE THAT ABOUT HER...BUT SOMETIMES, I WORRY.
I'M AFRAID THAT ONE DAY...HER KINDNESS WILL TAKE HER LIFE.
WE MUST NEVER REPEAT THE PAST...
VEENA KNOWS THAT.
VEENA'S POOR HEALTH...
BUT A SHINKI'S BETRAY-AL...

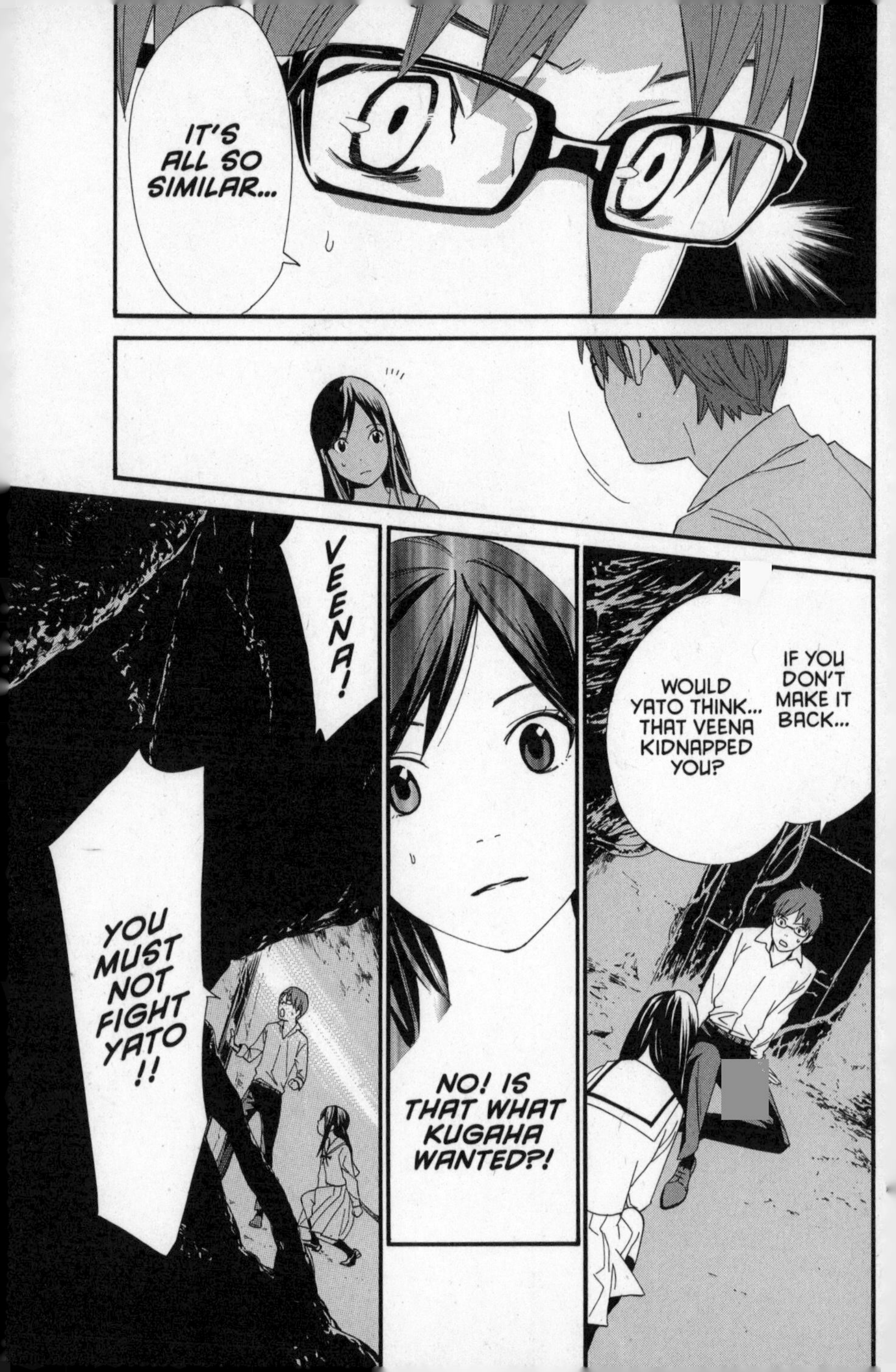
IT'S ALL SO SIMILAR...
IF YOU DON'T MAKE IT BACK...
WOULD YATO THINK... THAT VEENA KIDNAPPED YOU?
NO! IS THAT WHAT KUGAHA WANTED?!
VEENA!
YOU MUST NOT FIGHT YATO!!

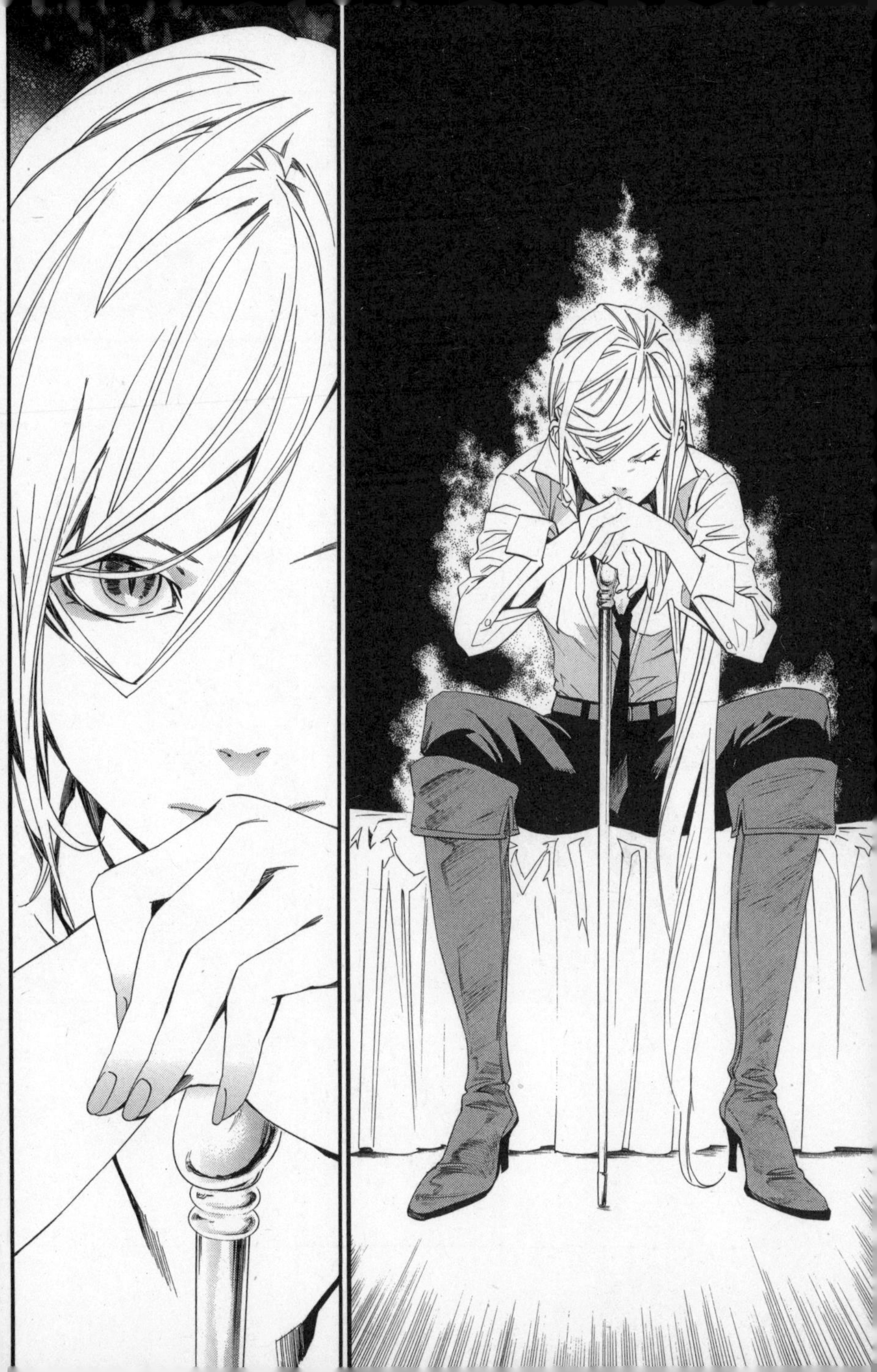

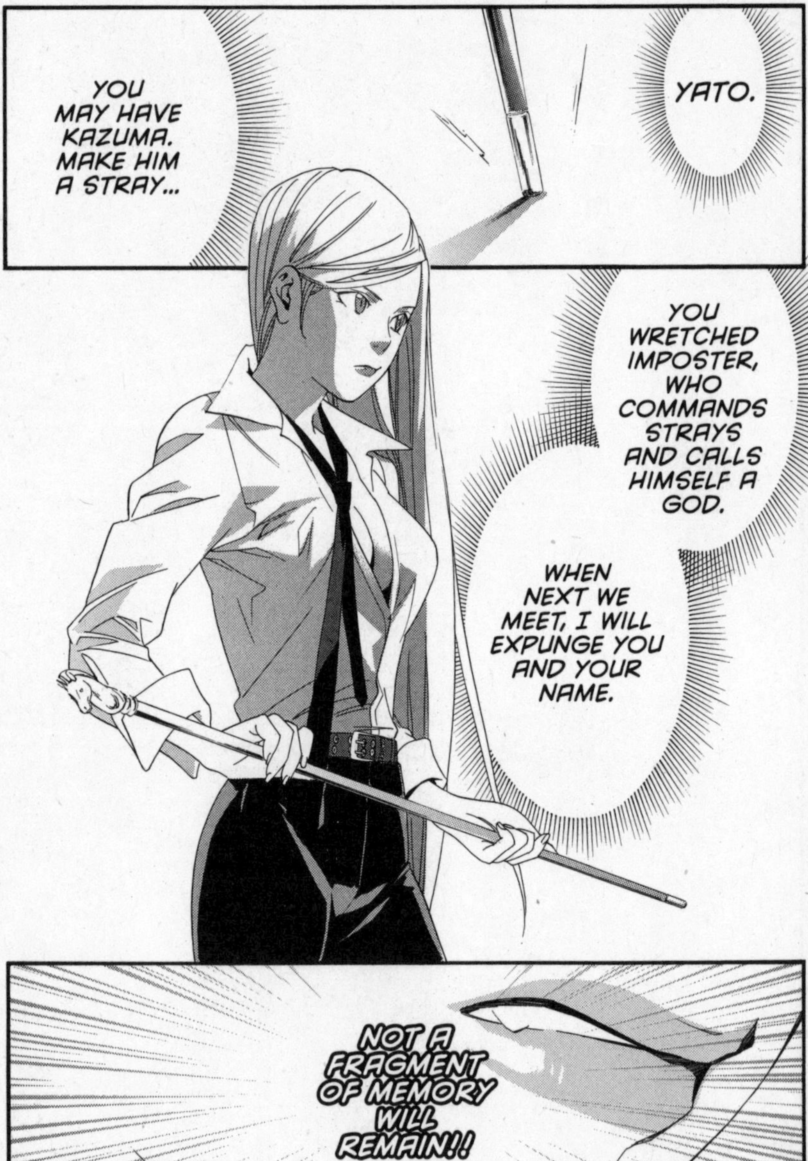
YATO.
YOU MAY HAVE KAZUMA. MAKE HIM A STRAY...
YOU WRETCHED IMPOSTER, WHO COMMANDS STRAYS AND CALLS HIMSELF A GOD.
WHEN NEXT WE MEET, I WILL EXPUNGE YOU AND YOUR NAME.
NOT A FRAGMENT OF MEMORY WILL REMAIN!!

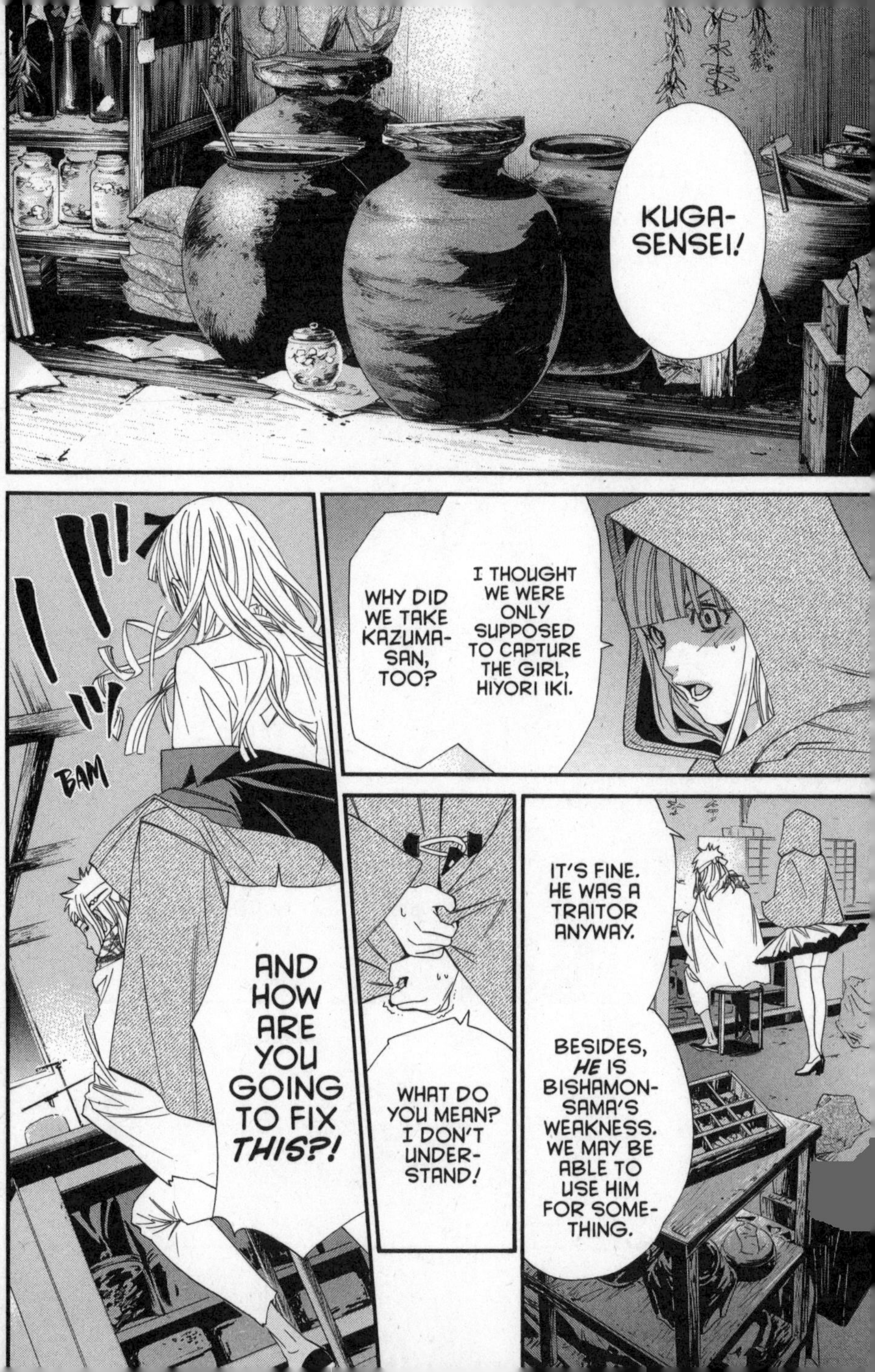
KUGA-SENSEI!
I THOUGHT WE WERE ONLY SUPPOSED TO CAPTURE THE GIRL, HIYORI IKI.
WHY DID WE TAKE KAZUMA-SAN, TOO?
IT'S FINE. HE WAS A TRAITOR ANYWAY.
BESIDES, *HE* IS BISHAMON-SAMA'S WEAKNESS. WE MAY BE ABLE TO USE HIM FOR SOMETHING.
WHAT DO YOU MEAN? I DON'T UNDERSTAND!
BAM
AND HOW ARE YOU GOING TO FIX *THIS?!*

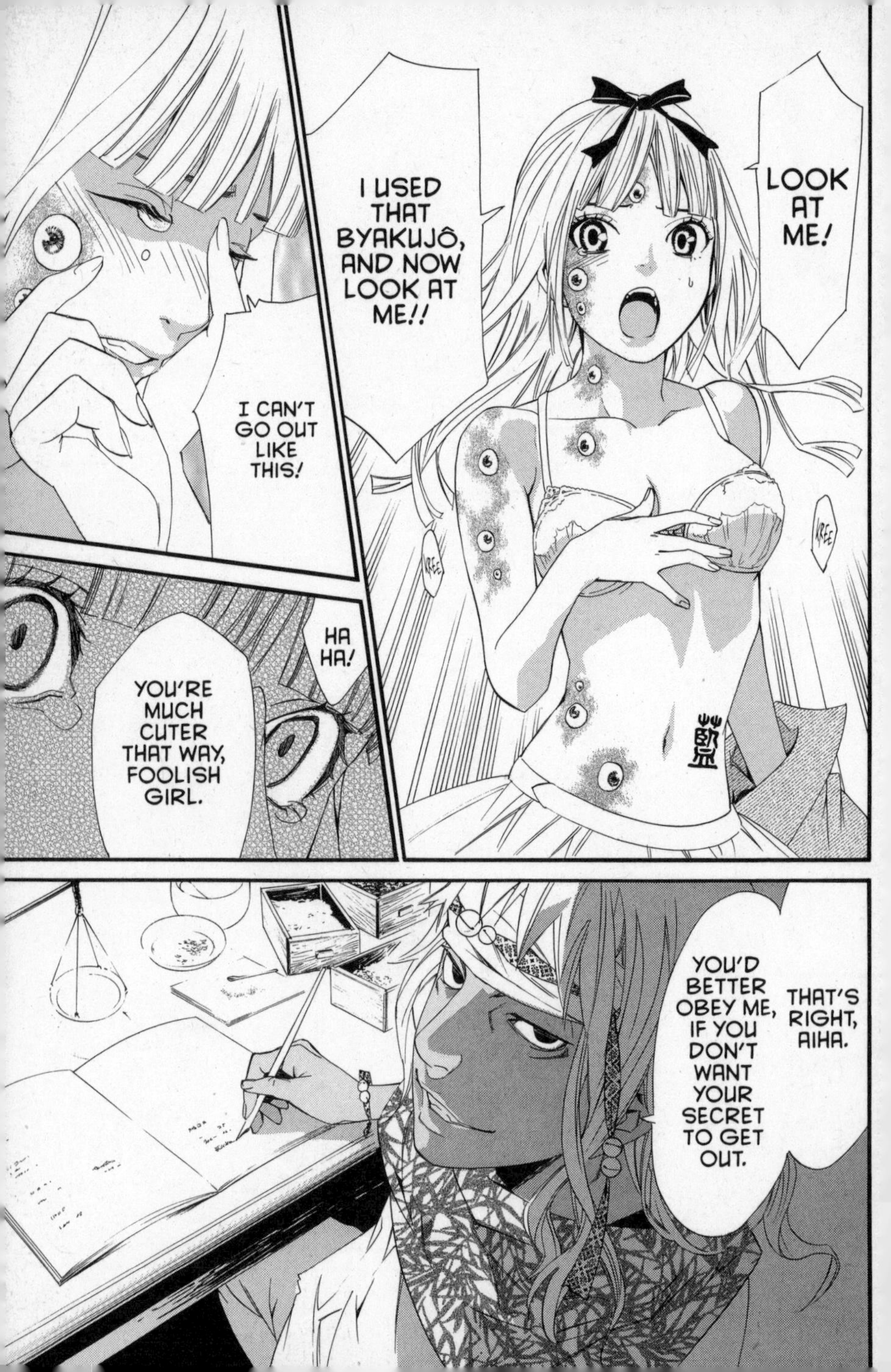
LOOK AT ME!
I USED THAT BYAKUJÔ, AND NOW LOOK AT ME!!
KREE
KREE
I CAN'T GO OUT LIKE THIS!
HA HA!
YOU'RE MUCH CUTER THAT WAY, FOOLISH GIRL.
THAT'S RIGHT, AIHA.
YOU'D BETTER OBEY ME, IF YOU DON'T WANT YOUR SECRET TO GET OUT.

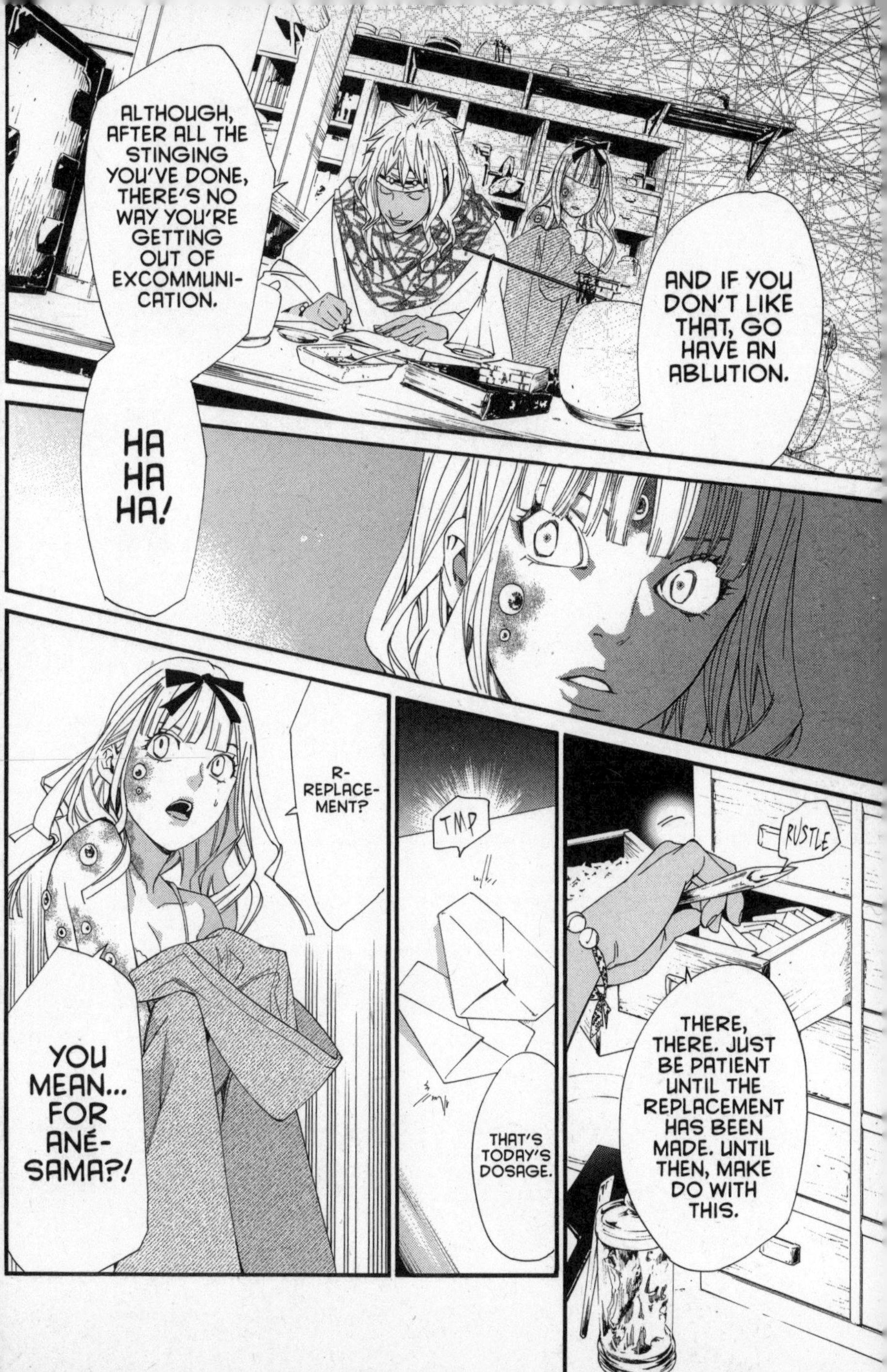

ALTHOUGH, AFTER ALL THE STINGING YOU'VE DONE, THERE'S NO WAY YOU'RE GETTING OUT OF EXCOMMUNI-CATION.
AND IF YOU DON'T LIKE THAT, GO HAVE AN ABLUTION.
HA HA HA!
RUSTLE
THERE, THERE. JUST BE PATIENT UNTIL THE REPLACEMENT HAS BEEN MADE. UNTIL THEN, MAKE DO WITH THIS.
TMP
THAT'S TODAY'S DOSAGE.
R-REPLACE-MENT?
YOU MEAN... FOR ANÉ-SAMA?!

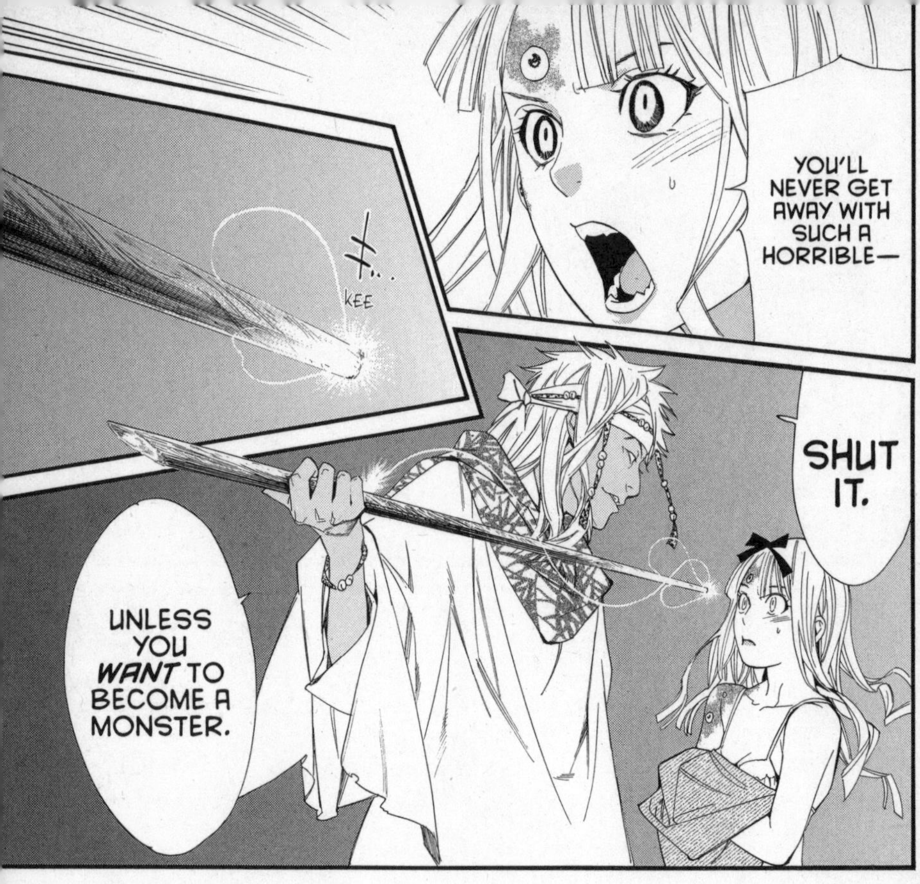

YOU'LL NEVER GET AWAY WITH SUCH A HORRIBLE—
KEE...
SHUT IT.
UNLESS YOU *WANT* TO BECOME A MONSTER.

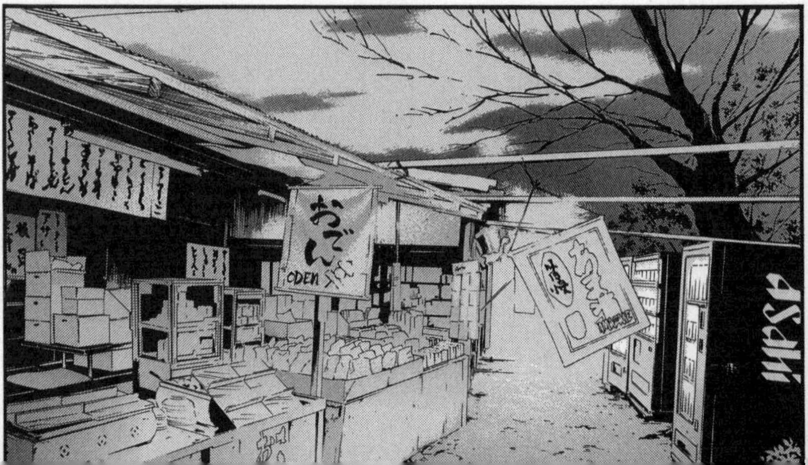

おでん
ODEN
ASAHI

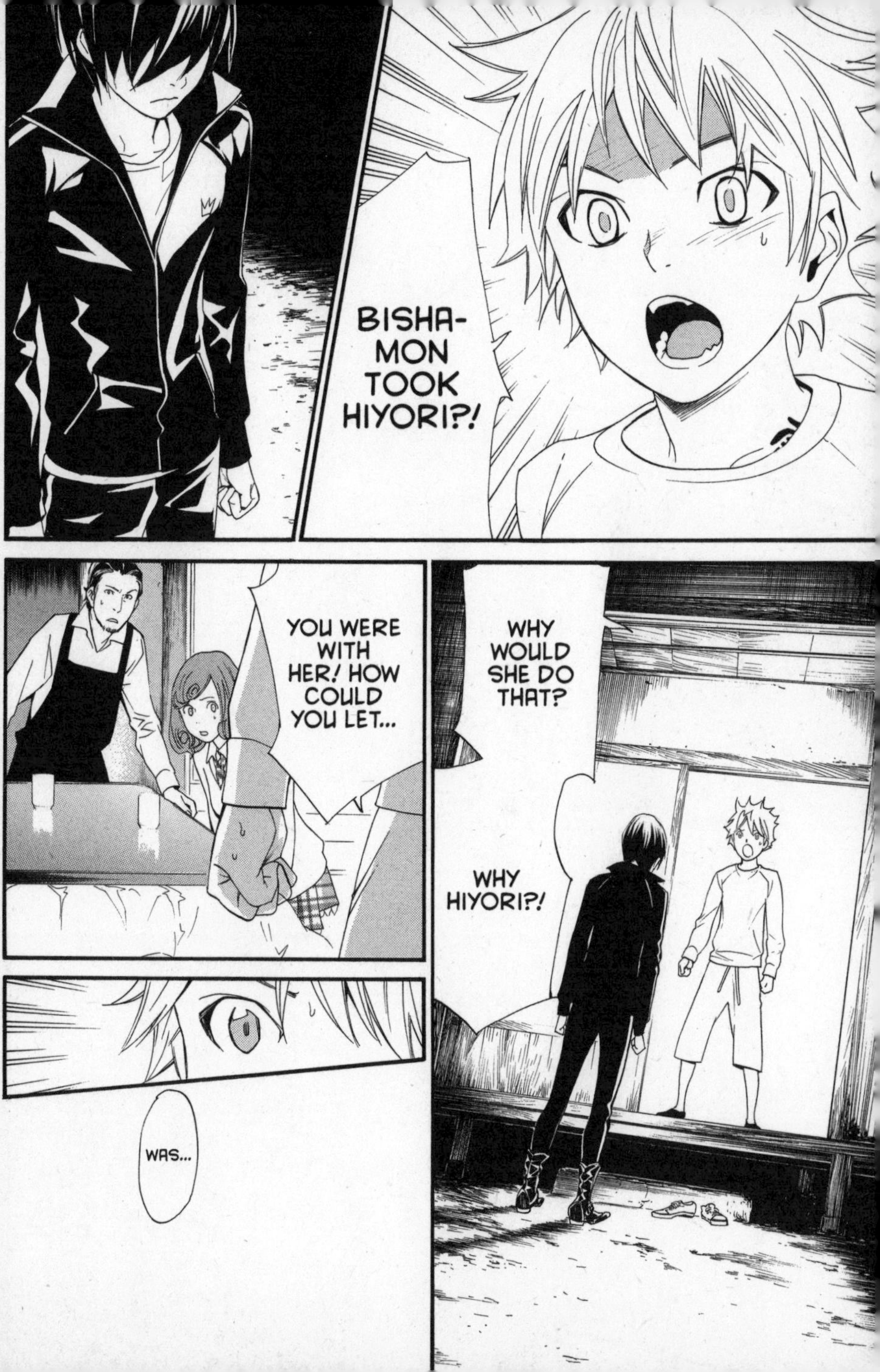
BISHAMON TOOK HIYORI?!
WHY WOULD SHE DO THAT?
WHY HIYORI?!
YOU WERE WITH HER! HOW COULD YOU LET...
WAS...

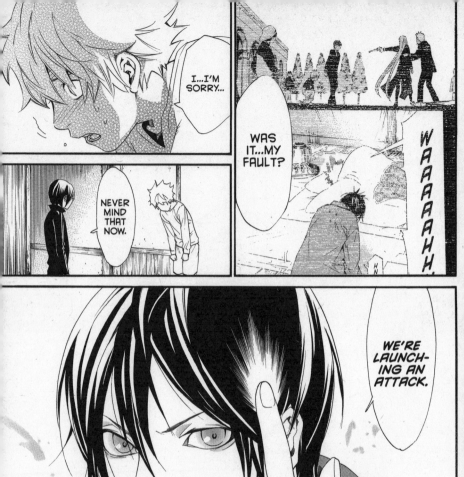

I...I'M SORRY...

WAS IT...MY FAULT?

NEVER MIND THAT NOW.

WAAAAAHH.

HN

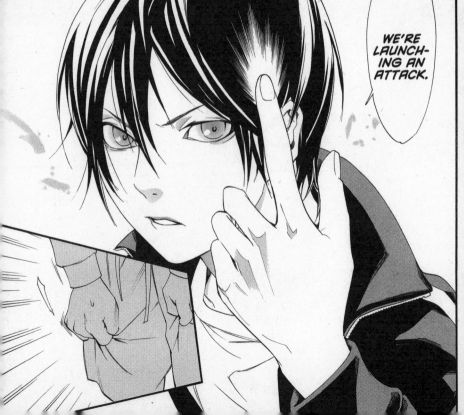

WE'RE LAUNCHING AN ATTACK.

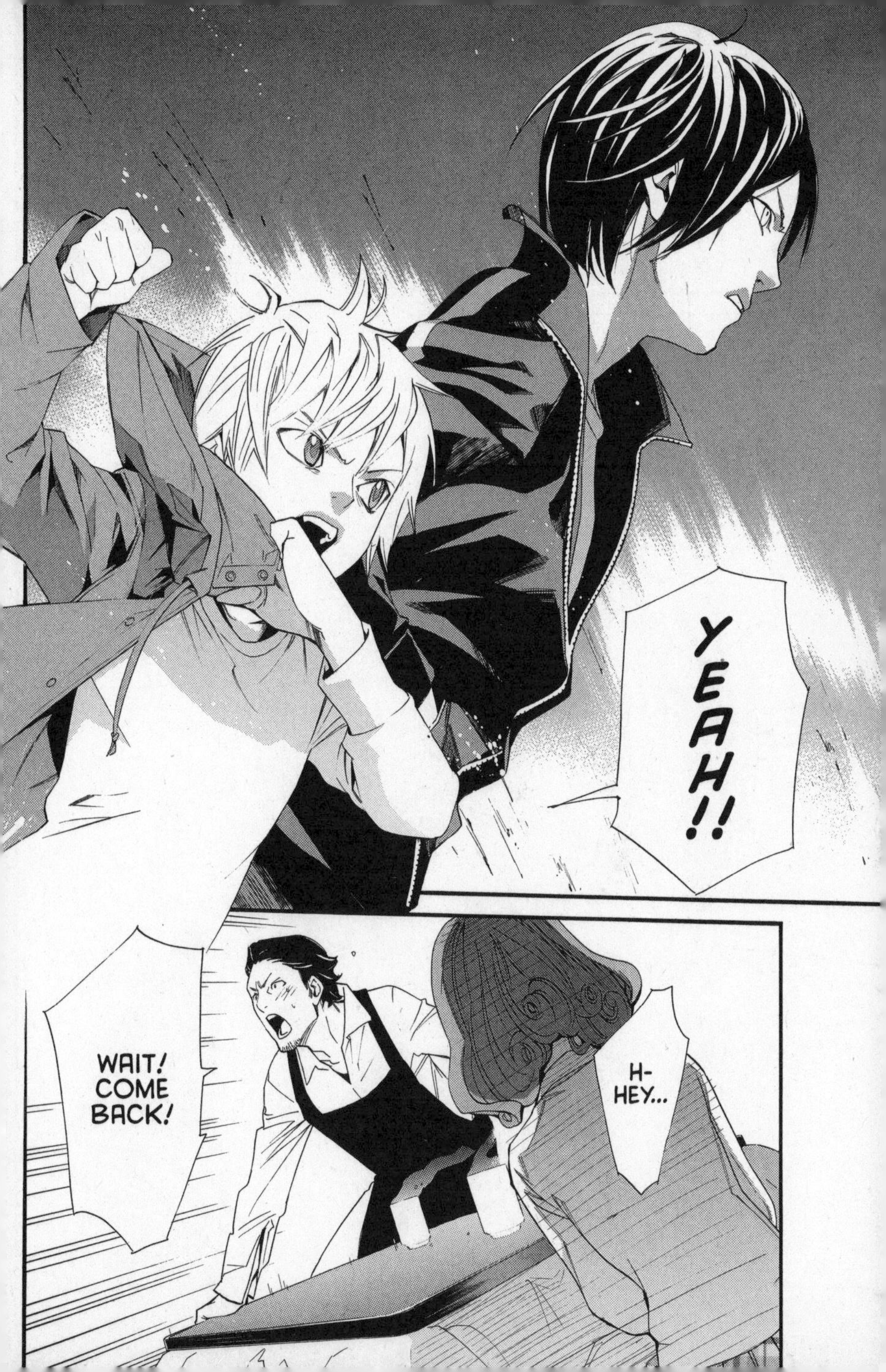
YEAH!!
H-HEY...
WAIT! COME BACK!

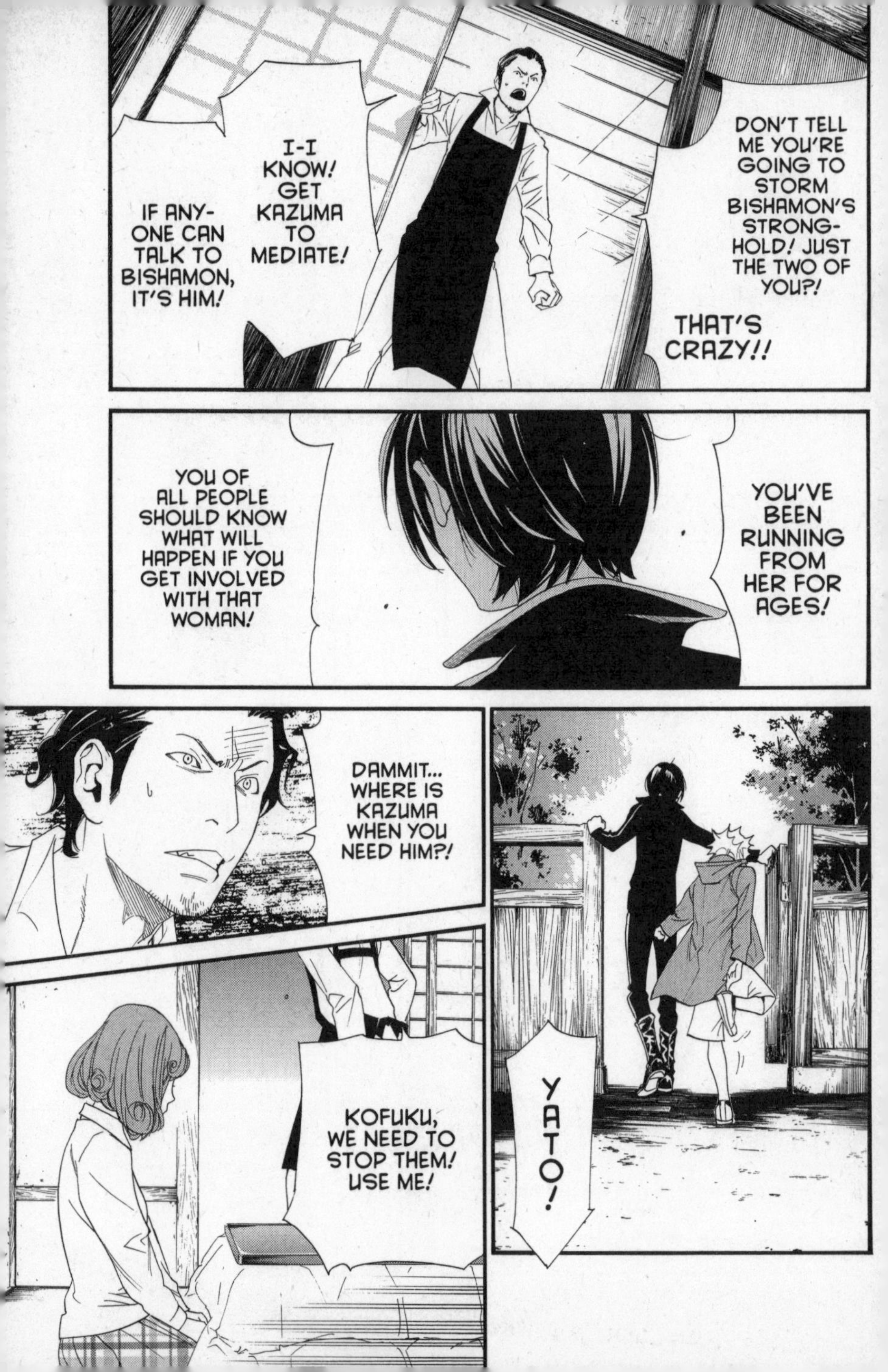
DON'T TELL ME YOU'RE GOING TO STORM BISHAMON'S STRONG-HOLD! JUST THE TWO OF YOU?!
THAT'S CRAZY!!
I-I KNOW! GET KAZUMA TO MEDIATE!
IF ANY-ONE CAN TALK TO BISHAMON, IT'S HIM!
YOU'VE BEEN RUNNING FROM HER FOR AGES!
YOU OF ALL PEOPLE SHOULD KNOW WHAT WILL HAPPEN IF YOU GET INVOLVED WITH THAT WOMAN!
YATO!
DAMMIT... WHERE IS KAZUMA WHEN YOU NEED HIM?!
KOFUKU, WE NEED TO STOP THEM! USE ME!

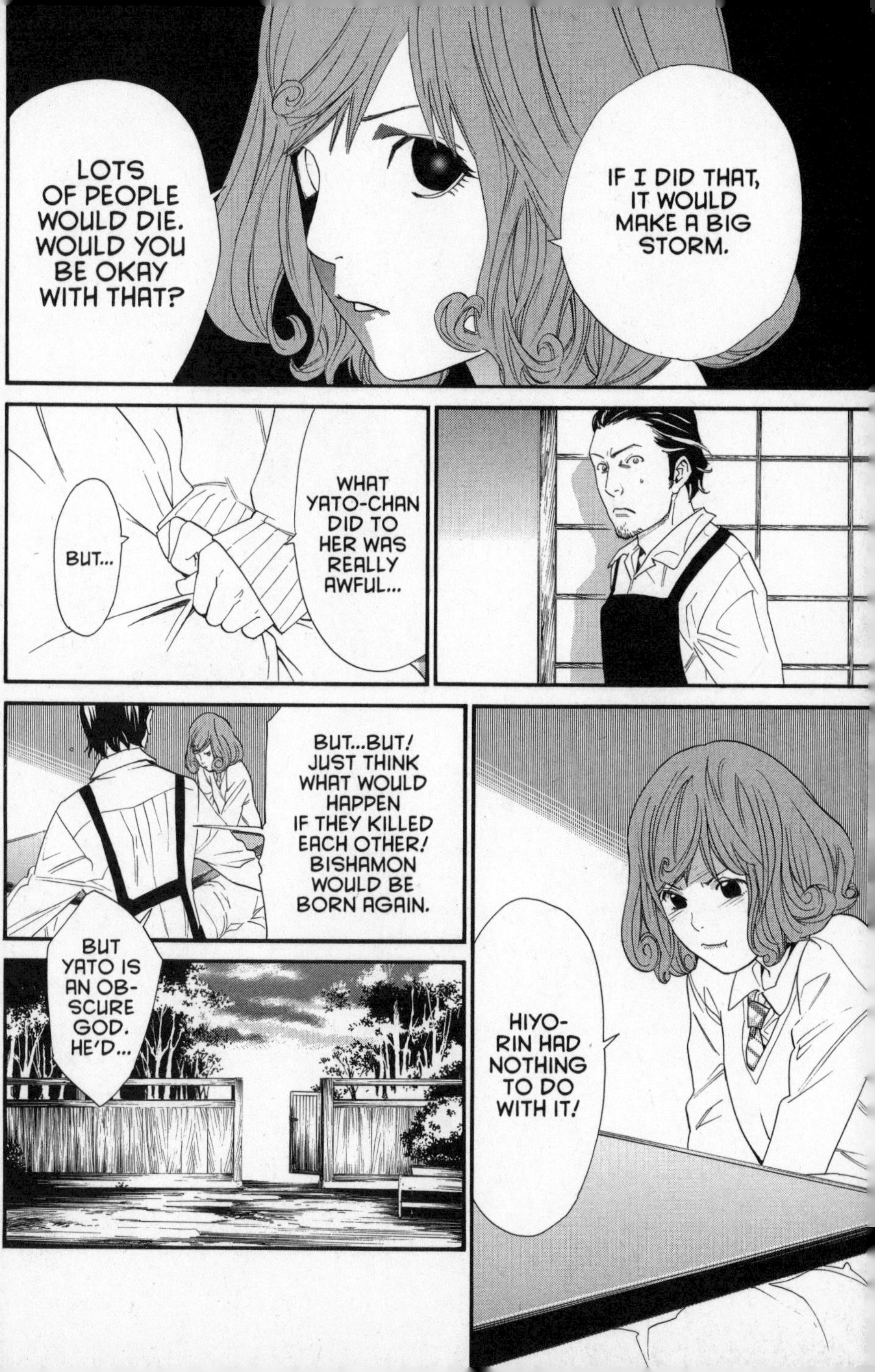
IF I DID THAT, IT WOULD MAKE A BIG STORM.
LOTS OF PEOPLE WOULD DIE. WOULD YOU BE OKAY WITH THAT?
WHAT YATO-CHAN DID TO HER WAS REALLY AWFUL...
BUT...
HIYO-RIN HAD NOTHING TO DO WITH IT!
BUT...BUT! JUST THINK WHAT WOULD HAPPEN IF THEY KILLED EACH OTHER! BISHAMON WOULD BE BORN AGAIN.
BUT YATO IS AN OB-SCURE GOD. HE'D...

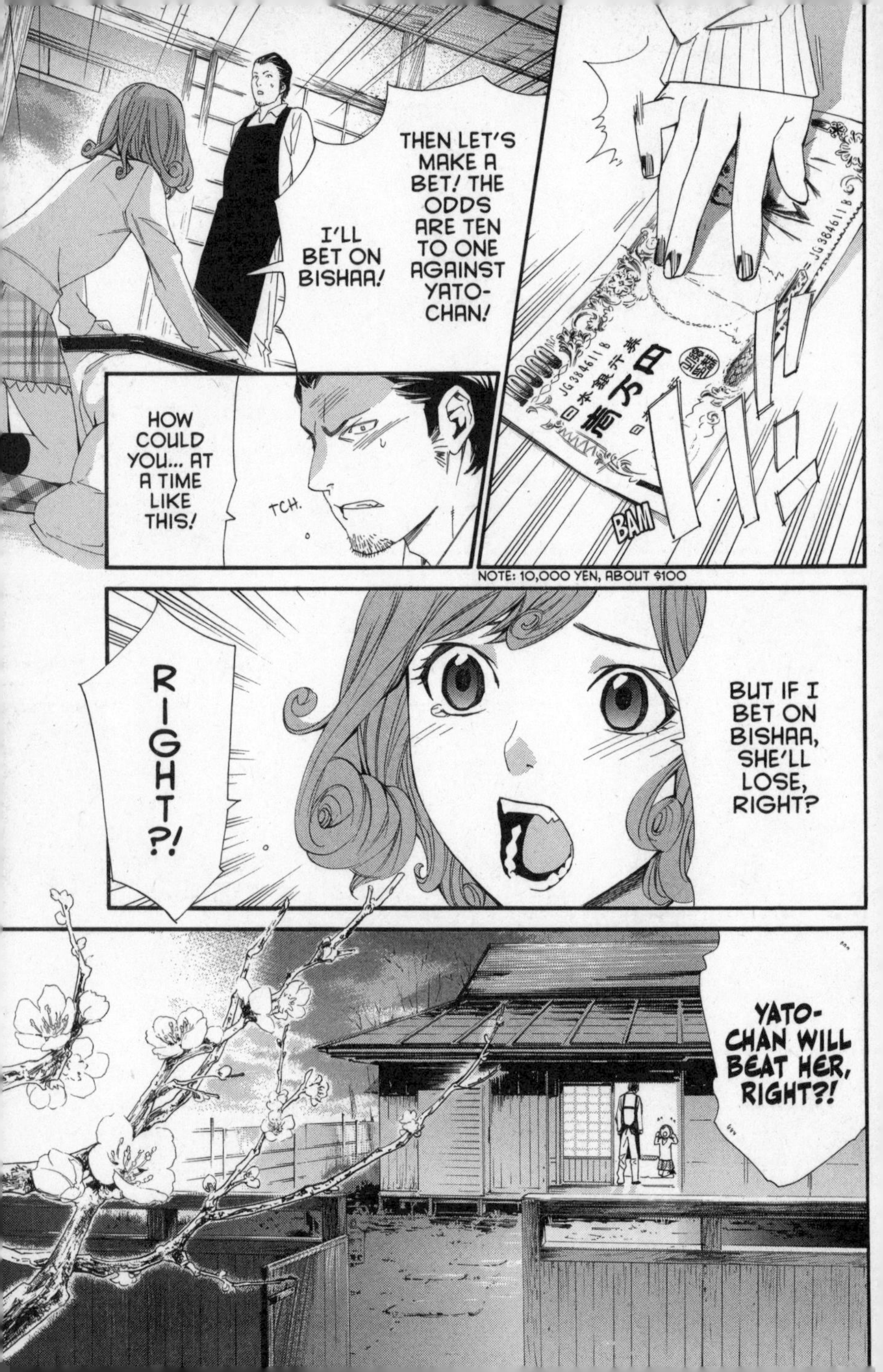
BAM
THEN LET'S MAKE A BET! THE ODDS ARE TEN TO ONE AGAINST YATO-CHAN!
I'LL BET ON BISHAA!
HOW COULD YOU... AT A TIME LIKE THIS!
TCH.
NOTE: 10,000 YEN, ABOUT $100
BUT IF I BET ON BISHAA, SHE'LL LOSE, RIGHT?
RIGHT?!
YATO-CHAN WILL BEAT HER, RIGHT?!

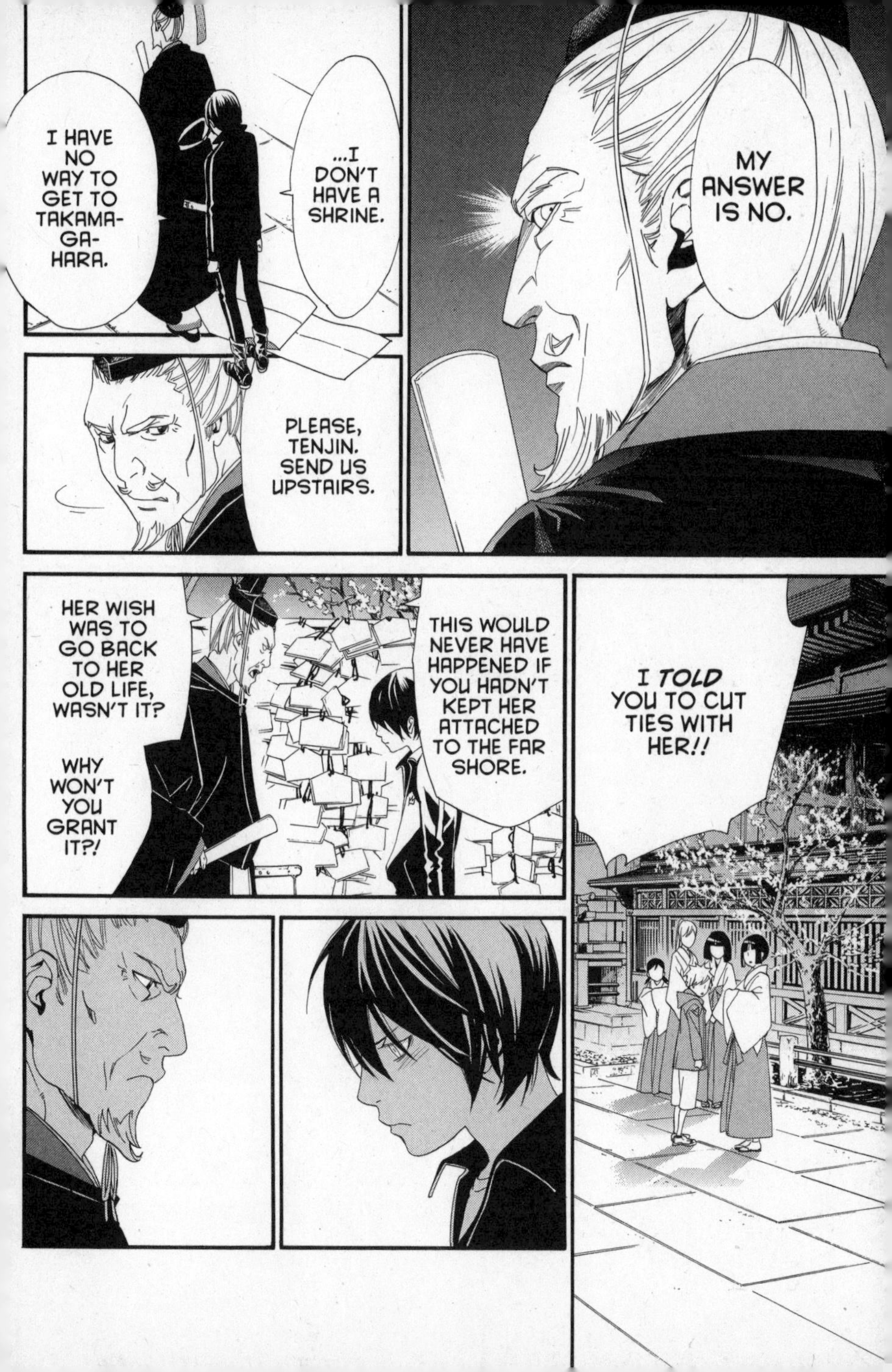
MY ANSWER IS NO.
...I DON'T HAVE A SHRINE.
I HAVE NO WAY TO GET TO TAKAMA-GA-HARA.
PLEASE, TENJIN. SEND US UPSTAIRS.
I *TOLD* YOU TO CUT TIES WITH HER!!
THIS WOULD NEVER HAVE HAPPENED IF YOU HADN'T KEPT HER ATTACHED TO THE FAR SHORE.
HER WISH WAS TO GO BACK TO HER OLD LIFE, WASN'T IT?
WHY WON'T YOU GRANT IT?!

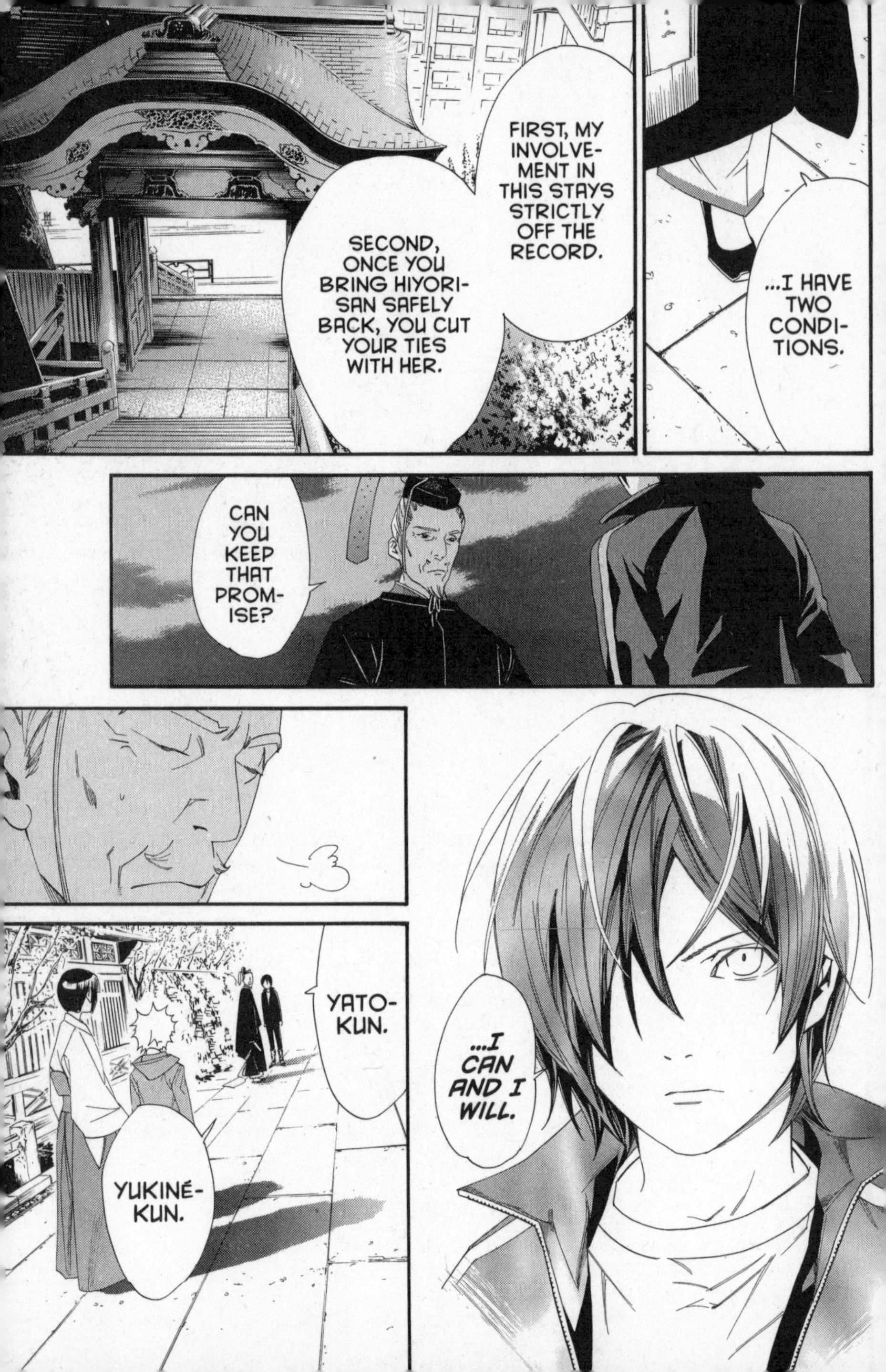
...I HAVE TWO CONDITIONS.
FIRST, MY INVOLVEMENT IN THIS STAYS STRICTLY OFF THE RECORD.
SECOND, ONCE YOU BRING HIYORI-SAN SAFELY BACK, YOU CUT YOUR TIES WITH HER.
CAN YOU KEEP THAT PROMISE?
...I CAN AND I WILL.
YATO-KUN.
YUKINÉ-KUN.

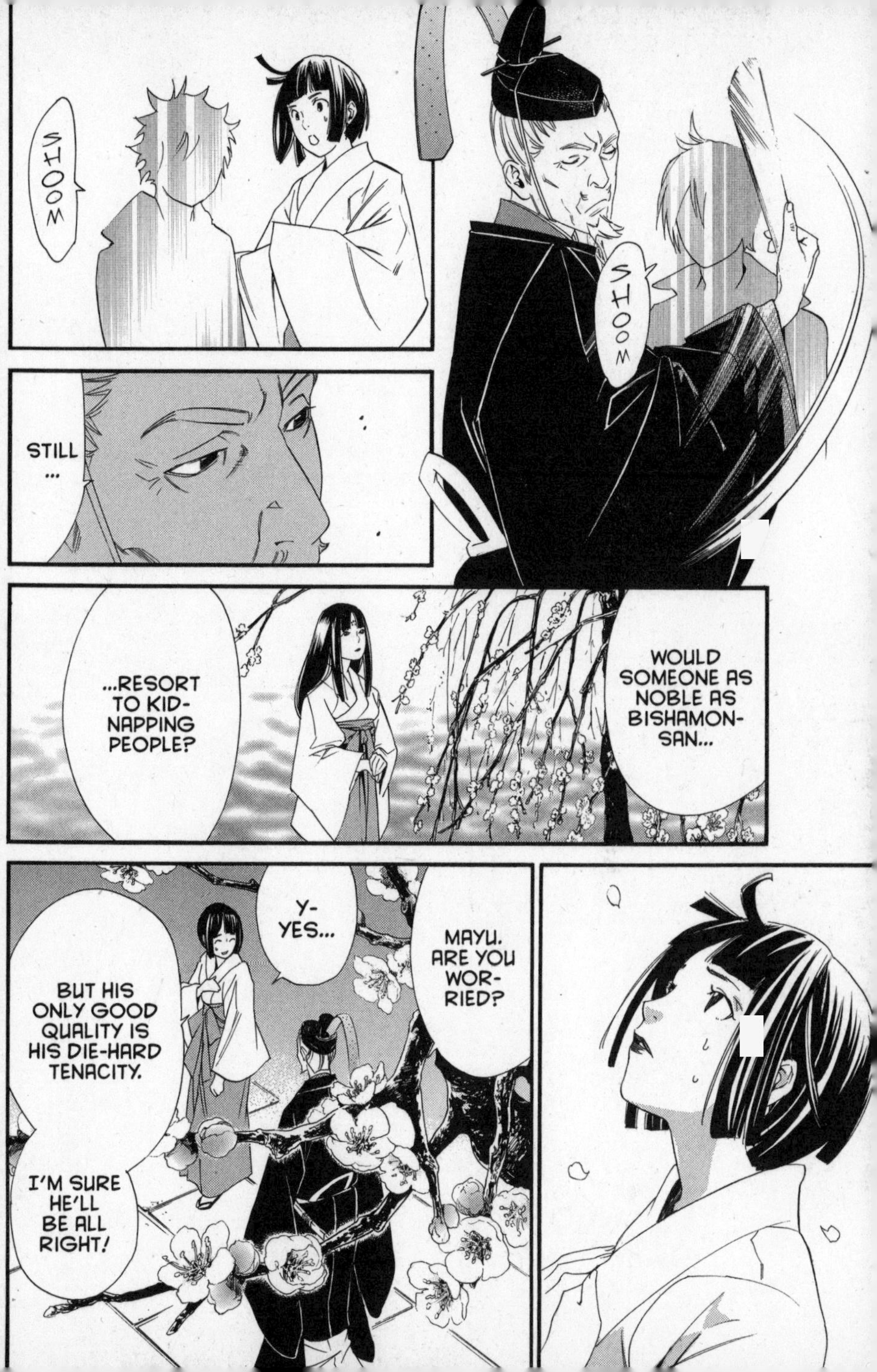
SHOOM
SHOOM
STILL ...
WOULD SOMEONE AS NOBLE AS BISHAMON-SAN...
...RESORT TO KID-NAPPING PEOPLE?
MAYU. ARE YOU WOR-RIED?
Y-YES...
BUT HIS ONLY GOOD QUALITY IS HIS DIE-HARD TENACITY.
I'M SURE HE'LL BE ALL RIGHT!

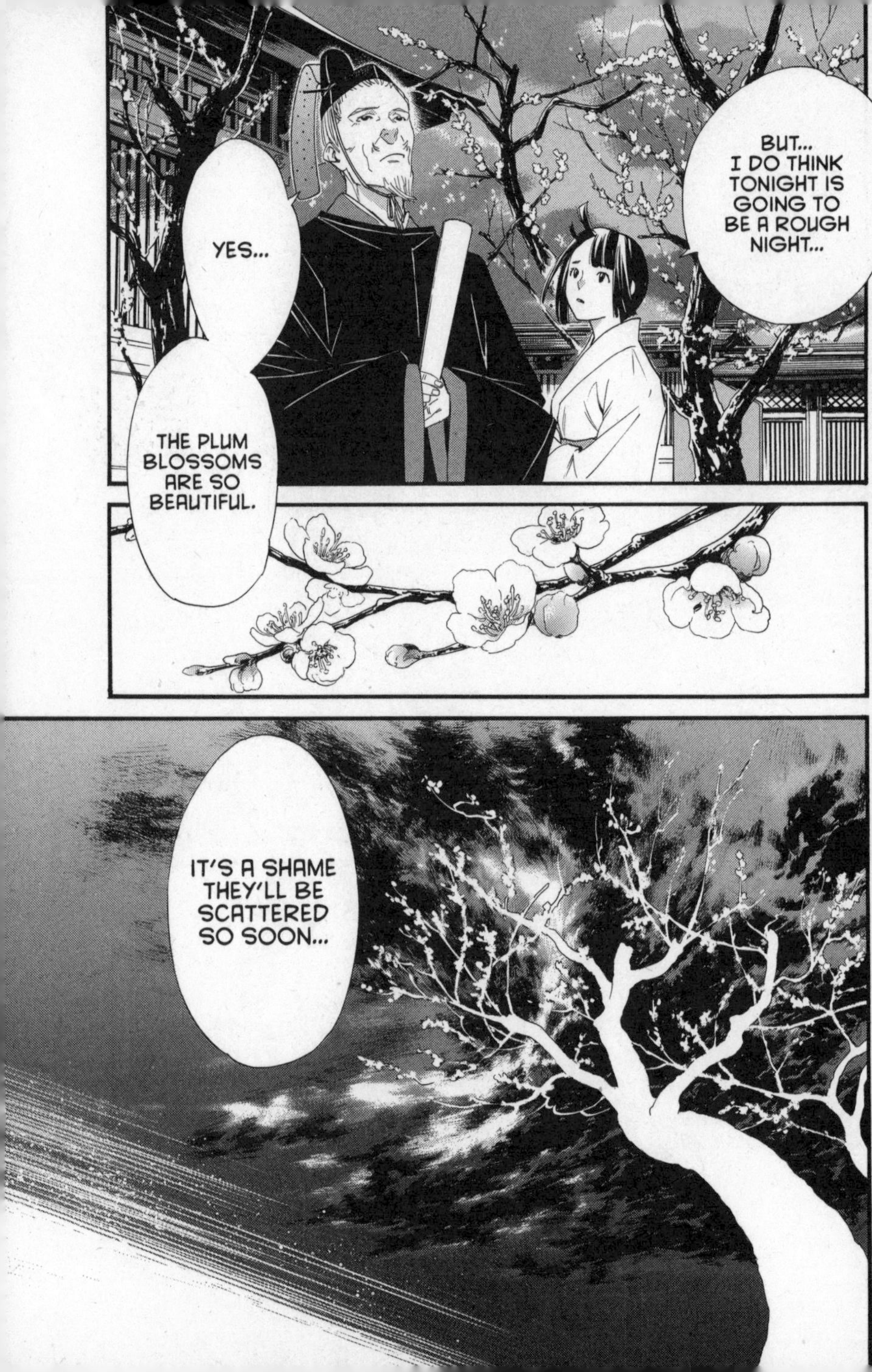
BUT... I DO THINK TONIGHT IS GOING TO BE A ROUGH NIGHT...
YES...
THE PLUM BLOSSOMS ARE SO BEAUTIFUL.
IT'S A SHAME THEY'LL BE SCATTERED SO SOON...

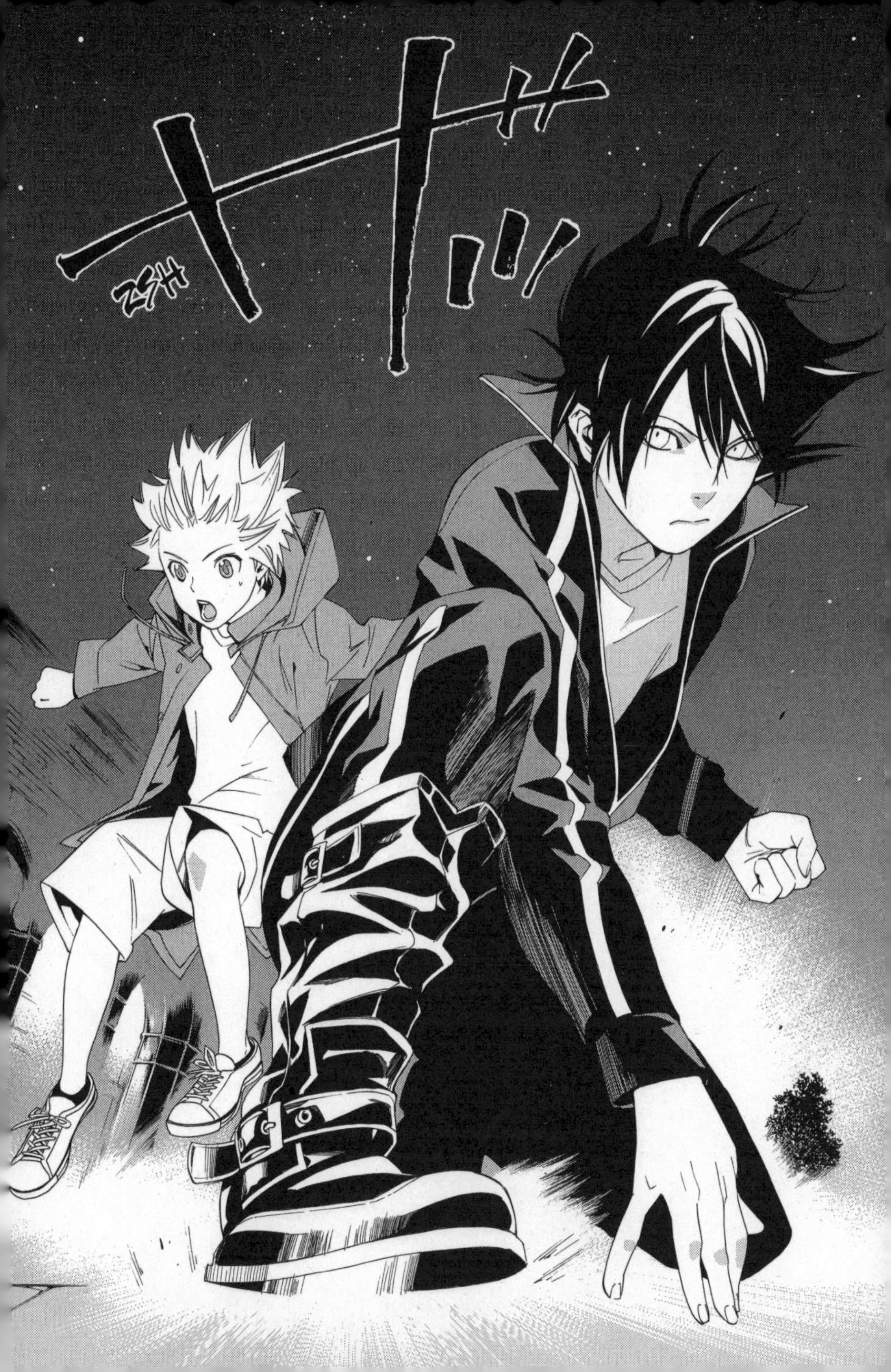
ザッ
ZSH

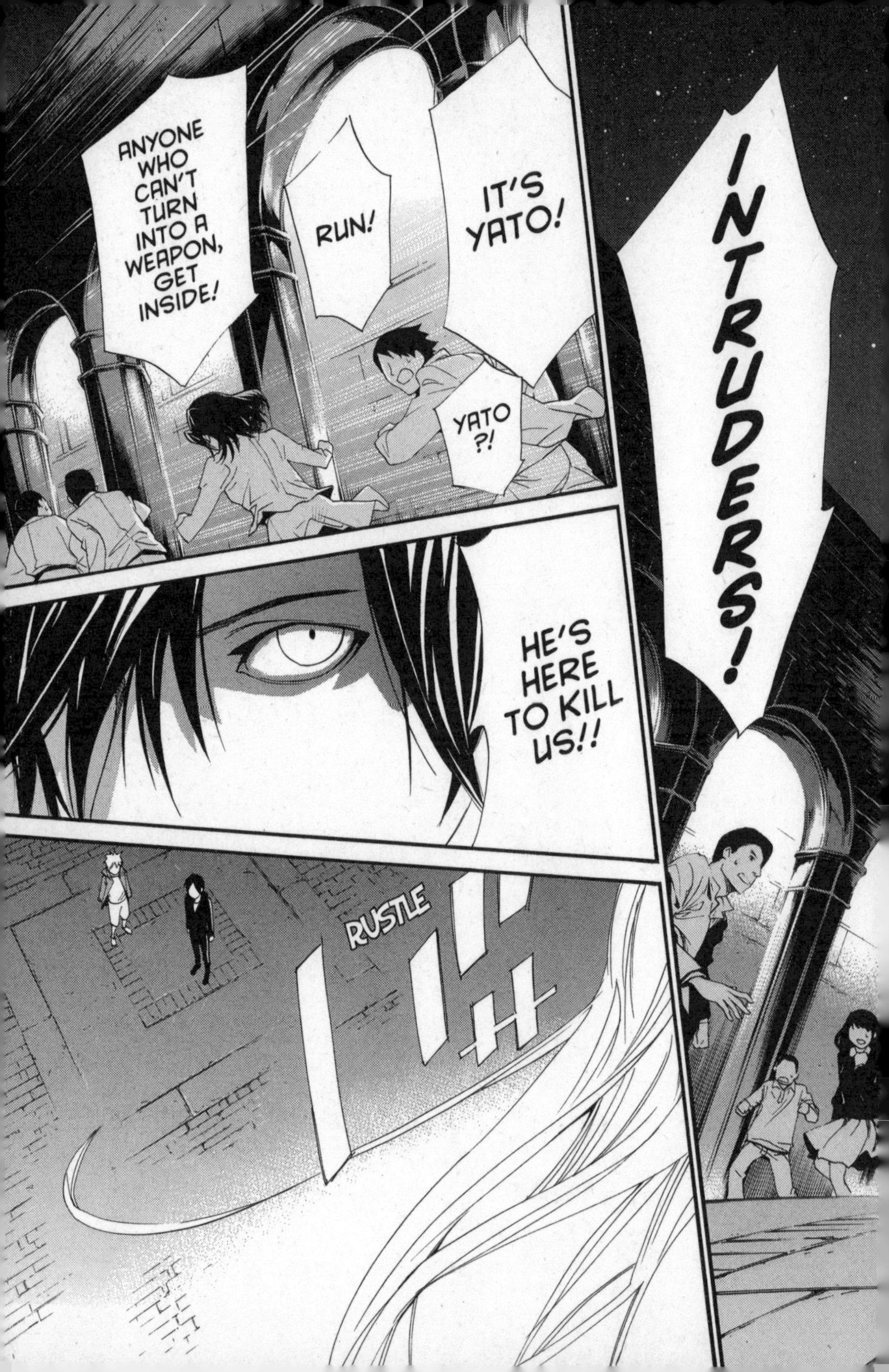
INTRUDERS!
IT'S YATO!
RUN!
ANYONE WHO CAN'T TURN INTO A WEAPON, GET INSIDE!
YATO?!
HE'S HERE TO KILL US!!
RUSTLE

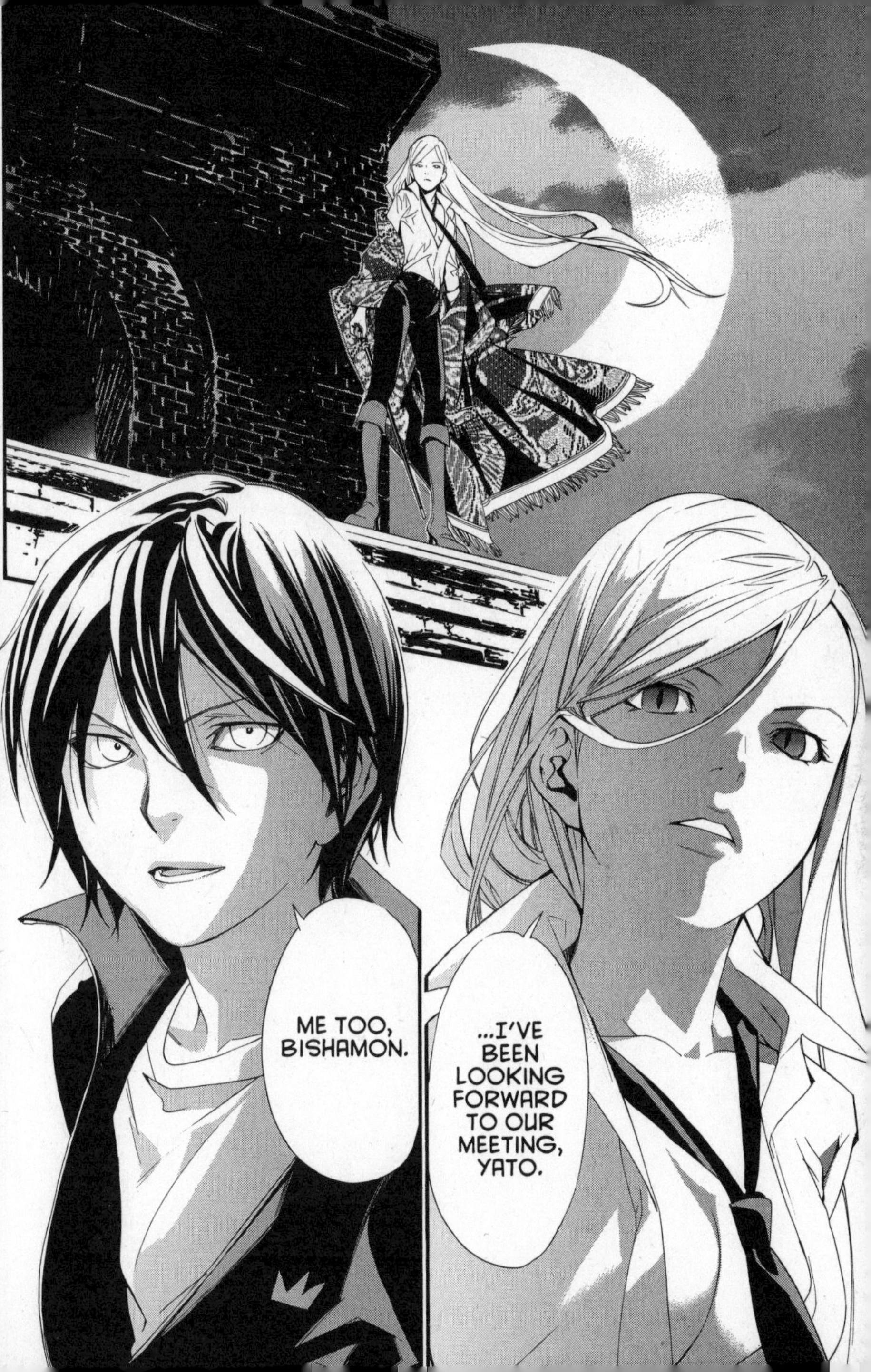
...I'VE BEEN LOOKING FORWARD TO OUR MEETING, YATO.
ME TOO, BISHAMON.

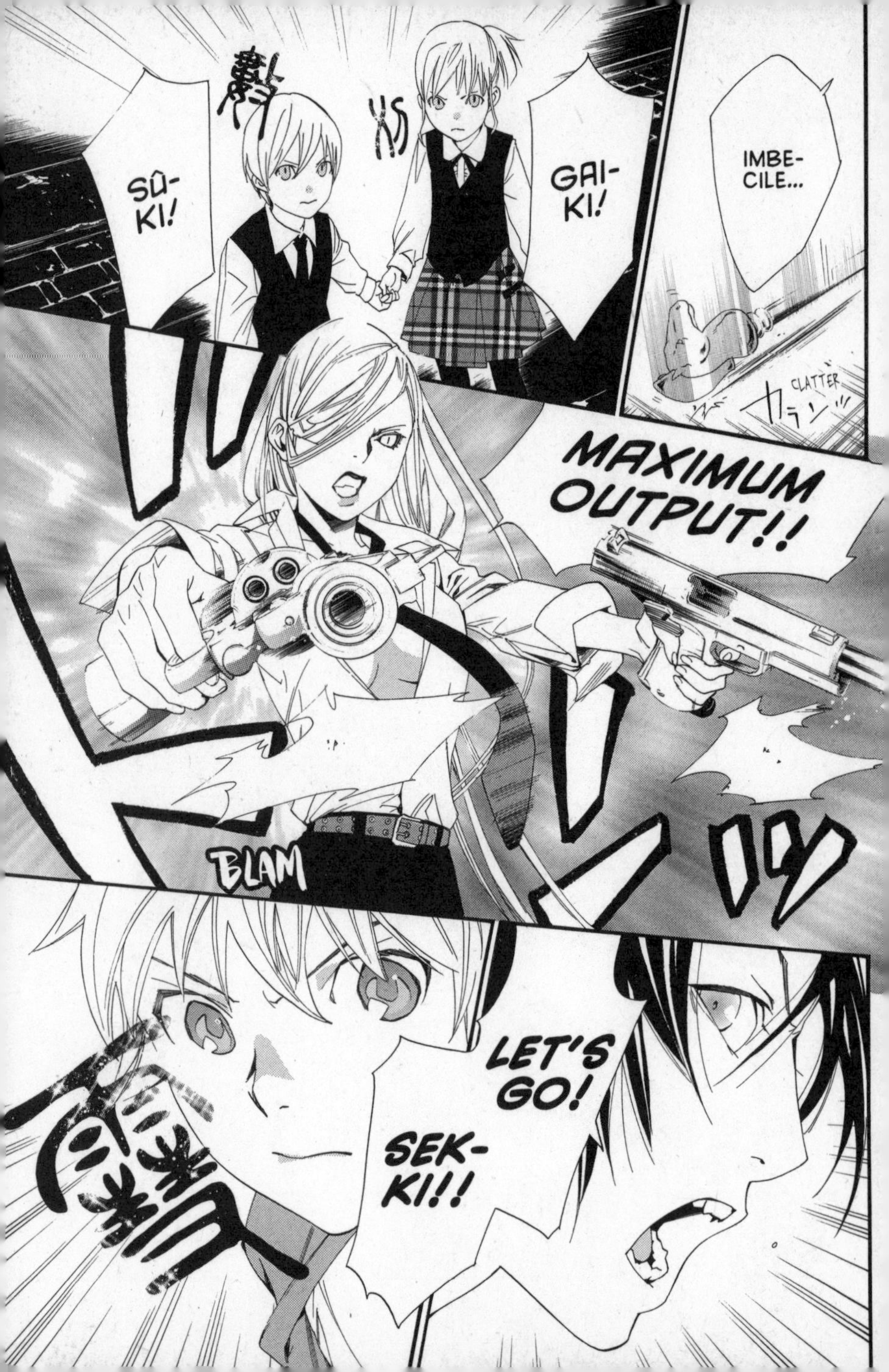
IMBE-
CILE...
CLATTER
GAI-
KI!
SÛ-
KI!
MAXIMUM
OUTPUT!!
BLAM
LET'S
GO!
SEK-
KI!!

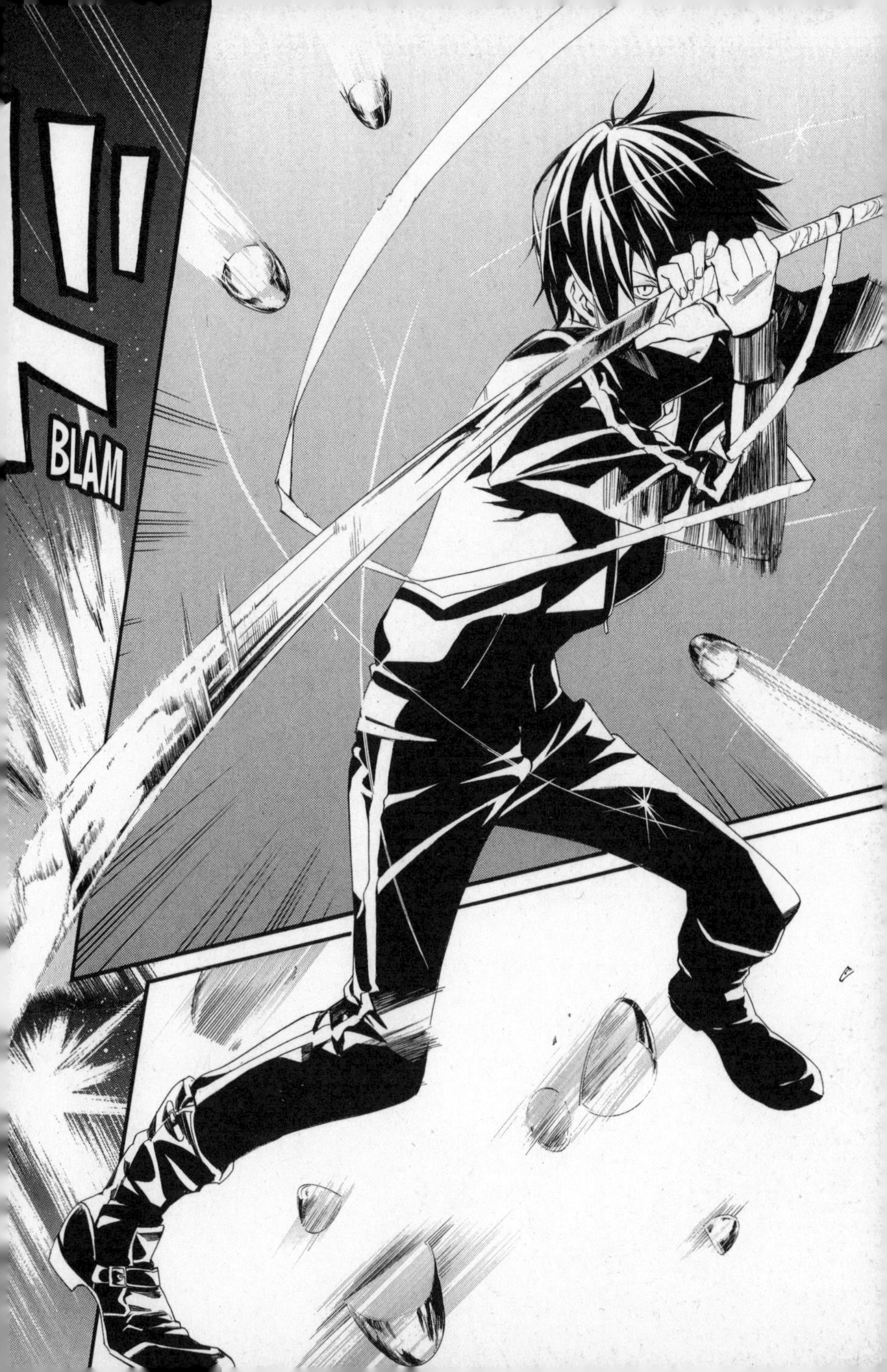

!!
BLAM

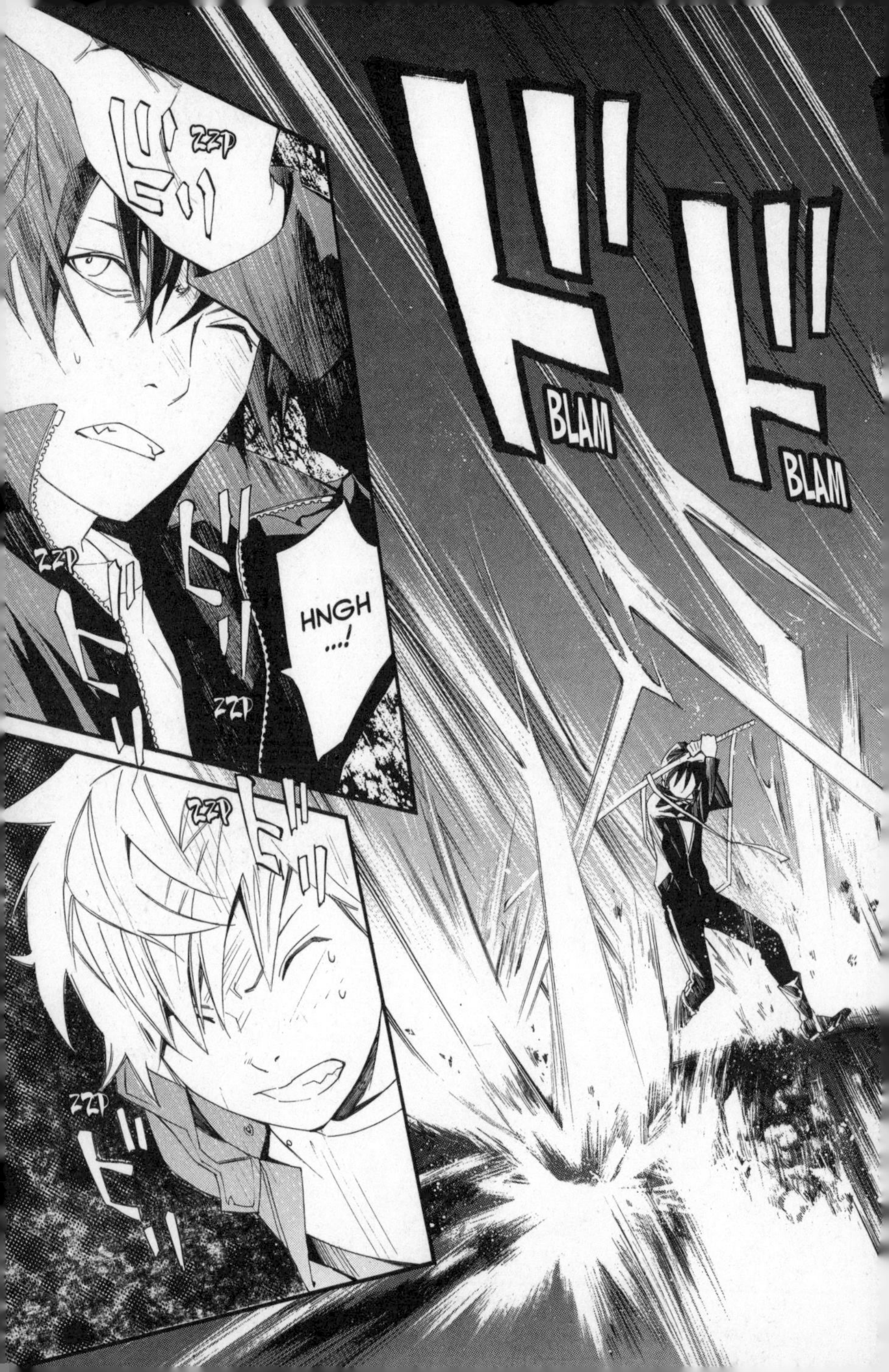
BLAM
BLAM
ZZP
HNGH ...!
ZZP
ZZP
ZZP
ZZP

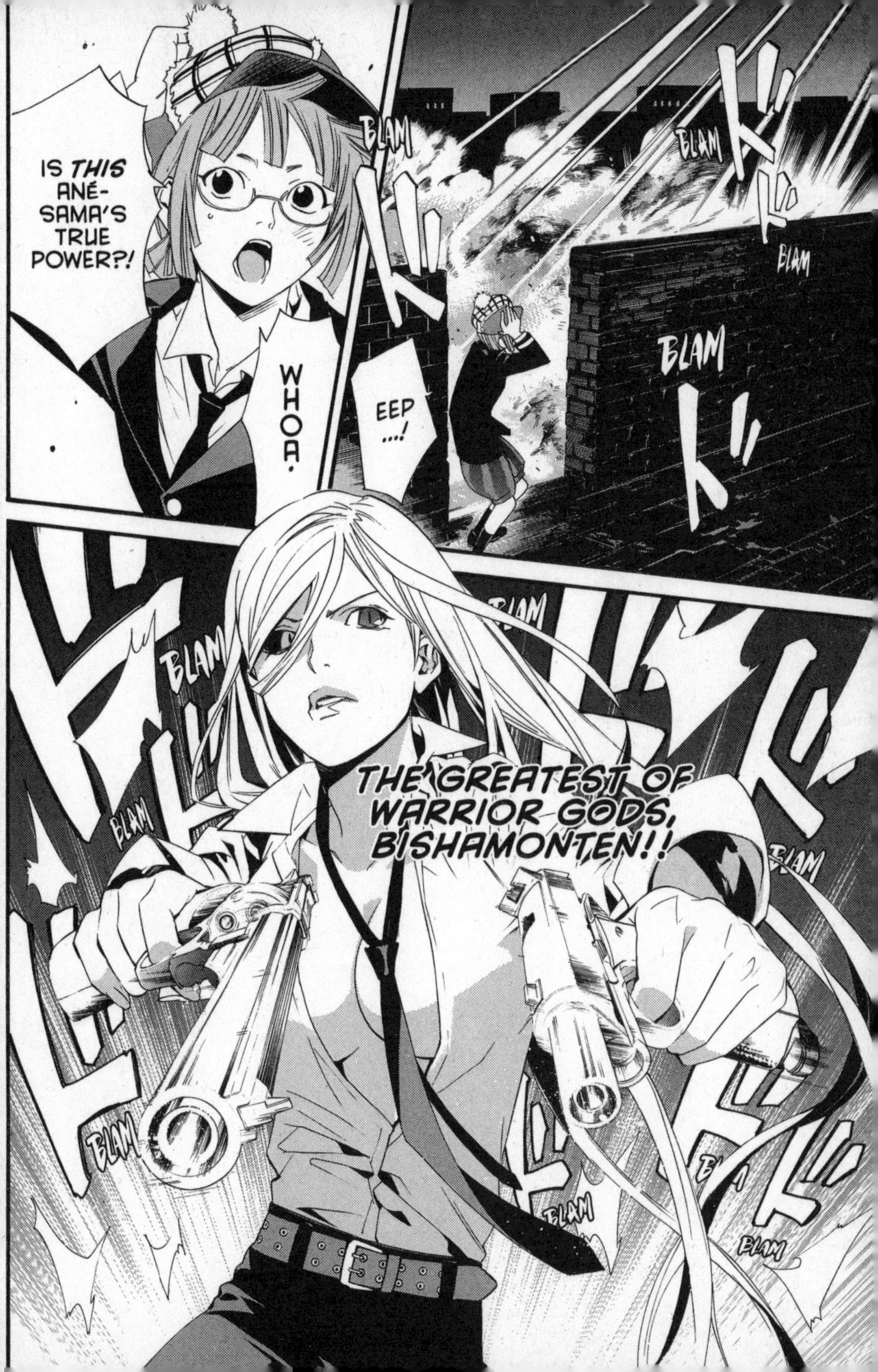

BLAM
BLAM
BLAM
BLAM
EEP ...!
BLAM
IS THIS ANÉ-SAMA'S TRUE POWER?!
WHOA.
THE GREATEST OF WARRIOR GODS, BISHAMONTEN!!
BLAM
BLAM
BLAM
BLAM
BLAM
BLAM
BLAM

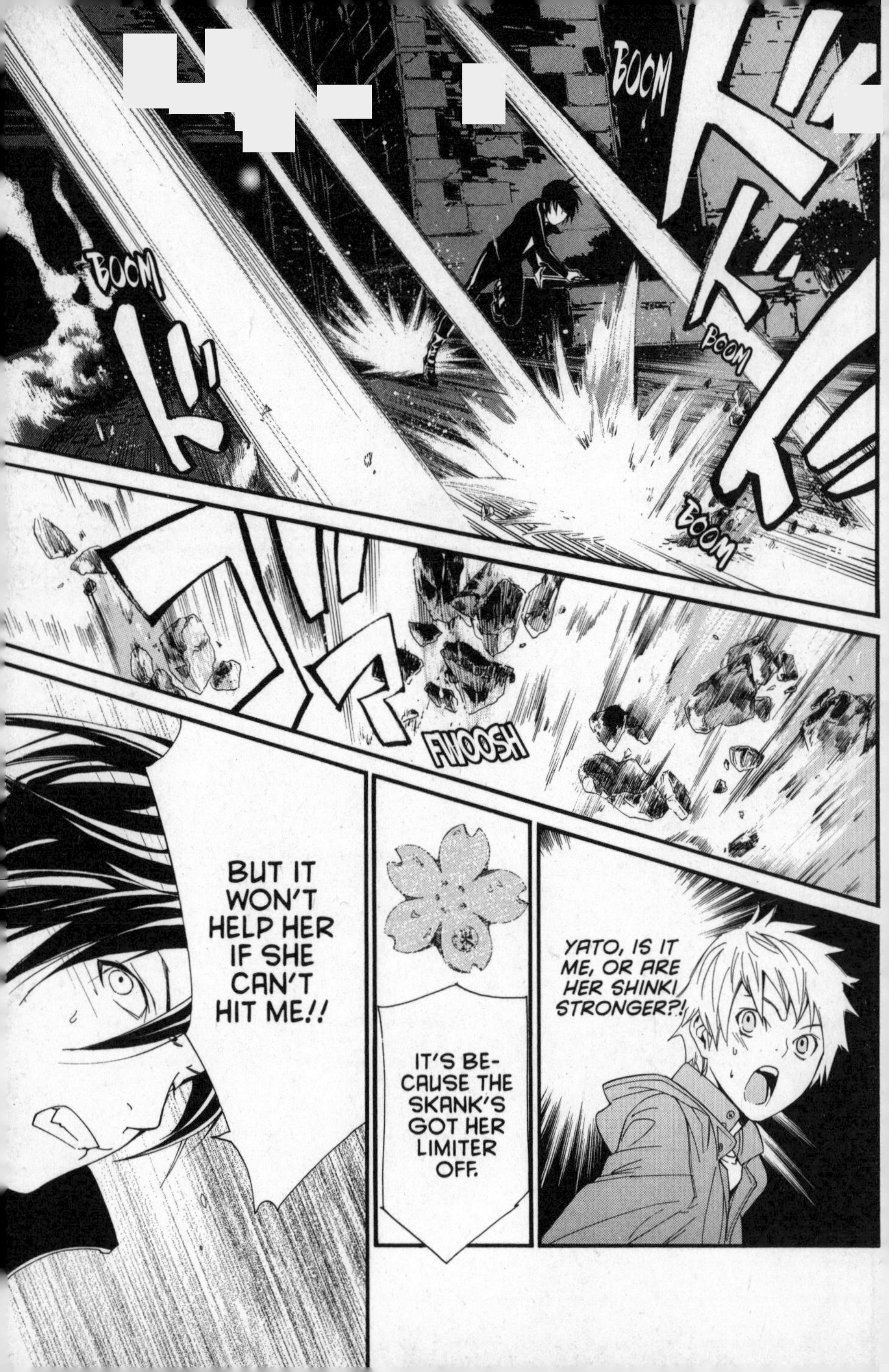
BOOM
BOOM
BOOM
BOOM
FWOOSH
YATO, IS IT ME, OR ARE HER SHINKI STRONGER?!
IT'S BE-CAUSE THE SKANK'S GOT HER LIMITER OFF.
BUT IT WON'T HELP HER IF SHE CAN'T HIT ME!!

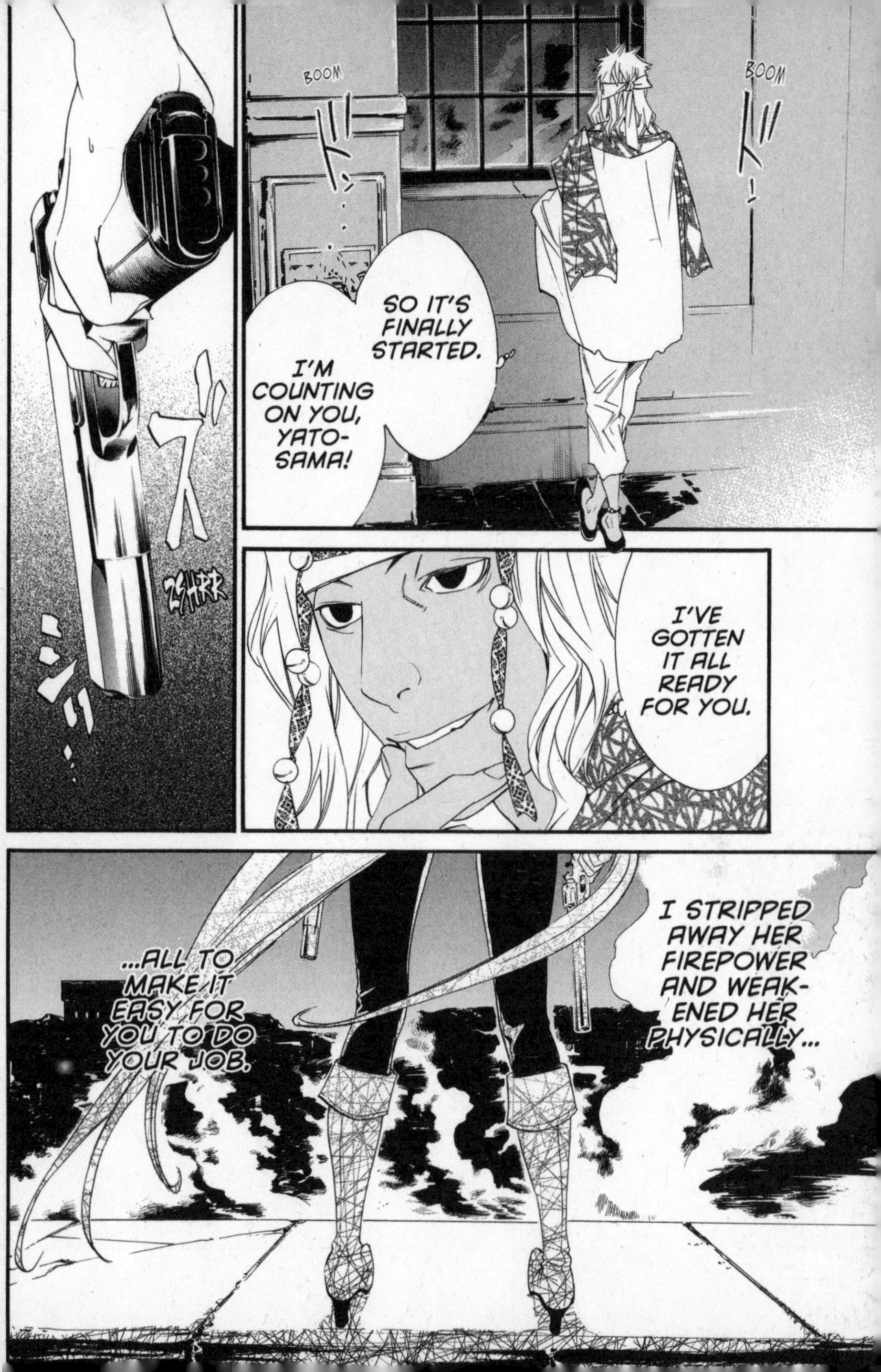
BOOM
BOOM
SO IT'S FINALLY STARTED.
I'M COUNTING ON YOU, YATO-SAMA!
I'VE GOTTEN IT ALL READY FOR YOU.
ZSHRR
I STRIPPED AWAY HER FIREPOWER AND WEAK-ENED HER PHYSICALLY...
...ALL TO MAKE IT EASY FOR YOU TO DO YOUR JOB.

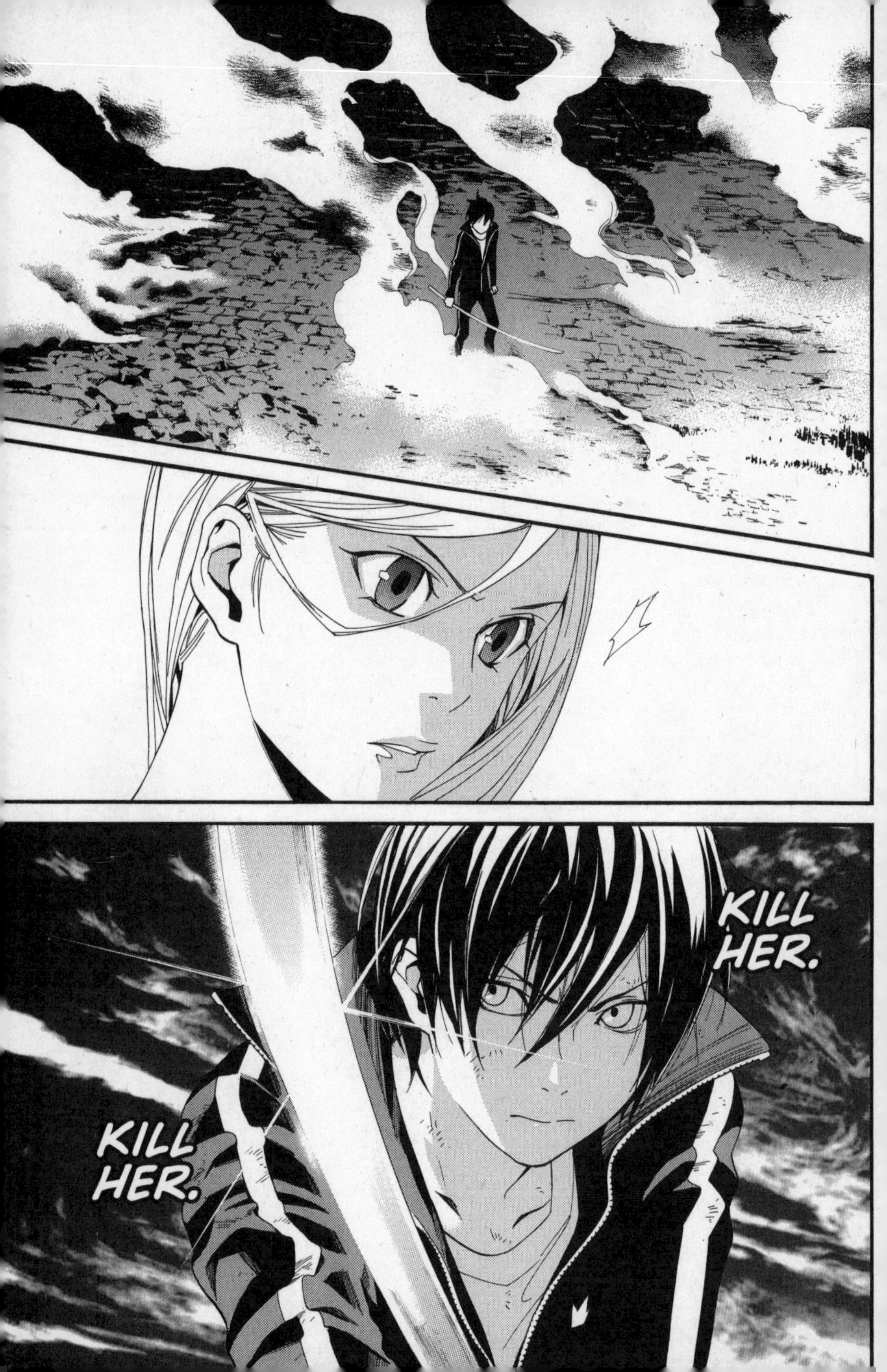
KILL HER.
KILL HER.

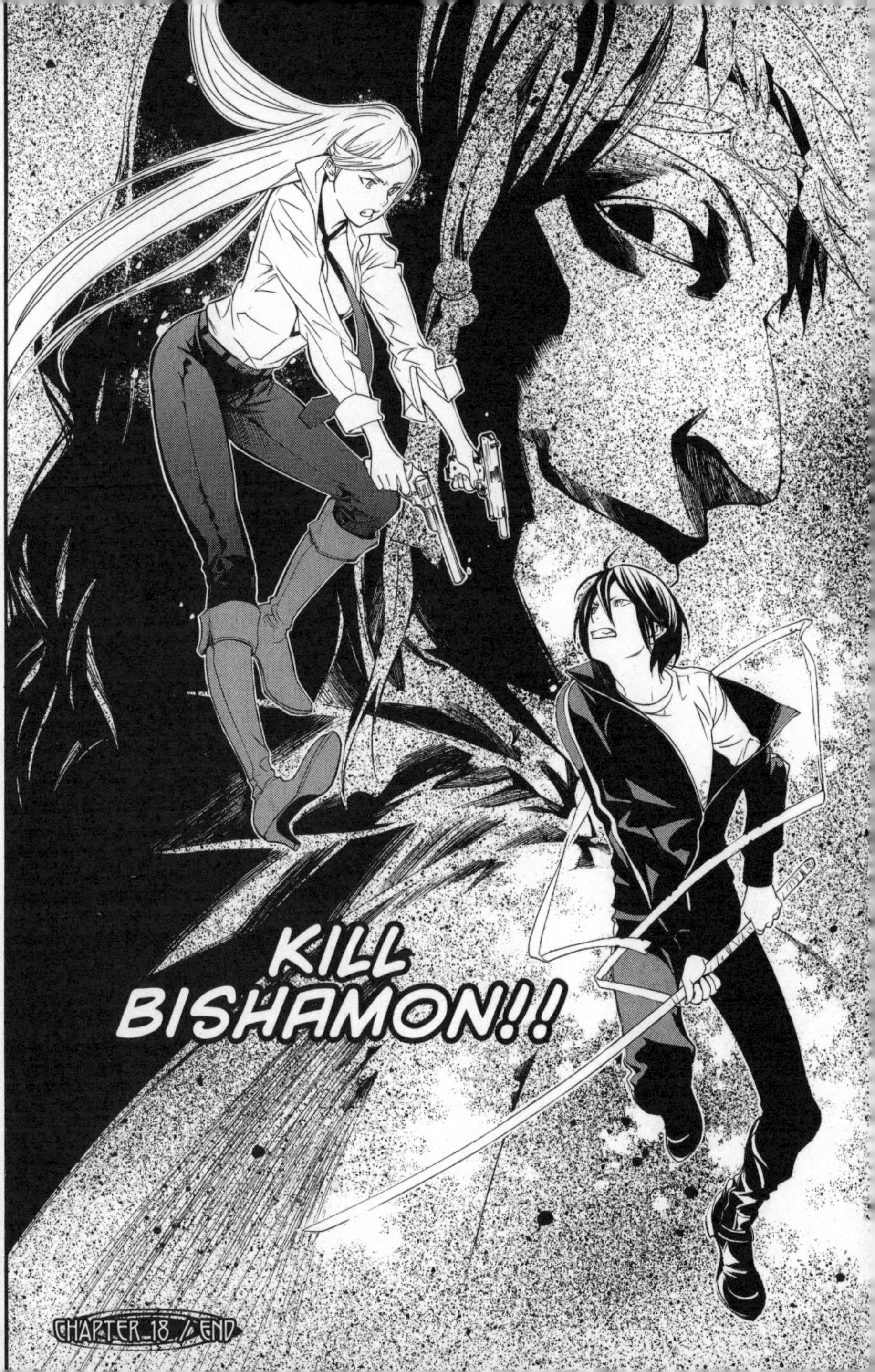
KILL BISHAMON!!
CHAPTER 18 / END

野

見

神

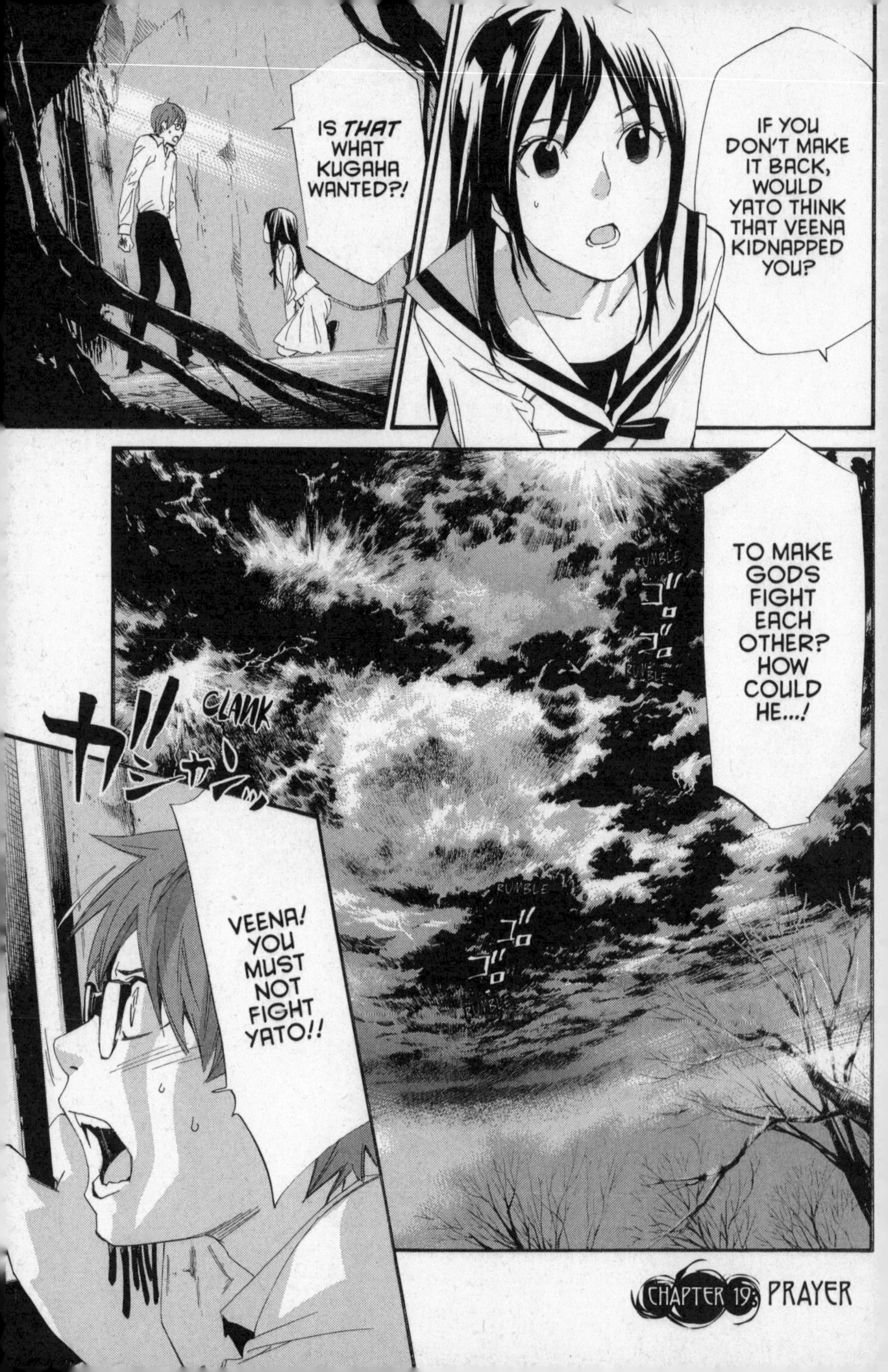
IF YOU DON'T MAKE IT BACK, WOULD YATO THINK THAT VEENA KIDNAPPED YOU?
IS *THAT* WHAT KUGAHA WANTED?!
TO MAKE GODS FIGHT EACH OTHER? HOW COULD HE...!
RUMBLE
RUMBLE
RUMBLE
RUMBLE
CLANK
VEENA! YOU MUST NOT FIGHT YATO!!
CHAPTER 19: PRAYER

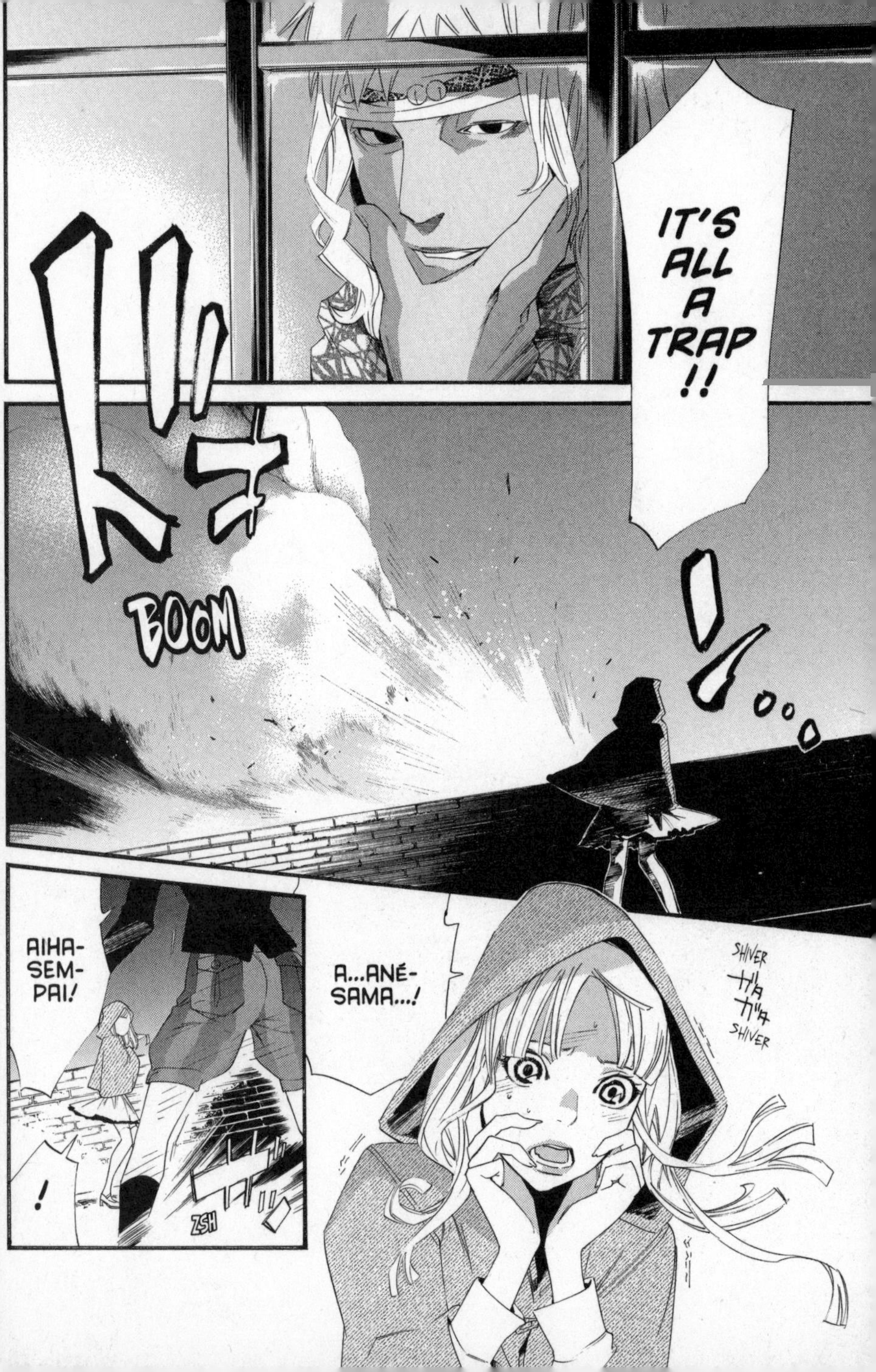

IT'S ALL A TRAP!!
BOOM
SHIVER
SHIVER
A...ANÉ-SAMA...!
AIHA-SEMPAI!
!
ZSH

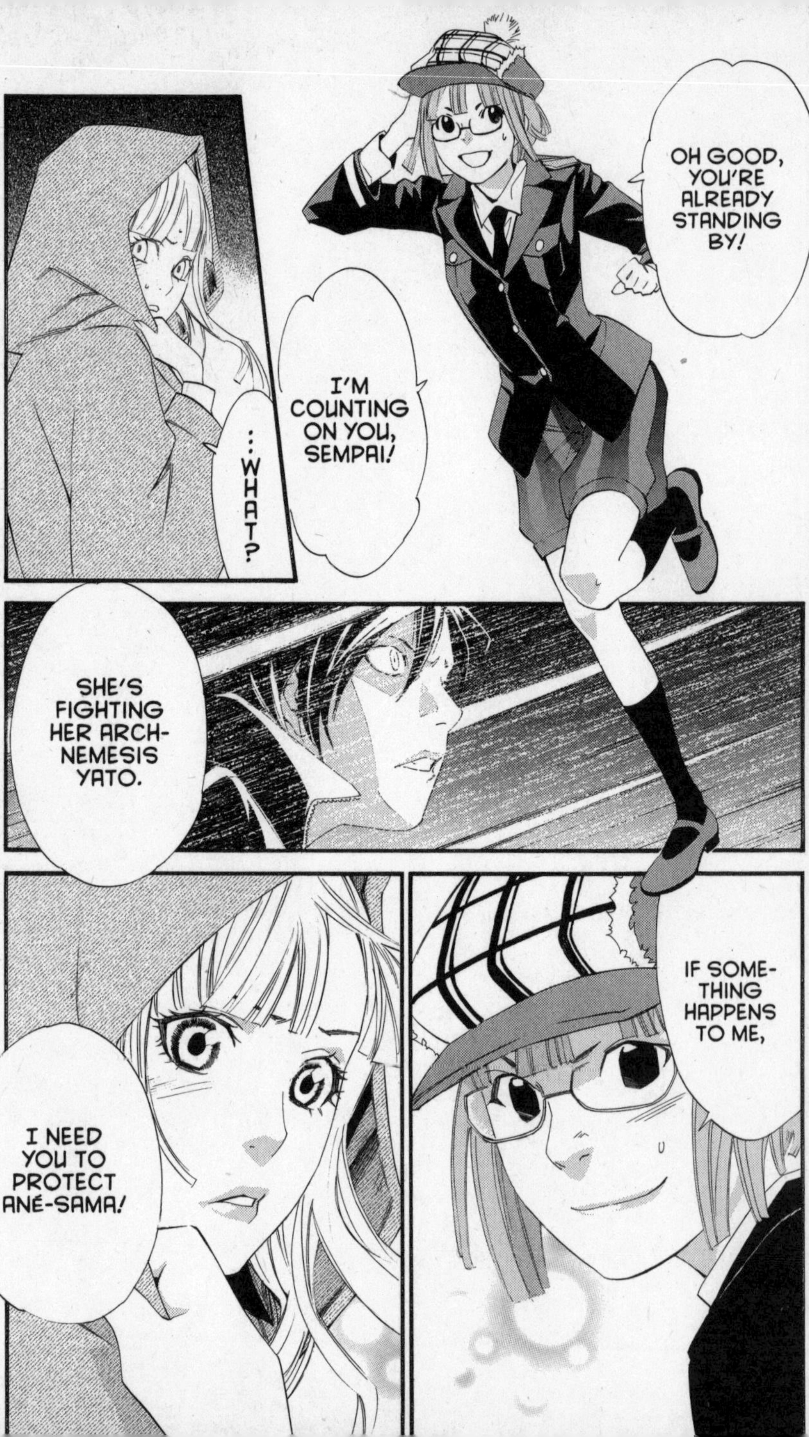
OH GOOD, YOU'RE ALREADY STANDING BY!
I'M COUNTING ON YOU, SEMPAI!
...WHAT?
SHE'S FIGHTING HER ARCH-NEMESIS YATO.
IF SOME-THING HAPPENS TO ME,
I NEED YOU TO PROTECT ANÉ-SAMA!

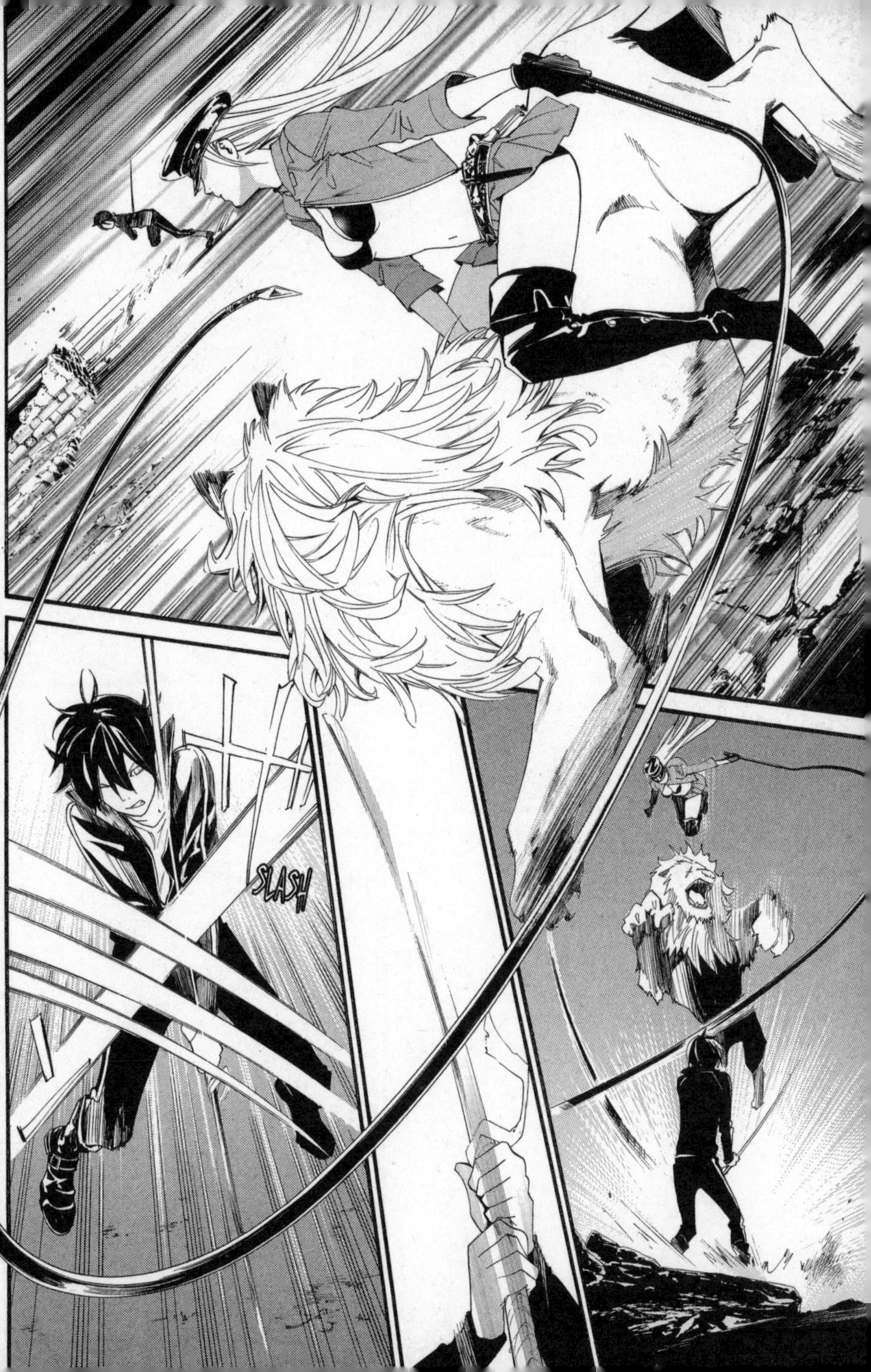
SLASH

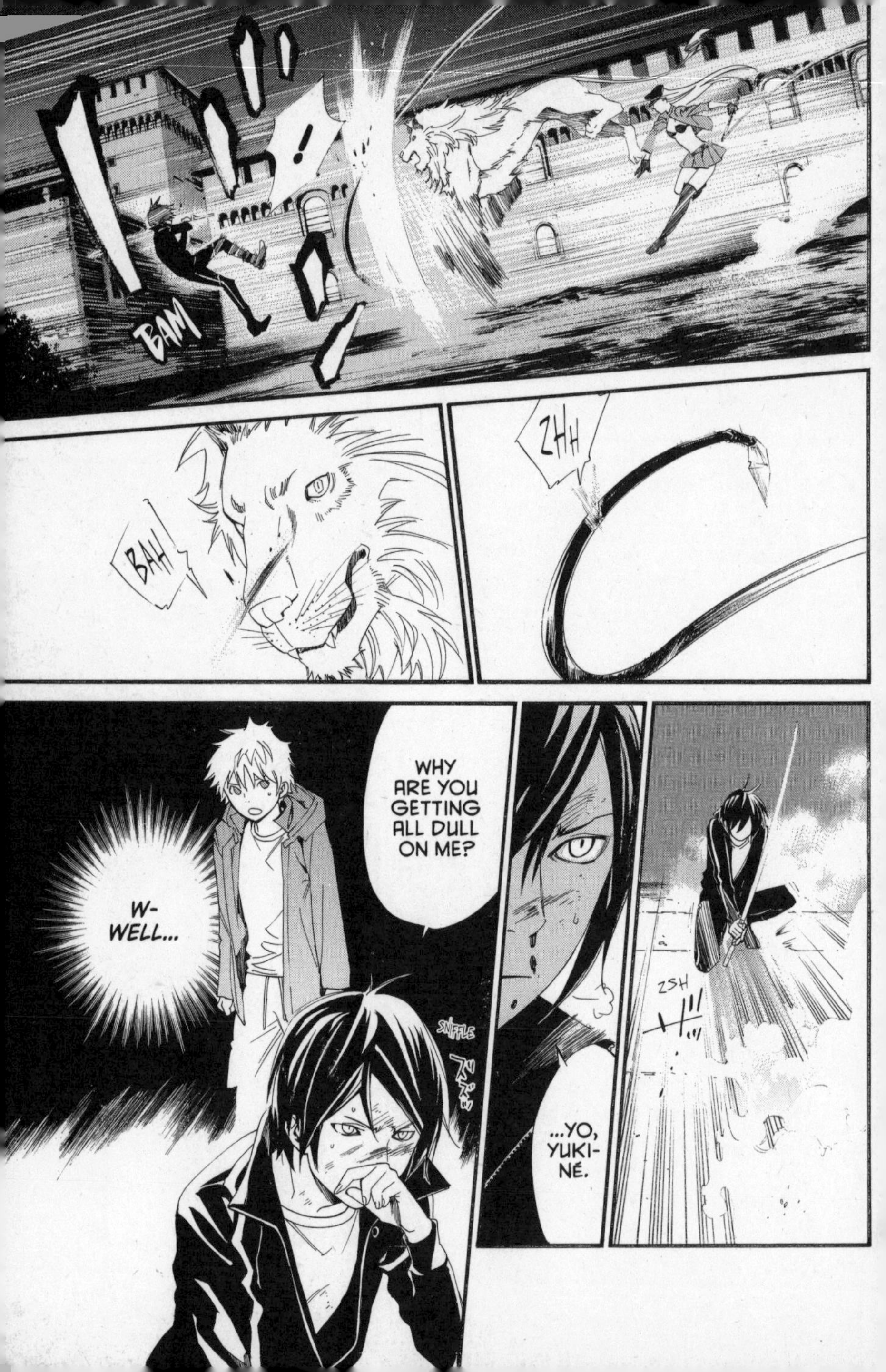
BAM
ZHH
BAH
ZSH
...YO, YUKI-NÉ.
WHY ARE YOU GETTING ALL DULL ON ME?
W-WELL...
SNIFFLE

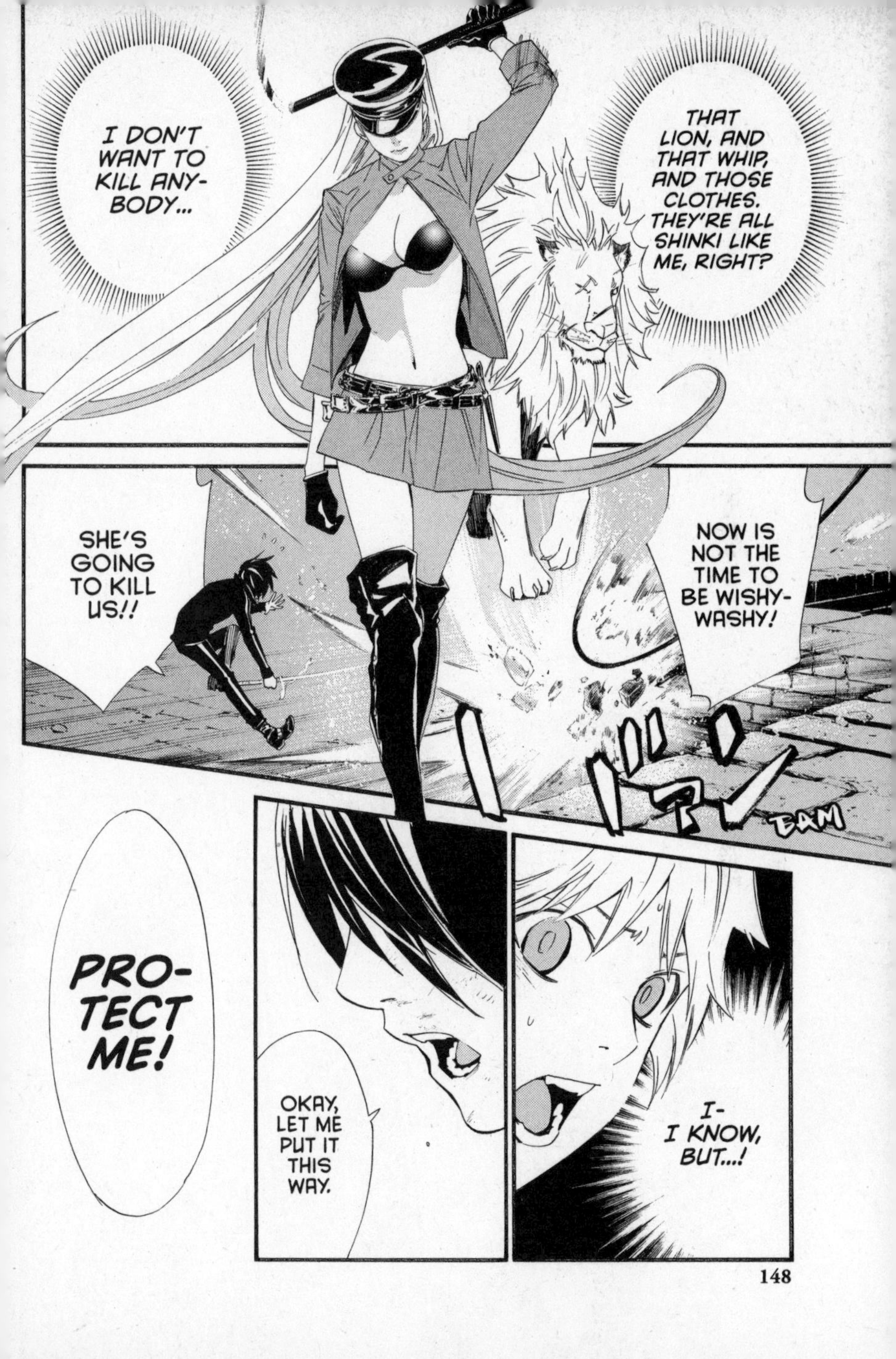
THAT LION, AND THAT WHIP, AND THOSE CLOTHES. THEY'RE ALL SHINKI LIKE ME, RIGHT?
I DON'T WANT TO KILL ANY-BODY...
NOW IS NOT THE TIME TO BE WISHY-WASHY!
SHE'S GOING TO KILL US!!
TAM
I- I KNOW, BUT...!
OKAY, LET ME PUT IT THIS WAY.
PRO-TECT ME!

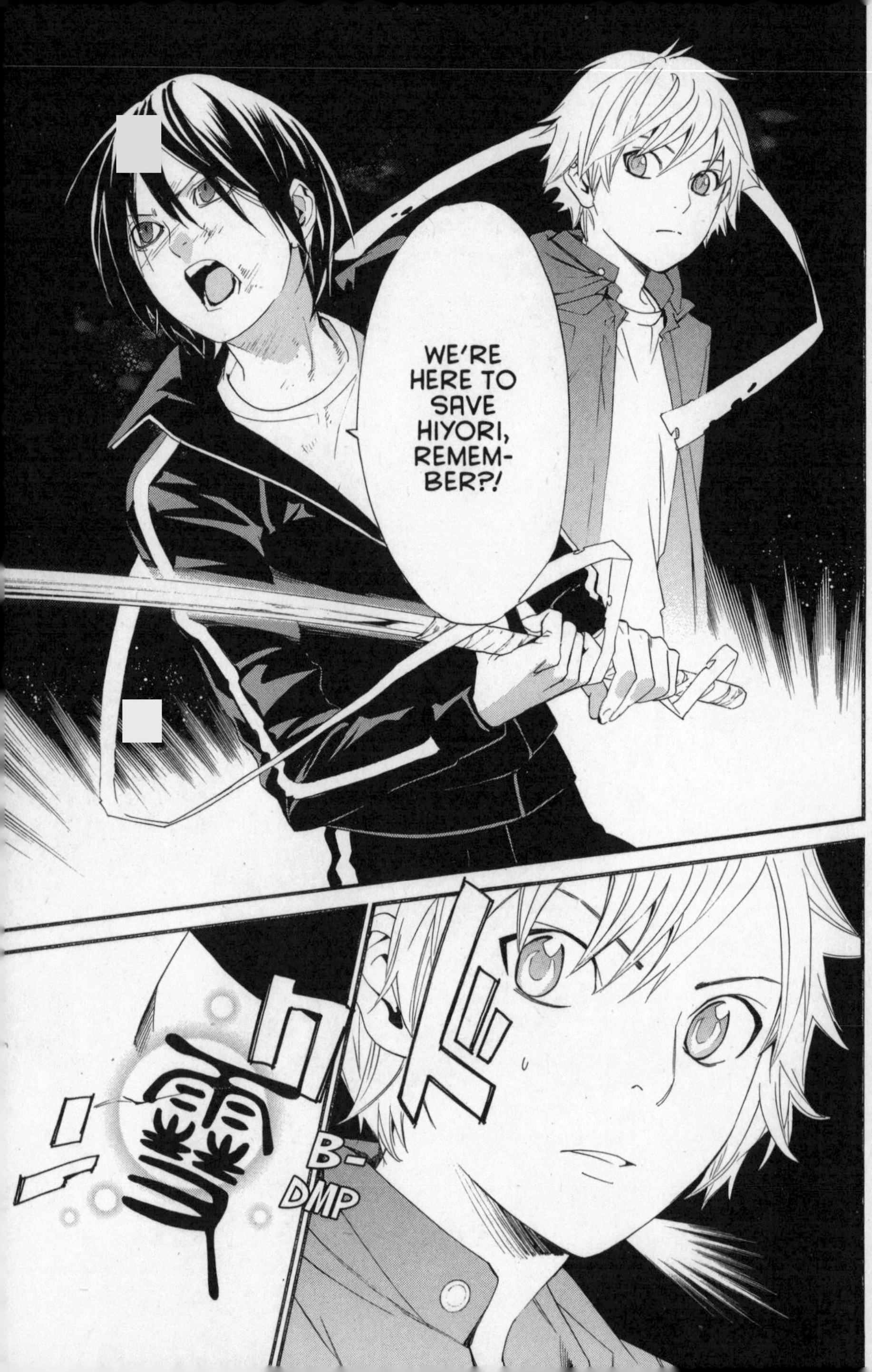
WE'RE HERE TO SAVE HIYORI, REMEM-BER?!
B-DMP

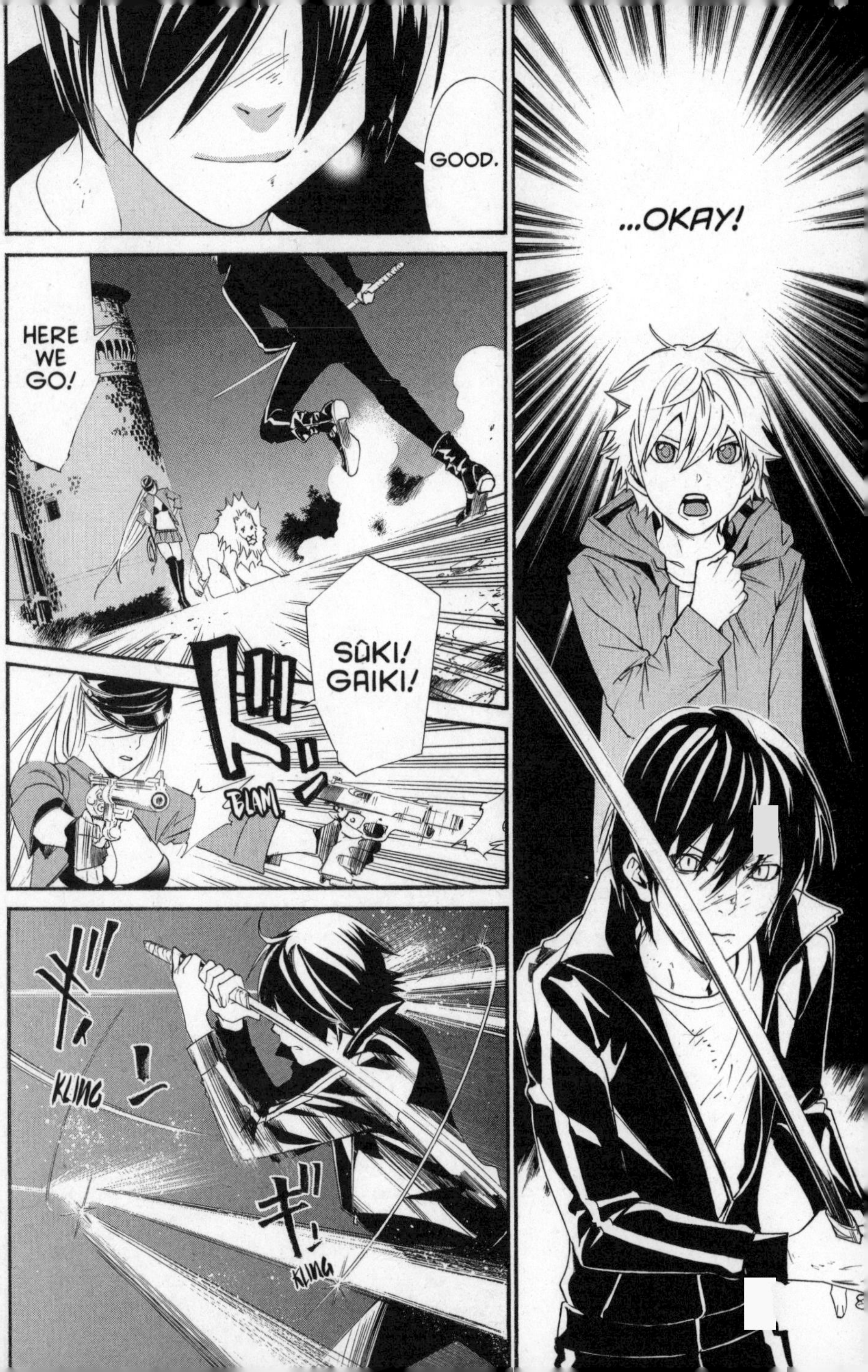
...OKAY!
GOOD.
HERE WE GO!
SÛKI! GAIKI!
BLAM
KLING
KLING

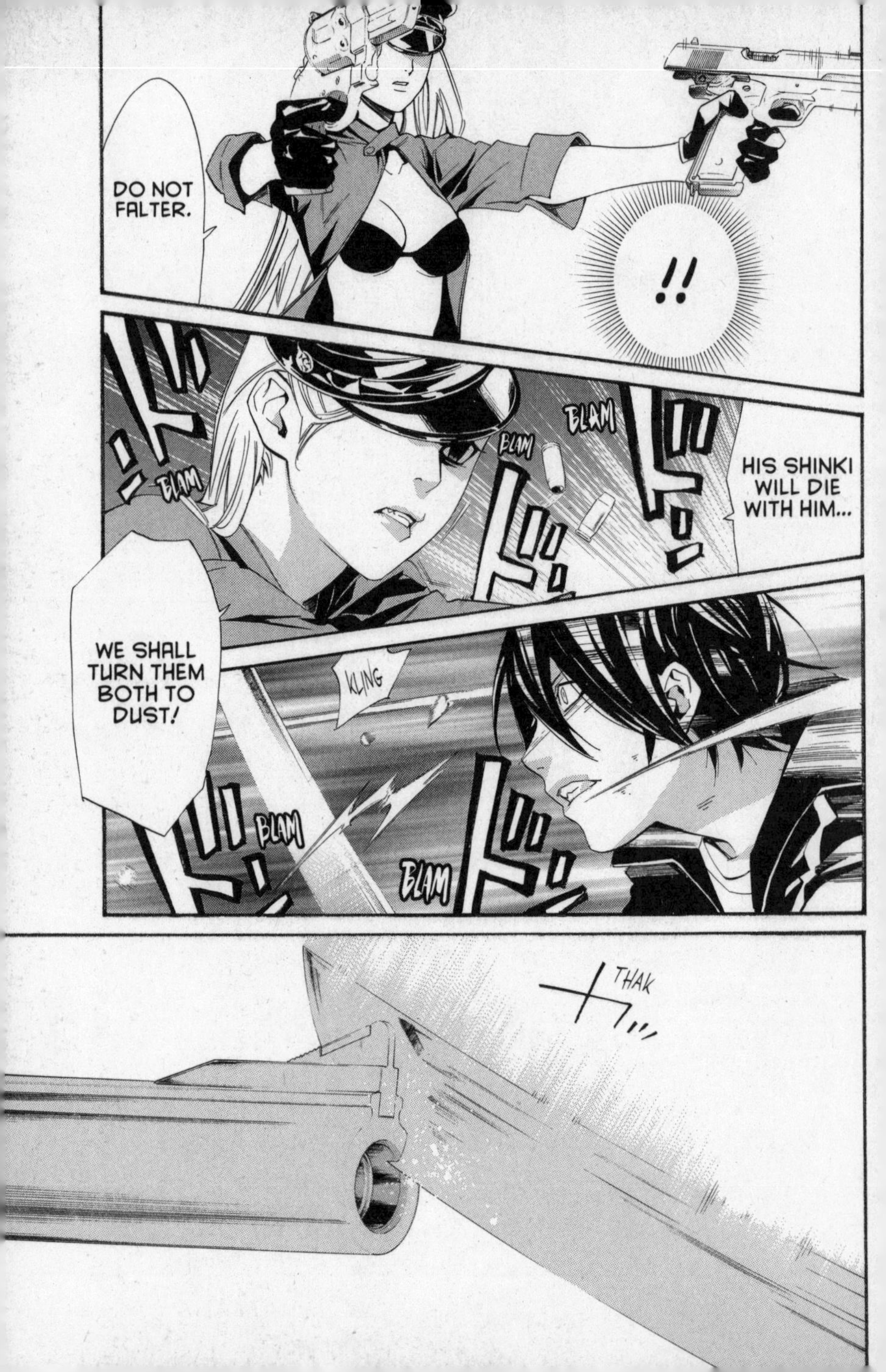
DO NOT FALTER.
!!
HIS SHINKI WILL DIE WITH HIM...
BLAM
BLAM
BLAM
WE SHALL TURN THEM BOTH TO DUST!
KLING
BLAM
BLAM
THAK

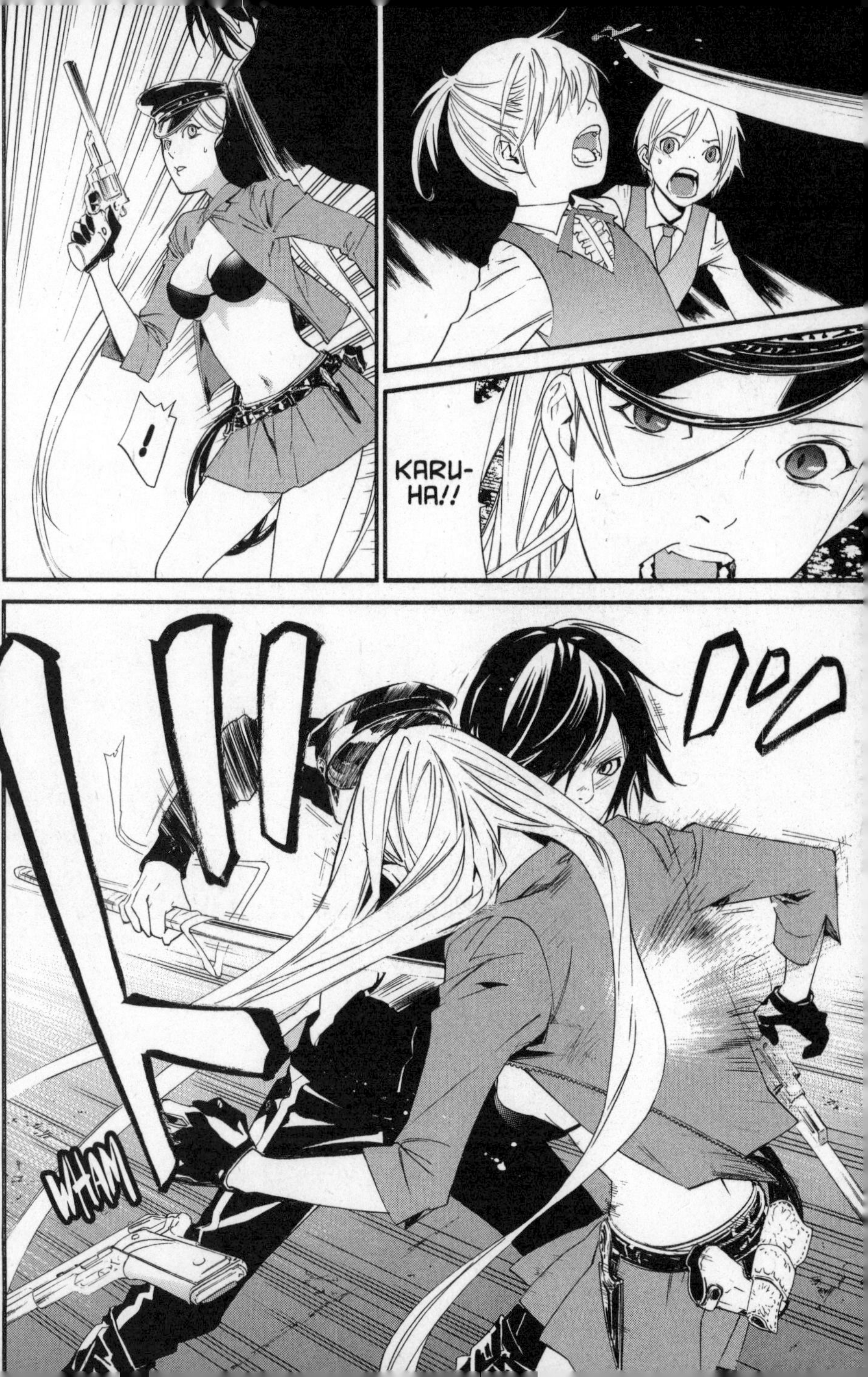
KARU-HA!!
!
WHAM

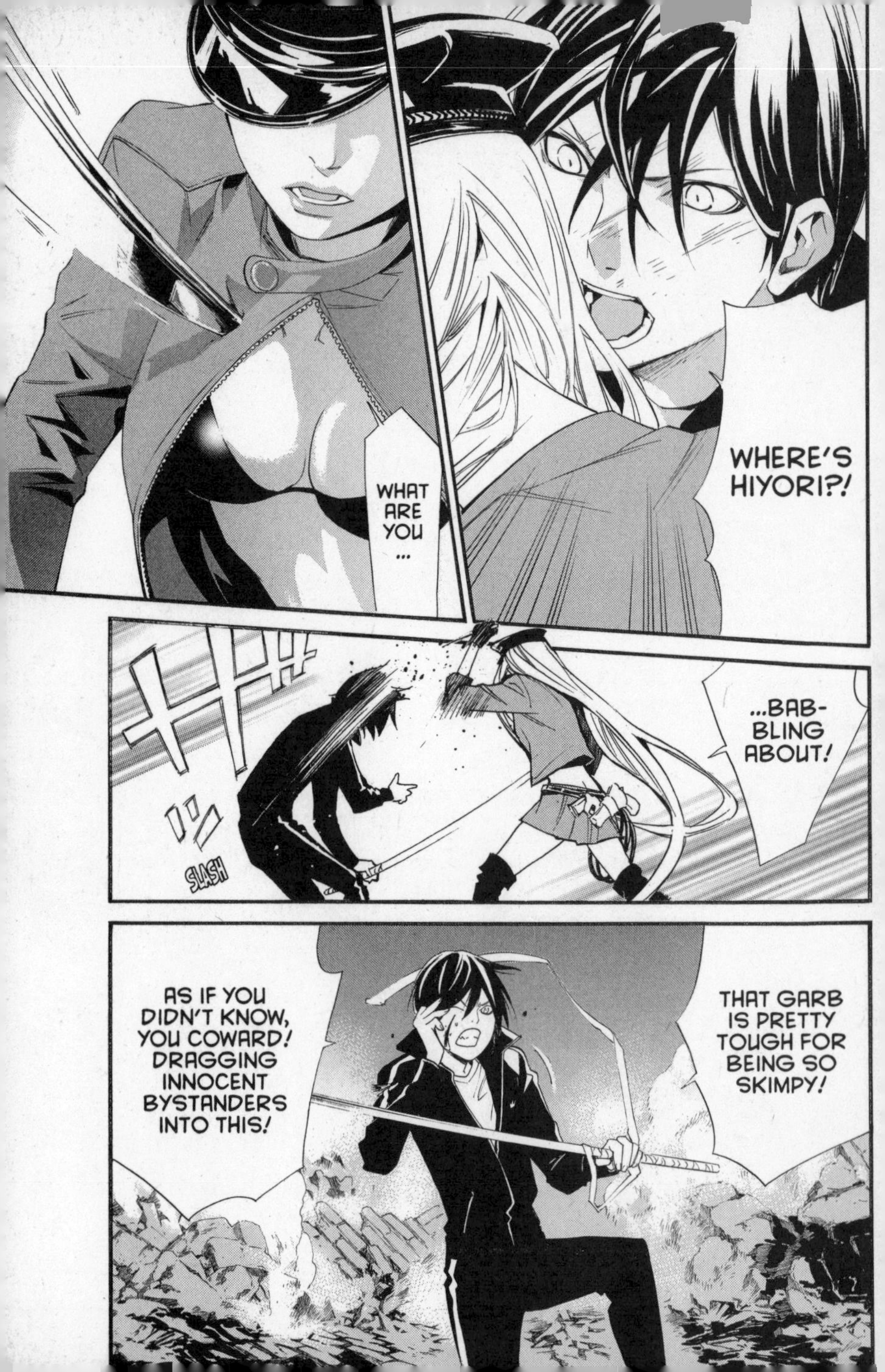
WHERE'S HIYORI?!
WHAT ARE YOU ...
...BAB-BLING ABOUT!
SLASH
THAT GARB IS PRETTY TOUGH FOR BEING SO SKIMPY!
AS IF YOU DIDN'T KNOW, YOU COWARD! DRAGGING INNOCENT BYSTANDERS INTO THIS!

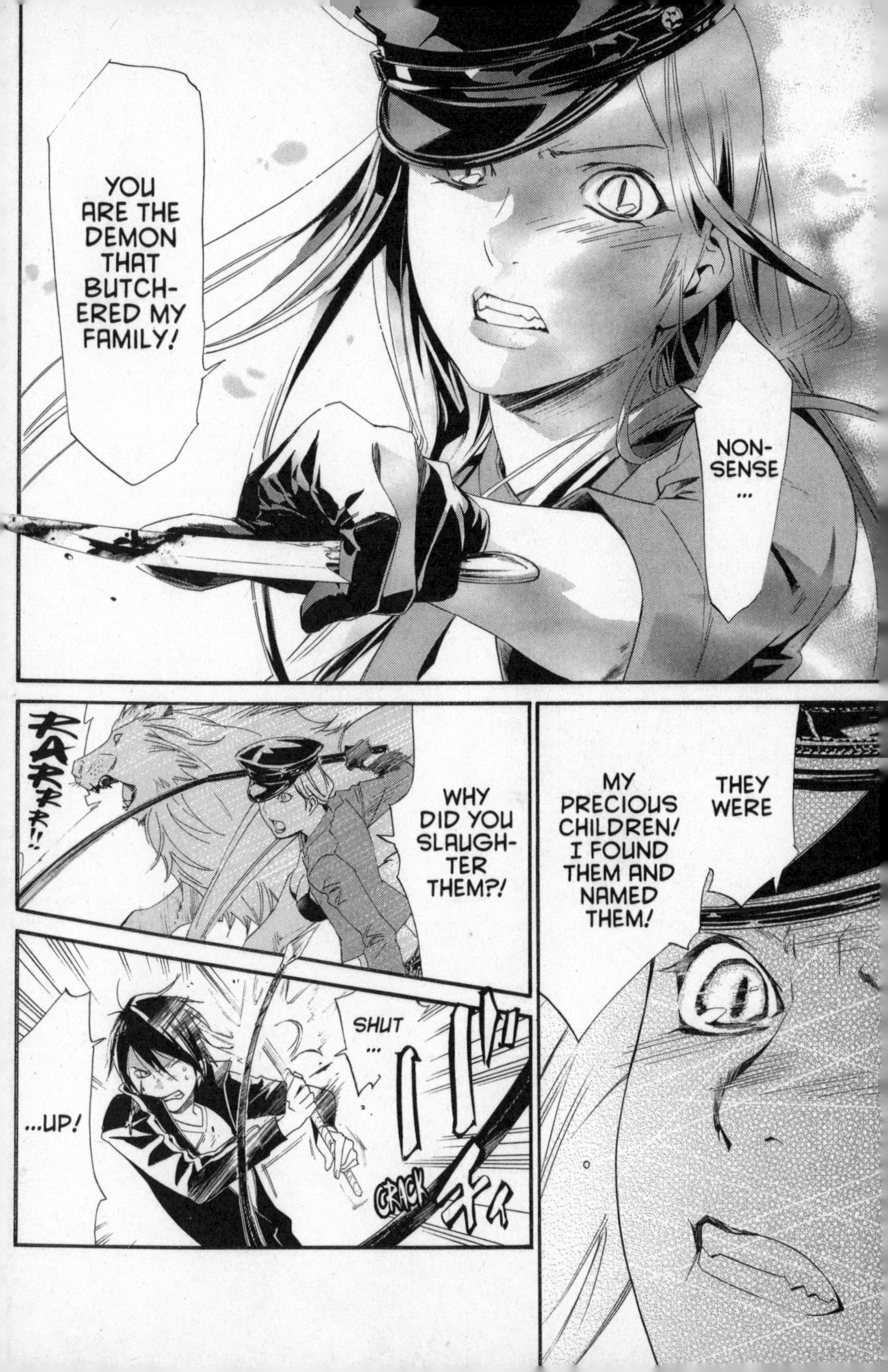
YOU ARE THE DEMON THAT BUTCHERED MY FAMILY!
NON-SENSE...
THEY WERE
MY PRECIOUS CHILDREN! I FOUND THEM AND NAMED THEM!
WHY DID YOU SLAUGHTER THEM?!
RARRR!!
SHUT...
...UP!
CRACK

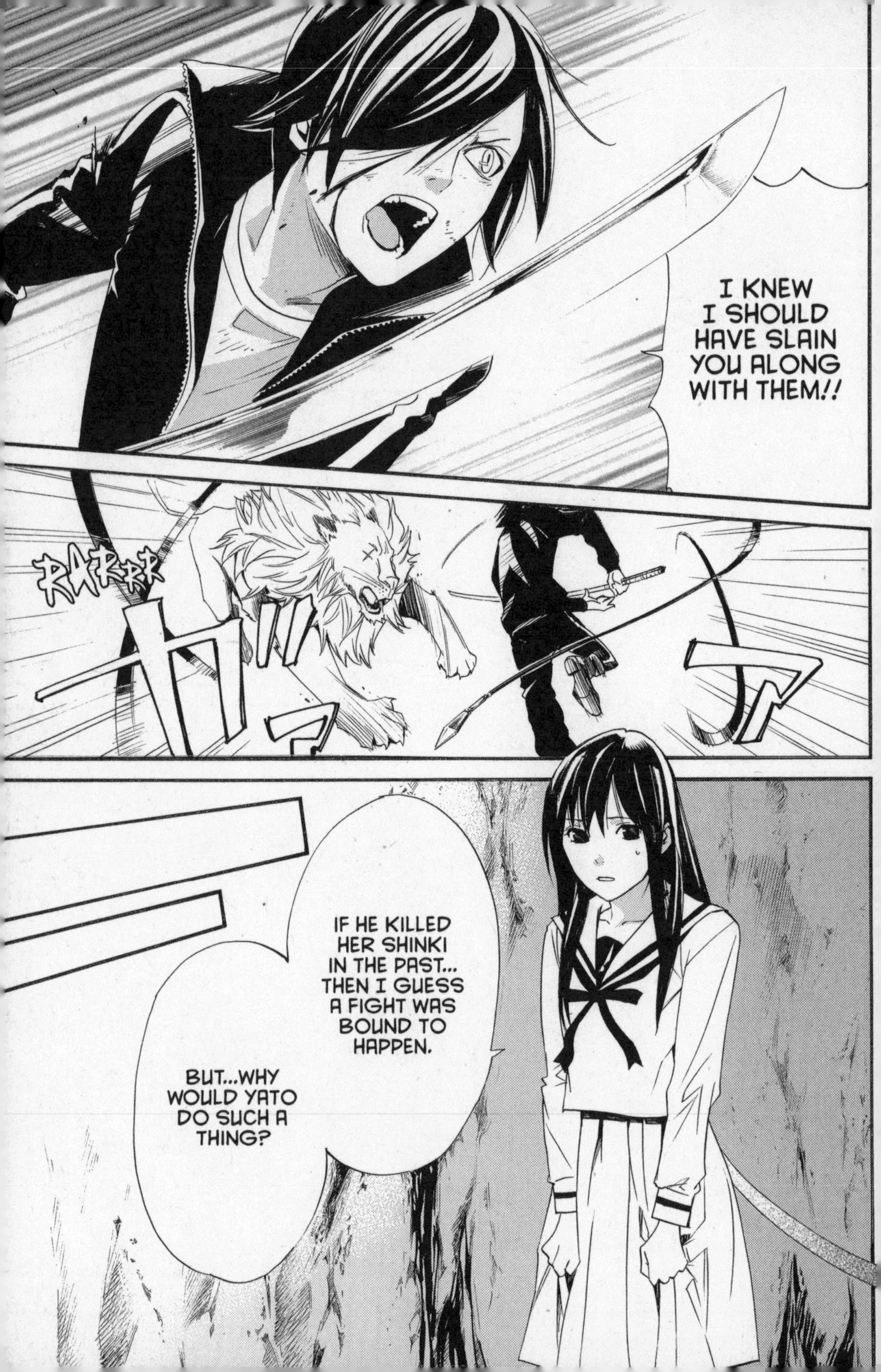
I KNEW I SHOULD HAVE SLAIN YOU ALONG WITH THEM!!
RARRR
IF HE KILLED HER SHINKI IN THE PAST... THEN I GUESS A FIGHT WAS BOUND TO HAPPEN.
BUT...WHY WOULD YATO DO SUCH A THING?

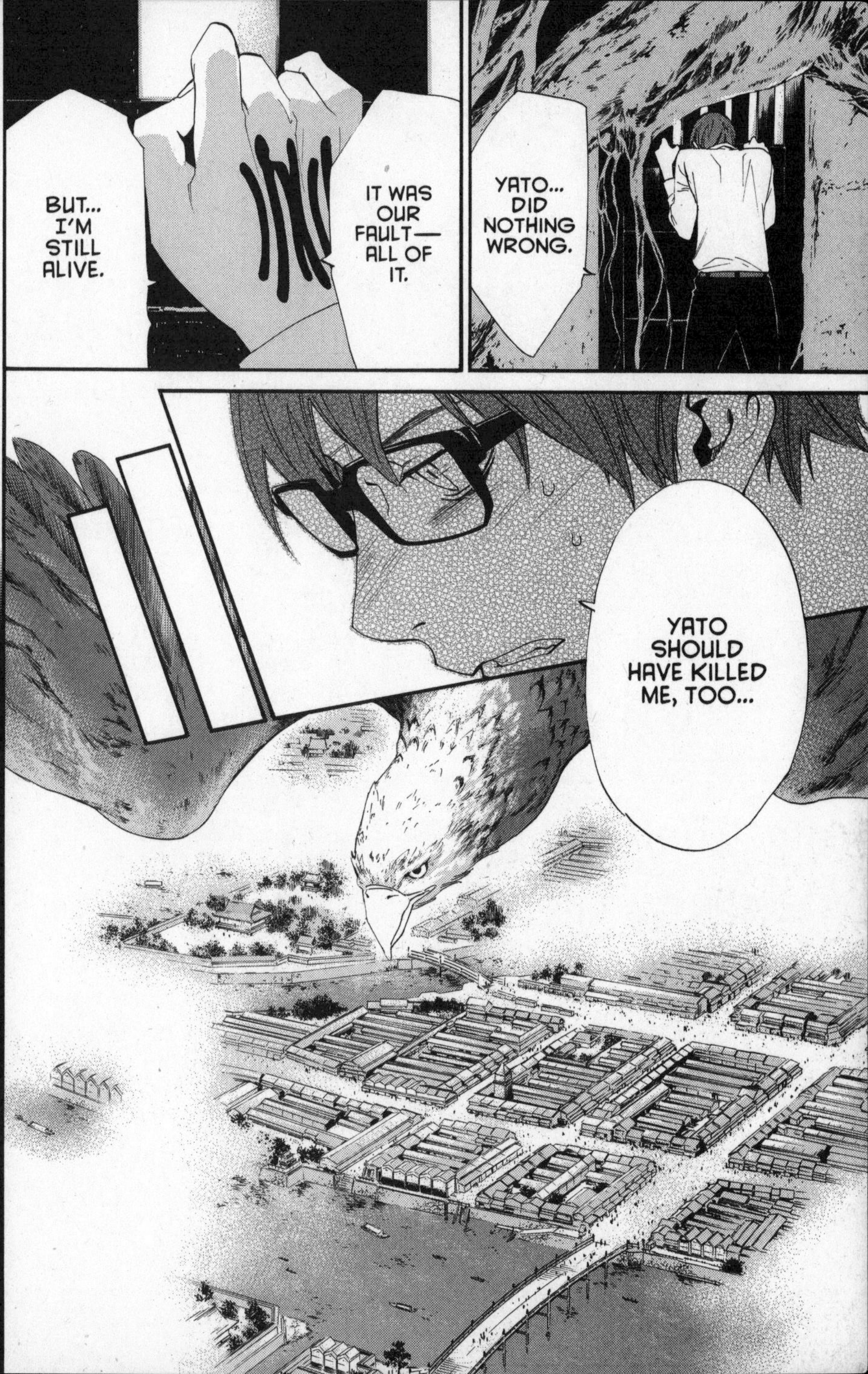
YATO... DID NOTHING WRONG.
IT WAS OUR FAULT— ALL OF IT.
BUT... I'M STILL ALIVE.
YATO SHOULD HAVE KILLED ME, TOO...

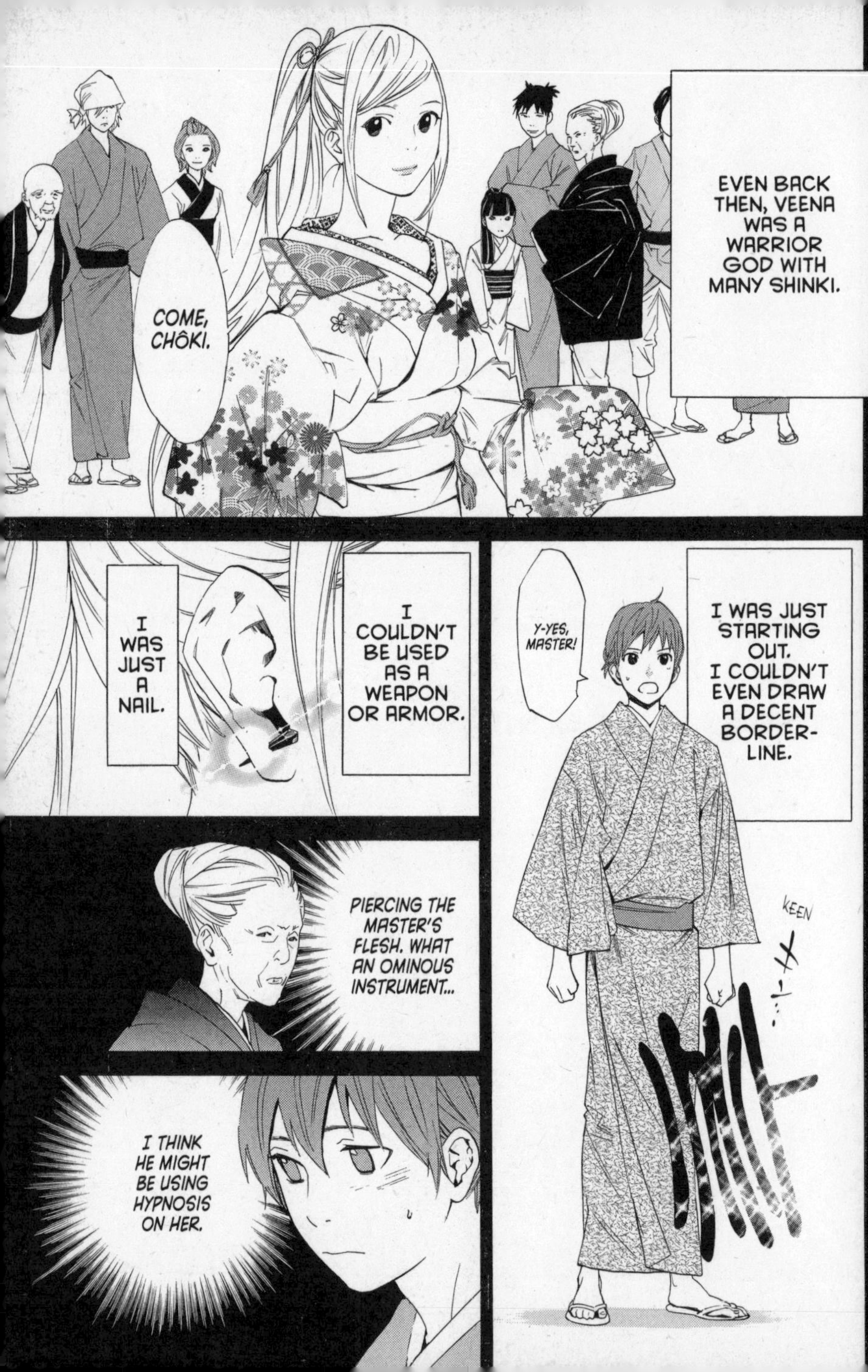
EVEN BACK THEN, VEENA WAS A WARRIOR GOD WITH MANY SHINKI.
COME, CHÔKI.
I WAS JUST STARTING OUT. I COULDN'T EVEN DRAW A DECENT BORDER-LINE.
Y-YES, MASTER!
KEEN
I COULDN'T BE USED AS A WEAPON OR ARMOR.
I WAS JUST A NAIL.
PIERCING THE MASTER'S FLESH. WHAT AN OMINOUS INSTRUMENT...
I THINK HE MIGHT BE USING HYPNOSIS ON HER.

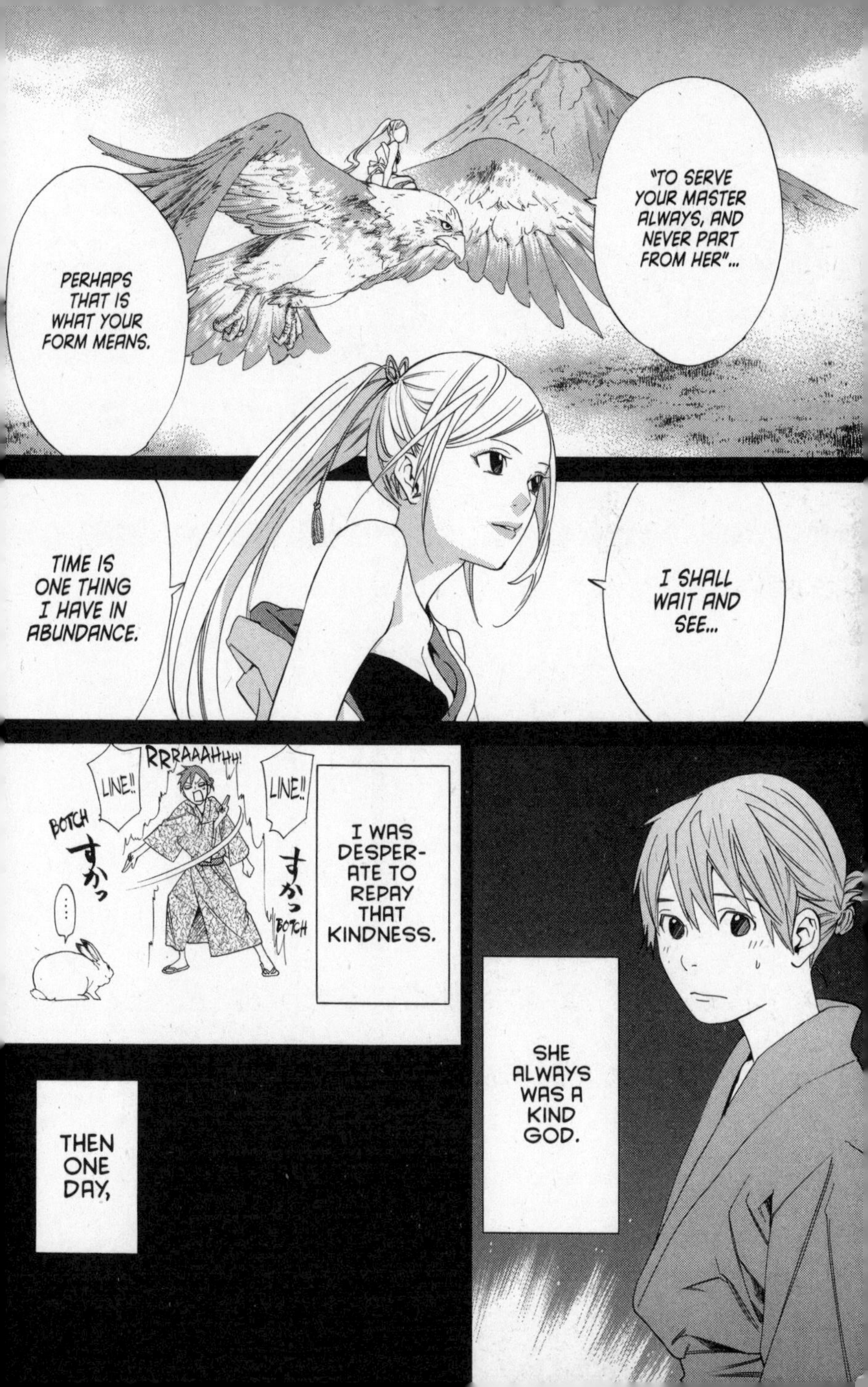
"TO SERVE YOUR MASTER ALWAYS, AND NEVER PART FROM HER"...
PERHAPS THAT IS WHAT YOUR FORM MEANS.
I SHALL WAIT AND SEE...
TIME IS ONE THING I HAVE IN ABUNDANCE.
SHE ALWAYS WAS A KIND GOD.
I WAS DESPERATE TO REPAY THAT KINDNESS.
LINE!!
RRAAAHHH!
LINE!!
すかっ
BOTCH
すかっ
BOTCH
...
THEN ONE DAY,

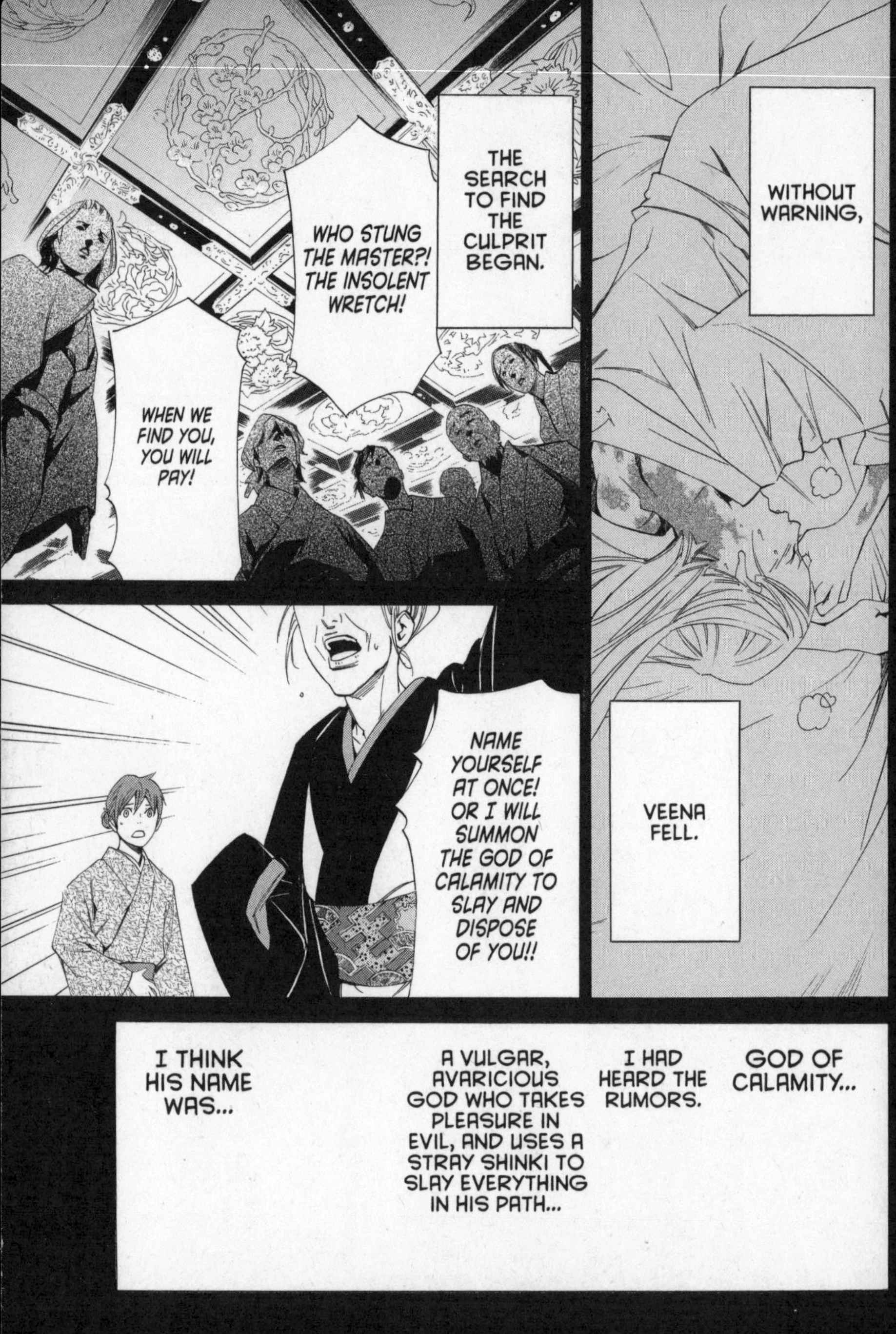
WITHOUT WARNING,
VEENA FELL.
THE SEARCH TO FIND THE CULPRIT BEGAN.
WHO STUNG THE MASTER?! THE INSOLENT WRETCH!
WHEN WE FIND YOU, YOU WILL PAY!
NAME YOURSELF AT ONCE! OR I WILL SUMMON THE GOD OF CALAMITY TO SLAY AND DISPOSE OF YOU!!
GOD OF CALAMITY...
I HAD HEARD THE RUMORS.
A VULGAR, AVARICIOUS GOD WHO TAKES PLEASURE IN EVIL, AND USES A STRAY SHINKI TO SLAY EVERYTHING IN HIS PATH...
I THINK HIS NAME WAS...

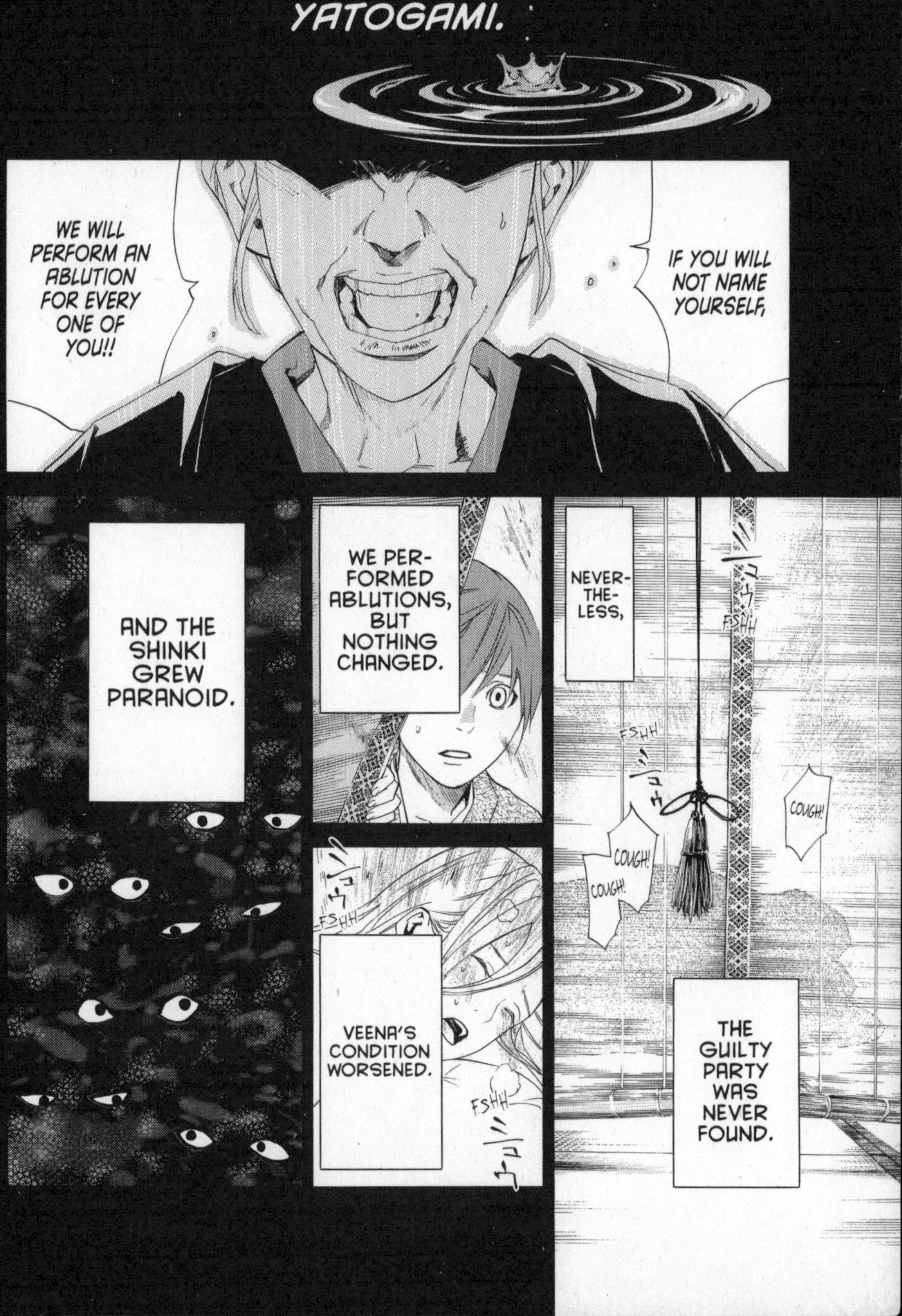
YATOGAMI.
IF YOU WILL NOT NAME YOURSELF,
WE WILL PERFORM AN ABLUTION FOR EVERY ONE OF YOU!!
NEVER-THE-LESS,
FSHH
FSHH
COUGH!
COUGH!
COUGH!
THE GUILTY PARTY WAS NEVER FOUND.
WE PER-FORMED ABLUTIONS, BUT NOTHING CHANGED.
FSHH
VEENA'S CONDITION WORSENED.
FSHH
AND THE SHINKI GREW PARANOID.

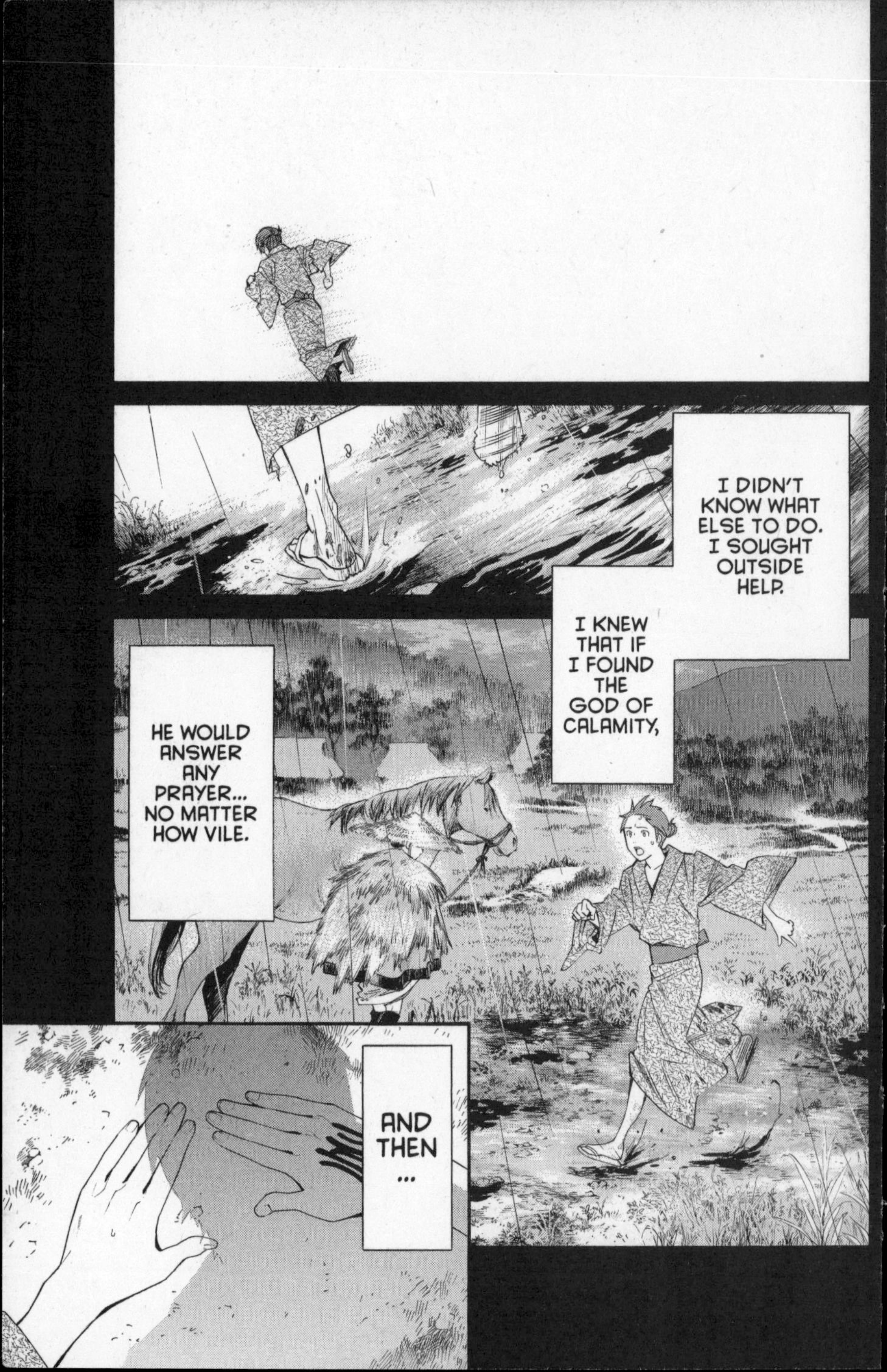
I DIDN'T KNOW WHAT ELSE TO DO. I SOUGHT OUTSIDE HELP.
I KNEW THAT IF I FOUND THE GOD OF CALAMITY,
HE WOULD ANSWER ANY PRAYER... NO MATTER HOW VILE.
AND THEN ...

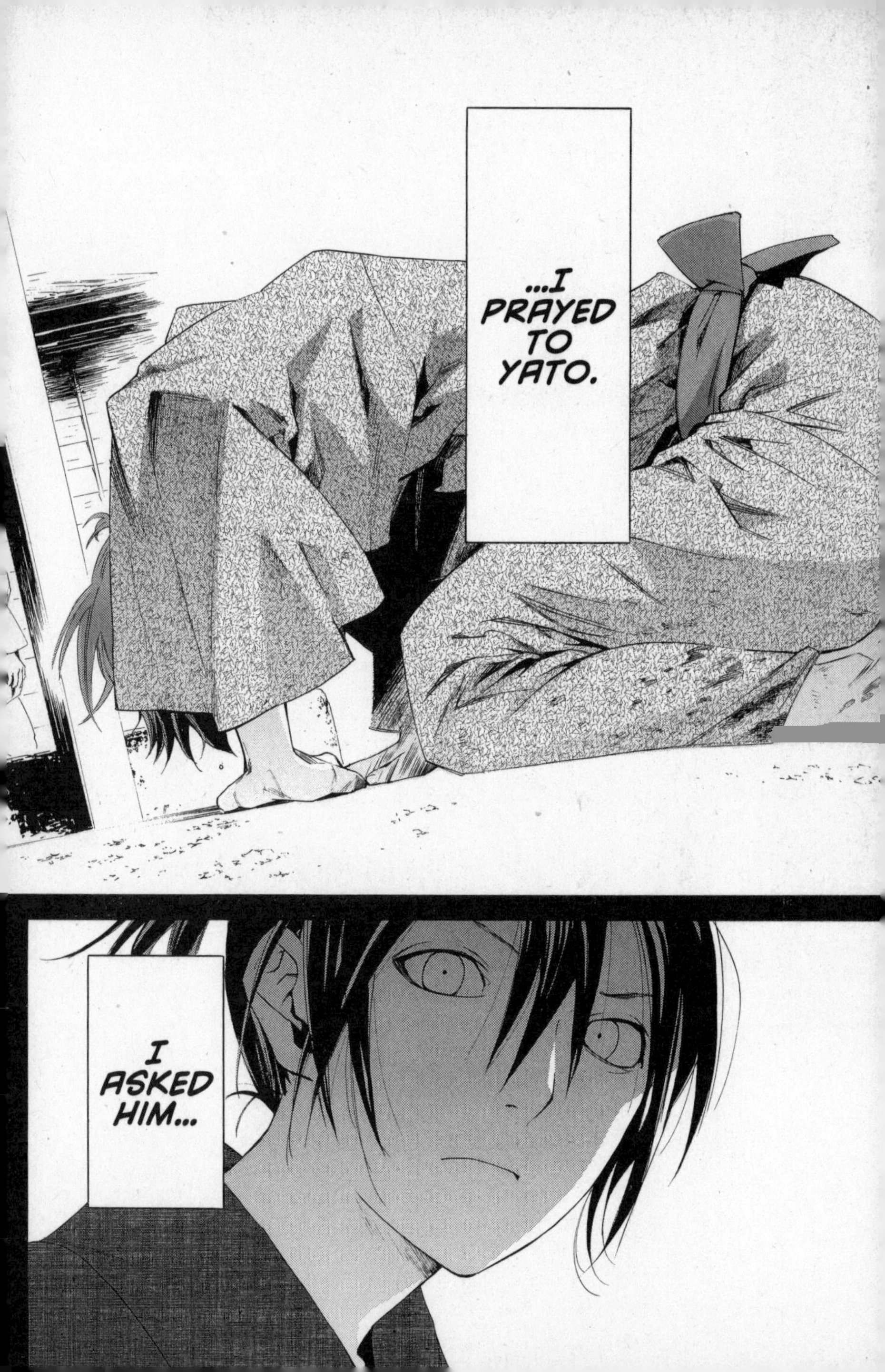
...I PRAYED TO YATO.
I ASKED HIM...

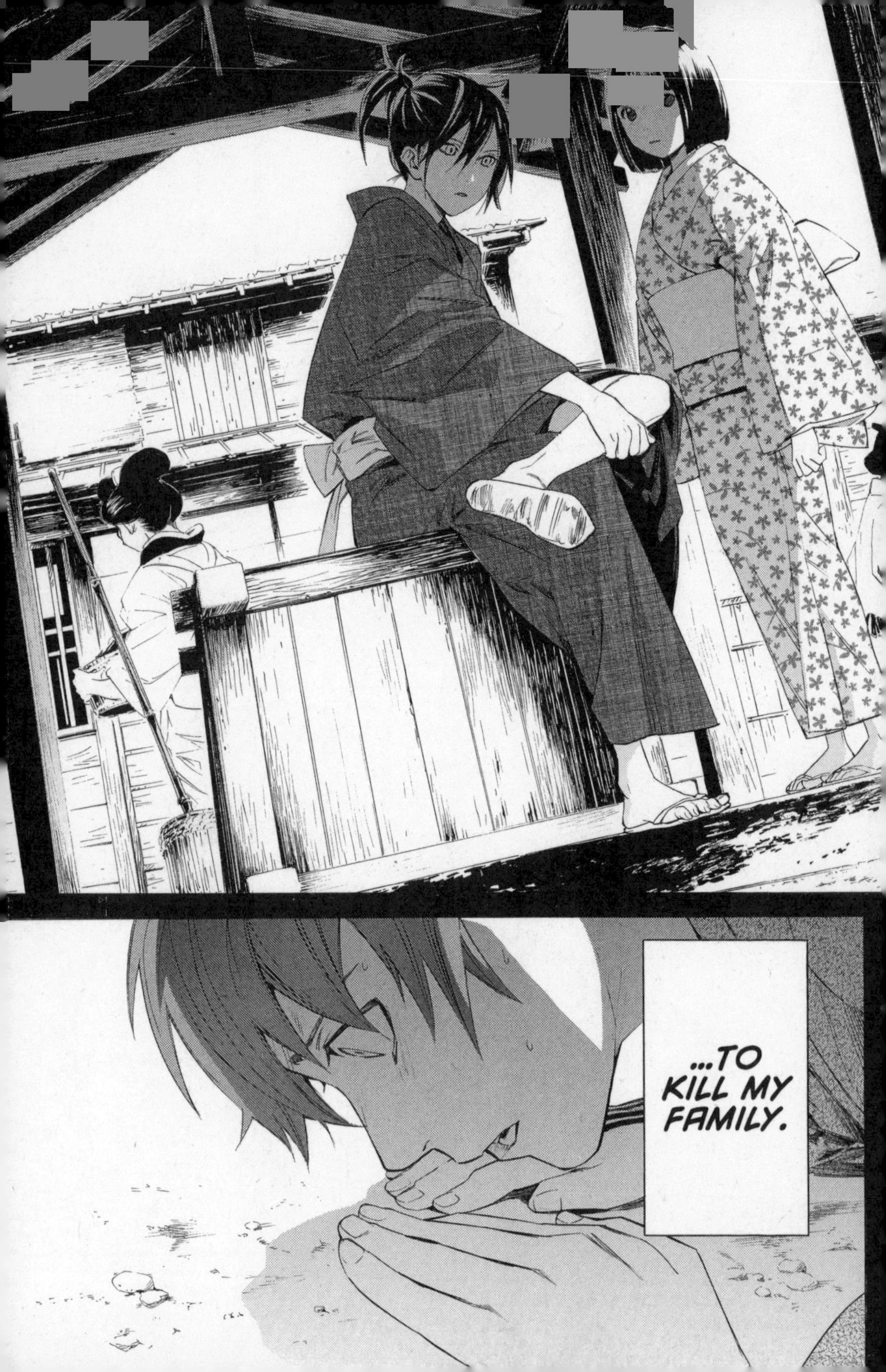
...TO KILL MY FAMILY.

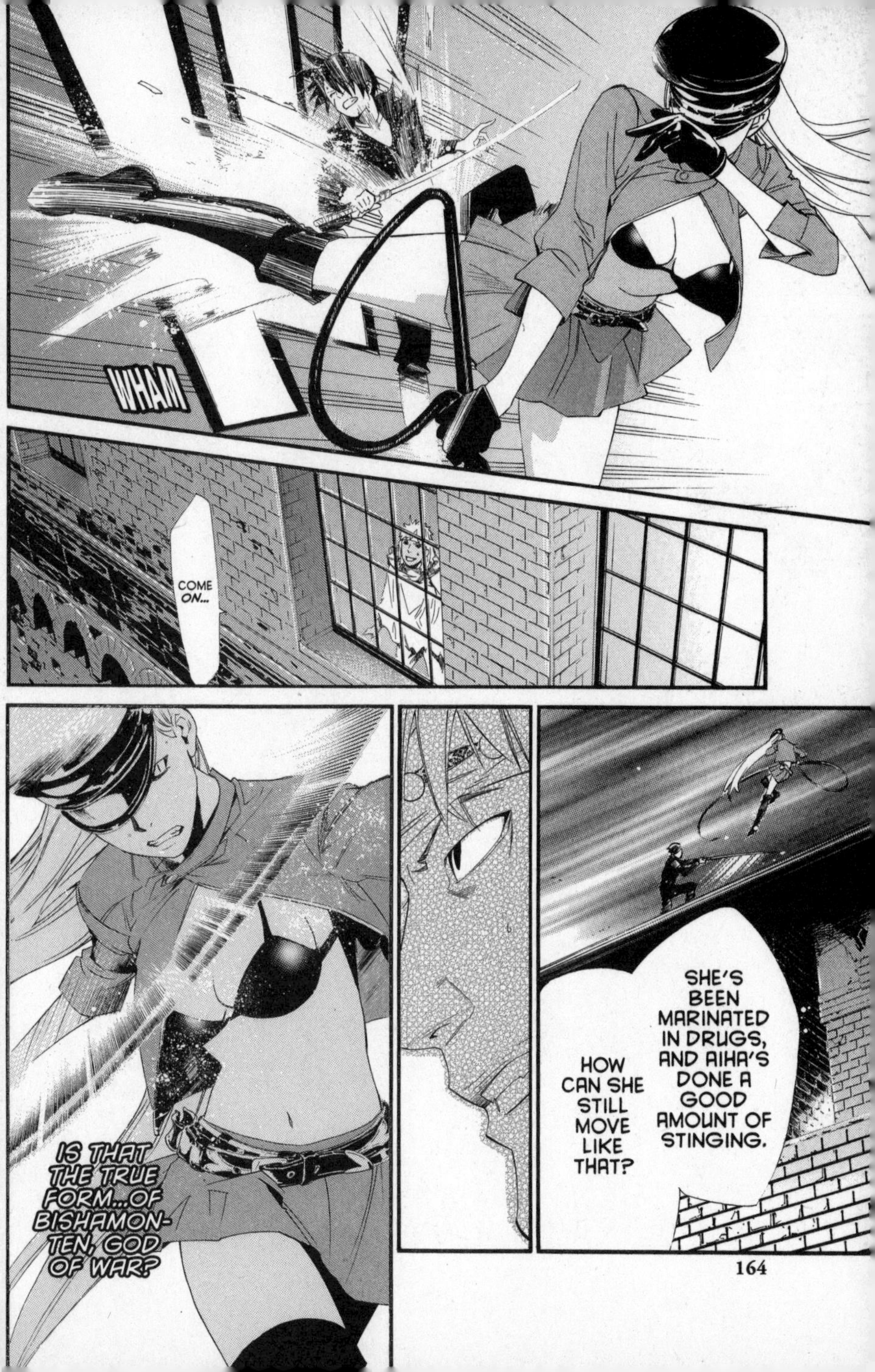
WHAM
COME ON...
SHE'S BEEN MARINATED IN DRUGS, AND AIHA'S DONE A GOOD AMOUNT OF STINGING.
HOW CAN SHE STILL MOVE LIKE THAT?
IS THAT THE TRUE FORM...OF BISHAMON-TEN, GOD OF WAR?

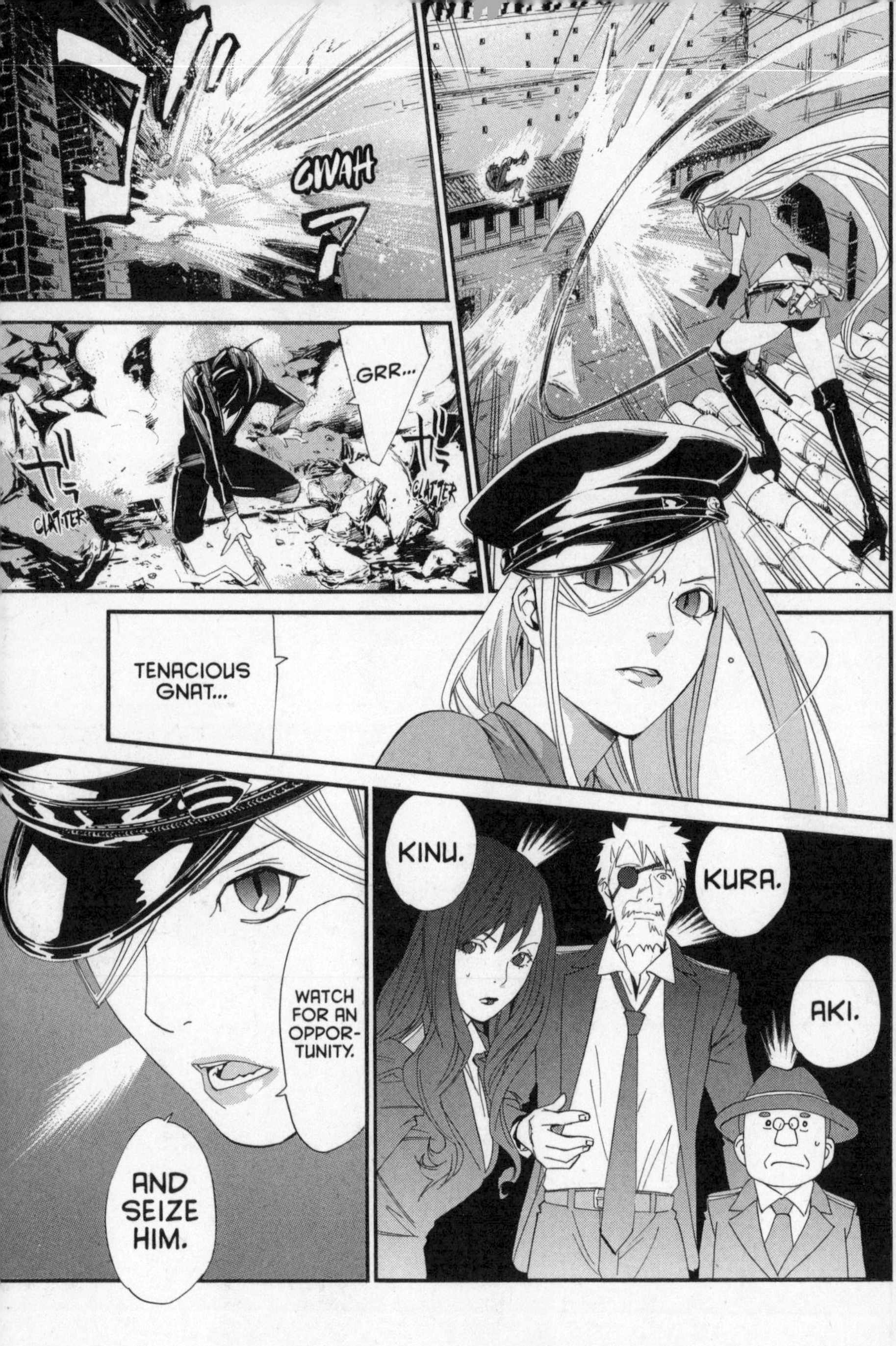
GWAH
GRR...
CLATTER
CLATTER
TENACIOUS GNAT...
KINU.
KURA.
AKI.
WATCH FOR AN OPPOR-TUNITY.
AND SEIZE HIM.

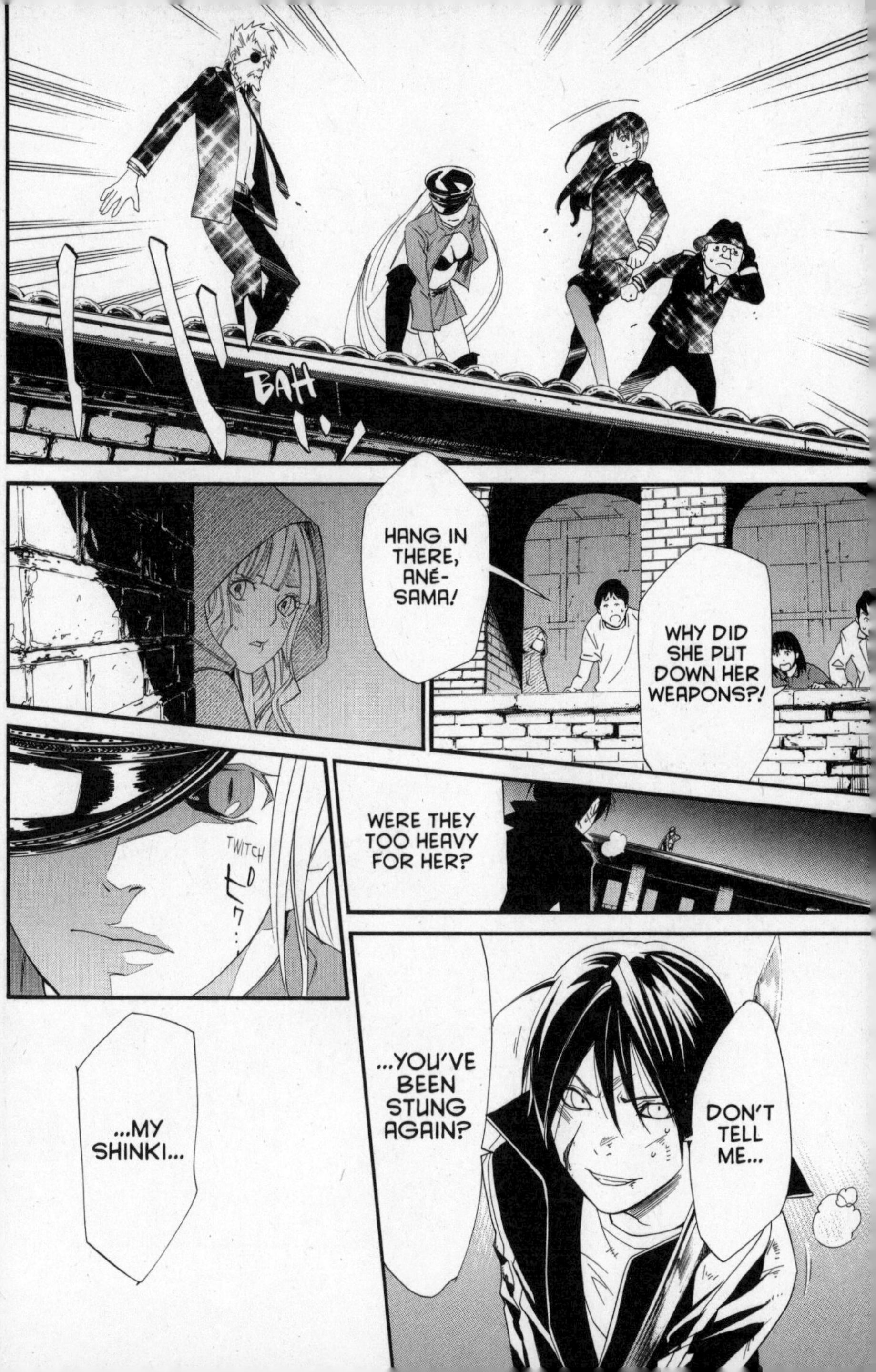
BAH
HANG IN THERE, ANÉ-SAMA!
WHY DID SHE PUT DOWN HER WEAPONS?!
WERE THEY TOO HEAVY FOR HER?
TWITCH
DON'T TELL ME...
...YOU'VE BEEN STUNG AGAIN?
...MY SHINKI...

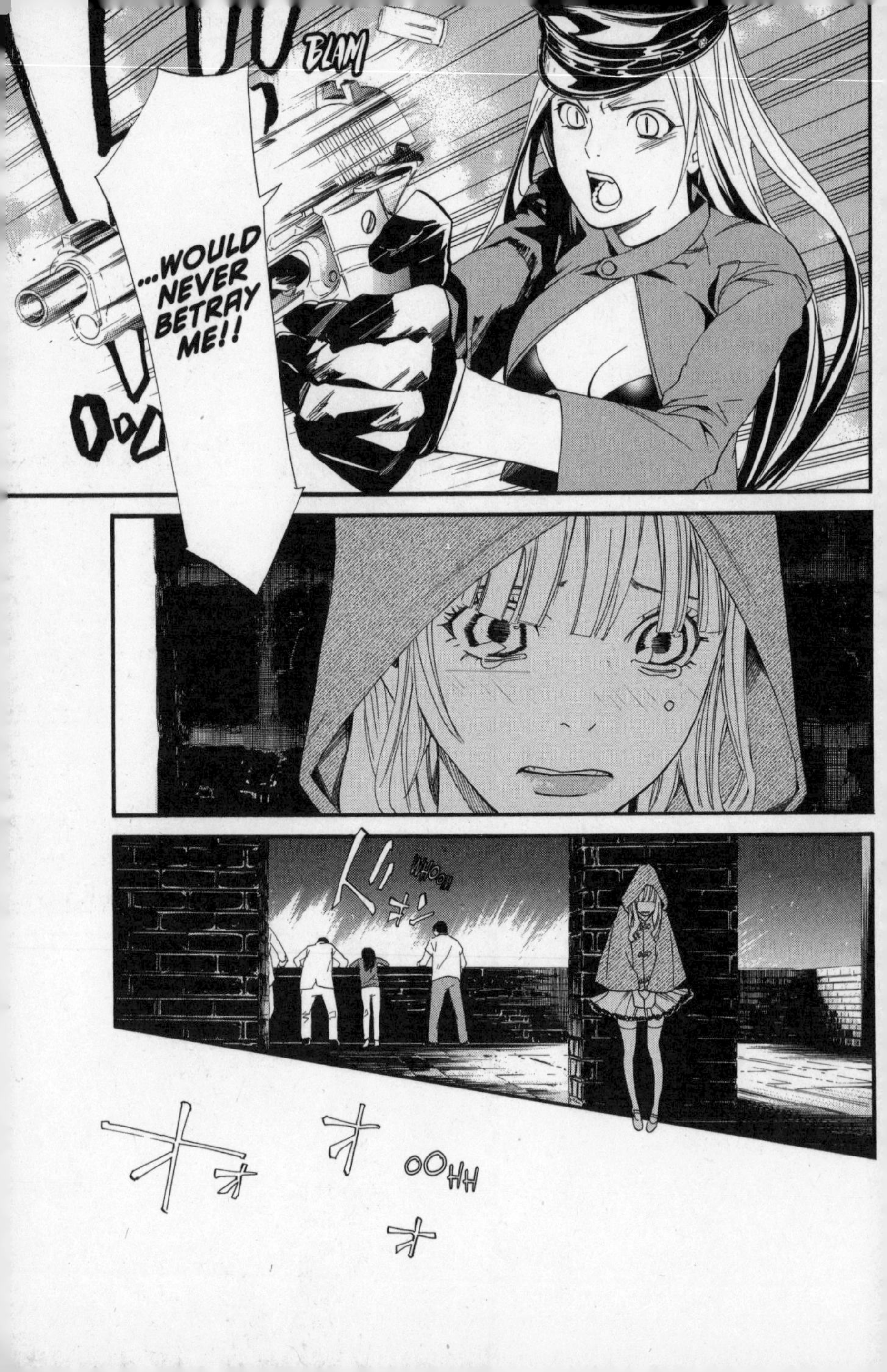
BLAM
...WOULD NEVER BETRAY ME!!
WHOO!!
OOHH

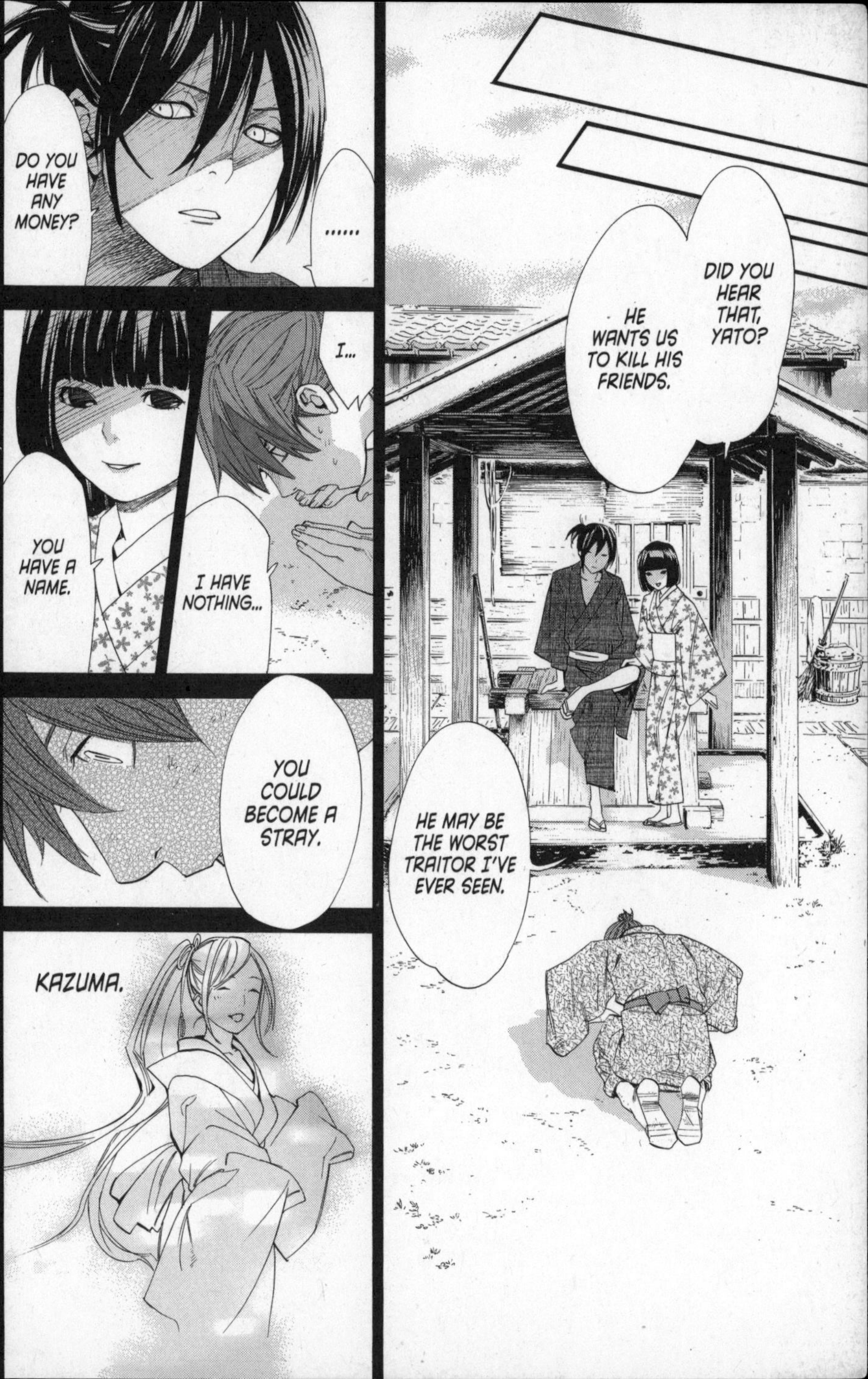
DID YOU HEAR THAT, YATO?
HE WANTS US TO KILL HIS FRIENDS.
HE MAY BE THE WORST TRAITOR I'VE EVER SEEN.
DO YOU HAVE ANY MONEY?
......
I...
I HAVE NOTHING...
YOU HAVE A NAME.
YOU COULD BECOME A STRAY.
KAZUMA.

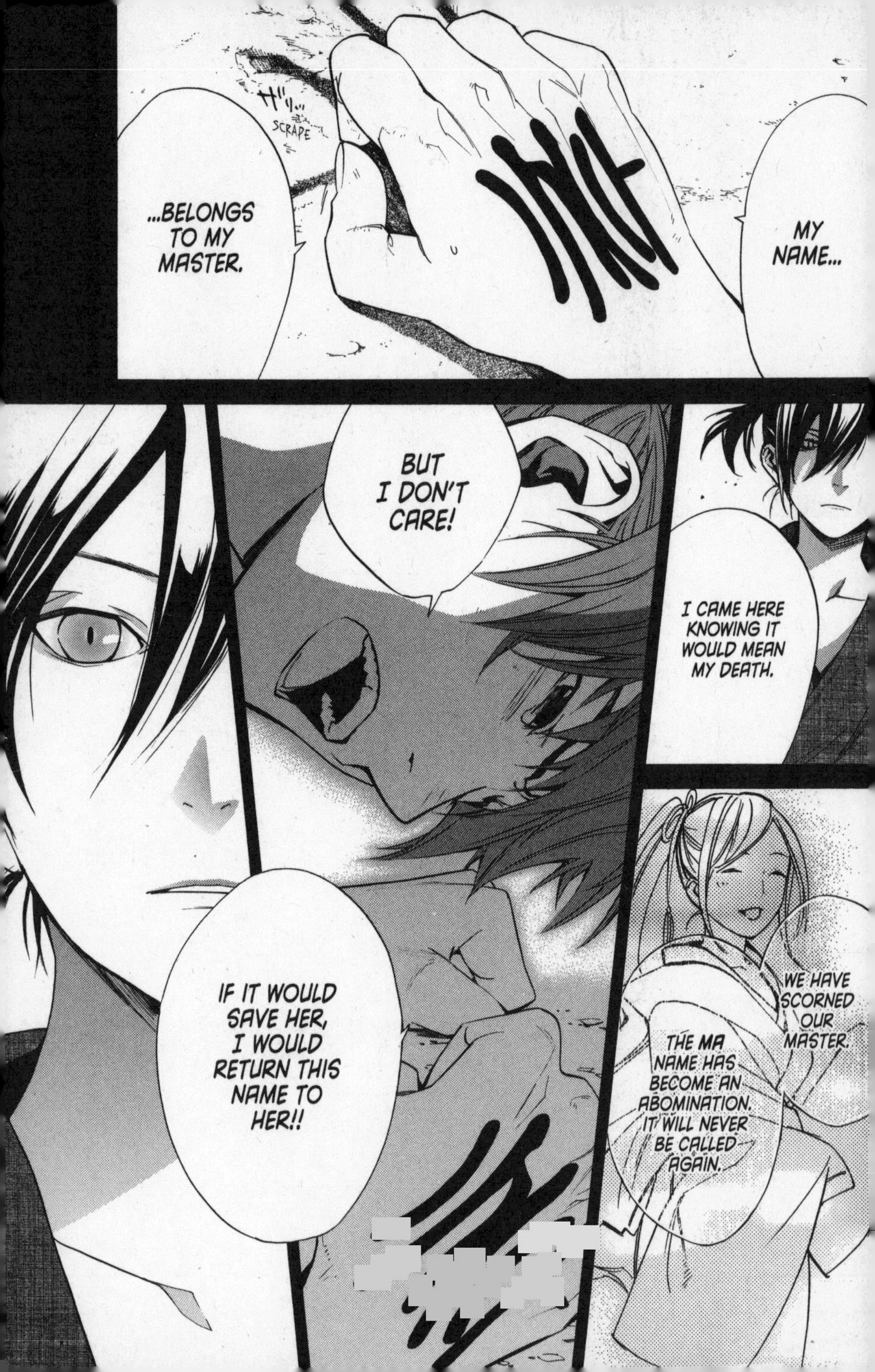
MY NAME...
SCRAPE
...BELONGS TO MY MASTER.
I CAME HERE KNOWING IT WOULD MEAN MY DEATH.
WE HAVE SCORNED OUR MASTER.
THE MA NAME HAS BECOME AN ABOMINATION. IT WILL NEVER BE CALLED AGAIN.
BUT I DON'T CARE!
IF IT WOULD SAVE HER, I WOULD RETURN THIS NAME TO HER!!

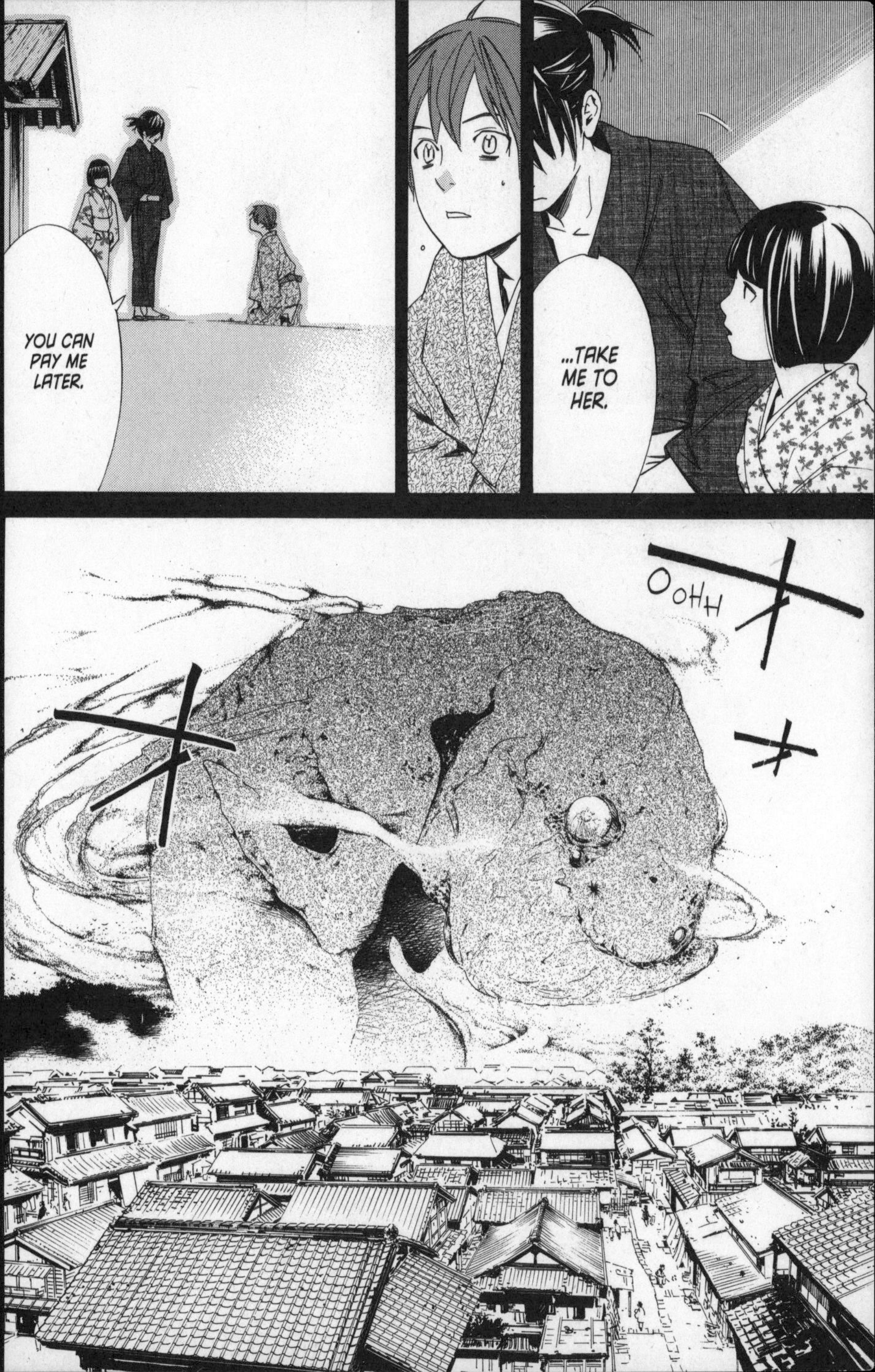
...TAKE ME TO HER.
YOU CAN PAY ME LATER.
OOHH

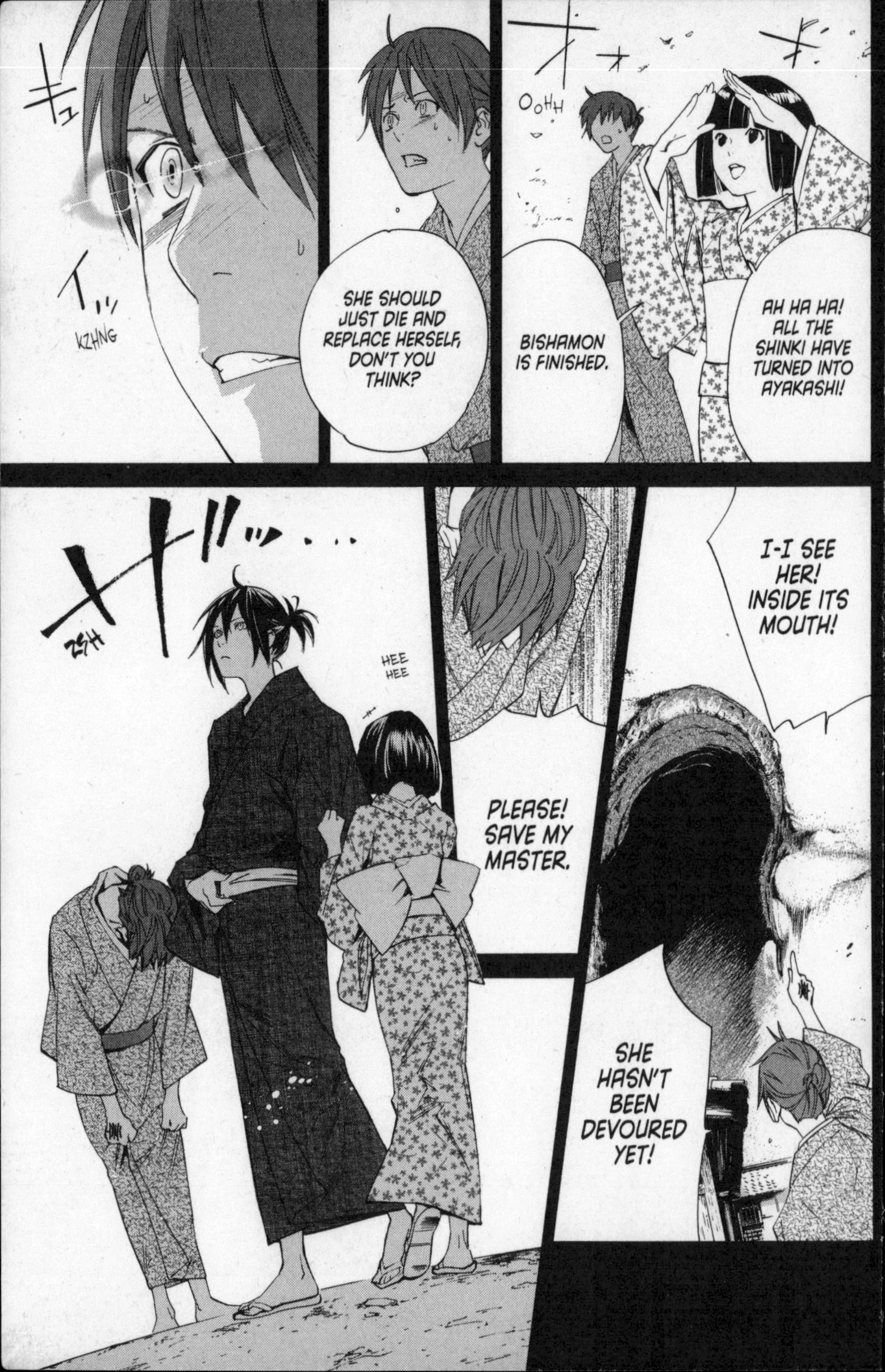
OOHH
AH HA HA! ALL THE SHINKI HAVE TURNED INTO AYAKASHI!
BISHAMON IS FINISHED.
SHE SHOULD JUST DIE AND REPLACE HERSELF, DON'T YOU THINK?
KZHNG
I-I SEE HER! INSIDE ITS MOUTH!
SHE HASN'T BEEN DEVOURED YET!
PLEASE! SAVE MY MASTER.
HEE HEE
ZSH

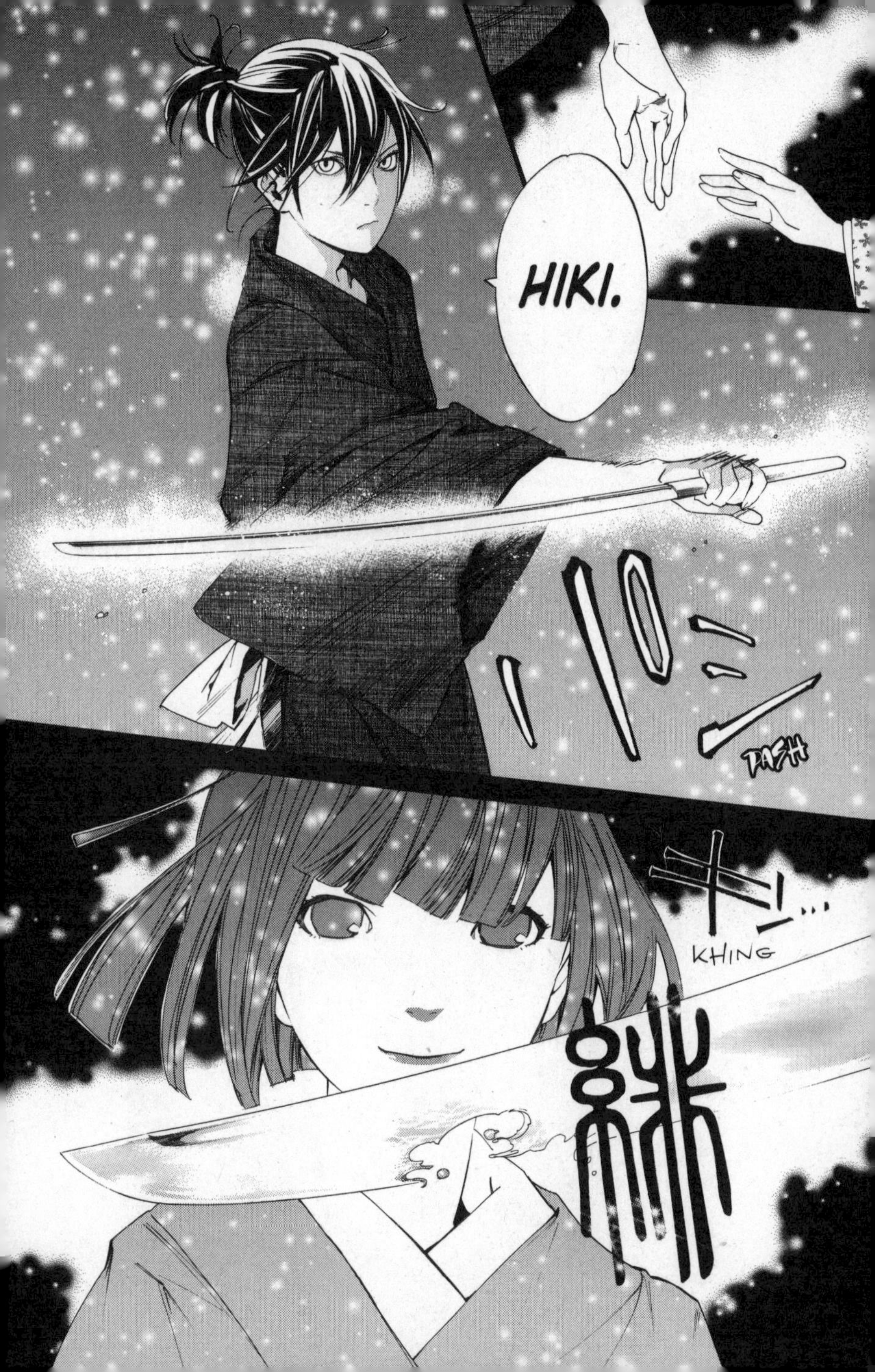
HIKI.
DASH
KHING

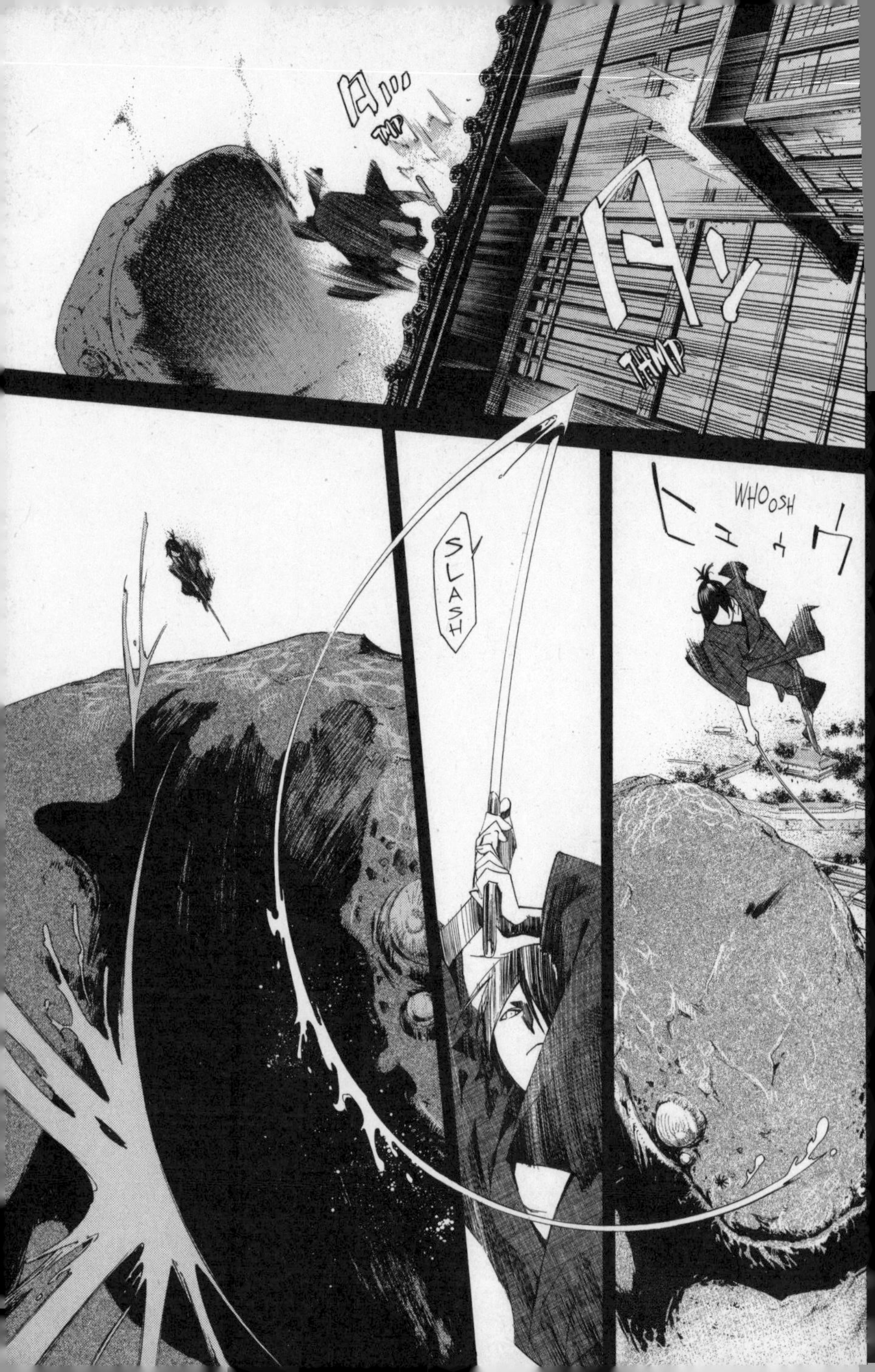
THMP
THMP
WHOOSH
SLASH

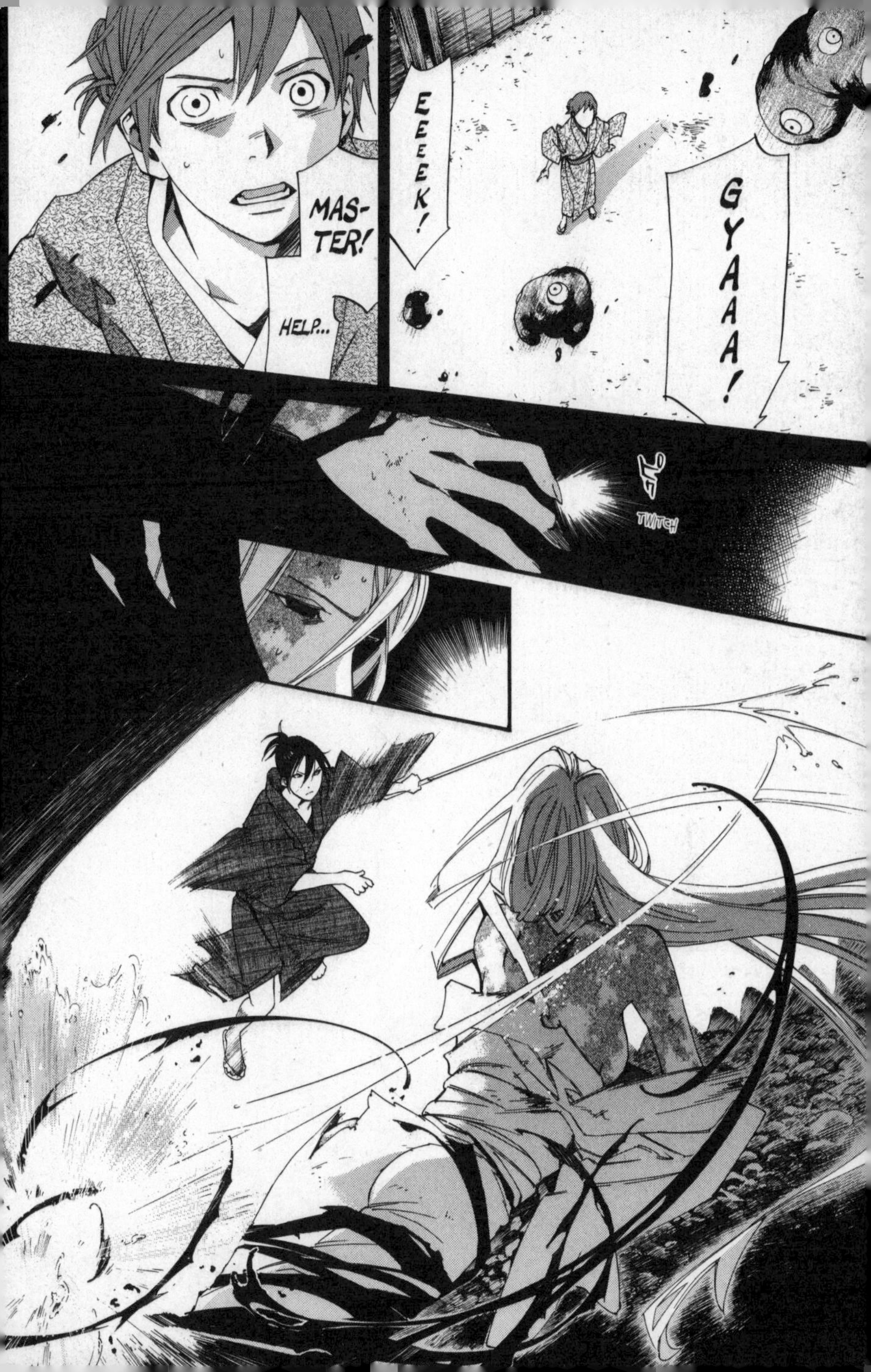
GYAAA!
EEEEK!
MAS-TER!
HELP...
TWITCH

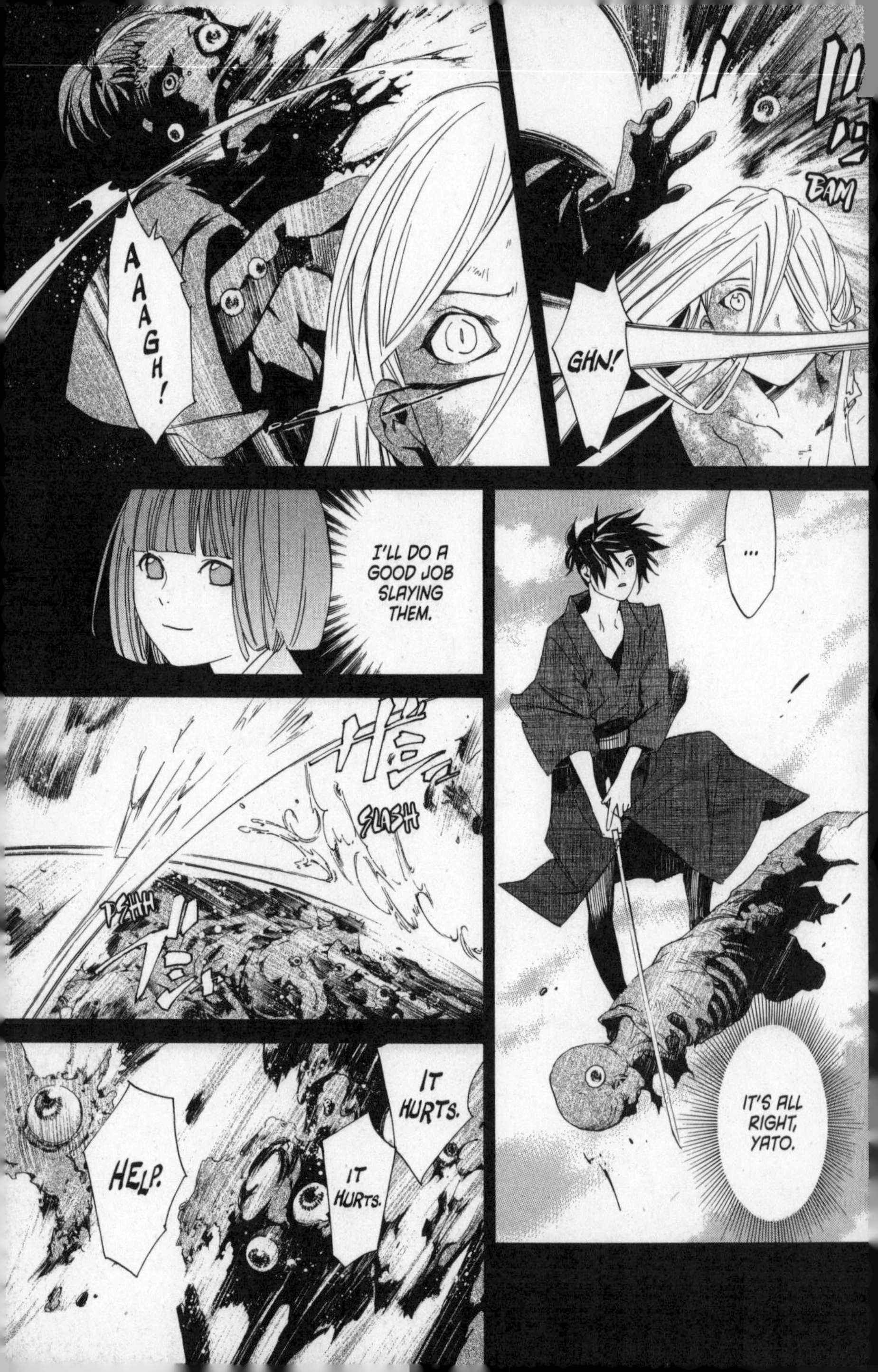
BAM
GHN!
AAAGH!
...
IT'S ALL RIGHT, YATO.
I'LL DO A GOOD JOB SLAYING THEM.
SLASH
PSHH
IT HURTS.
IT HURTS.
HELP.

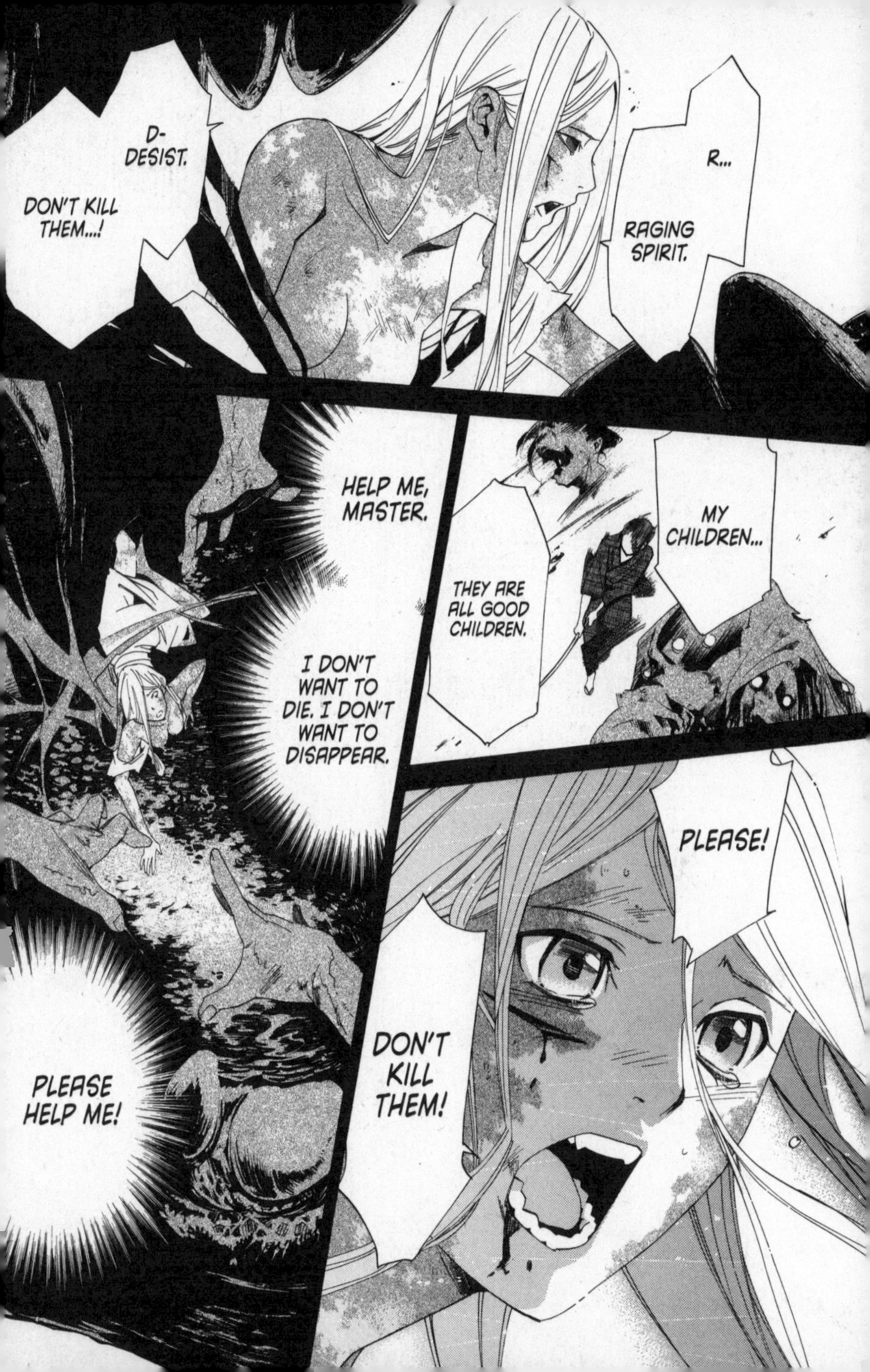
R...
RAGING SPIRIT.
D-
DESIST.
DON'T KILL THEM...!
MY CHILDREN...
THEY ARE ALL GOOD CHILDREN.
PLEASE!
DON'T KILL THEM!
HELP ME, MASTER.
I DON'T WANT TO DIE. I DON'T WANT TO DISAPPEAR.
PLEASE HELP ME!

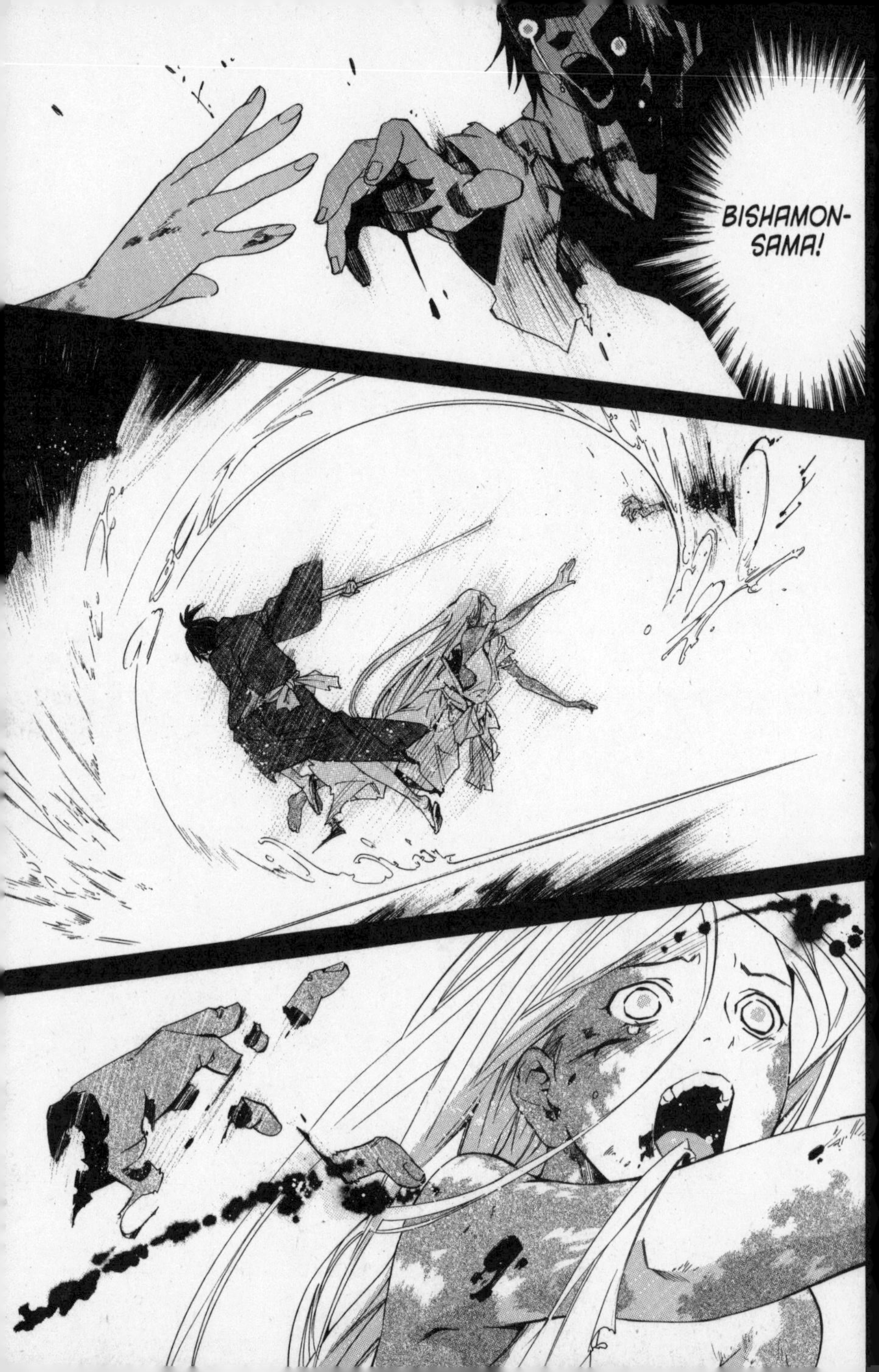
BISHAMON-SAMA!

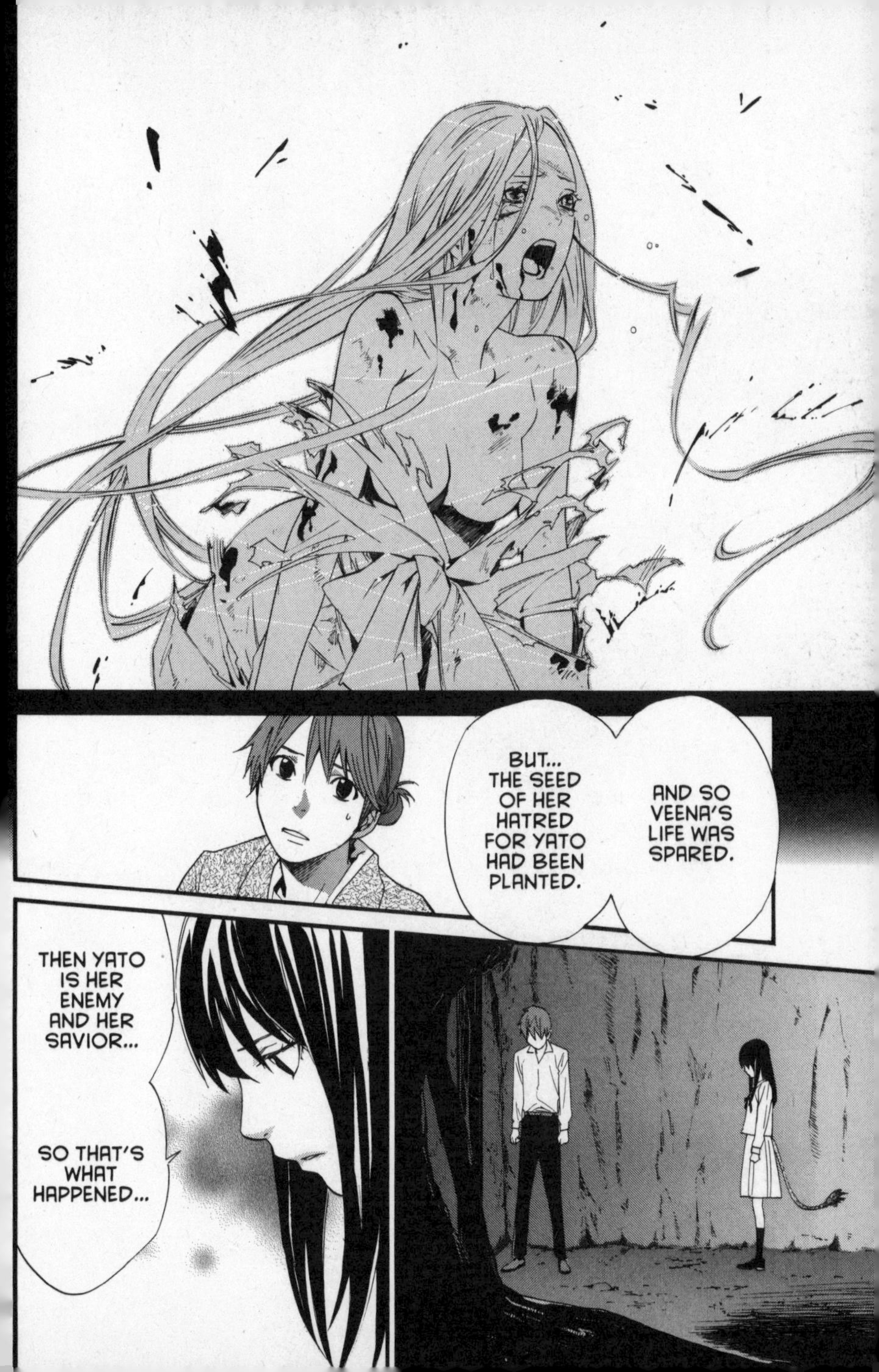
AND SO VEENA'S LIFE WAS SPARED.
BUT... THE SEED OF HER HATRED FOR YATO HAD BEEN PLANTED.
THEN YATO IS HER ENEMY AND HER SAVIOR...
SO THAT'S WHAT HAPPENED...

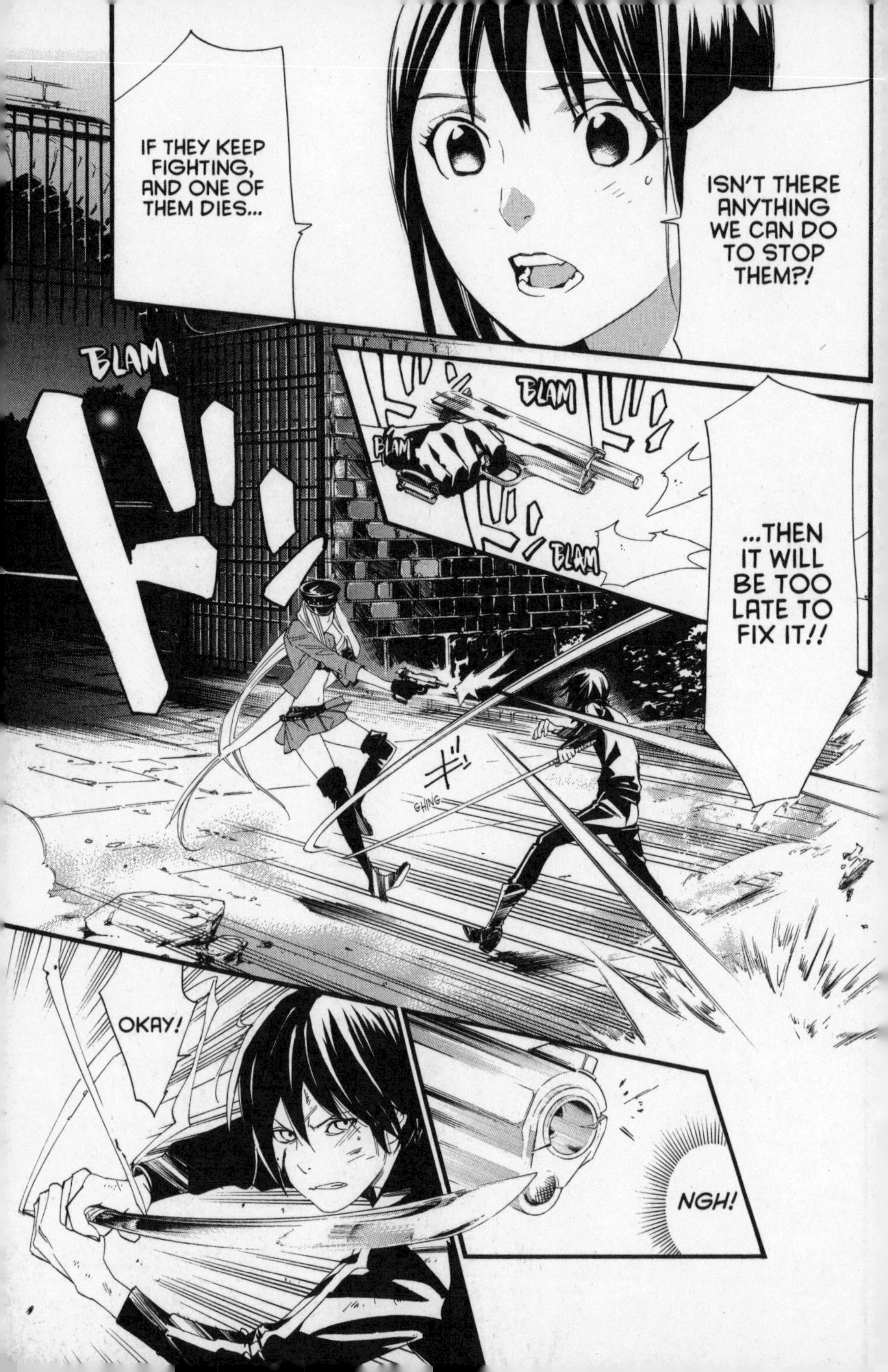
ISN'T THERE ANYTHING WE CAN DO TO STOP THEM?!
IF THEY KEEP FIGHTING, AND ONE OF THEM DIES...
BLAM
BLAM
BLAM
BLAM
...THEN IT WILL BE TOO LATE TO FIX IT!!
BLAM
GHING
NGH!
OKAY!

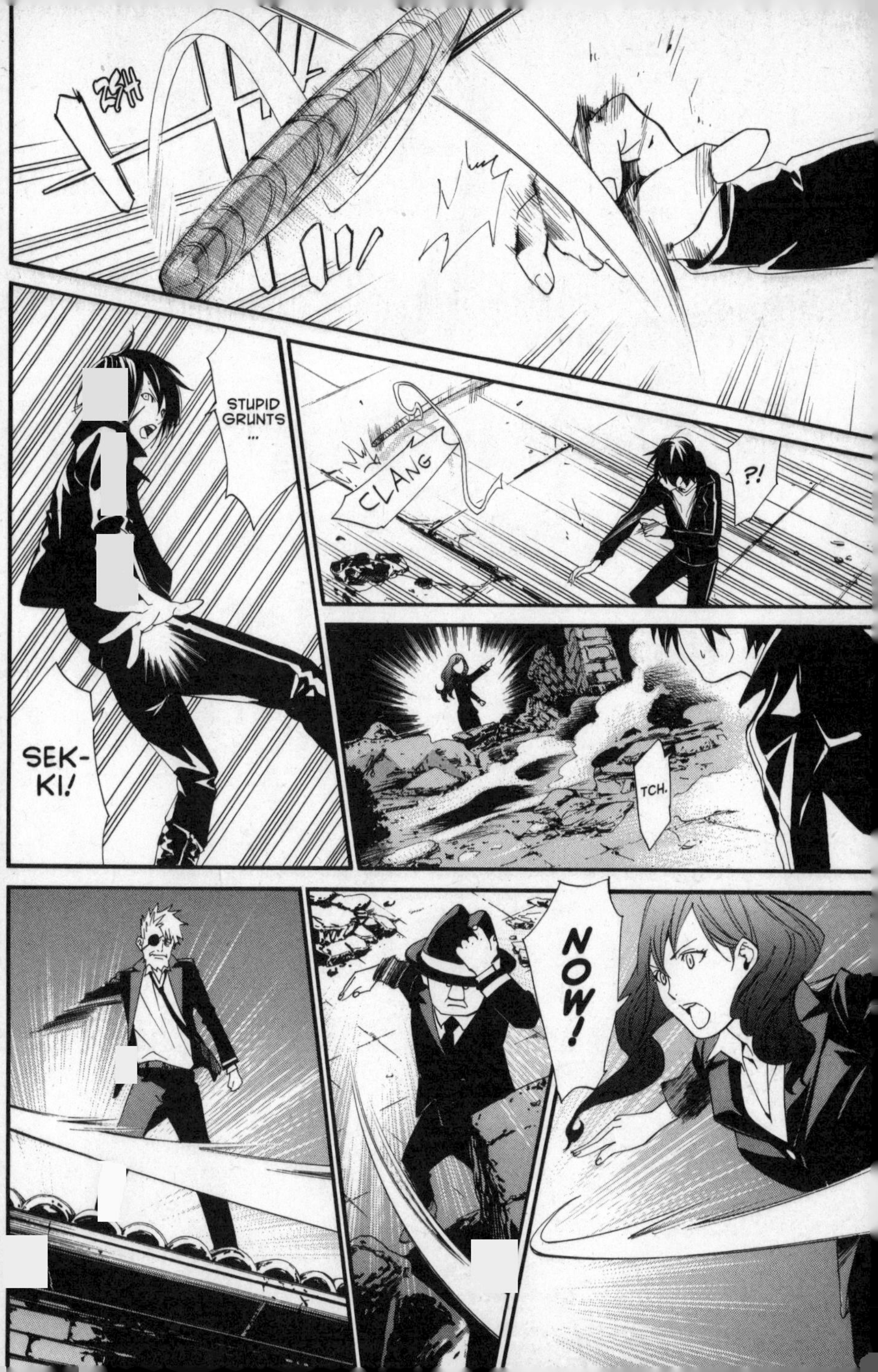
ZSH
?!
CLANG
TCH.
STUPID GRUNTS ...
SEK-KI!
NOW!

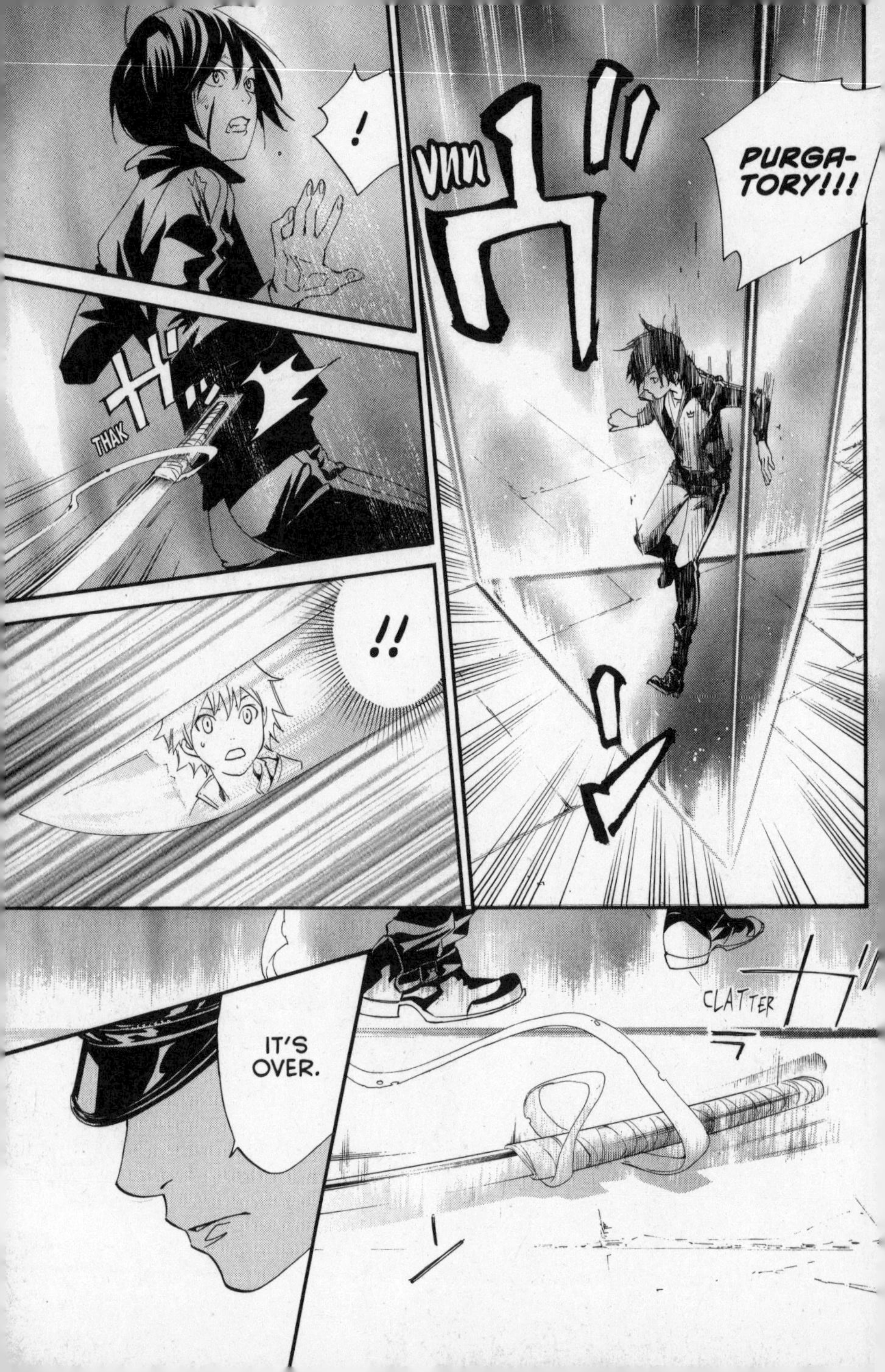
PURGA-TORY!!!
VNN
!
THAK
!!
CLATTER
IT'S OVER.

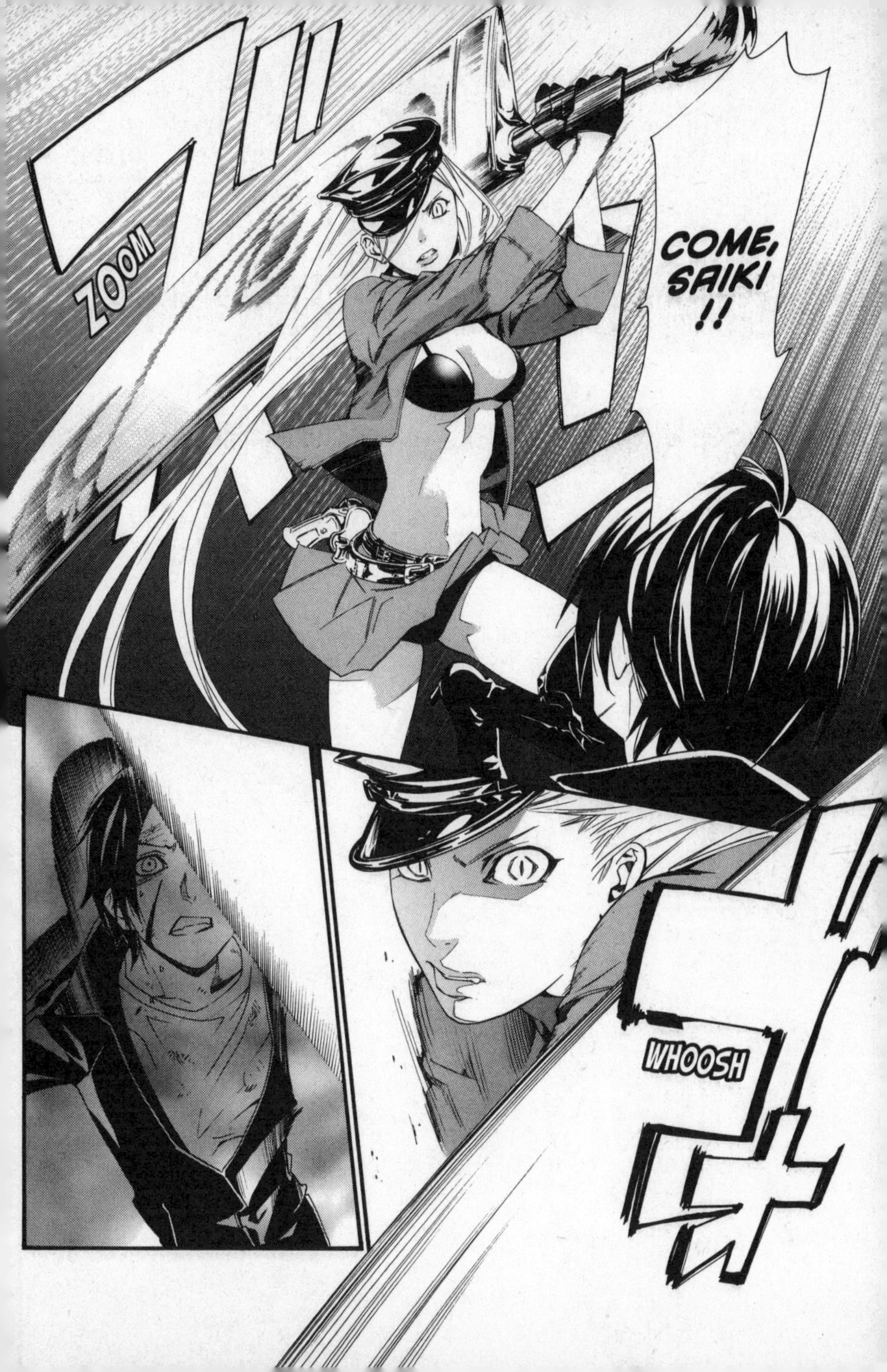
COME, SAIKI !!
ZOOM
WHOOSH

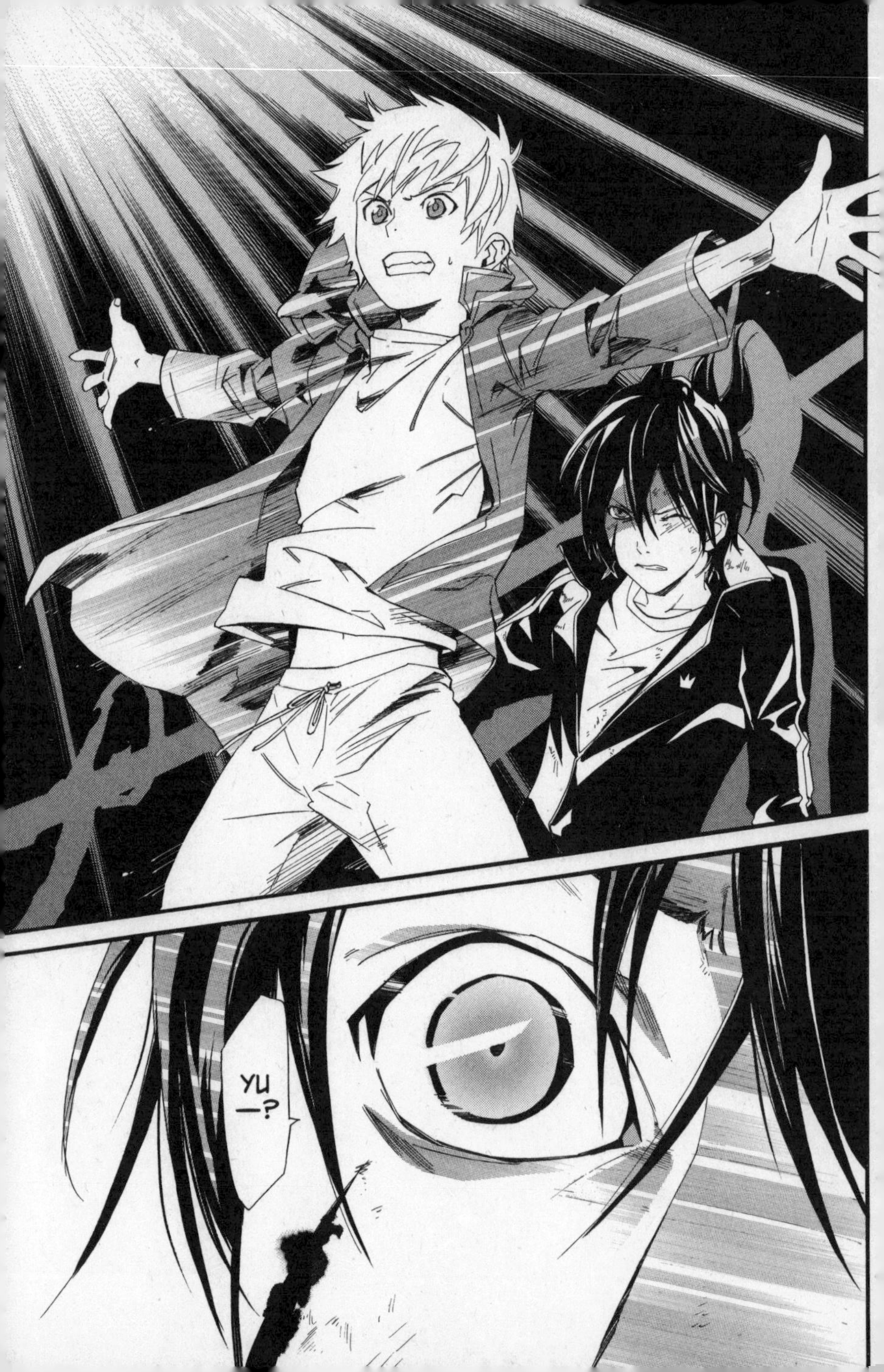
YU —?

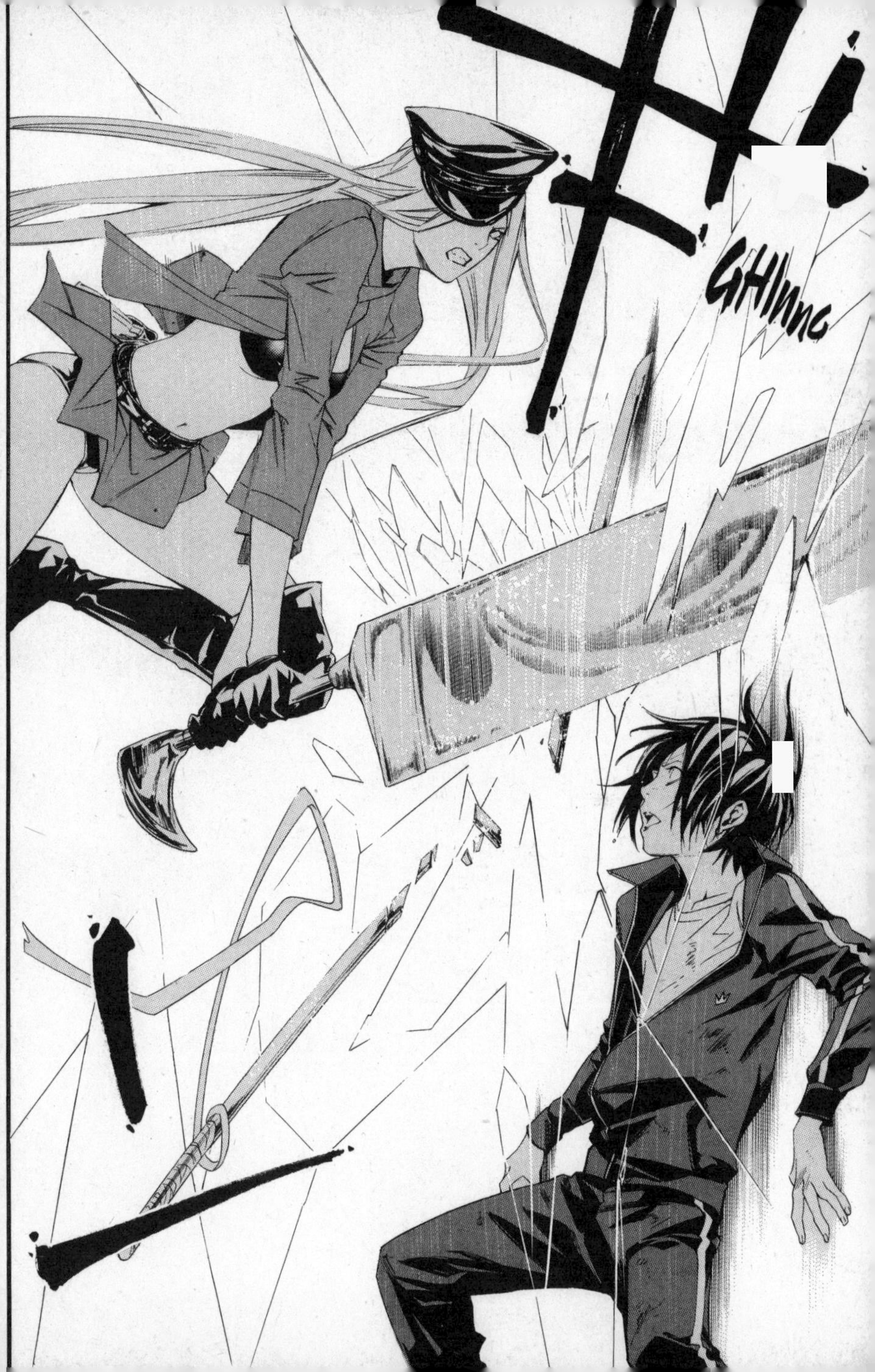
GHINNG

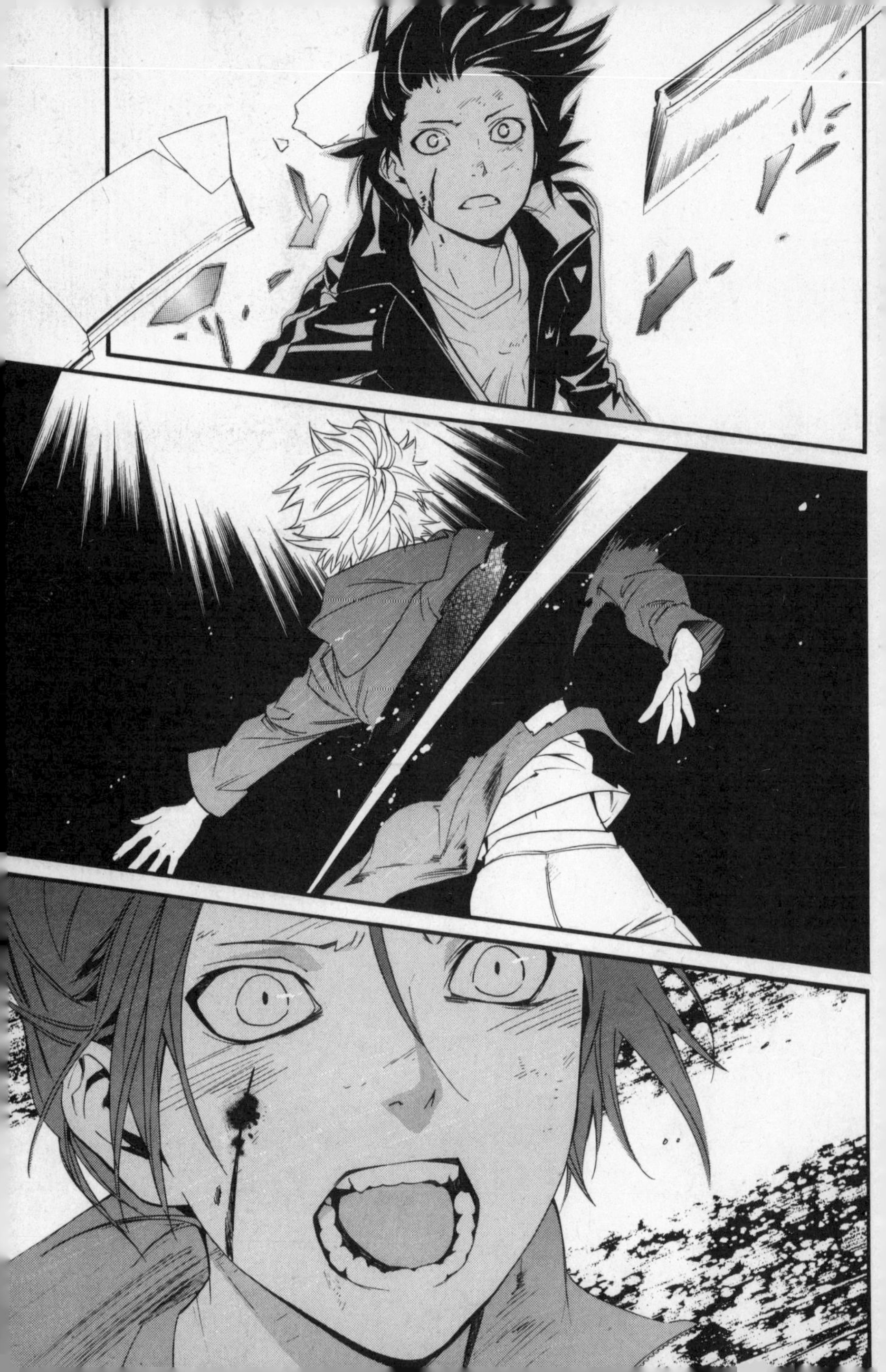

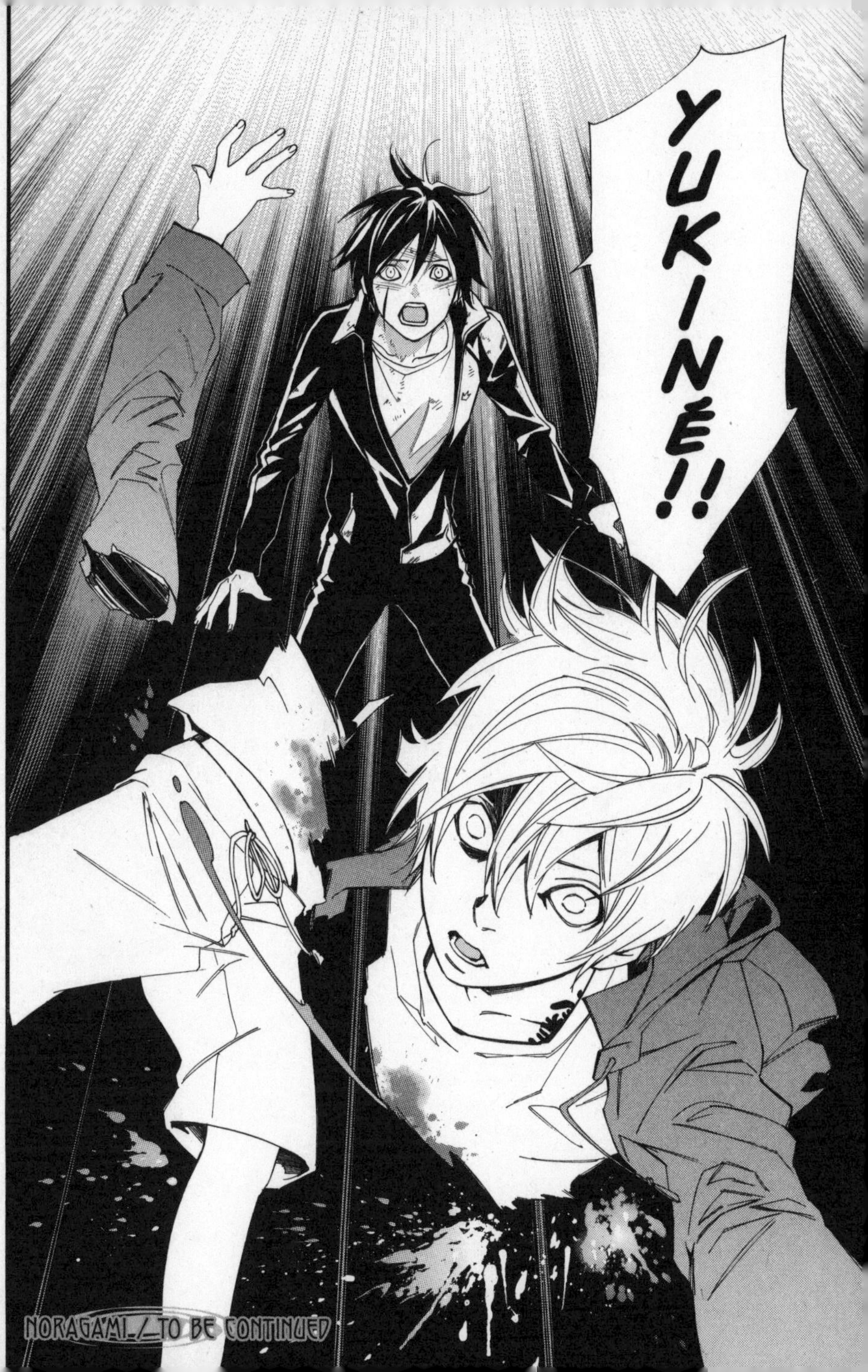
YUKINÉ!!
NORAGAMI 2 TO BE CONTINUED

野

兑

神

ATROCIOUS MANGA

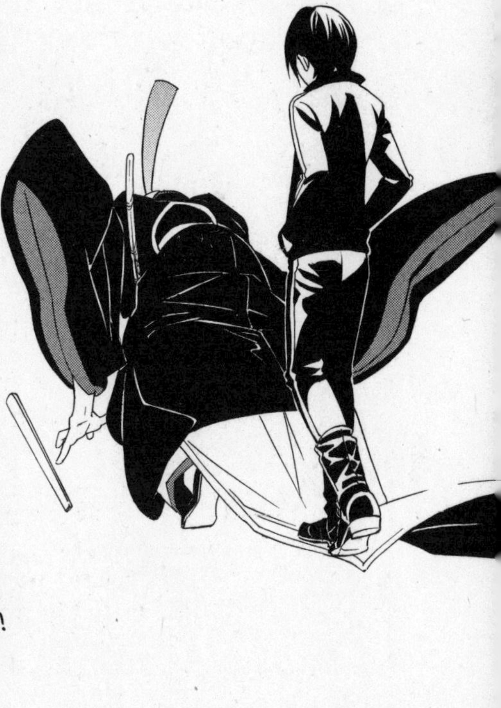

PAIN IN THE NECK

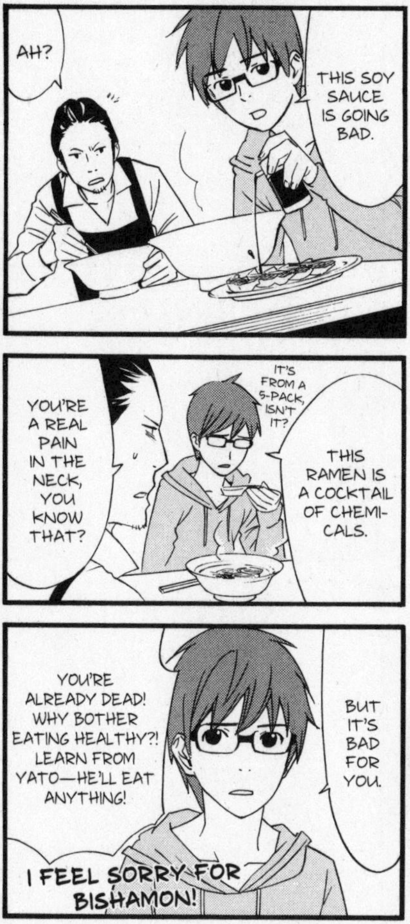
THIS SOY SAUCE IS GOING BAD.
AH?
IT'S FROM A 5-PACK, ISN'T IT?
THIS RAMEN IS A COCKTAIL OF CHEMI-CALS.
YOU'RE A REAL PAIN IN THE NECK, YOU KNOW THAT?
BUT IT'S BAD FOR YOU.
YOU'RE ALREADY DEAD! WHY BOTHER EATING HEALTHY?! LEARN FROM YATO—HE'LL EAT ANYTHING!
I FEEL SORRY FOR BISHAMON!
YATO, THAT'S SOAP!
WHAT ARE YOU, A TODDLER?!
YOU'RE BOTH A PAIN IN THE NECK!!

※ DON'T TRY THIS AT HOME, KIDS.

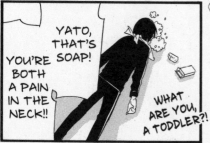

NOT LONG-DEAD FOR NOTHING

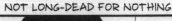

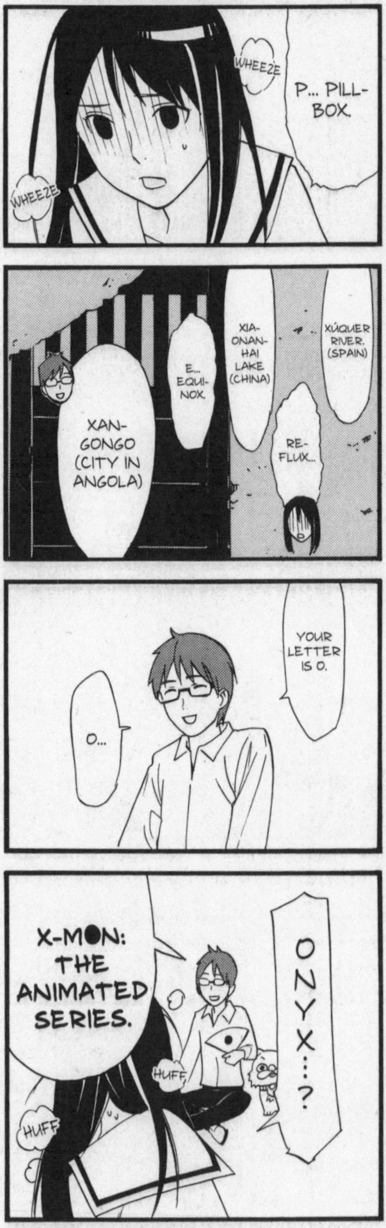
P... PILL-BOX.
WHEEZE
WHEEZE
XÚQUER RIVER. (SPAIN)
RE-FLUX...
XIA-ONAN-HAI LAKE (CHINA)
E... EQUI-NOX.
XAN-GONGO (CITY IN ANGOLA)
YOUR LETTER IS O.
O...
ONYX...?
X-MON: THE ANIMATED SERIES.
HUFF
HUFF

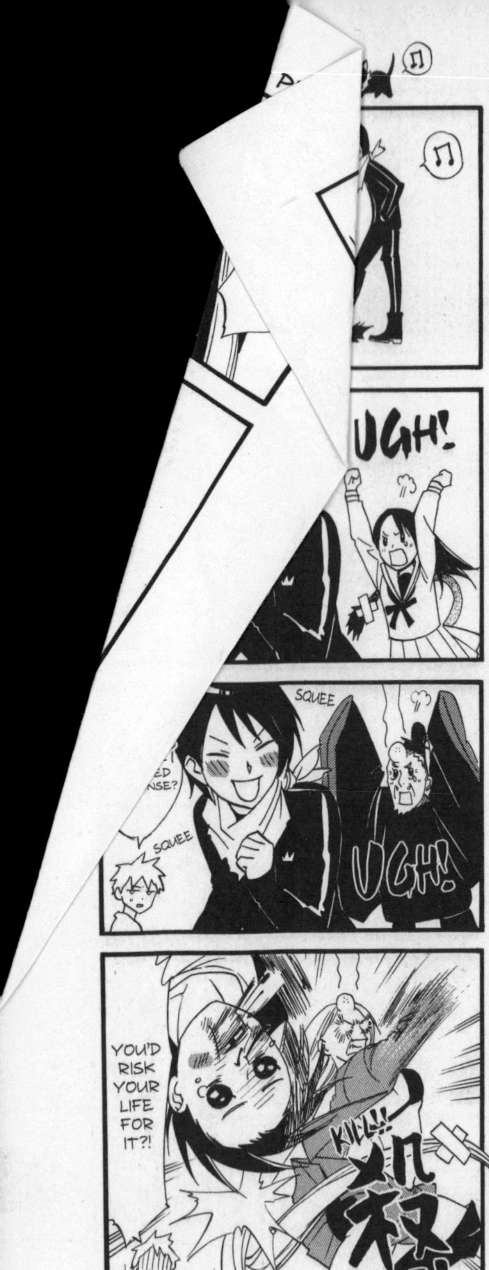
♫
UGH!
SQUEE
UGH!
SQUEE
KILL!!
YOU'D RISK YOUR LIFE FOR IT?!

KINKI IN A

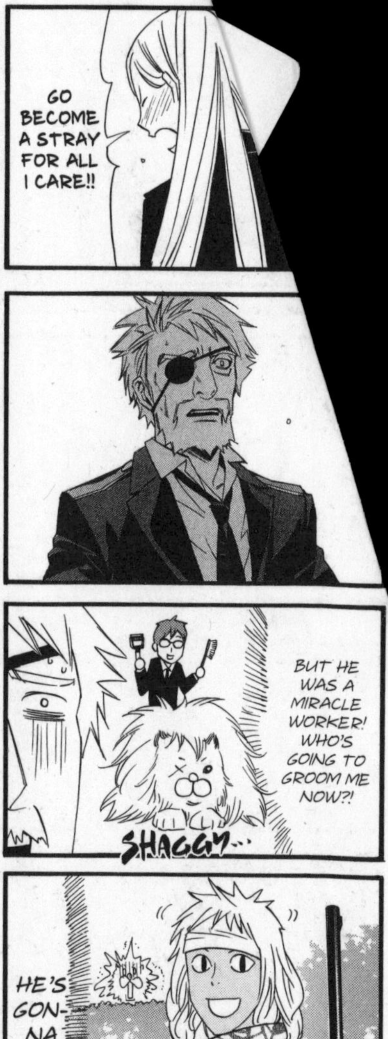
GO BECOME A STRAY FOR ALL I CARE!!
BUT HE WAS A MIRACLE WORKER! WHO'S GOING TO GROOM ME NOW?!
SHAGGY...
KURAHA! TIME FOR A SHAVE!
HE'S GON-NA TAN MY HIDE!
HUNTING RIFLE

KINKI PART TWO

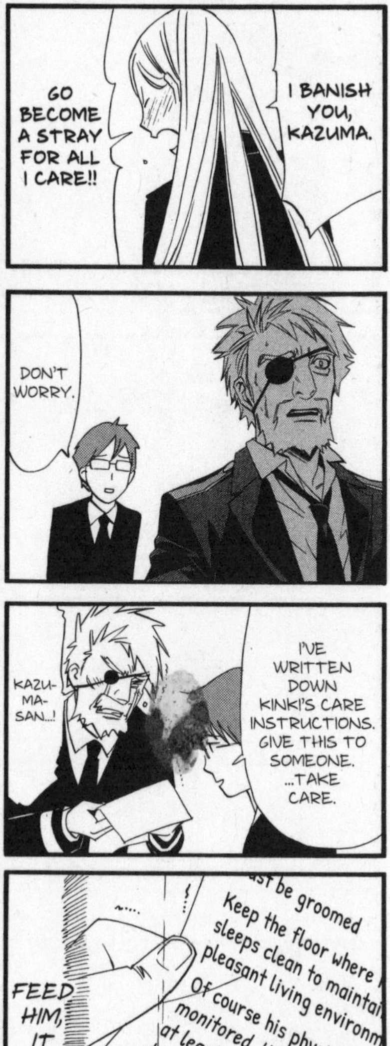
I BANISH YOU, KAZUMA.
GO BECOME A STRAY FOR ALL I CARE!!
DON'T WORRY.
I'VE WRITTEN DOWN KINKI'S CARE INSTRUCTIONS. GIVE THIS TO SOMEONE. ...TAKE CARE.
KAZU-MA-SAN...!
ust be groomed
Keep the floor where
sleeps clean to maintai
pleasant living environm
Of course his physique mus
monitored. His weight fluctu
at least once a week, so make
to feed him three times a day.
Be careful not to overfeed him.
FEED HIM, IT SAYS...!
DRIP-DRIP

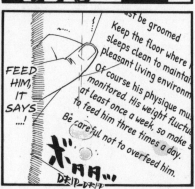

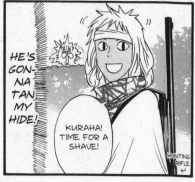

THE WORK OF A GUIDE

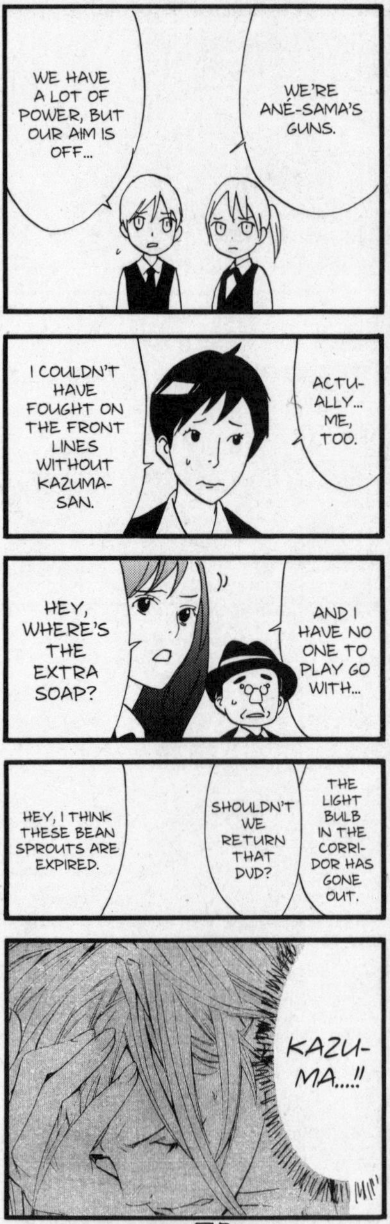
WE'RE ANÉ-SAMA'S GUNS.
WE HAVE A LOT OF POWER, BUT OUR AIM IS OFF...
ACTUALLY... ME, TOO.
I COULDN'T HAVE FOUGHT ON THE FRONT LINES WITHOUT KAZUMA-SAN.
AND I HAVE NO ONE TO PLAY GO WITH...
HEY, WHERE'S THE EXTRA SOAP?
THE LIGHT BULB IN THE CORRIDOR HAS GONE OUT.
SHOULDN'T WE RETURN THAT DUD?
HEY, I THINK THESE BEAN SPROUTS ARE EXPIRED.
KAZUMA...!!

MASTER'S TRAINING PLAN

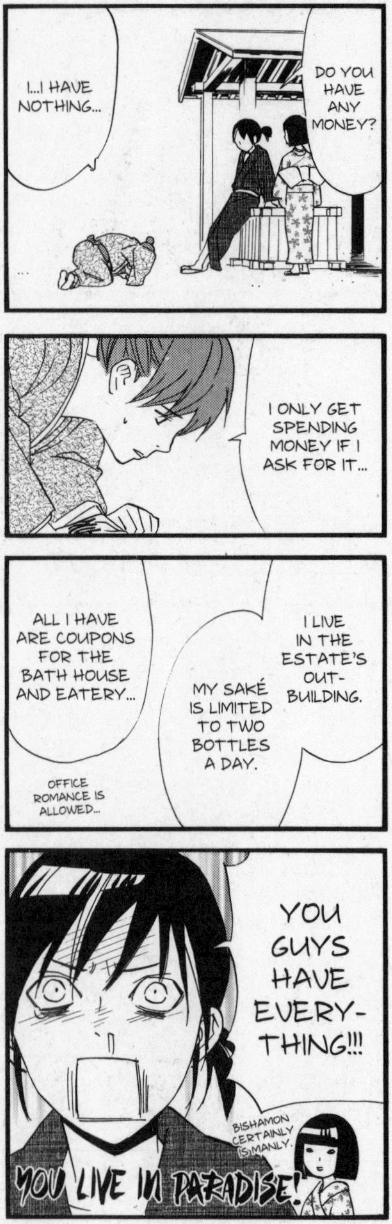
DO YOU HAVE ANY MONEY?
I...I HAVE NOTHING...
...
I ONLY GET SPENDING MONEY IF I ASK FOR IT...
I LIVE IN THE ESTATE'S OUTBUILDING.
MY SAKÉ IS LIMITED TO TWO BOTTLES A DAY.
ALL I HAVE ARE COUPONS FOR THE BATH HOUSE AND EATERY...
OFFICE ROMANCE IS ALLOWED...
YOU GUYS HAVE EVERYTHING!!!
BISHAMON CERTAINLY IS MANLY.
YOU LIVE IN PARADISE!

THANK YOU, EVERYONE WHO READ THIS FAR!!

TRANSLATION NOTES

Japanese is a tricky language for most Westerners, and translation is often more art than science. For your edification and reading pleasure, here are notes on some of the places where we could have gone in a different direction in our translation of the work, or where a Japanese cultural reference is used.

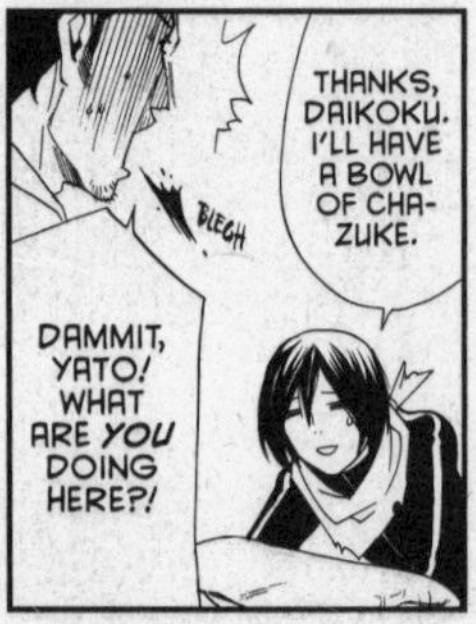
THANKS, DAIKOKU. I'LL HAVE A BOWL OF CHA-ZUKE.
BLEGH
DAMMIT, YATO! WHAT ARE *YOU* DOING HERE?!

Chazuke, page 14

Chazuke means, roughly, "soaked in tea," and, as the name suggests, is a dish of rice with tea poured over it. Think of cereal and milk, only with rice and green tea. Savory toppings are added, such as Japanese pickles, seaweed, or wasabi.

Deliciastick, page 29

This is the translators' attempt to replicate the name of the popular Japanese snack, *umaibō*, which means "delicious stick." As you might imagine, it's shaped like a stick. It's made of puffed corn, and comes in a variety of flavors. In the original Japanese text, the word was partially obscured to prevent lawsuits. The translators' chose to partially obscure the name in English by giving it an English equivalent.

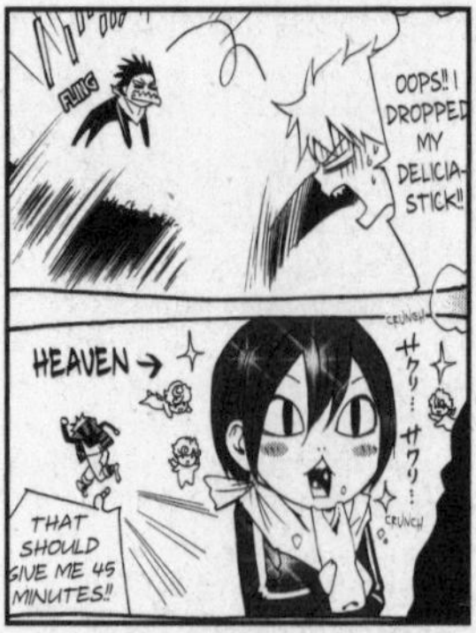
OOPS!! I DROPPED MY DELICIA-STICK!!
AUG
CRUNCH
HEAVEN →
CRUNCH
THAT SHOULD GIVE ME 45 MINUTES!!

***Byakujō* staff, page 74**

Byakujō is Japanese for "hundred staff." Search as they might, the translators were unable to find exactly what kind of a staff this is, or what the "hundred" is referring to. Perhaps this one staff is as strong as one hundred. Maybe one blow from it is equal to one hundred blows. It might be a reference to historical laws in Japan and China, in which one of the five punishments was caning—depending on the severity of the crime, the punished was beaten with up to one hundred strokes of a cane or staff. Either way, this particular weapon name seems to be unique to *Noragami*.

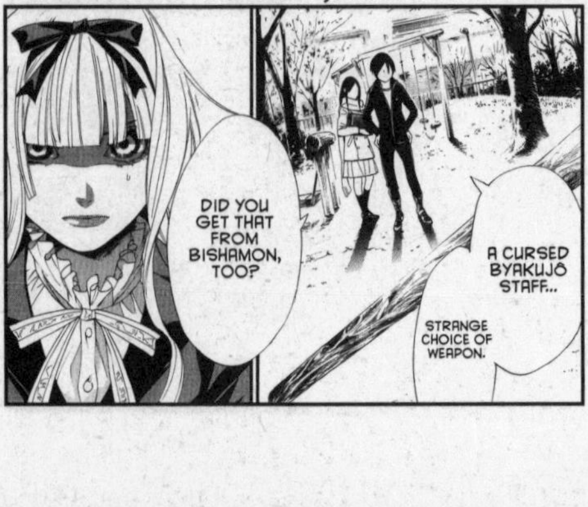
A CURSED BYAKUJŌ STAFF...
STRANGE CHOICE OF WEAPON.
DID YOU GET THAT FROM BISHAMON, TOO?

Shinki clans, page 107

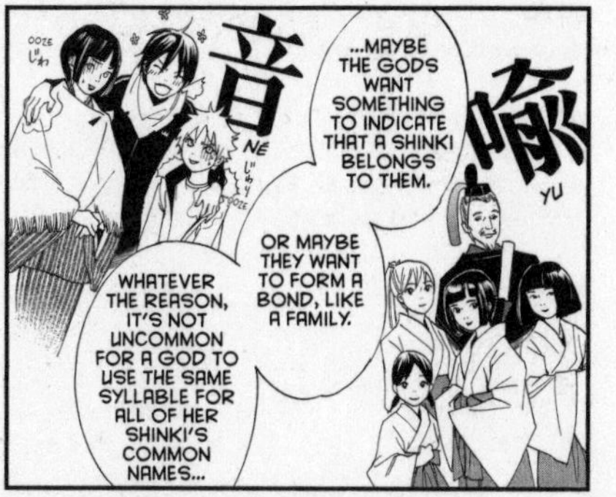
音
NE
...MAYBE THE GODS WANT SOMETHING TO INDICATE THAT A SHINKI BELONGS TO THEM.
喩
YU
OR MAYBE THEY WANT TO FORM A BOND, LIKE A FAMILY.
WHATEVER THE REASON, IT'S NOT UNCOMMON FOR A GOD TO USE THE SAME SYLLABLE FOR ALL OF HER SHINKI'S COMMON NAMES...

For anyone interested in what the clan names mean, here's a breakdown. As discussed in volume one, Yato's *né* means "sound," which is related to the words in the shinki ordination
(see volume one). As the god of learning, Tenjin uses *yu*, a rather complex kanji that means "metaphor." The reader is free to imagine any reason that Tenjin would choose this character, but it is the translators' opinion that it has to do with the fact that when calling, for example, Mayu, he is not using her true name, but a metaphor for who she truly is.

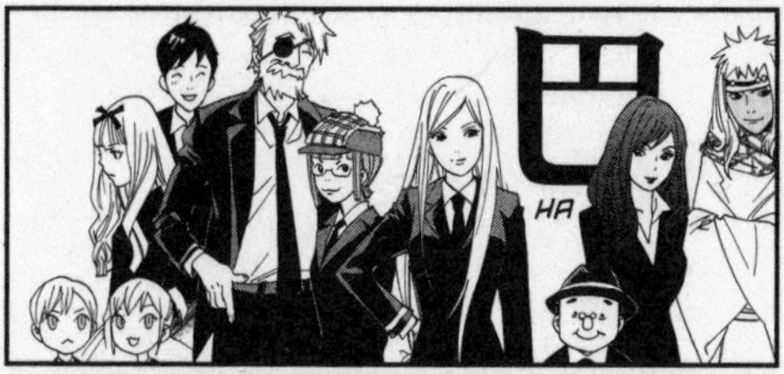
巴
HA

The *ha* that Bishamon uses in modern times has many ties to her as a warrior god. The character can be pronounced either *ha* or *tomoë*. Meaning-wise, it refers to a comma shape, as seen, for example, in half of a yin-yang symbol. The *mitsudomoë*, or "three *ha*" symbol, is an emblem using three comma shapes spiraling around the center of a circle. This symbol is associated with Hachiman, another famous warrior god, and is commonly used as a family crest in samurai families. Finally, Tomoë Gozen is a famous female warrior who is believed to have fought in the Genpei War—anyone living on the Far Shore who is familiar with that aspect of Japanese history might recognize the *ha* character and immediately connect it to a female warrior, and thus think of Bishamon.

The *ma* that Bishamon once used means "flax," which is a sacred plant in Shinto.

Yato and the *ma* clan, page 108

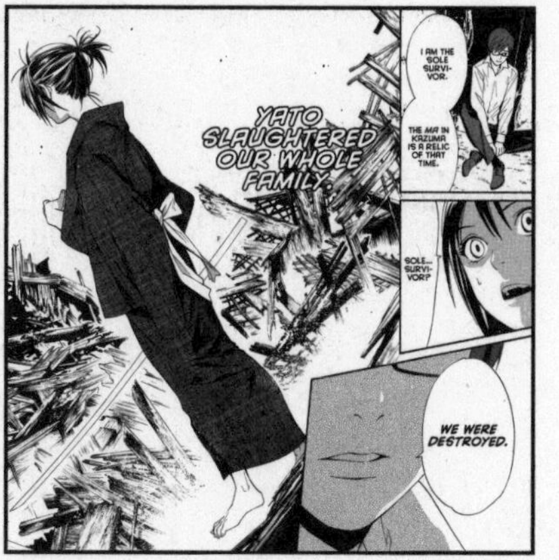
I AM THE SOLE SURVIVOR.
THE MA IN KAZUMA IS A RELIC OF THAT TIME.
YATO SLAUGHTERED OUR WHOLE FAMILY.
SOLE... SURVIVOR?
WE WERE DESTROYED.

There is an old Japanese record called the *Hitachi no Kuni Fudoki*—the ancient record of the Hitachi province (located in modern day Ibaraki). This record contains the story of the Yato-no-kami, snake gods that would destroy the entire family of anyone unlucky enough to see one. These Yato-no-kami infested a field that a man named Yahazu no Matachi wanted to cultivate. He drove off the Yato-no-kami and set up a borderline, marked by guide posts. This border marked the boundary between the world of men and the world of gods, and in exchange for the snake gods leaving his family

alone and staying on the other side of the line, Matachi agreed to erect a shrine to worship Yato-no-kami.

While this story is clearly connected to Yato, there are a few points that connect it to Kazuma as well. First, the *ma* in Matachi is the same *ma* of Bishamon's *ma* clan. And, just as Kazuma is a guide, Matachi used guide posts to create a borderline and protect his family.

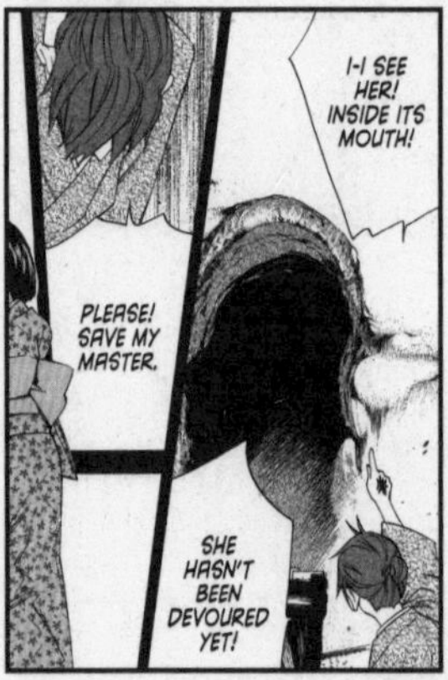
I-I SEE HER! INSIDE ITS MOUTH!
PLEASE! SAVE MY MASTER.
SHE HASN'T BEEN DEVOURED YET!

Save my master, page 171
It may be interesting to note that, while the ha clan lovingly calls Bishamon "Ané-sama," the ma clan refers to her as *nushi-sama*, which is one of many terms meaning "master." At this point, Kazuma is still calling her *nushi-sama*. The story as to why he now calls her Veena has yet to unfold.

Hiki, page 172
Because the stray commented earlier about how much she loved the name Yato gave her, the translators thought that some of the readers, like them, might be curious as to what it is. As you can see now, her instrument name is Hiki. The kanji *hi* 緋 means "scarlet," and is likely a reference to the color of everything after Yato uses Hiki. Most likely, her name in human form would be Akané.

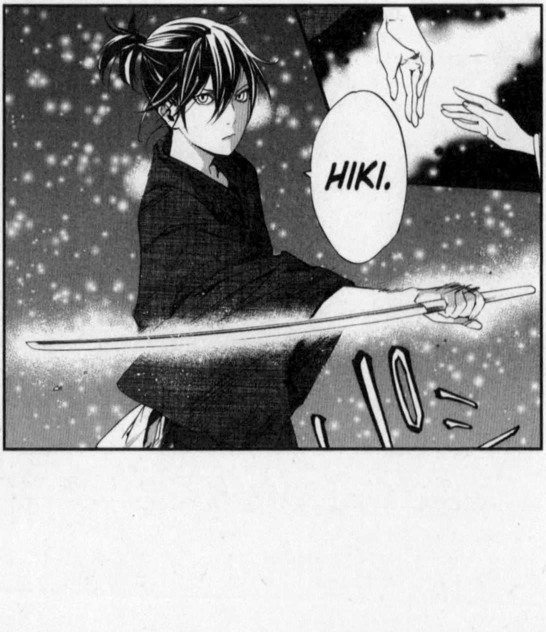
HIKI.

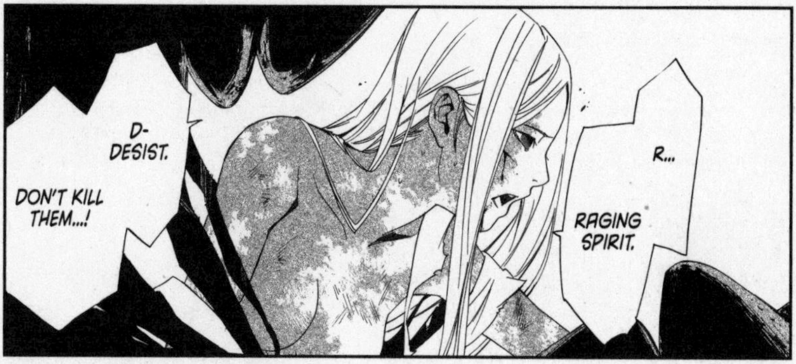
R...
RAGING SPIRIT.
D-DESIST.
DON'T KILL THEM...!

Raging Spirit, page 176
Here Bishamon addresses Yato as *ara-mitama*, which means, roughly, "raging spirit." The "spirit" can be a "great spirit" type of spirit, like a god, or the spirit of a dead person. In this case, it is the former, referring to an angry god bringing calamity to its hapless victims.

Kazuma and Hiyori killing time, page 189

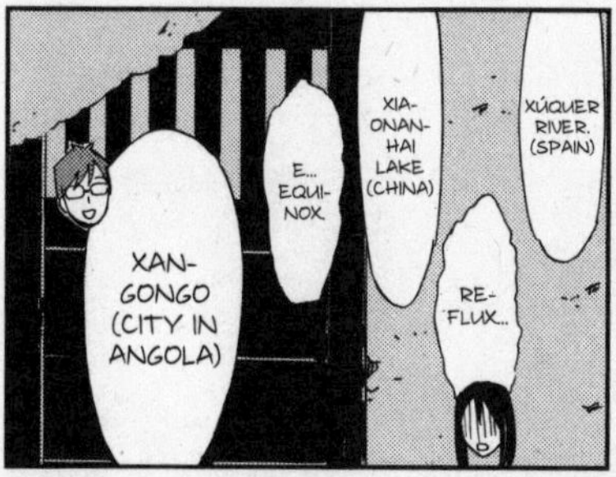
XÚQUER RIVER. (SPAIN)
XIA-ONAN-HAI LAKE (CHINA)
RE-FLUX...
E... EQUI-NOX
XAN-GONGO (CITY IN ANGOLA)

Kazuma and Hiyori are passing the time by playing a game called *shiritori*, meaning "take the end," and is like the English-speaking game Word Chain. The rules are simple: someone says a word, and the next person has to say a word that starts with the last letter of the previous word. In Japanese, the last letter will be a syllable, because the Japanese writing system is a syllabary, meaning each character (letter) represents a syllable. Hiyori is using the clever strategy of trying to stump Kazuma by choosing words that end in the one "letter" that never starts a Japanese word: *n*. This *n* is a syllable by itself, as opposed to the other N syllables: *na*, *ni*, *nu*, *ne*, and *no*, which are the characters used when a Japanese word begins with the N sound. Kazuma is forced to get creative, but fortunately for him, he's been around long enough to know plenty of *n* words.

In the Japanese version, the game of shiritori goes like this, starting with Hiyori: "*shinkansen* [bullet train]," "Ng'iro *gawa* [Ng'iro River] (Kenya)," "*wain* [wine]," "Ntomba *ko* [Ntomba Lake] (Congo)," "*koban* [a kind of coin]," "Ngorongoro (city in Tanzania)," "*rondon* [London]," "Nbaba *rabu songu* [Mmbaba Love Song] (opening theme to the anime *Papuwa*)."

The translators felt the easiest way to make an English version of this word chain difficult for Kazuma would be to end every word in X.

NORAGAMI

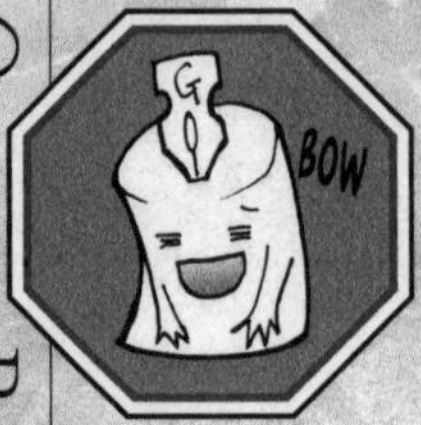
BOW

It may be a little late for this, but the correct pronunciation of *shinki* is actually *jingi*. The characters in *Noragami* all say "shinki," but this manga may be the only place where it's pronounced that way.

Adachitoka

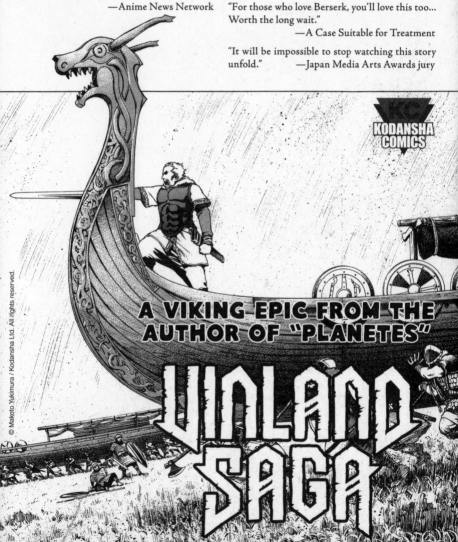

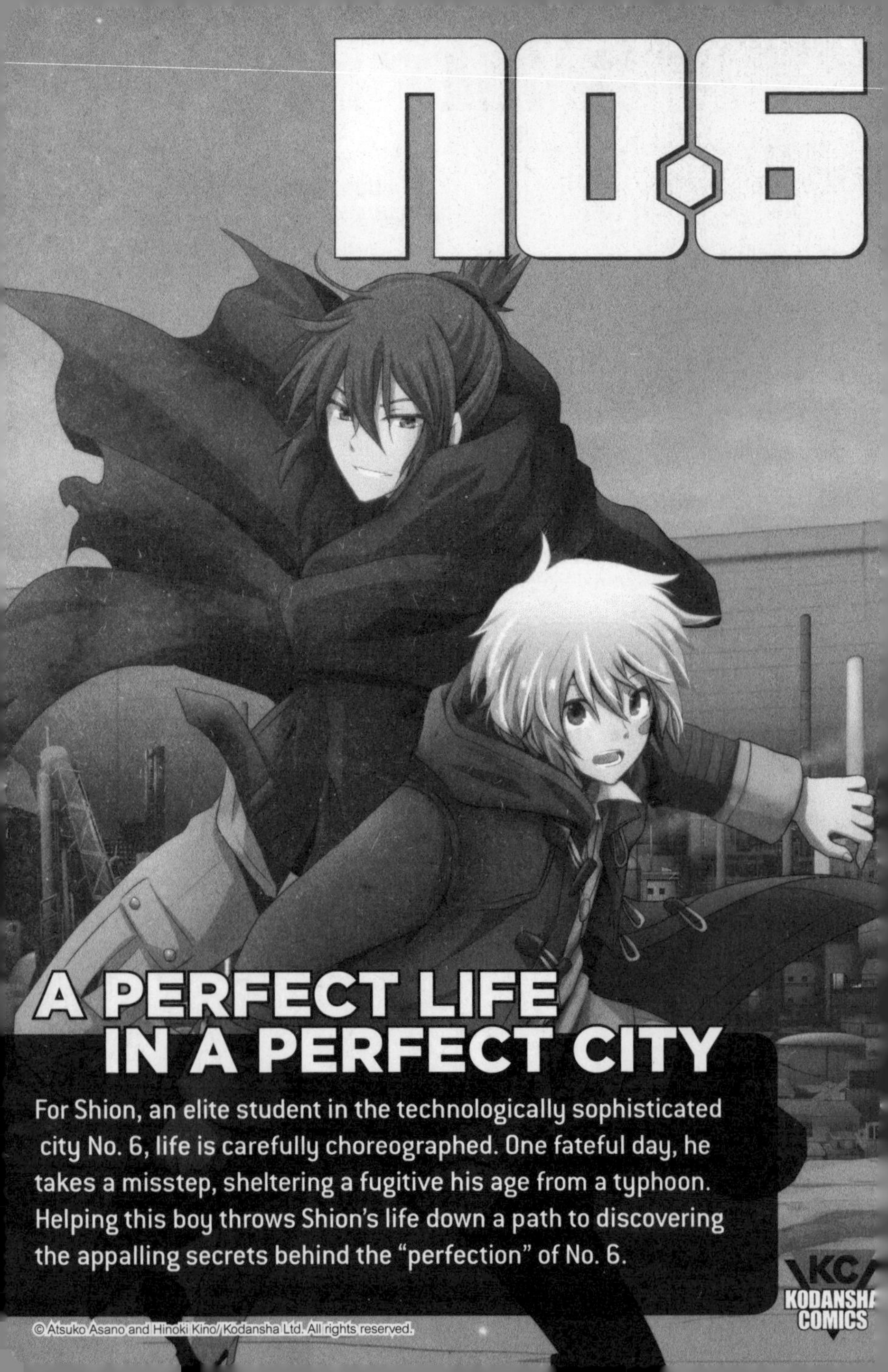
NO.6
A PERFECT LIFE
IN A PERFECT CITY
For Shion, an elite student in the technologically sophisticated city No. 6, life is carefully choreographed. One fateful day, he takes a misstep, sheltering a fugitive his age from a typhoon. Helping this boy throws Shion's life down a path to discovering the appalling secrets behind the "perfection" of No. 6.
KC
KODANSHA COMICS
© Atsuko Asano and Hinoki Kino/ Kodansha Ltd. All rights reserved.

Noragami: Stray God volume 5 is a wor
places, and incidents are the products of the author's imagination or are used fictitiously. Any resemblance to actual events, locales, or persons, living or dead, is entirely coincidental.

A Kodansha Comics Trade Paperback Original.

Published in the United States by Kodansha Comics, an imprint of Kodansha USA Publishing, LLC, New York.

Publication rights for this English edition arranged through Kodansha Ltd., Tokyo.

First published in Japan in 2012 by Kodansha Ltd., Tokyo, as *Noragami*, volume 5.

ISBN 978-1-61262-995-7

Printed in the United States of America.

www.kodanshacomics.com

9 8 7 6 5 4 3 2 1

Translator: Alethea Nibley & Athena Nibley
Lettering: Lys Blakeslee